T0065739

Praise for *Girl Singer*

"Remarkably candid, entertaining, and moving . . . Her memories of life on the road in the '40s, of her pal Marlene Dietrich, and of New York when it still dazzled are worth the price of the book!" —*Boston Herald*

"Dramatic. Such genuine and often sweet insight into one of America's most famous personalities that *Girl Singer* is a must for anyone with even a passing curiosity about Clooney." —*Kirkus Reviews*

"Engaging." —*Time*

"To know Rosemary Clooney is to love her. After reading this book, you will, too." —Tony Bennett

"Rosie, dear, you've got it all. You've had it all. You must read this book to know it all." —Dolores Hope

"Hearing Rosemary Clooney sing is like a taste of honey; reading her book is a full and delicious meal." —Stanley Donen

"A beautiful book. A beautiful American dream of a life, plus a large hunk of nightmare, plus the story of contemporary American popular music." —Betty Comden

"Rosemary Clooney is one of the great singers of our time, a truly wonderful comedienne on and off the stage, and as good a friend as you could hope for. *Girl Singer* brings out all these qualities—and many more." —Margaret Whiting

"*Girl Singer* is an extraordinary and heartbreaking book. This was my time in Hollywood, as it was Rosie's, and it brought back a lot of memories." —Joanne Woodward

"A great singer and a great lady, Rosemary Clooney now adds another jewel to her crown, that of great memoirist. She gives us the best picture we have of an often misunderstood era in popular music, and she lets us see the exactitude of celebrity and the bounty it places on the soul." —Gary Giddins, author of *Visions of Jazz: The First Century*

"Rosemary Clooney has been the outstanding girl singer of our century. Her autobiography is the vivid depiction of a fascinating life. I loved it!" —Kathryn Crosby

"With all due respect, there just aren't any more like her. As I have said before, she is the person I would love to live next door to." —Maria Cole

"*Girl Singer* is startlingly honest and beautifully written. At times, this book will break your heart, but throughout, it will open your heart." —Gavin de Becker, author of *The Gift of Fear*

"Just as Rosemary's voice has a unique, unforgettable quality all its own, so does her autobiography. In my book, she stands alone. A true American treasure." —Ann Rutherford

"Rosemary Clooney's eyes are illuminated by intelligence and mischief. Like her music, she is without guile or self-promotion. Amidst the hubbub of her stories, there are hints of longing, of missing people who are nourished in her special intimate ways. These vanished citizens are the motors of the songs. In her autobiography, they are revealed and revered. And of course there's the mischief and the music." —Jonathan Schwartz

"This book is a must for all who have loved the talent of Rosemary Clooney over the years as I have. The essence of this wonderful lady is captured beautifully within these pages." —Rose Marie

Rosemary Clooney
with Joan Barthel

Broadway Books

New York

GIRL SINGER

An Autobiography

Designed by Dana Leigh Treglia

The Library of Congress has cataloged the hardcover edition as follows:

Clooney, Rosemary.
Girl singer: an autobiography / Rosemary Clooney
with Joan Barthel. —
p.   cm.
Includes index.
1. Clooney, Rosemary.   2. Singers—United States Biography.
I. Barthel, Joan.   II. Title.
ML420.C58A3   1999
782.42164'092—dc21   99-24342
[B]   CIP

ISBN 978-0-7679-0555-8

145038997

For Betty

every day

GIRL SINGER

ONE

From the porch, the river looked smoky brown sometimes, rosy and lavender when the sun was going down, then slate gray, just before it turned pitch black.

From the porch, the lights of the *Island Queen* beckoned, like reachable stars.

From the porch, the river promised better times coming, faraway places just around the bend.

From the porch, the river was a wide tranquil ribbon, no hint of a dangerous current. All you could see from the porch were possibilities, not perils.

The porch was at my grandmother's house in Maysville, Kentucky, on the Ohio River. Although Maysville was called a port city, it was a classical small town, its life centered in a few downtown blocks between the train station and the bridge: Magee's Bakery, Merz Brothers Department Store, the diner with the swinging EAT sign and six stools at the counter, where we sat and watched our hamburgers—the size of half dollars—frying on the grill.

Now that house on West Third Street, high above the river, is spruced up, glistening white, with window boxes full of scarlet geraniums and trailing ivy, listed in *The National Register of Historic Places*. The side street leading down to the river is named Rosemary Clooney Street. Then it was a rented house, well-scrubbed, but the linoleum on the kitchen floor was peeling, curled up at the edges. There was no central heating, just little potbellied stoves and a fireplace with a grate where my grandmother cooked when the bills hadn't been paid and the gas was turned off. On winter days, my sister Betty, my brother Nicky, and I licked the ice that formed on the inside of the kitchen window.

But my grandmother loved that house, loved sitting in her high-backed rattan rocking chair on the porch, where she could look down at the river rolling by. She loved to cook—floured chicken pieces with lots of salt and pepper, fried to the crackling stage in bubbling hot Crisco; green beans boiled with a chunk of country ham; piles of cole slaw. Once she made strawberry shortcake on the fireplace grate. She loved listening to her daytime serials on the big Zenith console in the living room, always tuned to WLW in Cincinnati: "Stella Dallas," "Backstage Wife." She loved her little garden beyond the porch, with its straggling hollyhocks and snapdragons, late-summer rows of the juiciest tomatoes, the twisted hackberry tree at the far edge of the yard.

Best of all, she loved us.

My grandmother, Ada Guilfoyle, was my mother's mother, one of the strongest women I've ever known. I like to think—and I do believe—I've inherited some of her strength. When she was a young wife, expecting, she and my grandfather were working on a rented farm outside of town. She began to bleed and fell over in the tobacco field. The doctor came in his horse and buggy and carried her back to the farmhouse, where they hung clean sheets on the walls and spread them over the kitchen table. With warm beer bottles pressed tightly against her body, she was operated on for an ectopic pregnancy and warned not to have children. But she and my grandfather, Michael Joseph Guilfoyle, had planned on children, so they had nine: four boys and five girls. When my grandfather dropped dead on the street at the age of fifty-two—an aneurysm—their youngest was just three. So my grandmother had to get a job. Before she was married, she'd taught in a one-room rural schoolhouse, but now, with young children, she needed to be home during the day. She worked nights as a practical nurse.

Frances, my mother, was the third child, the second daughter after Rose, followed by Jeanne, Ann, and Christine. My Aunt Rose was always labeled—even honored—as the beauty of the family, while my mother wasn't even considered pretty according to the conventions of the time. She was straight and slim, with deep blue eyes and thick dark hair, but her features were sharp and angular. So she made up in flamboyance what she felt, and was often reminded, she lacked in looks. She would be the best dresser, the most stylish; she would have flair. She was barely five-foot-four but she seemed taller, with shoulder pads and spike heels and a way of holding herself proud and erect. When she walked to work as a sales-clerk at the New York Store, she wore a cartwheel hat and carried a showy purse. She almost always won the Charleston contests on the *Island Queen*.

She had grown up saying she would become an actress or a dancer. "I want to get out of Maysville. I want to *be* somebody." Instead, she married a charming, funny, handsome man, Andrew Clooney, who was eight years older and who had already decided that his dreams were submerged at the bottom of a bottle.

When I was born on May 23, 1928, she had just turned nineteen. She and my father had already separated at least once, then they had gotten back together briefly—a dismal pattern that would be repeated often, that would frame my childhood. I don't remember all of us living together under the same roof for more than a few weeks at a time. Sometimes I was with an uncle or an aunt, sometimes at Grandma Guilfoyle's, sometimes with my Clooney grandparents. Because my father was so rarely around, it was his father whom I called Papa. It was easy for my mother to decide where to leave Betty and Nicky and me when she needed a place for us.

She just left us with whoever had room. Whoever wasn't rock-bottom broke, looking for work. Whoever said yes.

~

"You're the oldest. You'll manage," my mother would say. "You'll be fine." She had been promoted from salesclerk to manager of the dress shop, but she yearned to get out of Maysville, so she got a job as a traveling sales representative for the Lerner chain. When her weekly envelope came, with a five-dollar bill, I'd scan the postmark to see where my mother was or where she had been: Dayton, St. Louis, Detroit. "I don't know when I'll be back," she would say. "But I know you'll be a good girl."

So I was. I was very careful never to say the wrong thing or do the wrong thing. I tried to figure out, early in a stay, what people expected of me, then I'd make sure I was just what they expected. If I wasn't a good girl, I wouldn't be able to live there anymore. Then Betty and Nicky wouldn't be able to live there anymore, either. Then what?

~

In all the comings and goings of those years in Maysville, my sister was the one constant. I was six years older than Nicky, and we became real friends later. But I was just three when Betty was born, so we grew up together. There was hardly ever a time when I didn't share a room with her, play with her, laugh and talk and fight with her. And there was absolutely no time when I didn't love her.

Betty always listened to me, always did what I said we'd do. One very cold winter day, when I was five and Betty just about two, we got dressed up in one of our aunt's long dresses. "Now we have to go down to the river," I told Betty, "because we're going on a long trip, and we have to wait by the river till the boat comes."

Somehow we managed to sneak down the stairs and out of the house without being seen. We scurried across Front Street, clutching the folds of our long gowns. We were standing at the edge of the river grading, and I was looking upriver, pretending I could just see the boat coming, when

Betty skidded down the slick grading into the river. The dark water closed above her head.

I leaned over, grabbed her hand, and dragged her out. She wasn't crying, just coughing and sputtering. I got her home and into the bathtub and then dried off, all by myself—my mother had told me I would manage, I would be able to do whatever had to be done. Betty and I formed a bond, very early, that I was sure nothing would ever break. "We'll always be together," I promised her one day, when we'd just been moved from one place to another. "I'll never leave you behind." I felt absolutely certain nobody else would ever come between us, and I was right. Nobody else did.

Grandma Guilfoyle's house was cozy, but my Grandmother Clooney kept a stylish house, perhaps because when she married an Irish shopkeeper, her family let her know how far down she'd stepped. My grandfather was a watchmaker, with a jewelry store where, in those Depression days, he had more merchandise than customers.

My grandmother was christened Crescentia Koch, called Cynthia, nicknamed Mawley by her grandchildren. At finishing school in Ohio, she'd learned crocheting and tatting and the piano, how to discern fine lace; she taught me needlepoint, the difference between Waterford and Lalique.

Papa was tall, with a mop of white hair, always dressed in a blue suit with a white shirt and a cream-colored silk handkerchief. He usually had his main meal in the middle of the day, sometimes at Caproni's Restaurant by the railroad station, with its wide view of the Ohio River. When he came home from an evening of talking politics with friends, he'd wake me up to join him in a late-night snack of potted shrimp, a wedge of Limburger cheese, orange slices arranged like a flower on the plate. He was the only person I knew who had an egg cup.

People said that Mrs. Clooney would go to unusual lengths to please a man. People also said that she took a lot of pills.

I inherited some of her traits, too.

She and Papa lived above the store on Market Street in an apartment with voile curtains and a gleaming piano. I never learned to play it—never even learned to read music—but I loved to stand by it and sing. My father had a vibrant singing voice, and when he was around—when he was sober—he'd take his ukulele and walk with Betty and me down to the riverbank, where we'd sit under a willow tree and sing. Never country music, which was so widespread in our little town. "Blood on the highway and dust on the Bible. Nothing good ever happens to those SOBs," he'd say, laughing. So we sang Cole Porter. At home, listening to the radio, he praised Bing Crosby, while I insisted that Frank Sinatra was better. Frank had such beautiful clear diction: He dotted the *i*'s and crossed the *t*'s in every word.

My father's sister Olivette led her own small orchestra, which played at parties at the country club. My mother's sister Ann sang in clubs, including Joyland in Lexington with Sammy Kaye's band. At home, she played Billie Holiday records: "Gloomy Sunday," "Strange Fruit." Sometimes she would come sweeping into the house, trailing a glorious scent and a glamorous black feather boa, laughing and singing, lighting up the house like a Fourth of July sparkler. But sometimes she would wander listlessly around the house, weeping. She swallowed a vial of pills one night, and her brother George raced her to the hospital. But the emergency room was jammed, and either they didn't have a stomach pump or they couldn't find it right away, so Uncle George tried to keep her awake. He walked her up and down the hall, but she just slipped out of his arms on to the tile floor and died.

I made my first public appearance when I was three, on the stage at the Russell Theater, the downtown movie house with twinkling stars on the ceiling. Aunt Olivette made me an orange crepe paper hat; I wore a white-dotted Swiss dress with a big bow and sang "When Your Hair Has Turned to Silver (I Will Love You Just the Same)." When I was four, Papa Clooney took me with him to a Rotary lunch, where I sang "Home on the

Range." At five, I sang at the high school in a revue, *Little Tots on Parade*. At St. Patrick's School, I played the wicked queen in an operetta version of *Snow White*.

I liked singing at home, too, even though my mother argued with me about it. When I started singing without any musical accompaniment, I'd wait for the beat, holding the four bars.

"Don't do that," my mother said. "Don't leave those holes."

"I have to, Mama," I said.

Then she was cross. "Why do you have to?"

I couldn't explain it. I was four, maybe five years old: How could I explain to a grown-up that I had to wait a certain amount of time before starting the next phrase? I didn't know how to explain the beats, didn't even know the word. "I don't know why, Mama. I just know I have to."

If my father happened to be there, he'd take my side. "She's right, Fran," he'd tell my mother. "She's doing it just fine." Then he'd grin at me. "You just keep on singing the way you want to."

I kept on. From the corner of Front and Market to the London Palladium, from porch swing to padded cell, strapped down in the violent ward, I never stopped singing. I always sang.

My Clooney ancestors came from Kilkenny, the Guilfoyles from Cork, part of the great surge of Irish who fled to this country from the hunger at home. Maysville had been settled by Presbyterians and Anglicans, members of the planter society—burley tobacco—who built themselves Georgian brick houses trimmed with New Orleans–style lacework balconies. But by the turn of the century, so many Irish had settled in that they built a Catholic church: St. Patrick's. I was baptized there, made my first holy communion there, walked to grade school there in my itchy wool jumper with white collar and cuffs, red tie, and knee socks.

Papa Clooney served on the city council, and for one two-year term was elected mayor. He was passionate about politics, an FDR Democrat, thrilled when President Roosevelt appointed one of Papa's friends, Judge Stanley Reed, to the Supreme Court. But Papa never really fit in with the Maysville establishment—not only because he was Irish Catholic, but because of his views, which many people considered eccentric at best, maybe downright dangerous. His volatile Irish temper flared most insistently when he argued social issues and injustices, when he felt a civilized code of honor had somehow been broken. He published a free newspaper once in a while, in which he urged people not to pay their water bills. "Water is given freely from God," he declared. "No man should be asked to pay for his water." I know he wanted to make an important social point, but the only point he made, as far as I was concerned, was that for a long time we didn't have running water in the house and had to go across the street to haul it back in buckets from the kitchen at the New Central Hotel.

He was an enthusiastic reader and student of history. Both Civil War presidents, Abraham Lincoln and Jefferson Davis, were born in Kentucky; Papa liked to tell us about Lincoln's wry reasoning at one of his first Cabinet meetings, with war looming. "I hope to have God on my side, but I *must* have Kentucky." There'd been a slave-holding pen in Maysville and at least two lynchings. Harriet Beecher Stowe had witnessed a slave auction near Maysville; in *Uncle Tom's Cabin*, Eliza inches her way across the frozen Ohio to Ripley, where in real life there had been a stop on the Underground Railroad. I never heard anyone say that the only good Negro was a dead Negro, but our daily paper's column of "Colored News" consisted mainly of flowery obituaries: "Friends, holding her in esteem as they did, will sorrowfully receive the news of her passing."

Papa's store was across the street from the New Central Hotel, where he took me to meet Lizzie Chambers, the black maid. "Lizzie didn't have a chance to go to school," he told me. "She didn't learn how to read because nobody would teach her. That was very, very wrong. When she was just about as old as you are now, she was working in the tobacco factory. Doesn't matter what people say, doesn't matter what color her skin is, and don't you ever forget that."

I never did. I became best friends with Lizzie's daughter, Blanchie Mae, who came to the hotel after school to wait for her mother to finish work. Lizzie worked late, so when I got home from my school, I'd go over and bring Blanchie Mae back to Papa's. Aunt Olivette, a born snob with a cruel streak, disapproved. "She shouldn't be bringing that colored child here. What will people think?"

"They'll think that these little girls are friends," Papa said firmly, reminding his wife to make some of her fancy sandwiches for us to eat as we played together after school.

When he took us to the Bethel Baptist Church some Sundays to join in the spirituals, we all sat together. But when he took us to the Russell Theater, Blanchie Mae had to sit upstairs in the "buzzard's roost." After the show, we'd walk home, stopping for ice cream cones. Blanchie Mae could eat with us if we were outside, but not indoors. Papa liked to have us put on impromptu shows in his store window—I'd sing and Blanchie Mae would tap dance—and if people passing by didn't like it, that was just too bad.

Between my mother telling me what a bad man my father was and my Grandmother Clooney telling me what a bad woman my mother was, I heard far more about grown-up life than I wanted to know. "She doesn't deserve to be married to my son," Mawley would say. "Your mother has boyfriends. Wouldn't you rather live here with me all the time? Where would you rather live?" Clasping her silk shawl around her shoulders, she would lower her voice as though sharing a secret, as though I were her contemporary and confidante, as though a second-grader could make that crucial choice.

"Your father was drunk again last night," my mother said. I was in the bathtub; she was sitting on the edge, washing my back. "He told me he would stop drinking, but he won't. Your father is a liar. Never trust your father." She scrubbed my back so hard that I squirmed. "Your father is a ladies' man. He has another child, but he's your father's child, not mine." I'd known there was a young man named Clooney working at Murphy's dime store, but it had never dawned on me that we were related. Every time I went to Murphy's after that, I'd hang around the counter and watch Andy Clooney. He looked amazingly like me: blond hair, blue eyes, same turn of the mouth. I never got to know him well. He was twenty-nine years old, still working at Murphy's, when he went on a picnic one summer Sunday, went wading in the Ohio River, walked into a step-off, and drowned.

I never heard Grandma Guilfoyle say mean things about anyone. I saw her really angry just once. My mother was sleeping in the bed with me when my father burst in and began dragging my mother out of bed. Grandma came running in behind him and grabbed hold of his arm.

"Get out and stay out!" she said. "Don't you come near my daughter again! Don't come near this house again!" As he stumbled away, she came around to my side of the bed, where I was huddled, and held me tight.

But I didn't have a frightening childhood, certainly not an abused one. I didn't even feel particularly poor. I never got a bike or roller skates for Christmas—but none of the kids I knew did, either. Lots of people were out of a job, lots of fathers and sometimes mothers were drinking moonshine or taking stuff to help them manage. As the black joke goes, a lot of folks were in the CIA: Catholic Irish Alcoholics. As I got a little older, I could laugh about it, too. One night when my father got up in the middle of the night to go to the bathroom, he was what was delicately called "under the influence," and instead of opening the bathroom door, he stepped out the second-floor window. The awning of my grandfather's store broke his fall. He rolled off the awning, picked himself up, opened the front door—in those days, never locked—walked back upstairs, and went to the bathroom. Later, Nicky made a joke of it, because he said we had to laugh about a lot of stuff or we'd never have gotten through it all. "Other people's ancestors were knighted. Ours were dazed."

Mawley died when I was eight. I don't remember the wake or the funeral. I remember people saying that Papa was taking it hard. Grandma Guilfoyle said it would be easier for him if we came to live with her. So I wasn't there when the flood came.

The Ohio was rising, but slowly. A small river like the Licking River, which tumbles down through the hills and hollows of northern Kentucky, can come jumping up twenty-five feet in a day, so a person better not be asleep or slow-moving. A big river will cause more damage, but not so quickly. So Papa stood outside his store, one hand holding a corner of the awning, smoking a cigar. When his friends tried to get him to move his things out, he shook his head. "The river's not coming any higher."

It was the worst flood in Kentucky's history. The water rose to seventy-nine feet; Blanchie Mae, waiting for her mother to finish work at the New Central Hotel, was taken out of a second-floor window in a skiff.

Most everything in Papa's store was either swept away or ruined by the thick muddy water. He opened another store later, higher up on Market Street, mostly repairing broken watches; people shopped for new watches and jewelry at Traxel's around the corner. I was in fourth grade that fall, Betty in first, and we tried to walk home from school by way of his shop so we could stop in and see him. Papa would stand in the doorway and watch us as we walked away, me holding Betty's hand. "Be careful," Papa would always say to me. "Watch out for your sister."

Nicky started writing songs when he was six. He walked around the house, singing: *Oh, Jesus / Jesus, Jesus, / I'm so lonely, / Lonely, lonely . . .* Uncle George couldn't stand it. "That song is too doggone sad," he declared. "Let's give you a song with some pep to it." Uncle George devised a specialty number based on "The Sheik of Araby." Betty and I would harmonize on a phrase of the song, and Nicky would chime in after each phrase with the distinctive refrain "without no pants on!"

All my uncles were musical. Uncle Neal won a contest at the Opera House in Maysville, singing "Melancholy Baby." Uncle Chick sang pop tunes nonstop around the house. Uncle William was riding the rails into Michigan, looking for work, when he wrote "South Boy" (*I look at the snow and dream about cotton / I long to go back where I'm not forgotten / South Boy wants to go home*). But it was Uncle George who choreographed our family musicals and coached us in the finer points of ensemble singing.

Uncle George was the youngest of the Guilfoyle boys, tall and lanky, with a wry grin and a wraparound heart: He gave up his scholarship to Xavier University to take care of us. Money was stretched thin; Grandma always wore the same black cloth coat and little black hat with a bunch of artificial violets in front, right over her forehead. Once, when my mother's weekly envelope was late, Uncle George took his high school class ring down to the pool hall and exchanged it for three dollars, just for a couple of days. He came home with a sack of potatoes and onions, which Grandma fried in her cast-iron skillet on the fireplace grate.

Mama was somewhere on the road, working; Dad was just somewhere, so when Uncle George got a job with the Baldwin Piano Company in Cincinnati on their loading dock, Grandma packed up and we moved downriver. To Nicky especially, Uncle George became a role model of responsibility and honor. Twenty years later, Nick named his only son after Uncle George.

Our house on Fairfax Avenue in Cincinnati was bigger than Grandma's house in Maysville. There was a living room on the first floor—we called it the front room—and a big kitchen. Two bedrooms on the second floor, and on the top floor, an attic room for Nicky and Betty and me.

Betty was only ten when we moved, but already sure of herself in a way I could only admire, never expect to achieve. When a kid down the block began bullying Nicky, and Nicky told Betty and me, my sister took action.

Betty marched down the block, Nicky and I trailing, and found the kid sitting on his porch steps. "You've been beating up my brother," she said fiercely, making a fist. The kid looked at this knobby-kneed, skinny little girl and laughed. Betty's fist shot out and clipped him alongside his ear. The boy ran into his house, howling.

That evening his parents pounded on our door. "Your granddaughter beat up our son," they informed Grandma. "We expect an apology."

Again, Nicky and I trailed along. Betty walked briskly up the steps, not a moment's hesitation, and knocked. Instantly the door was yanked open. The boy's mother loomed in the doorway, arms folded, glaring; her husband was a frowning figure behind her.

Betty regarded them for a moment, then folded her arms and turned to Nicky and me. "My, my," she said brightly. "Look what we have here! A reception committee!"

Our Aunt Olivette had once summed it up cruelly: "Betty has guts, but no talent. Rosemary has talent, but no guts." I was as angry as Betty about the bully, but I handled confrontation the way that worked for me even then: I avoided it.

Betty's "reception committee" line came directly from the movies. We spent nearly every Saturday or Sunday afternoon—sometimes both—

at our neighborhood theater, the Ritz at Hewitt's Corner. Sometimes we took the streetcar downtown to the Shubert or to the Albee, a magnificent movie palace, all gilt and cherubs and chandeliers. The urinals in the men's room were so imposing—black marble monoliths—that Nicky would go to the Albee only if Uncle George went, too.

Movies were our gateway to a boundless world. The screen glowed with the possibilities we'd always known must be out there—people to see, places to go—around the bend in the river. At night in our attic bedroom, three narrow cots in a row, scrunched under Grandma's worn warm quilts, we'd review the movie we'd just seen, quoting dialogue, planning trips we'd take together. To Singapore, after seeing Sydney Greenstreet under the ceiling fans at Raffles. To Venice on the Orient Express. To magical marvelous places. No matter where we went, we'd go together.

When we weren't replaying movies, we were listening to the radio. Grandma's big Zenith was the centerpiece downstairs, but in our private realm, we terrified ourselves with our little table model: "Suspense," "The Clutching Hand," "Lights Out." We were thrilled by the big band remotes: "Live from the Grill Room of the Hotel Roosevelt in New York City! It's the music of Guy Lombardo and his Royal Canadians!" Sometimes at midnight, long after we were supposed to be asleep, we listened to "Moon River," a program of poetry and music on WLW. We planned our own brilliant career: footlights, fans, and gowns with ostrich feathers for Betty and me.

Happily, we had relatives in town. Aunt Jeanne had moved to Cincinnati to find work and help support the family; she'd met her husband, Roy Dudenhoeffer, while they were both attending Hughes High School at night. Aunt Rose lived in Bond Hill with her husband, Isadore, and their daughters, Phyllis and Joan. Their home was bigger than anyone's I knew; it had a big downstairs room called a rathskeller, with a Ping-Pong table and a jukebox. Isadore had grown up in Maysville, but his family—the Middlemans—had opposed his marriage as strongly as the Irish Catholic Guilfoyles had objected to their daughter marrying a Jew. So the young couple had eloped to Cincinnati. Phyllis was four months old when her parents took her to Maysville, leaving her in a basket on Grandma's porch. Aunt Rose knocked on the door, then slipped around the side of the house as Grandma opened the door and saw her baby granddaughter.

When Uncle Isadore did the same thing at his family's house, everybody pretty much kissed and made up.

Betty and I loved having girl cousins our own age around. Phyllis and I started high school together that fall. The four of us were at the Shubert Theater seeing *The Barkleys of Broadway*—while Nicky, at the Ritz, watched Ida Lupino in *Ladies in Retirement*—on Sunday afternoon, December 7, 1941. At home, the news of Pearl Harbor crackled from the big old Zenith all that day and into the incredulous night.

Uncle George signed up for aviation cadet training, eventually to pilot a B-17 on bombing missions over Europe. Aunt Christine, who was still single, joined the WAVES. Uncle William signed up within weeks of Pearl Harbor, enlisting in the Army Air Force; he was later assigned to Wendover Air Force Base, where he was a part of what would be called the Manhattan Project, where crews were trained for the war in the Pacific, where the *Enola Gay* would be outfitted with the bomb.

Our cousin Tom Anderson lost his hands in a booby trap near Cologne. Uncle Roy, an infantryman, spent a year on the German front. Even Uncle Chick, who had a glass eye from a childhood bout with meningitis, joined the effort as an Army recruiter. When I made an album in 1991, *For the Duration*, I wanted to honor them all. Nick wrote the liner notes; on the cover, we put a photo of Uncle George in his jaunty pilot's gear.

Grandma moved to an old farmhouse on Indian Hill Road at the edge of town, with a big yard where she could keep a chicken coop and grow vegetables in a Victory garden. With Uncle George liable to be called up at any time, Mama came back. She moved us to a just-put-up apartment building on Clinton Springs Avenue. It had hardwood floors and, instead of the familiar brown paper shades on the windows, Venetian blinds; to us, it was palatial. I had to change schools, but I didn't mind. I didn't mingle much or sing in school shows as Betty did; in seventh grade, she gave the sultriest rendition of "Temptation" people had ever heard from a twelve-year-old. People thought I was shy, but it wasn't that simple. I was learning detachment as a protective measure. It was a much more accessible emotion than anger, I found, and useful.

Mama got a job managing a Lerner shop downtown; we all had supper together, and sometimes she'd bring home a coffee cake from the Federal Bakery in the Arcade. On most Sundays, Uncle Roy and Aunt Jeanne picked us up in their black LaSalle to go visit Grandma over on Indian Hill. Grandma would make fried chicken, then the grown-ups would play cards, alternating between the Irish game 500 and the Germans' pinochle.

Betty and Nicky and I were on Grandma's back porch with the Sunday comics when we heard the voices from the kitchen growing louder. We opened the screen door and slipped in. Nobody paid any attention to us.

"She's too old to be taking care of three children," Aunt Jeanne was saying.

"You simply cannot ask her to take care of them anymore," Aunt Rose said to Mama. "Absolutely not."

"Not three," Mama said. "I'm taking Nicky."

"I can do what I want to do," Grandma said stubbornly. "And I want to take care of them."

"It won't work, Fran," Uncle George said to Mama. "I'll be called up any day now."

Uncle William shook his finger at Mama. "You and Andy didn't mind making kids," he told her. "You just don't want to take care of them."

Betty started to cry. When I started crying, too, Uncle William turned around and glared at us. "Stop that!" he said. "Stop your crying! Be quiet!"

Nicky walked up to Uncle William and stood right in front of him. "No, Uncle William," he said in the sternest voice a seven-year-old could muster. "*You* be quiet. They can't help it."

It was the first time my brother had stepped up to defend me, certainly not the last. And he was right; we couldn't help crying. Mama was going to California to marry a sailor.

"Your father is coming to take care of you and your sister," she told me. "He has stopped drinking, and he says he'll never drink again. You can trust him."

I stared at her. What father was she talking about? Did she mean the father who was a hopeless liar, the man she'd warned us we could never, ever trust?

"I'm taking Nicky with me," Mama continued, "and as soon as I get settled, I'll send for you girls."

When the taxi came to take them to the train, she put her hands on my shoulders and looked steadily at me. "You're the oldest," she said. "You'll manage."

Nicky knelt on the back seat of the taxi, waving as they pulled away. Betty was crying as she waved. "We'll be going to California soon," she said.

I was crying, too. I kept looking down the driveway, although the taxi was out of sight. "No, we won't," I said.

Dad looked around and shook his head. "Too new, too fancy." We moved again, to a third-floor walk-up apartment in an old house on Elberon Avenue. I changed schools once more, and this time I made two friends: Marge Wehringer and Pat Jones. Pat and I met in home ec class; we formed a bond because we both hated home ec, where Pat made a pair of pajamas without enough room in the seat. After school we sat in booths at Peggy's Grill, with Cokes and french fries, smoking cigarettes and playing Sinatra records on the jukebox. I was more than a fan; I was obsessed. I saw the movie *Reveille with Beverly* seventeen times by actual count, because he sang "Night and Day" in the picture. I'd idolized Frank from the first time I'd heard him on the radio back in Maysville; I would stop whatever I was doing to hear him on "Your Hit Parade," savoring his exquisite diction and his supple sexy tone.

On weekends, Dad would take us downtown, to see a movie and hear a big band at the Albee, then have a milkshake at Fountain Drug and play the jukebox: still Bing Crosby for Dad, always Frank for me. He was working at the Wright Aeronautical defense plant, making good money and bringing it straight home. Some would go into the yellow bowl in the pantry to be used for groceries and bills; some he'd stash in the top dresser drawer until there was enough to buy a savings bond. There was a lot of money in both places the April evening he came in and emptied both the bowl and the drawer. A buddy had persuaded him to have a beer after work—just one—to celebrate V-E Day. He didn't come home that night, or the next, or the next.

When our food ran out a day or two later, Betty and I scoured the house for empty soda bottles and turned them in for the deposit. We could have called Aunt Jeanne, or Aunt Rose, or Grandma. But Mama had said, "You'll manage."

Radio Station WLW was one of the first stations in the country to begin broadcasting, in 1922. One of the first programs to be heard regularly was a series of swimming lessons, every Wednesday evening at eight o'clock, taught by an instructor from the YMCA. ("Don't take the radio into the pool with you!")

WLW called itself "the nation's station," an understatement for a while in the 1930s, when it was authorized to use a high-powered trans-mitter on an experimental basis. Transmitting at 500,000 watts—the legal limit today in the continental United States is 50,000—this radio station on Crosley Square at Ninth and Elm in downtown Cincinnati could be heard as far away as Calgary and Buenos Aires. Closer to home, people com-plained that they were receiving broadcasts on the banisters of their porches or in the fillings of their teeth.

Music was always a priority at WLW, which had a full orchestra on staff, along with a jazz combo. A large stable of musicians covered all the bases of genre and audience, almost around the clock: Chet Atkins started his country music program at four-thirty in the morning to reach his lis-teners, the farmers who were getting up then to milk cows, gather eggs, and do whatever else farmers need to do at four-thirty in the morning. The Mills Brothers had sung there, and the Ink Spots with their falsetto and their hilarious deadpan delivery. Fats Waller worked there until he was fired for playing jazz on the new organ that Powell Crosley, the boss, had dedicated to his mother. A Cincinnati girl named Doris von Kappel-hoff had sung on "Moon River" until she left town and became Doris Day.

But for Betty and me, flat broke and clean out of soda bottles, the best thing about WLW right then was the open auditions they held every Thursday.

"Where's your music?" the piano player asked us. All we had was our schoolbags.

He shrugged. "Well, then, what are you going to sing?"

We sang "Hawaiian War Chant." Some of the words we'd made up to replace the real lyrics we didn't know. But we were well matched to sing together. I was comfortable in the upper register, so I sang lead. Betty had a natural ear for harmony and a range about three notes lower, a voice close to mine in timbre, but a little darker and warmer. We thought we made a pretty good sound.

A man in a blue suit came out of a small room and asked us to sing something else. We sang "Patty Cake Man" and "Dream." He left and returned with another man. We sang one of our favorites, a Nat Cole tune, "Straighten Up and Fly Right." When they offered us a job, Betty smiled and asked for an advance on our salary.

I began singing for a living in April 1945. I was sixteen; Betty was thirteen. The Clooney Sisters were paid $20 a week. Apiece.

Now that we didn't need to ask for help, I had no hesitation about calling Aunt Jeanne; I'd managed, like Mama said I could. Aunt Jeanne was thrilled about our job, but dismayed that we'd been on our own. "You girls are coming to us," she insisted. And we were glad to agree, now that we could pay our way. When Dad turned up again, broke and contrite, he wanted us to come back. But we stayed where we were. I couldn't trust him again.

"Turn your head away from the microphone when you're sounding a *b* or a *p*," the engineer told us. "Otherwise, you'll make a popping sound into the mike."

That was the sum total of our professional vocal training at WLW. Neither of us read music—we could tell if the melody went up or down, that was all—but we had to learn the songs somehow. Aunt Jeanne and Aunt Rose chipped in to buy us a few lessons from Grace Raine, who'd been Doris Day's coach. Mrs. Raine would play the songs on the piano for us, lead and harmony; then, at the studio, we'd just keep an eye on the accompanist and follow the movements of his hands for the beat, the tempo, the rising or falling line. On our own time, we worked hard, rehearsing the songs we'd learned, working out intricate harmonies. Betty would come over and hum a line in my ear: "What do you think?" Then we'd go downstairs and sing for whoever was home, saying to each other, "Wait till they hear this at the station."

All that summer, Betty and I sang on "Crossroads Cafe" in the afternoon—talk and music, with a big band right there in the studio. The script was typed up on paper with yellow carbon copies behind, including commercials, with some words underlined and some all in capital letters to guide the announcer's delivery. Once when I was putting on lipstick in a break and didn't have a tissue, I blotted my lips on the corner of a carbon for a Vicks VapoRub spot: "It invites restful sleep. And brings such GRAND relief."

Nights it was "Moon River," with Hap Lee as organist. Aunt Jeanne would take us to the station in the LaSalle and wait to bring us home. Sometimes we'd stop for White Castle burgers—"sliders"—three for a quarter. In the backseat of the car, we applied makeup to our bare legs to get the look of stockings. "You're going on the *radio,*" Aunt Jeanne would say. "They're not going to see your legs." We'd laugh and try to draw seams with eyebrow pencil as the car bounced along. We knew the radio audience couldn't tell what our legs looked like; we were just caught up in the excitement of the performing world.

And the world was welcoming us. When Mary Wood, a writer at the station, took us to lunch at the Wheel Café, we talked shop. Over our club sandwiches with fancy toothpicks stuck through them, she gave us all the insider gossip. Because she was well known, she was constantly getting phone calls from listeners. When someone called her at two in the morning to ask, "How old is Loretta Young?" she changed her phone number and had it listed under the name of Buster Wood, her dog.

In the fall, Betty was a freshman and I was a senior at Our Lady of Mercy. It was close enough for us to walk to the station in our uniforms—plaid skirts, white cotton blouses, knee socks—carrying our schoolbags, just like the day we auditioned. We sang after school and into the evening, doing our homework in snatches.

But school had lost its urgency. I was a professional singer now, and I felt sure I would always be able to make my living that way. My confidence seemed to come naturally, based on my early and continuing interest in music. I'd listened so carefully to so many singers that I just somehow knew I could do it as well as almost anybody. I might never leave Cincinnati, but I knew I could always sing, I could always find work. Anyway, I loved to read, and I figured that anything I wanted to learn, I could learn on my own.

We began picking up side jobs around town. Billy Petering, a high school senior who lived around the corner from Aunt Jeanne and Uncle Roy, had organized his own combo. Betty and I sang at Saturday night dances in the high school gym while the kids spun and jumped and swayed on the gym floor with its basketball court markings, and I fell desperately in love with Billy. It's a cliché—the girl singer falling for the leader of the band—and it was glorious. Even after Billy left to join the Navy, he wrote letters calling me "sweetheart" and "dearest." On the backs of the envelopes he wrote the code of those days, SWAK (*S*ealed *W*ith *A K*iss), next to a little drawing of an anchor.

Billy's group may have been small-time, but with them we were band singers, and that carried a kind of glamour that transcended stuffy gyms. And it turned into a pathway when Barney Rapp, a local bandleader who'd discovered Doris Day, discovered us, too. We began singing with Barney's band at major venues in town—at Castle Farms, even at the Netherlands Plaza Hotel in downtown Cincinnati, which always had remote network broadcasts when the big bands came to town. Barney acted as our agent, too: He booked us into Moonlite Gardens with Clyde Trask's orchestra, and he recommended us when he heard that Tony Pastor was looking for a girl singer.

Tony Pastor's band was big-time: an established well-known big band, the real thing. Born Tony Pestritto in New Haven, Connecticut, Tony had been boy singer and tenor sax in the 1930s with Artie Shaw. When Shaw walked out on his band in 1939, heading for Mexico, Tony was good enough to be offered the top job. Instead, he struck out on his own, backed by a ballroom operator in Boston, Sy Shribman, who'd bankrolled a bunch of bands, including Glenn Miller.

Tony's road manager, a slick mustached guy named Charlie Trotta, knew Barney Rapp. So when the band was coming into Cincinnati to play a date, Charlie called Barney and came ahead to scout. Tony's vocalist, Virginia Maxey, was leaving; Cincinnati was a logical place to turn up a replacement. The city was known as a mecca for music: Local No. 1 of the Musicians' Union was formed in Cincinnati.

When Barney came looking for us, we were taking a dip in the community pool, and it was a soggy sister act that Charlie Trotta auditioned that early summer day in 1946. Our hair was uncombed and stringy; we wore shapeless cotton dresses and floppy sandals. That didn't faze Charlie, apparently; he reported to Tony Pastor that now the band had not one new girl singer, but two.

We were introduced to Tony when he came to town for his one-nighter. He was short and round, good-humored and easygoing. "You're good," he told us, "but your arrangements are corny. We'll get you some new arrangements—Ralph Flanagan will do some for you—and I'll see you in Atlantic City."

Betty and I had never been out of our tiny tri-state area: Kentucky, Ohio, and Indiana. We'd never seen the ocean. Now, within a year, we'd gone from schoolgirls in knee socks to big band singers in nylons—with contracts. It was almost too much to take in, an overflow of good luck. Up to that point, I'd been, it seemed to me, a burden to anybody I was left with; suddenly I knew I could take care of myself, and my sister, and my grandmother, and my brother, if necessary—and I could do it quite handily.

But it wasn't quite that easy, getting going. "You gals are underage," Charlie Trotta said when he presented us with the paperwork. "You need somebody in your family to sign for you, to be responsible for you on the road." Betty and I looked at one another, then made a beeline out to Indian Hill.

"We need somebody to take us on the road," Betty said to Uncle George. "We can't go by ourselves."

Uncle George played it straight. "Can't go by yourselves? What a shame."

Betty looked stricken, but I was pretty sure Uncle George was stringing us along. He was just home from the war, not yet settled, and besides, he'd always been our most musical uncle.

"Come on, Uncle George," I pleaded. "We need a legal guardian because we're not twenty-one. Wouldn't you like to travel with a band?"

"Not twenty-one?" he asked, deadpan. "How old are you girls, any-way?"

"I'm fifteen, Uncle George," Betty said innocently. I didn't answer; I knew he was putting us on.

"So you're asking me to be your chaperone," he said, looking stern.

"Yes," I said.

"You want me to drop everything and come on the road with you?"

"Yes," I said.

He shook his head, still frowning. But when he saw that Betty was about to cry, his face cracked into that wonderful wry grin. "When do we leave?"

Goodbyes were difficult, but there was a tremendous excitement— not just ours, but everybody's for us. Uncle Roy drove us down to Maysville in the black LaSalle, the backs of our legs sticking to the hot car seats.

Papa Clooney was standing on the sidewalk on Market Street, one hand holding on to the awning, cigar in the other. There were no cus-tomers in the shop.

"You're going to see more of the country than most people ever do," he said.

Betty laughed. "At least we're going to see the inside of a bus and lots of theaters."

"When you go to a new town, find something interesting," he urged us. "Go to a drugstore and look at the picture postcards. They'll tell you what's worth seeing." He hugged us. "Be sure and send me one."

We walked down Casto Street to say goodbye to Lizzie and Blanchie Mae. Blanchie was thrilled.

"I'm sure going to miss you," she said. "But I'm so happy for you."

I put my arm around her shoulder. "Don't worry, Blanchie Mae," I told her. "We'll always be best friends."

Her mother was less thrilled. "You haven't finished school yet, have you?"

"No, ma'am," Betty said.

"Almost," I said. I had spent four years in four different schools, but lacking two credits, I didn't have a diploma. Betty, with only one year of high school, was a true dropout.

"Well," Lizzie said, clearly disapproving. But she took our hands. "God bless you."

When we climbed aboard the George Washington, we were loaded down with boxes of Grandma's fried chicken, angel food cake, cardboard suitcases into which we had jammed everything we owned. Grandma had been sewing nonstop—stage outfits for Betty and me to wear—two by two, everything matching. We took along pictures of every relative who had ever stood in front of a box camera. And I had my own private stash of Payday candy bars.

Uncle George sat across from us on the aisle. "You can sit on the river side first," I told Betty. "When I'm ready, we'll switch."

When the conductor came by—"How far you folks going?"—Uncle George brandished the tickets, gestured toward Betty and me, and said the line he'd been rehearsing. "All the way," he told the conductor. "We're together, and we're going all the way!"

TWO

"*P*ut Nicky up front," Betty said. We lined up the family photos on the scratched veneer top of the dresser until they were all
arranged and there was no room for anything else. Then Betty
took the big brown scrapbook—the biggest we could find at the
dime store—and laid it on the bed. Before we left home, she'd
labeled the stiff cardboard cover with big white letters:

THE CLOONEY SISTERS
OUR LIFE WITH TONY PASTOR'S ORCHESTRA
JULY '46 TO ?

She pasted our train ticket stubs on the first page. "I'm not going
to forget a thing," she said.

The Albemarle was a no-star hotel. The double bed was
sinking in the middle, the light bulbs low-wattage, the floor

slanted, the bath down the hall. Our room was small and dark and absolutely splendid. We unpacked all our clothes, took baths and brushed our teeth, rearranged the pictures, and finally fell into bed, exhausted and wide awake, too keyed up to sleep.

On the next evening—July 10, 1946—we would open at the Marine Ballroom on the Steel Pier in Atlantic City. We were professionals now. We were big band singers. We were sure we were on our way to being stars, and we had the wire from Aunt Jeanne to prove it.

> BEST WISHES IN YOUR NEW ADVENTURE
> STOP KEEP GEORGE IN HAND STOP BE
> SEEING YOUR NAME IN LIGHTS

Atlantic City was a lovely place, a world removed from today's neon and casino glitter. Men wearing straw hats strolled the boardwalk with ladies dressed in a style that could only be called genteel. The grand hotels were set back from the boardwalk with cultivated gardens. The clubs and restaurants seemed festive, not flashy. The place was so tranquil, in fact, that writers regularly came down from New York City to work: George S. Kaufman and Irving Berlin were among the creative types who found Atlantic City happily conducive to concentration.

The Steel Pier stretched far out from the boardwalk, suspended over the Atlantic on enormous pilings I didn't quite trust. The main theater was toward the middle of the pier; we were appearing on the secondary stage at the end, where at regular intervals during the day a trained horse would dive from a forty-foot tower into a tank. As we walked the pier's length, Betty and I were both sure it was going to collapse under us. And when we were backstage, waiting to go on, a tiny part of me wished it would. Only our band work with Barney Rapp in Cincinnati kept me from being totally nervous. And I told myself that this was a dance band; people came to dance, not critique the singer.

Before I even realized I was moving, I found myself out of the wings and halfway across the stage, shaking in my unaccustomed spike heels, my plaid taffeta dress rustling around my ankles. Out of the corner of my eye

I saw Betty moving toward me from the other side of the stage. The lights blinded me so that I couldn't see more than a few feet from the stage, but I sensed the people—three thousand or more on the dance floor, waiting for the music to start.

I looked at Betty, the band struck up "It's a Good Day," and we sang.

For the most part, the arrangements on hand were in keys I could handle. "It's a Good Day" went without a hitch. But my first solo, "That's Good Enough for Me," was a little high in places. Reaching for one note, I felt and heard my voice break—badly. I thought I heard a faint collective gasp from the crowd.

So much for my career as a band singer. I knew in that moment it was all over, but I couldn't break down. I had to cover up for the audience, smooth it over, the only professional thing to do. I gave them my biggest smile, as if to say, *Wasn't that something?*

And they applauded. They clapped for me! Then I knew they were on my side. And I knew how much that mattered to me—something Betty, with her generous, extroverted warmth, had known all along, but I was just realizing. I wasn't singing to the wall of a sound-proofed studio anymore; I was singing to real people, lyrics they could understand, maybe even in some personal way.

Again that night, neither of us could sleep. When a gray light began to filter in our window, we dressed and walked out to the pier, right back to the end. We stood in the shadow of the empty pavilion carpeted with the litter of a big night, and we looked out over the Atlantic. Last night it had been dark and I hadn't been paying attention. Now, at dawn, I saw that it stretched beyond imagination, and the force of the waves as they crashed against the pilings made the pier tremble. I clutched Betty and we laughed, feeling the Atlantic wind on our faces, just laughed with the thrill of it all.

At the first rehearsal, Tony Pastor had introduced us to the band, then Uncle George introduced himself. "I am the big man," he said bluntly. "Keep that in mind at all times. If you want to take the girls to a movie and you ask me first, you will find me reasonable. But if you go behind my back"—he paused for effect—"you will not find me reasonable at all." Uncle George was only twenty-four years old, but the musicians seemed impressed, partly because of his strong stance and partly because they were so young themselves. Glenn Miller had made a movie, *Orchestra Wives,* but most of the boys in the band were bachelors, and most *were* boys—in their late teens, early twenties. Only a trombone player, Dave Maser, who was several years older, complained about us. "We're babysitting two little kids on the road, for God's sake. This is supposed to be a professional organization. What the hell is this, two teenaged kids with us on the road?" But Uncle George straightened him out, and we got along fine. Later, when Aunt Chris came to travel with us for a while, she and Dave got along so fine, in fact, that they got married.

Singing with a big band was a defining experience in my life. In the comfortable enclosure of the WLW studio, my voice could be contained, even cradled. The pacing was relaxed, the atmosphere flexible, even on a live show. Singing from a bandstand with a full orchestra demanded discipline and unbroken attention. The horns and drums rushed along like a locomotive—fall off the beat and that train would just keep going, run right over you. Before anything else, I learned timing and pacing, and I learned to keep up.

I learned refinements, too. How to work as part of an ensemble. How to modulate my voice against the background of the other instruments. How to go beyond just singing a song to phrasing it; how to emphasize unexpected words or leave a space where you'd expect a note to catch the listener's ear and make him wonder, *What next?* Betty and I weren't singing every second, and to draw attention away from the other performers, even by looking away, would have been unprofessional—so I learned how to sit still at the side of the stage and yet appear involved when the band was doing an instrumental number, or when Tony was singing by himself. He sang "I'm Confessin' (That I Love You)" every single night, and he always smiled when he sang.

Betty and I each made $125 a week; out of that we paid for our hotels and food, plus Uncle George's, and sent some home to Grandma Guilfoyle. Uncle George felt responsible for her, even though she had other grown children living nearby, even though Mama had come back from California with her husband and Nicky and a new baby, Gail. Betty and I visited them in Lexington, Kentucky, before we left because Grandma said we had to and because I wanted to see Nicky, who'd been away from us for four years. But I hadn't forgotten that Mama had broken her promise to bring Betty and me to California, so I still considered—always considered—Grandma's house to be home base.

The farther I got from most of my family, the closer I felt to Betty—and the closer Betty felt to almost everybody. More than ever, she wore her heart on her sleeve, and it was a heart as big as all outdoors—or at least as big as the band bus. She lavished warmth on everyone: the bus driver, Uncle George, the waitresses in the all-night diners. I teased her about how often she said, "I love you." One night in a hotel, she glanced at me—"Listen to this"—as she picked up the phone to leave a wake-up call. "Goodnight, operator," she said, winking at me. "I love you."

We embellished our scrapbook, pasting tiny cut-out photos of ourselves into the *o*'s in CLOONEY. Into the book went the DO NOT DISTURB sign from the Harrisburger Hotel and the complete menu from the dining room of the Lorraine Hotel in Philadelphia: A Tom Collins was fifty cents, a complete dinner with soup, salad, entrée, and two vegetables ranged from $1.20 for a mushroom omelette to $2.75 for a broiled tenderloin steak, the costliest item on the menu. I had eaten that mushroom omelette and it had hooked me; from then on, I ordered a mushroom omelette whenever I could, at any hour of the day or night.

Something I took care to leave out of the book was an article that a Cincinnati paper ran, reporting that "the older half of the singing Clooney sisters had been signed as the leading feminine vocalist with Pastor's band." No mention of Betty. Not that I wanted to hide it from her—she'd seen it and it hadn't ruffled her a bit—but I didn't want to highlight it, either.

I couldn't deny it was exciting to be singled out, though. In our first recording session with the Pastor band—our first ever, for that matter—we'd cut an album of songs from the Disney movie *Song of the South*. We sang together on "Zip-a-Dee-Doo-Dah" and "Everybody Has a Laughing Place," but I was the one who stepped up to the mike alone to record

"Sooner or Later." And when *Down Beat* reviewed that little platter, calling me "perhaps the nearest thing to Ella Fitzgerald we've ever heard," I was thrilled—and inspired. I figured if the critics liked that sound, I should concentrate on making that sound. We were playing a ballroom a few weeks later when I heard a strange cough and looked down from the stage to see Uncle George dancing past, trying to catch my eye. In a stage whisper, he called up to me, "Sing it, Ella!" He rolled his eyes. I must have been concentrating too hard; after that, I never again tried to copy any other singer.

I've never thought of myself as a jazz singer. I know a lot of people—musicians, mostly—do think of me that way, because I have certain jazz attributes that I can incorporate into whatever I'm singing; I have good time, and a certain way of phrasing, and I know where the beat is. But my definition of a jazz singer is an improvisational musician, like Ella, or Carmen McRae, or Mel Tormé. I have very little in the way of improvisational skill, because I don't read music—I don't know what the chord structure is—and I don't have the ear for it. I'd call myself a sweet singer with a big band sensibility.

The big bands were beginning to fade in that just postwar year; within six months of our signing with Tony Pastor, some of the biggest names in the business—Woody Herman, Harry James—called it quits. But Tony said a much longer goodbye. He kept going for another decade until he finally was forced to admit that the road was getting way too expensive for five saxophones, three trombones, four trumpets, drums, a bass, a piano, and a guitar, not to mention the vocalists. In 1957, he regrouped with a small combo for a settled stay in Las Vegas.

But for Betty and me, that summer of '46, no end was in sight. We felt we were on the threshold. The big bands were still what people went to hear at the theaters, played on the radio and the phonograph, danced to on a Saturday night. Some bands were built around a leader's personality and his instrument: Artie Shaw's clarinet, Count Basie's piano. Tommy Dorsey and Glenn Miller led what were called "sweet" bands; Kay Kyser's College of Musical Knowledge was a "novelty" band. Although Tony was sometimes called "the Louis Prima soundalike," he nonetheless had a talent for presenting a familiar song in a wholly new way: His big hit with

Shaw had been "Indian Love Call" in a jazz version of his own creation. Tony's band was warmhearted, listener-friendly; his theme song was "Blossoms."

It was a clean band on the whole—no heavy drugs, maybe a little pot, definitely some drinking. Once, in a dry town, a trumpet player ducked into an alley and came out smiling, holding a bottle of "Southern Comfort" with the label still wet. A few veterans lived for the road, even when they weren't traveling; our band manager, Danny Gregory, loved the life so much that even when he was at home in Harrisburg, he'd go downtown to a hotel and sit in the lobby to read his paper and smoke a cigar. For him and a few others, including Tony, the road was not just a way of life, but a way of being. And even though the life was often far from glamorous, no matter what movies of the 1940s suggested—especially for sidemen, who didn't lead a section or play a solo—they lined up to play for name outfits. Literally lined up: Members of the union local would hang out in the halls where a name band was rehearsing, waiting for a call for their instrument, an empty chair in their section. Waiting for the door to open and the manager to lean out: "Is there a tenor man in the hallway?" There was a great swell of satisfaction and professional pride in the calling, among the best musicians, and it was parceled out sparingly; it was a tremendous compliment for a vocalist to be called a musician, too.

A compliment and a challenge: Frank Sinatra once compared working with a big band to lifting weights, heavy ones. "You're conditioning yourself," he said. "A singer can learn—should learn—by listening to musicians." He'd learned the most, he said, not from vocal coaches or even from other singers. By paying close attention to Tommy Dorsey on the trombone, he'd learned his phrasing, his breathing. Certainly he had greater breath control than any singer I've ever known, but that wasn't what impressed me most. Could he do six bars without taking in air? That's Johnny-one-note, like Ethel Merman holding a note until people start to applaud. It's just a sideshow trick. What I was learning from Frank was his diction: It was stunningly clear, no matter what he was singing— standards or fluff. On the bandstand, I took my apprenticeship further.

Offstage, Betty and I quickly became comfortable with the routine: Check in, check out, make do. When our hotel room had swinging doors that wouldn't stay closed, we moved a heavy chifforobe up against them for the night. We learned quickly not to set up the family photos unless we were staying somewhere at least a week. We learned how to apply makeup in a moving vehicle and how not to: I'd once glued my eyelids shut with too much mascara. We learned to sleep whenever and wherever, which was often leaning against each other in our seat on the bus. We had the second seat; the front seat went to the band boy, Joe Mooney, who made sure all the instruments and equipment—and all the musicians—made it on and off the bus on time. Joe had a killer Lionel Barrymore imitation he would do if you asked him; it wasn't especially good, just funny.

Uncle George shared his seat, and his hotel room when we had hotel rooms, with tenor sax player Stan Weiss; trumpeter Al Quaglieri and trombone player Sy Berger sat nearby, and the six of us ruled over our own section of bus. When we weren't asleep or trying to be, we'd sing, or Uncle George would tell bedtime stories—Kentucky folk tales, like the one about the woman who walked out of the river clad in green leaves. Tony Pastor liked to reminisce. With Artie Shaw's band, he'd met and befriended Billie Holiday. Billie had sung with the Shaw band, always with a gardenia pinned in her hair. But she wasn't billed as the main vocalist and couldn't do the whole show because she was, in the labels of that time, "colored," a "Negro." When she needed a doctor once, while the band was playing below the Mason-Dixon line, it was Tony who found—and paid—a doctor willing to treat her.

We'd played the Steel Pier for two weeks, but the band made the most money from one-nighters. Sometimes we didn't even check into a hotel: We'd play the room, change clothes, and get back on the bus to ride and sleep the rest of the night and into the next day. We'd roll into the next small town and go straight to the auditorium, or the college gym, or wherever, sometimes to change in a dressing room, sometimes just in the ladies' room.

Nights on the bus, we couldn't see much out the windows except pale reflections of our own faces. Days, we watched as the country rolled by, beautiful or desolate, always more real and more varied than we'd ever imagined. The flat landscape of central Ohio rose up ahead of us into startling contours, gentle hills and green valleys full of welcoming towns, before it flattened out on the other side. In West Virginia, the mountains were a brooding presence; the road sliced through them in tunnels like the kind John Henry dug, plunging straight into the mountainside.

I woke up when the bus slowed down at the entrance to Lincoln Tunnel. "Betty," I said, shaking her. "We're almost there." Then we plunged into a deeper darkness, weirdly punctuated with orange lights. I scanned the curving tunnel walls, checking for cracks or drips; I could almost feel the weight of the Hudson River above.

On the Manhattan side, in the West 30s, we drove through a deserted industrial cityscape; our hotel in the theater district, the King Edward, had a funny musty smell and an odd collection of men in suits sitting around the lobby. Were they salesmen? Pimps? We weren't sure, but it was fun to speculate.

I was thrilled and excited by New York the first time I saw it, and I still am. My romance with Manhattan has endured now for half a century and counting. Betty and I scarcely slept that first night, waking before sunrise to watch the streets come alive. In Times Square, we stood stock-still, grinning at the puffs of smoke drifting up from the CAMEL cigarette sign high above the street. In Greenwich Village, we walked the narrow lanes, relishing the bumpy roundness of cobblestones under our feet, and stared unabashedly at the passing parade of characters. We'd heard of bohemians; we couldn't believe we were actually seeing them.

Whenever we weren't working or trying to sleep, we were exploring. Up Broadway to Columbus Circle, facing the wall of green that was the southern rim of Central Park. Down 57th Street past the ornate marquee of Carnegie Hall. "We'll sing there someday," we promised one another. The posters in the display cases would show THE CLOONEY SISTERS smiling together, larger than life.

Tony Pastor's home manager in New York was Joe Shribman, the nephew of Sy Shribman, who bankrolled the band. He had an office on Seventh Avenue, not far from our hotel, where we had to check in regularly. The floor directory pointed the way: right for Shribman and a law firm called Friend and Reiskind, left for José Ferrer Productions. "You think that's the famous actor?" we'd say to each other. Betty wasn't sure.

"Wouldn't he be in a fancier building?" It became a kind of shorthand whenever we stepped off the elevator: "You think?"

To add to the excitement, we were playing the Paramount Theater, where Sinatra had launched his spectacular solo career just a handful of years earlier on New Year's Eve, 1942. That performance had ushered in a new era of pop stars as idols; when Sinatra was introduced, the roar of the young crowd slammed into the stage, a solid wall of sound. No one had ever seen an audience in such a frenzy—screaming, swooning, grasping for the stage. Our audience was calm, though, and I was surprisingly calm, too. While it felt important to be standing and singing in the exact same spot where my idol had stood and sung, I was also feeling the rigors of the road. Our Paramount schedule was timed to the minute, a continuous loop of entertainment from noon to one the next morning. After four minutes of advance trailers, Tony Pastor & Band played for exactly forty-seven minutes, starting—according to one day's tattered timetable I've kept—at 2:06, 5:00, 7:39, and 10:27. In between: two intermissions, three shorts, a newsreel, and a feature film. And to keep us on our tired toes, a rehearsal before the first show, every morning.

On one of our rare days off, we'd gone out for a long late lunch and a longer walk. We were coming into the hotel lobby in the early evening when we met Tony Pastor going the other way. He took us each by an arm and swung us back out the door. There was someone he wanted us to see: Ella Fitzgerald at a club on 52nd Street.

We walked up Broadway to the block known as Swing Street, jammed with little jazz clubs. The Three Deuces, the Famous Door, the Onyx—one after another after another. I hadn't yet been to New Orleans, but later I thought that 52nd Street was very much like Bourbon Street, the club doors open with jazz spilling out, guys out front, smiling seductively, like carnival barkers: "Come in, come on in, we have a show starting in fifteen minutes, don't pass by, pretty lady, come on in!"

I don't remember the club where Ella was singing that night. "She says she has a bad throat tonight," Tony whispered to us. "Just so you know." But when she opened her mouth and sang—"Day In—Day Out" was the opener—she wasn't at all forgiving of her voice: She sang full-out. Sitting in that tiny club, listening to this legend, I could hardly believe my name had ever been linked in the same sentence with hers.

She didn't excuse herself or give herself an easy way out that night. She tried to sing the song as best she could, with her bad throat. She demanded of herself what she knew she had, and it didn't matter that she perhaps couldn't do it at that moment. She gave the audience everything she had, and I admired her for that. I learned from that.

But I learned something else, too, a little later on, when the word had gone around: She wasn't singing so well. It only happened that one night, but it can be a runaway thing; people talk, and it can hurt your voice and your work and your ability to get work. I learned that sometimes it's best to take one step back and perhaps not perform that night. Or at least take the easy note instead of the reach. Take the easy note because most people won't know the difference. Musicians will know, especially if they work with you all the time, because they know what usually happens at that point in the song, but in general the audience won't know and therefore won't mind.

I never talked about this with Ella, because when I got to know her, she never wanted to talk about work, about anything professional. She always talked as though we'd been in constant touch, even though I didn't see her often at all. She'd sit down and say, "My niece was on an airplane the other day . . ." and she'd talk as if picking up where she'd just left off. She moved immediately to the personal; we talked about family and our daily lives, never about music.

And yet music seemed to come to her with incredible ease. When she performed, there was no flamboyance, no theatrics: She just stood there with the little handkerchief she always held, kind of wadded up in her hand, and that sound flowed out with no effort at all. If I had never believed in God before, I believed when I listened to her sing.

⌣

Billy Petering was still sending me his sweet letters sealed with a kiss, but I was moving on. Uncle George's protective instincts weren't altogether off base: I found myself involved, more and more seriously, with the band guitarist, Milt Norman. I hadn't sought a connection for its own sake; I didn't feel that I needed a man. I'd spent most of my childhood without a father, and I knew I could be all right on my own. But with Milt, I fell truly, deeply in love. I had all a nineteen-year-old's capacity for strong feeling with a dash of overwrought romantic ardor. I thought our affair was a force of nature, history-making, bigger than both of us.

Which made it all the more difficult to keep it quiet. Uncle George was still my guardian and still very much my chaperone; romances were not part of his plan for Betty and me, and he took his plan seriously. He kept his eyes open during the day and often knocked on our door for a bed check at night. So I couldn't date Milt openly or associate with him except in the general way of the band. We saw each other secretly. "Rosemary's asleep," Betty would say when Uncle George came to the door, or "Rosemary's in the shower." She always covered for me, and it worked for a long time.

Milt sat with me on our plane trip all the way across the country to Hollywood. Neither Betty nor I had ever set foot on an aircraft, and some of the boys weren't much more seasoned travelers; it was unusual for a band to travel by plane or even by train. In those days, the cross-country trip was grueling, even by air: It took all day, with four stops, and each time we were sure that *this* time the plane was going to break up or *this* time the propellors would fly off, they were making so much racket. Uncle George laughed. "Relax," he said. "It's not a B-17. At least nobody's shooting at us!"

We reached the West Coast in one piece, and I loved it the moment I stepped off the plane. Stiff and groggy from sitting, I breathed in the soft air with pleasure and disbelief: it felt so *good*.

We set up at the Hollywood Palladium and dug in for a stay at the Vine Lodge, where all the bands stayed. As soon as we could, we headed down Sunset Boulevard to the ocean. If our first glimpse of the Atlantic had been a thrilling view of possibilities, tied up with the excitement of our new life with the band, the Pacific bookended us with a calm, palmy glamour. Betty and I—seasoned professionals now—leaned on the Palisades railing and watched the sun go down over the smooth surface of the sea, not feeling that we'd seen it all, just that we now appreciated the range of what there was to see.

We hadn't seen it all, far from it. We were still starstruck. One night we stood in the shadows in the courtyard of the Vine Lodge, waiting to catch a glimpse of June Christy, the girl singer with Stan Kenton's band.

We knew Kenton was playing in town and the band was staying at the hotel; we figured June Christy had to come in sometime. When she did, wearing a suede trenchcoat and laughing with her husband, Kenton tenor sax player Bob Cooper, I was actually tongue-tied for a moment: She was so stylish—and so close to us! Betty, the one with the guts, had no problem. "Hi, Miss Christy!" she called out.

June turned and smiled, that happy, wide, quirky smile of hers. "Hi, girls!" I couldn't believe it, but she knew who we were. "How's Tony treating you?"

Tony and Hollywood were treating us fine. Between shows at the Palladium, we made the rounds. We dropped in at radio stations to mingle with DJs, push the band's records—the kind of promotion that was best done in person. On Tony's instructions, we'd show up at the door at all hours—late at night, in the early-early morning—and introduce ourselves: "Mr. Pastor couldn't come, but he sent us!" Smiling till our gums hurt, we played the opening of a big Rexall drugstore at Beverly and La Cienega; as the mayor cut the ribbon, I kept sneaking looks around at the people who had gathered. Never in my life—not even in New York—had I seen so many beautiful people all in one place.

"I've got to come and live here someday," I said to Milt.

He reached for my hand. "Stay here with me now."

He was serious. He was going to quit the band, and he wanted me to quit, too. He wanted me to marry him and stay in California.

In my naïve romanticism, I hadn't imagined that any conflict could arise between the different things I wanted: to be with Milt; to sing with the band; to explore possibilities. I was stunned at the choice I had to make. But I'd always found it easiest to tell people what they wanted to hear. I knew there was only one possible answer.

"Yes," I said.

Tony had arranged for the band to record on the Columbia label. The first session came up on June 5, 1947, at the CBS studio in Hollywood. We did a few novelty numbers together—"My O'Darlin' My Lovely My O'Brien," "Tira Lira Li"—then I had a solo, "I'm Sorry I Didn't Say I'm Sorry When I Made You Cry Last Night." The convoluted progression of feeling in the title pretty well described my own state when I took the mike. I felt almost overwhelmed with emotion—fear, partly, because it was the first time I'd recorded for Columbia. But I was nearly choked by my feelings about Milt as he swung into the guitar intro with a sweet, knowing smile for me.

I loved him very much. But I knew I wouldn't stay here with him. I couldn't afford to stop in my tracks just when my career was beginning to move. I couldn't take on a husband. All this was swelling in my mind as the intro played, and I was almost in tears. When I opened my mouth to sing, the lyrics came out in something like a whisper. I couldn't help it; I sang the whole song that way.

I still wanted to enjoy the time I had left with him, and I took a certain poignant pleasure in living out the end of a lovely romance. An end only I knew was coming: I hadn't managed to tell him my decision. I didn't want to hurt him, and I knew that it would.

One night we walked around the empty streets long after the rest of the band was back in the hotel. I knew Betty would cover for me when Uncle George knocked on the door. So when I slipped into our room much later, turning the knob as quietly as I could, I was totally unprepared to find Uncle George sitting bolt upright on the edge of my bed, eyes glued to the door—and me. Betty was curled in a chair, looking miserable. She hadn't been able to fool him this time.

Tony fired Milt the next day, not knowing he'd been ready to quit anyway. Milt caught my eye while Tony was talking, and I knew what he was thinking—that now was my time to say I was leaving, too. I looked away.

I avoided Milt until the last possible moment. Then I told him I was going on with the band. I said I couldn't leave my sister; I said I needed the money; I said I wasn't ready. I don't know if any of those arguments made sense to him. I do know he believed that our separation would be temporary, that we'd be together eventually, because I didn't tell him otherwise. He didn't make a scene or even remonstrate with me at all, though I felt his disappointment weighing on me all the time we were packing up to go.

I felt it all the way to our next date in a small Texas town, where he'd said he would write to me care of general delivery—a sweet, sad letter I could barely stand to read. I still felt it when we drove into Virginia Beach, clear on the other side of the country, for a stint at the Cavalier Hotel.

That night Betty and I sat on the beach, and I talked to her about it, hoping that would help. I thought she might understand, because what was hurting me most was this: I knew I'd done to Milt the same thing Mama had done when we were children—insisting everything was fine, making us trust that it was, when all along it was just the opposite. It was just so much easier for me not to tell Milt it was really over, and I thought it would be easier for him, too.

I hadn't really believed Mama when she promised we would join her in California. I hated to think Milt had seen through me that easily. Still, I couldn't have confronted him. Somehow that would have been worse.

We were on the road almost continuously for three years. The union limit on mileage was three hundred miles a day, but I know there were many days when we drove five hundred. In one seven-day stretch, we played Syracuse, New York; Pottsville, Johnstown, and Greensburg, Pennsylvania; Morgantown, West Virginia; Steubenville, Ohio; and Ann Arbor, Michigan. We played parks, schools, state fairs. We played theaters: the Chicago, the Casino, the Seville, the Hippodrome, the Capitol. We played nightclubs: the Thunderbird, the Vogue Terrace, the Meadowbrook, the Boulevard, the Club Bolero. Presentation houses like the Albee, where Nicky had been afraid to pee in the urinals.

When Nicky was thirteen, in the summer of 1947, he went on tour with us; he spent part of the next summer with us, too. Uncle George wanted to make him a boy singer; he bought him a new suit and started to coach him. But artistic differences quickly arose, the very same differences I'd had with Mama: When Nicky finished a line, he'd wait out the rest of the musical phrase, just beating time, and this drove Uncle George crazy. "Don't do that," he'd say. "Do it my way!"

So Nicky's career never got off the ground, but he had good times with us. One day we had a rare day off, no travel, so we went to a movie: *Anna and the King of Siam*. Afterward we analyzed the film, the way we used to in the attic, talking about our favorite parts and daydreaming about traveling to someplace so foreign, so deeply exotic.

One night we gave an outdoor concert at the Virginia Military Institute to an all-male audience of cadets, by definition rowdier—and bawdier—than a co-ed school crowd. Under off-the-shoulder peasant blouses made by Grandma, Betty and I wore our everyday bras, with the straps slipped down and pinned in place. Betty had added her own embellishment: a set of truly enormous falsies. She had worn them before without incident, but on the stage that night, one suddenly flew out of her bodice and bounced on the floor. The audience howled. One cadet called out, "Whose is *that?*" Another boy, standing right below the stage, reached up and grabbed Betty around the ankle. Still singing—she hadn't missed a note through any of this—she yanked her foot away and brought her spike heel right down on the boy's hand.

Soon-to-be Uncle Dave came to accept and even respect us, as did the rest of the company. But that didn't mean we were in on all the fun, all the time. In St. Louis, we stayed and played at the Chase, a lovely old hotel at the corner of Kingshighway and Lindell Boulevard, with a ballroom at the top whose curving windows looked out over the whole city and the green spread of Forest Park. There was a farewell party for one of the boys who was leaving the band, and we were invited, but Uncle George wouldn't hear of it. So we had our own party: The band boy rustled us up a bottle of some kind of bourbon, we dug out some cigarettes we'd hidden, and we sat on our twin beds, smoking and drinking. Then we passed each other crawling back and forth to the bathroom all night long.

Uncle George tried hard to keep us practicing Catholics. In New York, he found us a place to eat on meatless Fridays that served thick, delicious clam chowder. We ate it with oyster crackers, and we didn't do too badly in other observances; even on the road, we went to church in the towns we landed in on Sundays—if we could. I liked the sound Betty and I made when we lifted up our voices amid the congregation—a joyful noise totally unlike the kind we made on the bandstand—and I admit I enjoyed the appreciative glances we'd sometimes get from the folks in the pew ahead. More than anything, I liked the way it made me feel: a little exalted, maybe even a little closer to God.

It was a time when observances, like fast days and feast days, were taken very seriously and when your religion defined your place in the world with a great deal of certainty. So the trombone man Sy Berger, who was Jewish, had a faint air of mystery about him, even as I got to know him better. I got to know him, in fact, quite a bit better. I'd believed—actually, assumed—that Milt and I were forever; I didn't know any other way to think of it. So losing him—and getting over it—had surprised me with the revelation that you could move on, that you could love more than one person in a lifetime, that the present good thing might not be the *only* good thing. Loving Sy just completed that particular learning curve.

Not that I took romance lightly as a result; far from it. I don't know how far my relationship with Sy might have gone—I do know he was serious about me, as I was about him—but in the spirit of the time, his family objected strenuously to a connection with an Irish Catholic girl. Years later, he did marry a Gentile, and his parents sat shiva for him.

Three years is a long time to be on the road, living out of a bus, ironing clothes on hotel room floors, away from people you love. For every spark of excitement, there began to be a twinge of discomfort, sometimes genuine pain. One winter day we climbed off the bus in a country town, virtually ignored by the greeters—girls who, in the guise of welcoming the band, flounced and flirted and made eyes at the boys. Betty and I were walking away with our suitcases when one of the girls from the hotel noticed us. "Oh, there was a phone call for you," she said offhandedly. "Your grandfather died."

We couldn't get home for the funeral. But Betty and I remembered his parting advice to us, and in his honor we went to the corner drugstore in that dreary town to see what postcards they had. The pickings were slim: a statue of a war hero and a well-preserved cabin dating back to pre-Revolutionary days, both photographed from many angles to make up a saleable selection. Hand in hand, we walked out of the store and visited them both.

Sometimes the road led much closer to home. When we played the Albee in Cincinnati, it wasn't just an engagement, it was a celebration. All our relatives came: Aunt Jeanne and Uncle Roy, Aunt Rose and Uncle Isadore, and all our cousins, sitting in the front row, with Grandma in the center. The next day she raided her chicken coop for the traditional feast: piles of crispy fried chicken, bowls of cole slaw, green beans with chunks of Kentucky ham, all passed along the picnic tables set up in her backyard. Besides the family, all the boys in the band came. Gene Cipriano, a young saxophone player from New Haven, was especially appreciative. "This is wonderful, Mrs. Guilfoyle," he told Grandma. "I didn't get this kind of food at home. We ate a lot of spaghetti."

Our road crossed and recrossed the heartland, with its motor courts—one with cabins shaped like Indian tepees—and bandshells on village greens. We read BURMA SHAVE signs out loud, including one I had to explain to Betty:

> A LEGITIMATE BUSINESS
> IS OUR DOWER
> NO CABINS RENTED
> BY THE HOUR

And it was on the road that I met Skitch Henderson.

I'm not sure just where we met, and Skitch doesn't remember, either. But I remember how seriously I fell in love with this funny, articulate, two-timing man who played the piano and led his own dance orchestra. He was the most sophisticated musician I'd met—he was a friend of Bing Crosby, who'd suggested that he put together a band. Skitch played the Café Rouge at the Pennsylvania Hotel in Manhattan, where Glenn Miller had made a hit of the hotel's phone number: "Pennsylvania 6-5000"! He went on the road then for a couple of years, but that was long enough for us to meet and for me, at least, to be swept away. "You are a beautiful woman, with an uncommon musical sense," he said, "and that's a hell of a combination! You can grow geranium beds with that!"

We were together whenever we could arrange it—at least once in Cincinnati, when he was playing Moonlite Gardens, and he came to Grandma's for fried chicken. At Aunt Rose's house, he shampooed the cocker spaniel in a washtub in the rathskeller while my cousin Phyllis played my latest recording, "You Started Something," on the jukebox. I lay on the couch, pretending to keep my eyes closed, but I peeked out between my lids so I'd see their honest reactions. Phyllis saw that I was peeking; Skitch looked thoughtful, listening to the arrangement, and I could tell he liked the sound. The wet dog kept slithering out from under Skitch's arm while the song swung on.

I'd kept that early Cincinnati article out of our growing scrapbook, but I couldn't keep away the knowledge that I was outstripping my sister as a singer. I hated to think that Aunt Olivette might have touched the truth in her harsh appraisal: the guts to Betty, the talent to me.

It's hard to pin down where the real difference lay. People who heard us individually would sometimes say we sounded alike, and I could hear a certain likeness of timbre, too, the way you can tell two different speakers are related. Though neither of us had perfect pitch, we both had good relative pitch—an ability to "hear" the relationship between one note and every other note in a key or in a song—which made us comfortable singing new pieces, doing harmony with each other, and matching the band. It's true I had a higher range, and with good control—all natural, none of it taught—I could sing three high notes in a row with no trouble. And more and more, as our time with Pastor went on, I was the one who stood out. I heard it from—the highest compliment of all—the other musicians. "Your intonation is perfect," Gene Cipriano told me. "You have great timing. And you're blessed with a great sound."

Uncle George thought so, too. He was now our manager as well as our chaperone, and in February 1948 he presented me—as a single—on "Arthur Godfrey's Talent Scouts." Among the competition that night was a young singer named Anthony Dominick Benedetto, whose stage name then was Joe Bari. I remember I sang "Golden Earrings," a number I'd sung with the band many times. And I won. That was the only time I ever won anything against Tony Bennett.

Backstage, Uncle George took my hands in both of his. "God has blessed you with the best voice any girl vocalist ever had," he told me seriously.

It was no longer an abstract concept: "making it on my own." I had already made something of a name for myself through my recordings with the Pastor band. The record I'd cut in a daze of fear and romantic agony in Hollywood—the whispered "I'm Sorry"—had caught the ear of Columbia's management in New York. If I wanted to move on, I had somewhere to move to.

But I'd have to move on without Uncle George. I selfishly knew—no, not selfishly—I *honestly* knew that he couldn't do me much good as a manager in New York. I'd need someone who operated on a different level. Someone like Joe Shribman.

I knew that would hurt my uncle, who'd pawned his class ring to buy food for us, who'd given up his college scholarship. I was torn about it. And on a purely practical level, I couldn't do anything, enter into any kind of contract, against his will. He was my legal guardian, and I was still underage; I wouldn't turn twenty-one until May of 1949.

Betty and I recorded for what would be our last time together with Tony's band in March 1949 at the East 30th Street studio in New York. Tony had arranged for the last cut, "Bargain Day," to be released under my name alone—not the band's, just Rosemary Clooney, solo.

Before long we were back in Virginia Beach, playing the Surf Club and staying at the Cavalier, the same place where I'd wrestled with my betrayal of Milt. Tradition held that performers should arrive for an engagement a day early to hear the act that was closing. So on our last night at the Surf Club, we met Merv Griffin, a young singer with the Freddy Martin band ("Music in the Martin Manner") who was starting the next day. The Surf Club was right on the beach, and between sets we sat on the sand and chatted.

We talked about working with big bands, about how much we'd both learned. Merv, like Betty and me, had been on the radio in San Francisco before he joined Freddy Martin. "I was locked in a studio with no audience," he said. "I had a big studio orchestra, but I'd never performed in front of people. The first time I played a theater, they had to turn the lights out when I walked onto the stage, because I didn't have a theatrical gait or a theatrical *anything*. I just walked like anybody else." He kicked up sand and laughed. "Do you know that when I started with Freddy, our first tour, we played seventy-four one-nighters in a row in seventy-four different towns?"

Back on the bandstand for the close of the show, I thought about what Merv had said. Not just the seventy-four days on the bus, staring at the back of the bus driver's neck, but the connection you felt with the audience when you could see them in front of you, dancing to the sometimes impossibly sweet music the boys were making, listening to the words and—you hoped—finding them true.

As the last song wound to a close, a remarkable thing happened. The whole band stood up and walked off the stage and into the Atlantic Ocean. Just marched right into the water with their instruments. "My God, that's a classy band," Merv said.

I can still see them standing there, up to their knees in the sea in their powder-blue sport jackets and checked trousers, Tony in his dark suit. Betty was standing next to me, dipping her toe in the surf; the air was mild, but the water was still achingly cold. I took her hand and we waded into the water together.

Joe Shribman took me aside. "I had a call from Manie Sachs," he told me. "This is it, Rose. It's your big break!"

He talked quickly. I just listened. Manie Sachs was the head of Artists & Repertoire at Columbia Records, and he was offering me a contract. Not the Clooney Sisters. Just me.

I couldn't bring myself to write the ending date on our scrapbook. But Betty smiled brightly when I started to tell her and interrupted me before I could get the news out. "I'm tired of being on the road," she said. "I want to be one of the girls wearing a formal and dancing while the band plays—not just the girl who sings while the other girls dance." She hugged me tightly. "I love you, Rosie," she said.

Betty didn't come to the meeting in Joe Shribman's office. Uncle George sat in a straight chair to the side of Joe's desk, with me on the opposite side, facing him. Charlie Trotta, Tony's road manager, was standing at the window, looking out on the street.

"You wouldn't have been able to go on the road without me," Uncle George said. "You know that, don't you?"

"Yes," I said.

"You'd never have met any of these people who have offered you a record contract," Uncle George said. "Am I right?"

"Yes," I said.

"And now you want to leave your sister and me behind. You want to be on your own."

"If she stays with you, she'll always be small-time," Joe Shribman told him. "She wants to come to New York with me."

"I want to hear it from her," Uncle George said. He turned to me. "Is that what you want?"

I looked at Joe. I looked at Charlie Trotta. I looked at the corner of the ceiling where a fine crack made a semicircle in the plaster. Then I looked at Uncle George.

"Yes," I said.

THREE

*E*ven with the windows closed, I could hear the street sounds: horns and brakes and raised voices, sometimes a siren wailing. I heard the traffic, but I felt the silence.

I'd never lived alone before. At home, our attic room was sanctuary for the three of us. Then, on the road with the band, Betty and I had been comforted by our close quarters. Now I was alone, with a city of millions all around me. I loved it, and I regretted it.

I loved my address, because even the name of my building, taken from a square in Paris, seemed impossibly sophisticated: the Parc Vendôme, Parc with a *c*, Vendôme with a circumflex over the *o*, not that I knew what a circumflex was. I loved my sublet apartment, because even though it was one tiny room, with a Murphy bed that pulled down from the wall, it was furnished in white leather, with a white shag rug, white blinds at the window, and an ornate plaster mantle over the fireplace. I thought it was about the most high-class place I had ever seen.

I loved the city, with its glamour, its energy and promise. I wanted to take it all in and to fit myself in: I rushed down Fifth Avenue in my navy suit and white gloves, trying hard to keep up with the crowd, because then I'd look—and feel—as if I belonged.

My building, at 340 West 57th Street, was within sight of Carnegie Hall. But if I had to go down that block, I'd walk on the opposite side of 57th Street. I didn't need to be reminded of the plan Betty and I had made: to sing there together someday. I knew I'd made the right choice, but I was saddened that I'd had to make that choice. And in choosing for myself, I'd inevitably chosen for my sister, too. Tony Pastor had hired a sister act, not a single; Betty and Uncle George went back to Cincinnati. Years later, recording "Have I Stayed Too Long at the Fair," I'd remember the way I felt now: *Here in New York, I'm many worlds away from people who are dear to me.* The fact that I'd made the decision myself only made it harder. I'd always known there must be a price to success; now I knew there was a price to ambition.

I'd signed the Columbia contract as soon as I legally could, May 24, 1949, the morning after my twenty-first birthday. That first contract paid me $50 a side, with a guarantee of eight sides a year. Royalties kicked in after the cost of making the record—in those days, about $5,000. After a 10 percent deduction for "breakage and returns"—those records were shellac—I would earn about three cents per record, payable every six months.

Manie Sachs, head of Artists & Repertoire at Columbia, was one of the dearest men I've ever known. He understood singers and liked them, no matter what. He was mentor and friend to Frank Sinatra during some of Frank's most turbulent times.

Whether because Manie knew of the rift with my family and sensed my melancholy or simply because he was such a good man, he went out of his way to befriend me. He could have left me to fend for myself; I had a manager to look out for me. Before I moved to the Parc Vendôme, I'd camped out on the couch in Joe Shribman's apartment. But it was Manie who cared most, who introduced me to the musical world of Manhattan. When he took me to the Waldorf to see Dinah Shore, she came to our table to talk with me. I was enchanted by her, especially by the way she sang "How High the Moon." Another singer would have thrown her arms up into the air with an extravagant motion: *How high is the sky?* But Dinah sang with great economy of movement, with nothing to distract from the grace and elegance of her singing. I knew I could learn from that.

One place Manie didn't take me, though I'd have loved to go, was to the weekly card game in his duplex apartment at the Hampshire House. It was a wonderful Art Deco building on Central Park South, its lobby decorated by Dorothy Draper, with rose-colored marble floors and a formidable fireplace. In the mezzanine restaurant, the tables were so discreetly tucked that it seemed like a private hideaway.

Manie ran the oldest established permanent settled gin game in New York, every Monday night. He kept two teams going, ten men each—agents and managers, music publishers, songwriters and singers, a critic from *Billboard*—any guy in the music business whom Manie considered deserving. An invitation to Manie's gin game wasn't just a Monday night out; it was a prize to be earned, a welcome-to-the-club. The Hampshire House itself was a kind of club for entertainment world names. Sinatra, Ingrid Bergman. Barney Balaban, the head of Paramount Pictures, lived in a twenty-two-room house in a moneyed suburb, but kept a roomy pied-à-terre at the Hampshire House; I'd see his daughter Judy kissing Montgomery Clift in the lobby, just inside the revolving door.

Most everything I liked or needed and most everyplace I wanted to be seemed to be in the neighborhood. Except when I went to Columbia's main recording studio, in a converted church on East 30th Street—considered "downtown"—I lived and worked between, roughly, Sixth Avenue and Eighth Avenue, between 50th and 60th streets. Those twenty-odd square blocks contained the Columbia offices; the Brill Building, music headquarters; Joe Shribman's office; his apartment; my apartment; the clubs on 52nd Street; and Patsy's.

When the little restaurant opened in 1944, the owners, Pasquale (Patsy) and Concetta Scognamillo, couldn't afford their own phone.

Everybody used the pay phone just inside the front door. There was a private table there, enclosed behind a frosted glass panel; that booth came to be always reserved for Sinatra, and he'd sometimes answer the phone.

Patsy, whom we called Papa, was a skinny little gray-haired guy with glasses and a limp who wore a gray cotton waiter's jacket. The restaurant was a hangout for local politicians—Carmine DeSapio was always there, wearing dark glasses. But Patsy, who played the mandolin, had a special soft spot in his heart for underpaid musicians. He understood when they'd come in, after a show, order a plate of spaghetti, then keep asking for more bread and butter. Mario Lanza never would check his coat because he couldn't afford the tip. Buddy Rich came in often with his sticks; he'd start tapping them on the table in the middle of the meal. Then Tommy Dorsey would join in with his instrument. Joe Shribman took me there the first time, introduced me to Patsy, and from then on I was a regular. Often a nonpaying regular; Patsy would cuff us, on a pay-when-you-can basis. Once I ran a tab for four months.

Without the security of a weekly paycheck, I had to concentrate on making ends meet. When Joe Shribman lined up an out-of-town club for me, I'd sing standards the band would know, so I wouldn't have to pay for new arrangements. Or I'd use arrangements from Tony's band or from recordings. I'd earn maybe $250 a night, which sounds like a lot, but I had to pay my piano player and my own expenses, and often I wasn't sure of my next booking. Payment could be eccentric, too; on one TV show, I was paid with 100 pounds of frozen food.

Still, it was a good time for singers. Large orchestras were less and less feasible economically—it was getting to be too expensive to take all those people on the road—and television was beginning to encourage a closer, more intimate focus. With the lights starting to go down on the big bands, vocalists were emerging on their own, like hopeful butterflies from cocoons: Peggy Lee from Benny Goodman's band, Jo Stafford out of Tommy Dorsey's, Joe Williams and Johnny Desmond from Count Basie and Glenn Miller. I was starting out on my own at the right time. The competition was tough; I'd landed in the big pond now, and so many people were after the same thing that I couldn't be sure how far I would go. With her wildly successful "Tennessee Waltz," Patti Page won the Best

Record in a *Cash Box* poll. Nevertheless, I was sure of myself and my own talent, sure I'd made the right choices.

From the day I hit town, Joe Shribman tried to keep my dance card filled: with dates in the city as well as outside it—Philadelphia, New Jersey, Baltimore. With occasional work on radio shows like "Camel Caravan," which Vaughn Monroe broadcast on weekends from a traveling van. And with television. I made my TV debut on "The Ed Sullivan Show" in the fall of '49 before I had any kind of hit record, before there was any real reason for me to be on the show. But Manie Sachs wanted me to have that boost, and Ed Sullivan seemed to like me. He wasn't a starmaker then in the sense that as soon as you appeared on his show, you were immediately going to sell all the records in the world. But it was national exposure, even though I was on for about twenty seconds, wearing long white gloves and a string of pearls and singing "Boy Wanted" after the opening act with a trained seal. And I was lucky to be working. I was one of the few singers of the time who never needed a day job: Peggy Lee had worked as a hired hand on a farm, Eddie Fisher as a fruit vendor.

For a manager, Joe Shribman was an unusually passive man, not given to demonstration. But on the phone that day, he couldn't keep the elation from his voice. "Sinatra wants you to make a record with him."

I'd been in New York less than a year, had made just a handful of records. Now I was getting a phone call that signaled the beginning of a lifelong relationship with Frank Sinatra.

I'm not sure what adjective to use to describe our relationship. We were never lovers, though many people thought so. I think I'd always been in love with him, at least a little, since I was a bobby-soxer. I'd never forgotten hearing him sing "All or Nothing at All" with Harry James, then "The Night We Called It a Day" with Tommy Dorsey. But he was never attracted to me, only to my sister. I rarely saw him socially, never at one of his famous Palm Springs house parties. And I was deeply hurt and angered when he later ridiculed my material in public, onstage in Las Vegas.

But I always felt a connection. Beneath our differences and the complications and even the occasional enmities, it was the music, I think—his music, mine, ours; not just our attitude and approach to it, but our embedded belief in it, our dependence on it—that established and maintained that connection.

The words mean everything to me, as they did to Frank. I always understood that, respected it, copied it. He was the conduit between the songwriter and the listener—the only instrument in the band that had the words. I was always impressed by his impeccable pronunciation and phrasing, his evident determination to have the listener understand and absorb not just every word but every syllable. Sometimes more syllables than the lyricist had intended: I once heard Cole Porter complain, "I threw that word out! I didn't want that word!" Whenever Frank did that, he did it to set up something he wanted to do rhythmically, and, as far as I was concerned, he was never wrong. I was always thrilled at the way he was able to invest a lyric with the most extreme yet still credible human emotion.

I was less thrilled when I found out he hadn't asked for me because he wanted me. He'd wanted Dinah Shore to record with him; she'd declined for the most basic and the most convincing reason: She hated the song. As the song's publisher, he was determined to show Dinah—and everybody else—that he didn't need her. "Who's the last girl singer you signed?" he asked Columbia. "Who's the last female?" Sinatra knew that the newest kid on the block couldn't afford to say no.

Still, I was nervous when I showed up at the Hampshire House for a rehearsal, whispering my name to the desk clerk in the lobby. *Yes, I am expected, yes.*

Sinatra: just as I'd pictured him—bone-thin, his face noticeably scarred. I'd heard that at birth, he'd weighed almost thirteen pounds, and the doctor had needed forceps to deliver him. He said hello in an offhand manner, then walked over to the piano player and started discussing the music. I came to understand that this was Frank's style: There was a reserve—a coldness—about him at first; he didn't warm up until he got to know you.

I didn't tell Frank I'd listened to him since I was a kid, never missed "Your Hit Parade," and had been, in fact, madly in love with him for as long as I could remember. Most male singers I've known didn't want to hear those compliments, except Tony Martin, who could stand still for a day and a half and listen to you praise him.

Besides Frank's customary reserve, there was additional tangible tension. Just as I was beginning what looked to be a promising career, Sinatra's was waning. He had throat trouble, and it sometimes showed in his performance. His enormous successes of the war years, when screaming fans had to be restrained behind police barricades, had diminished to the point where he could walk around the city, if not unrecognized, at least unimpeded.

Sinatra blamed Mitch Miller, who'd moved from Mercury Records to take over from Manie as head of A&R at Columbia. He complained that Miller forced him to record inferior songs, novelties like "Mama Will Bark," with a background male voice imitating a barking hound. He complained that he was being forced to record songs published by Broadcast Music, Inc., which was affiliated with Columbia, rather than better material published by ASCAP. In my early years in New York, Sinatra never seemed to pass up a chance to make fun of Miller and his singers: At the Paramount, he cracked a whip, mocking Frankie Laine, Miller's find in Chicago who'd done "Mule Train."

Mitch Miller blamed Sinatra himself—specifically, his turbulent personal life. When Sinatra left his Italian Catholic wife Nancy and their three children early in 1950 to romance the sultry Ava Gardner, the press had turned on him; parish priests were telling folks in the pews not to buy his records. Besides, Miller said, neither he nor anybody he knew could force Francis Albert Sinatra to do anything he didn't want to do. He pointed out that Frank had refused to record two songs Miller had lined up for him—"The Roving Kind" and "My Heart Cries for You"—both of which had made an instant star of the newest male singer in the Columbia stable, Guy Mitchell.

In any case, the record I cut with Sinatra did nothing for either of us. Dinah was right: When "Peachtree Street" hit the stores in April 1950, it was dead on arrival.

Tony Bennett and I were close in age—he was two years older—but we weren't close friends. Now I've come to treasure his friendship. But back then, in 1950, when we were both under contract to Columbia, energetically pursuing our careers, we were in competition, even though we sometimes worked together. On a primitive radio/television simulcast called "Songs for Sale," we performed amateur songs chosen for the interview value of the people who had written them. The people were funny, or interesting, or old, or young—something that emcee Jan Murray could exploit. Some of the songs were all right, but many were downright awful. Songs would compete every week, with the champion going on to defend its title. I got stuck with one champion song—something about a spinning wheel—that would not be defeated. I sang that wretched tune over and over for weeks until my own head was spinning. And the show's minuscule budget kept production values down: In one shot, I touched another singer's head and my hand came away smeared with the makeup they'd used to save money on a hairpiece.

But I loved watching Tony draw. In the breaks, he'd sit down with a sketch pad and draw me, or Jan Murray, or the band. Sometimes he'd give us the sketches, always signed BENEDETTO. And I was pleased with the publicity the show brought—Tony and Jan and I did some touring, and when Tony and I appeared at the Capitol Theater in Washington, D.C., *The Washington Post* sent a photographer, Jacqueline Bouvier.

I was happier—and so was Tony—with a summer replacement radio show that began in July 1950. "Steppin' Out" was a fifteen-minute show, 7:45 to 8:00 P.M., five nights a week. We worked with Johnny Guarnieri, a brilliant pianist who'd been a star with big bands, including Benny Goodman's. With no commercial sponsor, it was only a "sustaining series," but it certainly sustained my faith in radio.

In the early '50s, radio was still the arena in which records were made or broken. So I continued the relationship-building Betty and I had started with Pastor, paying courtesy calls on the DJs who had the ear of the young buying public, led by an elite in a few breakout towns: Gil Newsome of KWK in St. Louis, Bill Randle of WERE in Cleveland, Bob Clayton of WHDH in Boston. These broadcasters had the special ability to make a record fly out of the stores just by saying on the air, "This is going to be a tremendous hit, and if it isn't, it should be. Get out there and buy it." Martin Block of "Make-Believe Ballroom," WNEW in New York, was crucial in making my name known; practically by himself, he'd made "I'm Sorry I Didn't Say I'm Sorry When I Made You Cry Last Night" into a turntable hit.

It was important to keep the ball rolling, because these relationships were ongoing: Not only could a DJ "make" the record that was in stores today, he could, if properly encouraged, be counted on to give my next platter good play. I was coining a currency of favors. When I recorded a song Nicky wrote called "It Happened to Happen to Me"—a cute number and a big improvement on his early work (*Oh, Jesus, I'm so lonely*), but in need of support—I dashed off a note to my friends at the stations:

> You have always been nice to me.
> Won't you just listen to our little plea?
> Play "It Happened to Happen to Me,"
> 'Cause my brother Nicky wrote it just for me.

Romancing the jockeys was a tribal ritual, promotion disguised as socializing—for me, absolutely nonsexual, although a little harmless flirtation could go a long way. But "romancing" sometimes had sinister connotations: The payola scandal hadn't yet hit the headlines, but the practice of buying or giving commercial favors on an extracurricular basis was common. Whether it was called "ice" or "hot stoves" or, more prosaically, a payoff or kickback, a gift to a DJ or to a power player at a record label could mean the difference between obscurity and renown. One music executive I knew had given his wish list to certain art galleries for the convenience of music publishers—something like the bridal registry at Tiffany's. When I visited his country house, it was like walking into a museum. On a smaller scale, a prominent DJ frankly described the greenback that came with a new record as no different from a headwaiter's tip for a good table. So many records were being turned out that there was no way they could all get equal airtime; some DJs justified a payment on the grounds that they had to choose which records to play, and thus could be considered "consultants." I don't know if my managers bribed DJs or paid them off; I know I didn't.

I couldn't pick and choose the songs I recorded, but that was all right; I was happy to be singing and loving it. The first record I cut on my own was "Lover's Gold," at Columbia's East 30th Street studio—the former Adams Memorial Presbyterian Church, where they'd removed the stained glass and the pipe organ but left a wonderful acoustic. I recorded with Norman Leyden's orchestra, and with the handsome Canadian arranger Percy Faith, who had once worked as a theater organist, accompanying silent films. He had a distinctive style, with unusual voicings—lots of woodwinds—and Latin-inflected rhythms. I had a big crush on him.

I was also working with the children's department at Columbia. The field was booming—Capitol was making a third of its revenue from children's records—so companies loaded up on market research with kids, parents, and educators and invested their top musical resources. I recorded songs like "Suzy Snowflake" and "Me and My Teddy Bear" with some of the best jazz musicians in the world.

Children's recordings seemed genuine and direct, without the gimmicks often used on pop records—schmaltzy arrangements, multiple vocal tracks laid down on top of one another. A children's song told a story, so the song had to be simple and logical, and the diction had to be perfect. You couldn't talk down to children because they'd sense it right away and stop listening, stop trusting.

I wasn't happy to be singing just because I needed the work; I was enjoying myself. I knew I had a good instrument, with a long, graceful tone. Critics were saying so, using phrases like "almost cello-like evenness," "a cinnamon flavor," "robust and fresh, with an undercurrent of seductiveness." I could hold notes a long time, and my range was good. I could sing anything anyone put in front of me.

Later on, when I knew Billie Holiday, she told me that when she sang a song, it was run through the sensibilities of that particular time in her life; whatever was going on in her life was parallelled in her singing. Without knowing it, I think I was doing the same thing. I was happy, and it showed in my sound.

I was able to call home and chat as though nothing had happened, because my parting with Betty had been smoothed over. Betty was too loyal ever to say I'd broken up our act. She always told the press what she'd told me—that she'd gotten tired of traveling, yearned to go home to pick up the life she'd missed.

Betty didn't go back to school, though. She was eighteen years old with three years of traveling and professional singing behind her, way out of reach of high school sophomores. She began appearing on one of the early TV shows on WLW, "Boy Meets Girl," a fifteen-minute show with the theme of a young couple meeting somewhere—a diner, a grocery store—then singing about it. She sang occasionally at Moonlite Gardens with Clyde Trask and the house band. Mama had moved with her husband and Gail to Wilmington, Delaware; Betty was living with Grandma Guilfoyle in a house Uncle George had bought with a G.I. loan in Newtown, Ohio, population 800. *Down Beat* did a piece on her in December 1950. "Rosemary likes the big cities and I guess she will always be around New York, especially since she is going so well," Betty was quoted as saying. "For me, I'm real happy here in Newtown."

I did like the big city, especially in that carefree time. In the wave of free-spending relief that came in the wake of war, nightclubs were flourishing. There were big splashy clubs: the Latin Quarter, with a couple of dozen chorus girls and two dance orchestras; El Morocco, with red stars twinkling on the ceiling; the Stork Club, expensive and snobbish and racist. I liked the smaller clubs, what Skitch Henderson called "the Mabel Mercer rooms," intimate and sophisticated, smoky and throbbing: Goldie's New York; the Blue Angel, with its chic black-and-white bar, named for Marlene Dietrich's classic film, where Harry Belafonte, in half-buttoned shirt and tight pants, sang calypso before anyone else did. In Greenwich Village, the Bon Soir, where Mildred Bailey played one of her last engagements, and Café Society at One Sheridan Square, a proudly integrated basement room, its name intended as a dig at the snobbish uptown clubs.

Perhaps the most stylish was the Copacabana, which had three shows on Friday nights; Sinatra called the 2 A.M. show "the torch show." He sang mostly ballads, and it was absolutely magic. When I was dating Skitch, who was conducting Frank at the Copa, I'd go up a back elevator after the show—the elevator opened into the Hotel Fourteen, next door to the Copa, a dumpy place where the dressing rooms were. I'd find Frank and

Skitch and we'd sit around, talking and laughing, then Skitch and I would walk around the city as the sky turned from black to pearly gray. That was magic, too.

Nicky came to visit me in the summer of 1950, between his sophomore and junior years of high school. He thought my tiny Parc Vendôme studio was the greatest, even when he had to squeeze onto the couch for the night; I had rights to the Murphy bed. I loved showing Nicky the city, wanting him to feel the excitement I'd felt when Betty and I emerged from the Lincoln Tunnel the first time. And I think I wanted to convince both of us that we could still have good times. I realized he and Betty were closer to each other now than either of them was to me.

Nicky earned his keep, at least a little of it. Columbia paid him seventy-five cents an hour to be the jukebox police. He'd go up to jukeboxes all over the city and make sure the records Columbia wanted in there were actually in there. He'd check the frequency of play and compile statistics for each tune. Then he'd shove in a bunch of coins and play them all again.

During Nicky's visit, I began having pains in my stomach. Joe Shribman insisted I see a doctor, who informed me I was pregnant.

"No, I'm not," I said.

"Yes, you are," he said.

Nicky had come with me to the doctor's office, and since I was never in the habit of censoring myself around him—or around family at all—when I came out into the waiting room, I told him what the doctor had said. Nicky erupted. "He said you were pregnant?" he cried. "Well, he just better take *that* back!" He was outraged that the doctor would think I was pregnant without being married. It was the first time I saw Nicky let fly with the hereditary Clooney temper, a legacy straight from Papa Clooney. I knew I had inherited a touch of it myself, but I was always careful not to let it show; when I was upset, I tried to say nothing until I'd cooled down. If I had to vent, maybe I'd take a shower, and the air in the shower stall would be blue for a while. Then I'd be fine.

Indeed, I wasn't pregnant, but I could have been. I was having my share of romances. I had a few near-misses at Patsy's, coming in with one boyfriend and finding another already there. Sometimes Patsy, seeing the difficulty, would rush over to steer us clear of the obstacle and toward a more private table.

As it turned out, I had an ovarian cyst as big as a grapefruit; my uterus tilted in such a way that the doctor mistook it for pregnancy. I had surgery to remove it at Leroy Hospital, near enough to the Colony Restaurant that patients who could afford it got meals delivered. My room was more like a club than a post-op ward, full of food and flowers, and wall-to-wall people like a commuter train. Percy Faith could hardly get in the door. "Excuse me, miss," he said, leaning down to me. "What time does this room get to Newark?"

Even when I knew deep down that a romance wasn't forever, I didn't treat it as a fling. I treated each one seriously, because at the time, it was almost a requirement. If you told yourself that you loved a guy, even that you were going to marry him, somehow that made it all right; it validated the relationship. People talk about the hypocritical morality of those years, but for me at least, the point wasn't only to convince others, to keep up appearances, but to convince myself that what I was doing was all right.

I'd thought Skitch Henderson and I would marry—until I was chatting with a singer in his band, and she let slip that he had a girlfriend in California. She looked as stricken as I felt when she realized her mistake. It was the first time a man had broken my trust, and it was a revelation to me that such a thing could happen—that not every romance was built on good intentions or built to last.

"I have a friend I want you to meet," Joe Shribman said, so softly it was hard to hear him; he rarely spoke above a whisper. He wanted to introduce me to his friend Jake. He wasn't setting me up: Jake was Jacqueline Sherman, a friend of Joe's from Chicago. Jackie was one of the original Quiz Kids, educated at Francis Parker, the kind of progressive school where, if a student was bored in class, she could walk out or just climb out the window. She came from a well-heeled, well-traveled family; on vacation at the

Biltmore in Arizona, she'd played golf with Clark Gable. I was twenty-two, and Jackie was only two years older, but Joe thought I had a lot to learn from her, and he brought her into my life as a mentor of sorts, an assistant of sorts, a chaperone of sorts. Maybe he wasn't as comfortable as I was with my social life. Maybe he just didn't quite know how to handle a girl singer.

Jackie took over. Together we moved into an apartment in the Hampshire House her mother had bought for $6,000. The studio was not much bigger than my white-leather lair at the Parc Vendôme, but it was a very, very good address. It had a view of the air shaft, but it also had a big dressing room and two Mies van der Rohe chairs. Jackie had taste and standards in equal measure. Two daybeds with big bolsters, a bookcase between them with an inset mirror, a huge coffee table. "All you need is a piano," our musician friend Buddy Greco said, and he found one on 58th Street for $25, delivery included.

Now when I went on the road, Jackie came along. She drove the car; she went to newspaper offices with my glossies, saying, "I represent Rosemary Clooney." She made the arrangements, from hotel discounts to stage lighting. Having learned that Anna Sosenko, the mentor to the singer Hildegarde, always insisted on a Shubert Pink gel over the pinpoint spot, Jackie did the same for me, calling up to the lighting man, "I want Shubert Pink on her!" She handled my mail, answered the phone, started Clooney fan clubs. She wrote letters for my signature in a down-home idiom: *I was real happy that you liked your gift so much.*

She became a friend. We went shopping—her taste, so much more developed and determined than mine, dictating what and where. We went to museums, where she pointed out her favorite Turners and Vlamincks. And I met her friends. She introduced me to Dave Garroway, who lived in Chicago, and I began going out with him, staying with him whenever I played the Midwest. He was low-key and mellow, one of the most interesting guys I'd ever met; he knocked back liquid Dexedrine and B-1 in a shot glass every morning. I was excited when he brought me a quartz ring from Mexico and gave it to me in the bar of the Hampshire House, even though Jackie, upstairs, said, "It looks like a Ludens cough drop." Then one weekend Jackie and I went out to visit friends on Fire Island; Dave had told me he'd be out of town, but there he was with another girl.

One day Jackie and I were sitting on the daybed, watching television, our faces smeared with blue gentian because we'd picked up ringworm from Jackie's Siamese cats, when there was a knock on the door. "Don't answer it," I said. "Let it go." But Jackie was already up. "Hi, Buddy, how are you?" I heard her say, and then Marlon Brando came into the room. I nearly fell off the bed in my rush to the bathroom to wash the ointment off my face.

Jackie and Marlon—"Buddy"—had been friends since their families were neighbors, back in Libertyville, Illinois. Now he was the talk of the town. *A Streetcar Named Desire* had just finished a resounding run: 855 performances at the Ethel Barrymore Theater on Broadway. He sat around with us all afternoon. He told funny stories about his part in *I Remember Mama* when he was twenty years old, playing a Swedish kid in short pants. He talked about how he'd landed the *Streetcar* part—he'd hitchhiked up to Provincetown to see Tennessee Williams, and he not only got the part, but he fixed the playwright's leaky toilet.

I was getting used to moving in colorful circles. I remember meeting the extravagant new singer Johnnie Ray at a party with his hetero flame, Dorothy Kilgallen, the newspaper columnist. They sat together on the piano bench, and people couldn't keep from glancing their way. Johnnie was something of a curiosity then, making a splash on stage with the kinds of antics rock stars would pick up later—he was the thin edge of the wedge. Joe Shribman and his partner, Joe Galkin, had had a chance to manage Johnnie, and they'd turned it down: He was just too far out. Jackie and I went to see him in his first important show at the Copa.

That was quite a night. Frankie Laine was there, Tallulah Bankhead, the Duchess of Windsor. Dietrich was devastated that she couldn't sit with Yul Brynner, with whom she was having a blazing affair. He'd come a good way in half a dozen years, since he'd sat on the piano at the Blue Angel, strumming his guitar and singing folk songs; by 1951, he was so spectacular in *The King and I* that Dietrich had decorated her rented Park Avenue love nest in Siam silk and gold. But he'd vowed never to leave his wife, so when she came with him to the Copa, Yul didn't even acknowledge Marlene's presence. Meantime, Johnnie sang "Walking My Baby Back Home" and "The Little White Cloud That Cried," and everyone waited for him to fall down on his knees and cry and do all the outlandish things that people had never seen done on the Copa stage before.

I made a certain splash myself at the party at Phyllis McGuire's afterward, arriving in a slacks suit made entirely of beige leather. "Have you got a beige motorcycle outside?" one wiseguy cracked. I didn't mind, because I was having fun—so much fun that I decided I had to try out Johnny's hearing aid. "I want to see what it sounds like," I told him. He put it on me, someone screamed in my ear, and I couldn't hear clearly for five days.

The leather outfit had come to me by way of Marlene Dietrich, who had the same flair for cutting-edge Parisian design that she had for complicated couplings. I'd met her for the first time on Tallulah Bankhead's "The Big Show," where I was booked to promote a record.

It poured rain the night of the show, and a woman came in the back door of the theater enveloped in a long shapeless raincoat and big galoshes, swathed in a scarf. *Who's showing up looking like that?* I wondered. But when she peeled off the layers of functional outerwear, lo and behold, Marlene Dietrich emerged, perfectly coiffed, exquisitely turned out in chiffon and gold.

"You sing very well," she said to me. "Now we really should keep in touch, because I think you have a great future."

"I hope you're right," I said. "I haven't had a hit yet."

"You will," she said. "You will."

Dietrich was fifty then, with a daughter my age; we were an unlikely pair, but we became friends. Mitch Miller thought it would be fun to put the elegant chanteuse and the Kentucky kid together on a record. Over the next several years, we did a number of sides together, from ballads to novelties: "Too Old to Cut the Mustard" and "Dot's Nice Donna Fight." That title came from what was supposed to be a well-known dirty joke. But no one ever told me the punch line.

Dietrich knew the ropes in such fine detail that she could tell you the *two* best dry cleaners: one for the everyday, tough clothes that could take a beating, and one for the delicate stuff. She had dressers' names, maids' names, even somebody to fix the leaky sink. She had the lowdown on the most highbrow and the most mundane concerns, even some I'd never realized I should be concerned about. "You should wear only underwear that matches your skin, darling," she said. "It must never show through your clothes." But in stores you could only get pink, black, or white—so she made strong tea and soaked white underwear in it until it turned beige.

It was a heady time, when my life and the city both bubbled with exuberant glamour and pure, simple fun. I could call a guy and say, *Let's go for drinks at the Plaza,* or *Let's go to dinner, then catch the torch show at the Copa.* We'd order champagne and sip it while Sinatra sang. If the bottle wasn't empty, we'd finish it walking home, then put the bottle in a flower box outside a Plaza window. The streets were full of high-spirited people, and it seemed we knew them all.

At Thanksgiving, Jackie and I decided to serve a traditional dinner. The catch: We would prepare it in our Pullman kitchen with the two-burner stove and no oven and serve it in our one room, where there was barely enough space for everyone we'd invited—twenty-two people—to stand.

An enormous turkey went into the only available appliance, our electric roaster. Robert Preston came; Brando showed up with a furry bundle under one arm, his pet raccoon named Russell. We set out a buffet service, divided between the coffee table and the piano lid. A young keyboard man named Stan Freeman, who was getting ready to do a stand-up act at the Blue Angel, buttonholed Jackie and tried out some comedy material on her. When I sidled up to listen in, he broke off and turned to me.

"I've heard you on the radio, on 'Milkman's Matinee,'" he said. "They always play 'Mixed Emotions.' It's a lovely song." He shook my hand earnestly. "Your voice has a wonderful richness to it. A velvety honey voice."

"Thank you," I said. "I have to make the salad dressing now."

"Not like that," said Jackie at my elbow. She began whisking oil and vinegar together in the bowl of a spoon. "Like this," she instructed. "This is the best way."

Jackie always knew the best way. And I listened, because I was trying hard to figure out all the ins and outs of my new life—to learn how, and even who, I was supposed to be.

My first instinct in any situation had always been to ask myself, *What is the coin of the realm? What is the currency in this country, with this person?* I couldn't conceive of speaking or acting freely, without first asking and answering that question, and by now it was almost automatic. Since child-hood I'd been programmed to couch things in the right terms, to present the right face. I would divine from people what "right" meant to them, and then they would not be disappointed in me, because I was what they wanted me to be. I didn't think I was deceiving anyone, not even myself; it seemed a necessary step in living my life. It seemed natural to learn from people like Jackie what was expected in the world I lived in now.

Then I met another teacher.

FOUR

José Vicente Ferrer Otero y Cintrón spoke seven languages with such regional precision that he sounded different in Paris than in Provence. The son of an aristocratic family in Puerto Rico, he possessed an astonishing range of talents and a fierce intellect: He'd been accepted into Princeton at fourteen, studied in Switzerland, written his master's thesis on the role of the peasant in the late-nineteenth-century Belgian novel. He won a Tony, then an Oscar, for the stage and film versions of *Cyrano de Bergerac*. Altogether, he was so accomplished that even in a year when he didn't win anything—at the 1950 Academy Awards ceremony at the Pantages Theater, he presented the Technical Awards—his theme music was "You're the Top."

I was promoting a record on Robert Q. Lewis's TV variety show early in 1951 when I saw him, and he saw me. My half-sister Gail, just six years old, was with me, visiting from Wilmington, a treat for me as well as for Gail. She was a sweet, winning kid, and though I hadn't had a chance to get to know her well, I wanted to hold on tight to any family connection.

I noticed José Ferrer watching us from across the set, because I was watching him, too. He wasn't what you'd call handsome, not in a conventional way. But his features came together with a distinguished appeal. And when he spoke, he could hold people spellbound. Except for Bob Lewis. When José drew him aside, Bob kept glancing in my direction.

"Joe Ferrer asked about you," Bob said the next evening. He was taking me to see Ferrer and Gloria Swanson on Broadway in a revival of the 1932 farce *Twentieth Century.*

"He noticed you were with a child," Bob went on. "He wanted to know whom you were married to. He thought that was your daughter." I felt a pleasurable thrill. I'd been noticed by the most famous actor in the country.

"Watch out," Bob said half-seriously. "He plays fast and loose with the ladies. And he's married."

I knew Bob was getting ahead of himself—I hadn't said ten words to José Ferrer—but the very suggestion was exciting. It lodged like a small warm bulb in the back of my mind that lit up every time I passed over it. I sat through the whole show like that, smiling a little to myself while they hammed it up onstage. The play was pure farce, set in a Pullman car: Joe, wearing a villain's pencil mustache, tried to convince his old flame, Gloria, to play Mary Magdalene in a Passion play with real sand and camels. There was even an over-the-top deathbed scene. I could tell Joe was having fun.

When the curtain came down, Bob and I went backstage. But instead of the Ferrer dressing room, he took me to see Gloria Swanson. He said hello, then left me there.

Gloria Swanson was charming and pleasant, but after I'd told her how much I enjoyed the show, I couldn't think of a thing to say. I sat uncomfortably until Bob Lewis came back and we left. I was disappointed that I hadn't met José Ferrer, but I was still too unsure of myself to say so.

Next day the phone rang. "I expected to see you last night," José Ferrer said. "I sent Bob those tickets. Do you think he's jealous?" I didn't know what to say; the bulb was glowing again, warm and bright. "I'll be seeing you," he said as he rang off.

It was hard to believe a man of this stature, with this history, could take an interest in me. But our paths kept crossing. I ran into Joe in the hallway of his office building, where he still shared a floor with Joe Shribman, where Betty and I had lingered by the directory, wondering if that could possibly be *the* José Ferrer. We went to lunch in the company of other people a few times, then just the two of us.

And at first it was simply that: I enjoyed his company. He was sixteen years older than I was; I was dazzled by all he'd seen and done, by the range of subjects he could talk about. He loved to teach; I wanted to learn. He found in me a yielding student. Travels, books, the sciences: He knew so much, and there was so much I wanted to know. Over drinks, he talked about Thomas Hardy and how drastically the Industrial Revolution had changed the society he was depicting. Walking in the park, he talked about traveling in the South of France, the stony beaches and little hill towns. At the museum, he talked about representational versus abstract art. In bed, we talked about everything.

He'd been married twice, starting with the actress Uta Hagen. He wasn't living with his second wife, Phyllis Hill, but he wasn't divorced. And I didn't want to sneak around. So we compromised: We went out together openly, but not flamboyantly. Merv Griffin and Judy Balaban sometimes made up a foursome with us, so our excursions would have the look of a party, not a Ferrer–Clooney date. "We'll be the beards," Merv said. "Don't worry if I don't talk much." He said he was so overwhelmed at being in the company of such a powerful actor that he could hardly speak in Joe's presence. But he managed.

We ate out often. Joe had an exceptional appetite, slim as he was, to match his exceptional energy. He favored prime steakhouses: Toots Shor's; Gallagher's, with richly marbled meats displayed in glass cases just inside the front door; and especially Al & Dick's on West 54th Street, well known for its musical showbiz gloss. Nat Cole had his bachelor party there in the early spring of 1948; the men's room was said to be a discreet spot for the passage of "folderoo"—greenbacks folded to the size of a matchbook cover—from a musical favor-seeker to a DJ. One night at Al &

Dick's, Joe ate a shrimp cocktail, a thick porterhouse steak, potato, mushrooms, and sliced tomatoes. When the waiter asked if there'd be anything else—he meant dessert—Joe nodded and waved his hand over the empty plates. "I'll have this whole thing all over again," he said.

"Buddy" Brando somehow got word that Joe was jealous of him because he hung around the Hampshire House so much. I'd also heard that at one time they'd clashed over another woman. The next time Joe and I saw him, he made a big point of drawing me away from the group, then leaning toward me as if we were conferring secretly.

"I had a really good dinner the other night," he whispered.

"Why are we whispering?" I whispered back.

When we rejoined the group, Joe was bristling, wanting to know what he'd said to me. After that, whenever we were in a group together, Brando acted as though we had something to hide. We never did—never any romance—but Brando thought it was a great game.

"Frustration, nostalgia, and love!" Mitch Miller liked to say. "Those are the prevailing moods in American songs today. 'I love, you love, we all love, why do we love, who do we love, how much do we love, where do we love, why did you stop loving me?'"

By training, Mitch Miller was a classical musician, an acclaimed oboist who had attended the Eastman School of Music, played while Stravinsky conducted, and premiered some of the most important orchestral works of the century. By vocation, he was an equally gifted maker of pop records—and stars. Patti Page, Vic Damone, Guy Mitchell, and Johnnie Ray were all Miller "finds," rescued from varying degrees of obscurity. Guy Mitchell was living in a five-dollars-a-week furnished room, singing for free on demo records, when Mitch brought him in to record the set of songs Sinatra had turned down. He was Albert Cernick then, but Mitch argued that no one would know how to pronounce or spell that Yugoslavian surname. "I'll give you my name," he said. As for the first name: "I don't want to be Rock or Chip," the singer protested. Miller agreed: "You're always calling people 'guy,' like 'How's it going, guy?' So you'll be Guy."

Mitch's genius was a unique blend of musicianship and marketing. He had the pulse of the listening audience and a sure hand with a success, however gimmicky. He'd gambled $90,000 of Mercury's money on "Mule Train," with its whip-cracking sound effects, ordering 200,000 advance copies to ship to DJs. "If you're not going to take any risks, you're not going to do anything!"

He knew technical tricks as well: to cut through the deadened, woolly quality that had plagued earlier vocal tracks, Miller ran a line from the studio to the bathroom and placed a loudspeaker in there, along with a mike to pick up the speaker's sound and run it back to the main line. "You know how you sing great in the bathroom?" he'd explain. The idea was to pick up that echoey acoustic and put a little halo of it around the singer's voice—to make the song an intimate conversation between the singer and one listener, something that wouldn't have been possible in the days of the megaphone—and it worked beautifully.

Miller wanted his records to play louder than anybody else's on jukeboxes. But he wasn't allowed to touch the controls in the recording booth—only the engineers could adjust them, and anyway it was a given that the loudest sound determined the recording level of the whole record. So he devised a way to manipulate the dynamics and fool the ear while he conducted, playing soft parts a little louder than written, then falling off when a genuine *fortissimo* was coming, so that it would sound loud in comparison, but not register high enough to skew the levels. As a result, the whole record turned out louder than most, and folks listening to the jukebox would wonder, *What kind of microphone is he using?*

Once, when Mitch Miller played oboe at the recording of Sinatra's "Try a Little Tenderness" for Columbia, Manie Sachs had banned him from the studio because of a disagreement over the length of the side. Now Miller was back with a vengeance: He'd taken over Columbia A&R when Sachs left for RCA Victor. With intense dark eyes and a goatee that gave him a slightly sinister look, he presided over "Mondays with Mitch," a procession of music publishers peddling their wares. Occasionally one would leave smiling, having pressed a piece on him successfully.

At Columbia, Anthony Benedetto had become Tony Bennett, so I wondered if Mitch Miller would want me to be someone else, too. "I wouldn't let Tony change his nose," he told me. "Why would I want you to change your name?"

Tony had a powerful, versatile instrument that Mitch Miller didn't let him exercise fully; he encouraged Tony to sing in just one style, one texture, forceful and full-bodied. But what I respected Tony for most was his artistic integrity in the face of commercial demands and Mitch's designs. Tony always took the high road, never compromised; when everyone else was doing novelties, he held firm. He wasn't being obstinate; he just could not record those songs.

"I liked your recording of 'Grieving for You.' Nice sounds," Mitch said to me the first time I met him. He set out to make me—lucky me—all I could be, which he thought was a lot.

"All I can do is show you the talent that you have," he told me. "You can't put something there that isn't there. Nobody has it, that curvaceous sound you have." He walked me through a recording almost line by line, encouraged by what he *didn't* have to teach me. "With Johnny Mathis, I was telling him how to breathe! You're a natural singer. You just don't know all the shades and nuances you have." He'd play back what we'd just laid down: "See how you sound here? Why don't you do it all with that kind of sound?" And when I went back to do it again, it made sense. In the trade, he was called a Svengali of singers; his knack was called a Midas touch. I wasn't superstitious, but as my career started to move under his power, I started to believe a little.

The farther I moved, the more I tried to keep in touch. I called Grandma twice a week and asked after everyone, even Mama, though I didn't call her directly. Grandma's voice on the line, with the faint echo of home in the background, made me aware of what I was missing, how dangerously close I was to being *out* of touch. I tried to make up for that by asking a boatload of questions, detailed ones: *How's Nicky's cold? Are you keeping the rabbits out of the garden? Did you fix the sticky doorknob?*

Grandma didn't want to talk about rabbits or doorknobs; she wanted to talk about me. "You're working too hard, Rosie."

"I like it this way," I assured her. "I really do."

"Rosie, how many people have you been nice to today when you were too tired to be nice?"

The more things changed for me, the more I wished they could change for Betty. She was still doing local TV shows with names like "Teen Canteen" and "Going Steady with Betty Clooney," with Uncle George as her manager. For myself, I was still trying to find a way of dealing with our breakup. I kept telling her that any day now, Joe Shribman would find something terrific for her. I kept telling myself that, too.

I brought her to New York to stay with me as often as I could. Just before New Year's, 1950, we'd joined up with Tony Pastor's band again for a recording session, such a hefty slug of *auld lang syne* that I couldn't help remembering me and Betty standing on the Steel Pier. My horizon was still limitless, but I was afraid hers might not be, and it hurt me to think that. Three days after the Pastor session, she and I went into the studio together with Percy Faith to record a duet: "I Still Feel the Same About You."

While Betty was visiting, Joe Shribman took us to Patsy's one night. I was tackling my tagliatelli when suddenly Frank Sinatra was leaning against our table, looking steadily at Betty. "I don't believe we've met," he said in the silkiest tone I'd ever heard him use. I stopped eating, the pasta still twisted around my fork, as Joe Shribman introduced them. Frank took Betty's hand. She was wearing one of my dresses, a deep forest-green silk with a V neck; her dark hair was a tumble of curls. She looked fresh and lovely, wide-eyed, absolutely charming.

"Can you have dinner with me tomorrow night?" Frank asked Betty, still holding her hand. I just stared.

"Well, yes. I guess so," Betty said. Then she smiled widely. "Sure."

Frank released her hand then with obvious reluctance. "I'll call Mr. Shribman and get your phone number," he said. He turned and disappeared behind the frosted glass panel of his private booth.

"Don't get your hopes up," I muttered ungraciously to Betty. "He's crazy about Ava Gardner." She just smiled and went on eating.

Betty went out with Frank the next night, and the next. When she announced they were going out the third night in a row, I couldn't stand it. "Not without me," I declared. "Tell him we're a sister act."

Frank didn't blink an eye when I came down in the elevator with Betty. We had a terrific dinner at Toots Shor's, then I tagged along with them to the Astor Roof, where Tommy Dorsey was playing.

I loved the buzz, the swiveling heads as we walked in and were led to a band-side table. Frank ordered champagne; he talked about his time with the Dorsey band some ten years earlier. "I wish I'd heard you sing with them," Betty said wistfully.

I could have smacked her upside the head, I was so jealous of the smile he gave her—that slow, vaguely dangerous smile. "Wishes can come true," he said softly. He got up from the table and walked to the bandstand. He said something to Tommy Dorsey, then he turned and sang the song that had been such a hit for him with the band: "I'll Never Smile Again." The crowd went wild, but Frank never took his eyes off Betty. Their feeling for one another was something striking. When we left the club, we all got into a taxi. Then they dropped me off.

For the next several years, even after she was married, Betty got a tall bottle of Arpège, her favorite perfume, at Christmastime: no card, no note. "Who's sending you the perfume?" her husband would ask. "My sister," Betty would fib, because her husband was a jealous man. Then she'd smile. "For old times' sake."

I recorded "Beautiful Brown Eyes" in January 1951 with Mitch conducting, and with sales that eventually reached 400,000, it became my first hit. He upped my royalty from 3 percent to 5 percent, with a guarantee of $250,000 over five years. When my face appeared on the cover of *Down Beat*, glamorized almost beyond recognition and looking soulfully into the distance, I guessed I might be on my way.

But one magazine cover and one hit record didn't change my professional life overnight. I was still working hard, singing whatever and wherever I could. I was in no position to argue when Mitch Miller proposed a song for me to record: a quasi-Armenian pseudo-folk number called "Come On-a My House." William Saroyan and songwriter Ross Bagdasarian, creators of the Chipmunks, had cooked it up on a cross-country drive, supposedly inspired by the bounty and variety of the American landscape they were traveling through; in my opinion, they'd had a little too much time on their hands. They'd grafted their idea onto a genuine, ancient Armenian folk music tradition. Kay Armen had already recorded the product of this experiment, a record that went exactly nowhere. In its entirety, the song ran as follows:

Come on-a my house-a my house
I'm gonna give-a you candy
Come on-a my house-a my house
I'm gonna give-a you apple-a plum
And a apricot-a too eh
Come on-a my house my house-a come on
Come on-a my house my house-a come on
Come on-a my house-a my house
I'm gonna give-a you figs and-a dates
And-a grapes and-a cakes eh
Come on-a my house my house-a come on
Come on-a my house my house-a come on
Come on-a my house-a my house
I'm gonna give-a you candy
Come on-a my house-a my house
I'm gonna give-a you everything
Come on-a my house-a my house
I'm gonna give-a you Christmas tree
Come on-a my house-a my house
I'm gonna give-a you a marriage ring
And a pomegranate too eh
Come on-a my house my house-a come on
Come on-a my house my house-a come on
Come on-a my house-a my house
I'm gonna give-a you peach and-a pear
I love-a your hair
Come on-a my house my house-a come on
Come on-a my house my house-a come on
Come on-a my house-a my house
I'm gonna give-a you Easter egg
Come on-a my house-a my house
I'm gonna give-a you everything
Come on-a my house-a my house

I'm gonna give-a you my house!
Come on-a my house-a my house
I'm gonna give-a you poem and a dance
And a phonograph too
Come on-a my house my house-a come on
Come on-a my house my house-a come on
Come on-a my house-a my house
I'm gonna give-a you all-a my wage
And a bird in a cage
Come on-a my house my house-a come on
Come on-a my house my house-a come on
Come on-a my house-a my house
I'm gonna give-a you candy
Come on-a my house all-a your life
Come on, come on and-a be my wife

I didn't have any appreciation for the song's slightly tongue-in-cheek, self-parodic edge. I thought the lyric ranged from incoherent to just plain silly, I thought the tune sounded more like a drunken chant than an historic folk art form, and I hated the gimmicky arrangement: It was orchestrated for jazzed-up harpsichord, of all things, with a kind of calypso rhythm. I was afraid once people heard it, they wouldn't take me seriously as a singer capable of more than "I'm gonna give-a you candy." Maybe I took *myself* a little too seriously then; I wanted to sing death-defying love songs like "Tenderly," not weird novelty fluff. I'd worked too hard honing my diction to waste it on the cheesy accent Mitch wanted me to use, which was actually written-a into the lyrics. (When I had the chance to record a country number with Gene Autry, I had the same scruples about the word 'winder'; I insisted on pronouncing it 'window' until the producer pointed out that I could say it however I wanted—after I'd sold a million records. Until then, 'winder' it was.)

"I don't think so," I told Mitch.

"Know what I think?" he replied. "I think you'll show up because otherwise you will be fired."

At dinner that night at Al & Dick's, I complained to Joe. "It's just so empty," I repeated for at least the tenth time. "The lyrics are nothing but nonsense."

Joe swirled the Côtes du Rhône in his glass. "Actually, Rosemary," he said, "they go back a long way."

"I know, it's a folk song, but they've—"

"There's a play Christopher Marlowe wrote," he interrupted, "around 1590. Listen to these lines: *No, thou shalt go with me unto my house.*" He looked at me to see my reaction. "*I have an orchard that hath store of plums, brown almonds, services, ripe figs, and dates.*"

"No kidding," I said. "Figs and dates?"

Now that I knew the lyric had roots in the Renaissance, the harpsichord made a little more sense to me. Not a whole lot, but a little. And Mitch Miller had his heart set on it. Johnny Guarnieri had made some harpsichord jazz recordings with Artie Shaw and the Gramercy Five, but those mostly appealed to aficionados; a harpsichord in a pop record was Mitch's kind of novelty. He'd managed to turn up an instrument after several days' looking, finally renting one for $200 a day from a teacher at Juilliard. He'd turned up a guy to play it, too: the keyboard whiz and aspiring comedian Stan Freeman.

Like Mitch, Stan had a classical background. He'd never thought of playing pop music professionally until he joined the Army; Uncle Sam put him in a jazz band and his career took a whole new turn. Back in civilian life, he played on Tony Bennett's first recordings, "Because of You" and "Boulevard of Broken Dreams"; he'd go on to conduct for Ethel Merman. He not only conducted for Johnnie Ray, but acted as lookout, helping Johnnie and Dorothy Kilgallen dodge the press when they stopped off at her place after a night on the town. Stan would keep watch from the limo, reflecting that Johnnie might be gay, as people said, but clearly not all the time.

"Hey, Stan," I called to him when he came into the studio. "What gives with the harpsichord?"

Stan laughed. "Mitch called me up and said, 'Have you ever played the harpsichord?' I lied and said sure." He led me over to show me the instrument. "See, it has two keyboards, not one," he said. "And stops, like an organ. You can't really do crescendos, as you can on a piano—you do it with the stops. Listen to this." He played a middle C and pulled out a stop; a high C resonated from the strings. "Instant octaves." Under the lid, instead of the hammers that hit the strings on a piano, there were quills that plucked them, giving the instrument its distinctive sound.

"How do you plan to play this marvelous instrument?" I asked.

"It's a keyboard, right?" Stan smiled. "I'll play it like a piano."

Even after Joe's explanation, I was having trouble investing the lyrics with genuine feeling. The silly words were also uncomfortably suggestive—"I'm gonna give-a you everything"—and I didn't know how to work the combination of playfulness and seductiveness; it didn't seem to mix. Mitch gave the band a cutoff during the fourth take and came over to me.

Mitch had a way of helping singers make songs work, make them immediate and meaningful, by suggesting scenarios to help the interpretation along. He'd done it for Frankie Laine with "Lucky Ol' Sun." "Look at it this way," he'd told Frankie. "Just imagine you're sitting on your front porch and the steps are sagging and the house needs a coat of paint and you're in your undershirt and sweaty, probably need a bath. Make believe the kids next door are listening."

Now he put his arm around my shoulders. "Look at it this way," he told me, as if he knew exactly what wasn't clicking. "You are asking this boy over to your house because you're going to marry him."

It was simplistic; it was pretense; it was quintessentially '50s. And it worked. After the fifth and final take, Mitch Miller jumped up on a chair, flung his arms out wide, and trumpeted, "I'll get them to ship a hundred thousand of these in three days!" That was June 6, 1951.

The sign posted backstage at the Olympia Theater in Miami was very large and very serious:

NO HELLS OR DAMNS IN YOUR ACT
PLEASE KEEP IT CLEAN

"Oh, damn," I said to Jackie. "What the hell am I going to say in my damn act now?"

But Jackie wasn't listening; she was talking on the pay phone. She hung up and turned to me. "Joe Shribman says they've shipped three hundred thousand," she said. "But we haven't heard it played once."

I didn't hold out much hope for "Come On-a My House." In fact, I didn't think much about it; I was busy waiting for my cue. I was going on after Burns' Birds: trained parakeets who pushed miniature baby carriages and, for an encore, fired a miniature cannon. Right now I could hear little riffs of applause from the house for the man who played the accordion on the flying trapeze.

The Olympia was one of the last of the presentation houses, all-day showcases for film and vaudeville acts, with bands mixed in. Once there were thousands of theaters like that all across the country, but now there were perhaps a dozen left. This one stood on a corner in the heart of Miami's downtown, a Spanish-style edifice falling into genteel decay. Inside was a world apart: Stuffed birds watched over the box seats, stars glittered in the ceiling, a machine in the rafters gave out puffs of smoke to represent clouds drifting by. When the lights went down and the curtain went up, day was indistinguishable from night, so I wore white strapless evening gowns even at the 1 P.M. show.

While I was there, Shribman had arranged for me to appear on a radio show made up of kid performers who played, sang, and interviewed grown-up stars. I was in good company there. Bob Hope and Ethel Merman had preceded me in the slot—and I met a charming young man, Ronnie Schurowitz. He was bent on a showbiz career; later, he'd change his name to Ron Shaw to fit a marquee. He was thirteen years old, and he became a friend to last a lifetime.

"You know when you first came in the studio?" he said to me. "It was like a best friend or a cousin had just showed up again." For me, meeting Ronnie was like finding a long-lost brother, a kid brother you could take to the movies and the park, sit and talk to.

He became the founding officer of the Rosemary Clooney Fan Club, Miami Branch. Using letterhead typed up on a stencil, he organized mailings encouraging members to call radio stations and request my songs. He sent out letters addressed to "Dear Friend," requesting fifty cents in annual dues in exchange for an autographed 8x10 glossy, a journal, and a membership card: *You will be kept up to date on all the happenings of Rosie, and this will no doubt help build up her morale.* The night Ronnie and the other radio kids came to the show, I arranged to have them seated in the first row; when I introduced them from the stage, Ronnie led them in standing to take a bow.

He told me frankly that he hadn't heard of me before I showed up at the Olympia. But we got along famously from the start. He hung around the theater, taking calls for me backstage, when Brownie, the stage manager, would yell, "Telephone call, Rosemary Clooney!" Often it was Joe Ferrer calling, and he always identified himself on the phone. Ronnie couldn't get over that. "I've seen so many of his movies, I know his voice," he said. "He doesn't have to say who he is!"

After the Olympia, I was ready to head home, but Jackie had an idea. "We're so close," she urged me, "let's go over to Havana for a day or two."

Leaving the country! It was a novel idea to me. But if you were going, Havana was the place to go. Just ninety miles from Key West, the city was a short hop by plane but a world away from the straitlaced States in those days before Fidel Castro turned out the lights—an extravagant playground of sun and sin, sex and scandal. In the shadow of an eighteenth-century cathedral, the narrow streets of the old town wound among relics of colonial splendor, but at the Tropicana, rum flowed like water, tourists sipped their drinks from coconut shells, and chorus girls danced with chandeliers on their heads. We dropped our bags at the Hotel Nacional and tanned on the Trocadero until it was party time. Then we headed for a pleasure palace where real trees grew from the stage, their tops out of sight, platforms concealed in the foliage. "Jackie," I whispered, "there are chorus girls coming out of the trees!"

An exhausting thirty-six hours later, slumped in a cab heading home from the airport, I heard a familiar voice. I sat up and looked out the window; we were rolling up Broadway. There was the voice again: *I'm gonna give-a you figs and-a dates and-a grapes and-a cakes eh . . .*

My voice. Coming from the door of a record store propped open in the summer air.

. . . poem and-a dance and a phonograph too . . .

There it was again, pulsing out of another door down the block.

"You go on," I said to Jackie as I got out of the cab. "See you at home."

I crossed three lanes of traffic in a kind of daze, mesmerized by the sound of my own voice, coming from all sides now. As I walked up Broadway, it seemed that every record store—and there were a great many—was playing my song.

At first I was acutely embarrassed, as if I'd started this myself by mistake. I went into a store, thinking I should tell them to turn the record off, or stop the customers and explain to them that the song wasn't my idea in the first place. Then I realized that the customers were pressing around the counters, reaching out to clerks who handed records over without even wrapping them.

Come on-a my house my house-a come on . . .

Up until a few hours, even a few minutes before, I'd been just one of hundreds of struggling young singers trying for a big break. Now I was watching, part bewildered and part elated, while the break took place before my eyes. And nobody knew it but me. One of the clerks noticed me standing there, listening to my song play. "Hey, kid," he called to me. "Don't try to memorize it. Get one before they're all gone!"

The desert heat smacked me in the face as I walked down the steps from the plane onto the tarmac, past the honor guard at Nellis Air Force Base, with their white gloves and shiny young faces. I winked at the kid on the far end—he kept looking straight ahead, fighting a grin that was trying to twist the corner of his mouth. The brass band—enthusiastic, insistent—kept playing as the lieutenant governor of the state of Nevada came forward with a hearty handshake, followed by a little girl who thrust an armful of roses at me. A trio of cops on motorcycles whisked the white limo out of the airfield, heading for the Strip.

My first appearance in Las Vegas had been booked early in the year, for $3,500 a week. By the time I opened, at the end of my "Come On" summer, I'd gone from being just another girl singer to a full-page photo in *Life,* from "Rosemary who?" to a household word. My fee had quadrupled. But I played Vegas at the original price. A deal's a deal, my manager explained, especially when it's a deal made with Jake Lansky of the Meyer Lansky family.

Just a few months before, I'd been sleeping—or trying to—in a room over the clattering kitchen in a honky-tonk in Wildwood, New Jersey, where Dizzy Gillespie was working on his tan in the parking lot, wearing only a leopard-skin thong. Now I was swaddled in the silence of an air-conditioned suite: ankle-deep snowy carpet, silver bucket of champagne, more roses. I'd been walking up Broadway, anonymous and unrecognized. Now I was checking in with my office every day to see where I had to be when; I was a hot property, too hot to handle by myself. Suddenly my life was running on a different time clock, constantly ticking and ticking fast.

My three-week run at the Thunderbird was announced with a big splashy newspaper ad in Vegas-speak: THE SUPREME SHOW PRESENTATION OF THE YEAR. Standing in the pinpoint spot in my white lace gown and elbow-length gloves, I couldn't see faces, but I knew the Navajo Room was packed. We'd made sure that the local DJs had given "Come On" plenty of airtime before I arrived, so I knew my audience was waiting for it. I made them wait. I opened with "From This Moment On," slowed into "Because of You," turned uptempo with "The Lady Is a Tramp" and "Shotgun Boogie." I set them up, finally, with "Beautiful Brown Eyes," before rollicking into "Come On-a My House." And that, a reviewer said, "tears up the house."

Las Vegas was just beginning to rise up from the desert horizon then, in 1951. Down the road was the Desert Inn, where Sinatra had opened the day before. Ava Gardner was with him, along with her sister and her maid.

I liked Ava as soon as we met. She came from tobacco country, like me; a sharecropper's daughter who liked to go barefoot and stay up late. "My daddy always said I'd better get a job where I could work nights," she told me when we talked after my show. She was fresh and funny, so beautiful it hurt your eyes to look at her. Every night she'd go to Frank's show, then come to mine in time to hear me sing Gershwin: "They Can't Take That Away from Me." "I just love that song," she told me, and she sang a line: *The way you wear your hat . . .* "Every time I get a chance, I'm going to come down here and listen to you sing it, even though the old man doesn't like it much."

I knew that Sinatra liked Gershwin, so either he didn't like her coming to see me or he didn't like that particular tune, which had been a major hit for Artie Shaw, Ava's ex-husband. Although she'd been divorced for several years, Frank was still gripped by jealousy. The two of them had a wondrous talent for tormenting one another. One night at the Hampshire House, Ava had deliberately left her phone book open to Shaw's number—leading Sinatra to think she was going back to him—then paid an innocent visit to Shaw and his current love. Later that night, Frank phoned her from his bedroom, just across the suite from hers. "I can't stand it any longer. I'm going to kill myself now!" She heard a shot; the phone went dead. When she ran screaming into his room, she found him lying on the bed, smiling at her; he had fired into the mattress.

When we were appearing simultaneously in Vegas, Frank's career at Columbia was nearly over. His contract was not being renewed; he would leave the label still owing six figures in advance royalties. Even Manie Sachs was having no luck trying to find Frank a spot at RCA Victor. So Frank was taking potshots at those of us who were selling records. Even though he and I had recorded together, even though he knew Manie cared about me, Sinatra stood onstage in the Painted Desert Room and ridiculed the singer down the road: *sings the most awful music, the worst thing that's ever happened to music in this country, the worst fake accent you've ever heard.*

I never called him on it; confrontation wasn't my style. But I felt vindicated when a column appeared on the front page of the Vegas daily, the *Morning Sun,* criticizing him. It wasn't a review of his show—that piece, on an inside page, was a rave ("one of the greatest showmen ever seen in these parts"). The front-page article reproached him for his attitude and condescension, for standing there "with his mouth open and his capped teeth showing."

Anyway, I had other things to think about. In the middle of my second week, Joe Shribman came to my dressing room before the first show, looking pleased but nervous. "There's a talent scout from Hollywood out front tonight," he told me. "Second table from the right, center. Sing to him. Give him a great big smile."

FIVE

*P*aramount Pictures sprawled over ninety acres, edged with spiky palms and high hedges, in the heart of Hollywood. Driving through the main entrance, the De Mille Gate, I caught sight of the familiar logo: a snowcapped mountain encircled with stars. "The mountain is the whole company, and the stars are the people here, and the sky is our future!" the talent scout said. He turned to me and smiled.

In 1952, Hollywood was still a small town—ersatz Norman Rockwell, with tinsel around the edges. Beverly Hills was a cozy enclave of bungalow courts, with two old-fashioned hardware stores, Beverly Hardware and Pioneer; a dime store, Newberry's; and a fabric shop, Beverly Hills Silks and Woolens, on Rodeo Drive. I bought a glove-stretcher at Livingston's, a variety store on Beverly Drive that sold what in Maysville we called "notions": shoelaces, safety pins, hairnets. Jackie and I met a friend of hers, the actress Ann Rutherford, at Morley's at the corner of Beverly Drive and Little Santa Monica, where we sat at the marble-topped soda fountain and ordered milk shakes, just like at home.

Jackie and I rented an apartment on Wilshire Boulevard in a charming building called the Château Colline—stained glass, a fireplace, and a breakfast nook splashed with morning sun. We sublet the apartment by the month from Bill Dozier, a producer who was going to New York to work for CBS. He moved out with the wardrobe trunk so popular then—shaped like a Log Cabin syrup tin, so it could never be turned upside down.

Mitch Miller was dead set against my making a movie. "They're just using you, Rosie," he declared, thumping his fist on the desk. "They're just using you for your name value! Your singing will be great, but the picture will be a piece of shit."

But my manager wanted me to go. He'd have a private office on the Paramount lot. "You can keep making records," he reminded me. "They have recording studios in California, I'm pretty sure." Jackie liked the idea; she didn't approve of my relationship with José Ferrer. Jackie was as bright, as well educated and well read as he was, which made her a competitor with him when it came to me. Joe's work was in New York; in California, I'd be out of his reach.

In fact, Joe was in Europe, making a movie, *Moulin Rouge*. I thought if I made a movie, I'd have more in common with him, a shared experience. I had no illusions that I'd ever come within shouting distance of his artistic level, but it would be fun. And as soon as my picture was finished—a five-week shoot—I planned to join him in Paris.

Cecil B. De Mille's office was at the end of the corridor in the one-story main building, white stucco covered with climbing roses. I didn't meet Mr. De Mille that first day, but I met a studio publicist, A. C. Lyles, a charming gentleman who took me on a tour of the lot. It was a town within itself: A maze of narrow streets led to dressing rooms, a barber shop and a beauty salon, sound stages. I drank it all in. Ginger Rogers and Fred Astaire worked here. Alan Ladd had just made *Shane*. Crosby and Hope and Lamour and all their *Road* pictures. A.C. told me about a flick in the works, with Bob Hope and a new Paramount hire named Jane Russell: "Bob is in love with Jane, who's in love with Roy Rogers, who's in love with Trigger."

We had just turned a corner when a man on a bicycle came pedaling toward us. A.C. held up his hand. The man stopped, but stayed on the bike, resting one foot on the ground. "Meet Rosemary Clooney," A.C. said, as the cliché "needs no introduction" came to instant life. Bing Crosby was wearing a blue shirt that matched exactly the blue of his eyes.

"I understand we're going to be on the radio together," he said.

"Yes," I stammered, flustered. "Sometime in the twenties." I wanted to clap my hand over my mouth as soon as the words were out; I meant that I was scheduled to be on his show in the latter half of the month— around the twentieth—but his presence caused a short circuit somewhere between brain and mouth. Worst of all, I knew he hated people to fawn over him because he was a star, and I felt my reaction was just as bad. Maybe because I had nothing left to lose, I had the nerve to knock on his dressing room door later and explain myself. "I was really in awe of you," I told him, "but I don't feel that way anymore, and I'd like us to be friends." Beginning then, we were. After his wife Dixie died in late 1952, there was even speculation about a Crosby–Clooney match. But we never had a romantic involvement, not even a one-nighter. The famous men I *didn't* sleep with remained my friends always.

Every year Bing sponsored a golf tournament at Pebble Beach, with a musical show called the *Crosby Clambake*. He invited me to sing there, and he began inviting me to dinner at his house on Mapleton Drive, down the block from Lauren Bacall and Humphrey Bogart. His twenty-two-room house was lavishly furnished, with some antique pieces he'd bought from the Hearst estate, including a complete drawing room of wonderful French gray wood and chairs covered in needlepoint. When I visited, we'd watch the fights on television in the library, with dinner brought in by Georgie, the housekeeper, and served on card tables. All the place lacked was a swimming pool, which Bing had had filled in. Wherever he lived, he had the pool filled in and I never knew why. Maybe it was a mystery I didn't want to solve.

For all its grandeur, the house had an empty, echoing feeling. A large photograph of Dixie was centered on the piano; lighted cabinets displayed her collection of Copenhagen china, his collection of pipes. Bing's son Lindsay was about fourteen when Bing took him along to a film location in France, and Lindsay began writing me long, wistful letters from the set of *Little Boy Lost*.

In *The Stars Are Singing*, my first Paramount picture, I played Terry Brennan, who does dog food commercials but wants a singing career and tries to explain that to the young man who wants her: "I'd rather have my picture on the cover of *Down Beat* than marry you and have a houseful of kids . . . I gotta make it in this racket or die tryin'!" The plot, for lack of a more precise word, involved two other singers: a teenaged soprano and an aging tenor. Terry did indeed make it in her racket, of course, illustrating her success with a blasting "Come On-a My House." *The New York Times* confirmed Mitch Miller's grim prediction, though in gentler terms: "a musical mishmash of operatic and long-hair arias by Lauritz Melchior and Anna Maria Alberghetti . . . hot numbers by Miss Clooney . . . the script is so weak that Miss Clooney virtually has to get under it and lift it when she isn't in there singing." The trade journal *Exhibitor* chronicled the film's fate at a theater in Oklahoma: "I had so many walkouts and complaints that I called the exchange and asked them to send me another picture. I took a loss on it," the manager was quoted as saying.

The reviews didn't seem to matter to Paramount, though. What mattered to them was that their shining light, Betty Hutton, had just torn up her contract and walked away. What mattered to them was that they had some planned pictures that needed a brand-name singing star. But what mattered to me was my planned rendezvous with Joe. When Frank Freeman, a vice president of Paramount Pictures, heard that, I was invited to his office.

Mr. Freeman had thin sandy hair, rimless glasses, and a ministerial gaze. "José Ferrer is a married man, Rosie," he reminded me. But Joe had assured me his marriage was over, I pointed out; he was just waiting for his wife to agree to a divorce. Freeman shook his head. "Nobody loves a homewrecker," he said dolefully. "Have you read your contract?"

I admitted I hadn't.

"Mr. Shribman has a copy," he said. "You think about this, Rosemary. Mr. Shribman should think about it, too."

The Paramount contract wasn't as rigid as the MGM contract, which established Louis B. Mayer as godfather, prosecutor, and jailer—Ava Gardner's contract there required her to obtain his permission if she wanted to get married. But my contract contained the standard morals clause, studded with "if's." A person's contract was in jeopardy:

IF she would "do or commit any act or thing that will degrade her in society."

IF she did something that would bring her "into public hatred, contempt, scorn, or ridicule."

IF what she did would "tend to shock, insult, or offend the community or ridicule public morals or decency."

IF she flew to Paris to be with somebody else's husband.

A phrase such as "public hatred, contempt, scorn, or ridicule" sounded very general, but it translated into the painful particular. Ingrid Bergman had brought down upon herself all of the above when she became pregnant by a man to whom she wasn't married.

Actually, Ingrid Bergman was never pregnant. No woman was. She was either "expecting" or, more delicately but less specifically, "in the family way." It was the era of euphemisms, of the timed kiss—three seconds, tops—when married couples slept in separate beds. As the decade progressed, the Production Code became less potent; the town of Peyton Place was being erected in the background. But when I arrived, the Code was still enforced, a reaction against the days when Jean Harlow obviously wore nothing under her clinging, bias-cut satin dresses, when Mae West overflowed her tops and talked in tingling dialogue.

And it was thorough beyond belief, a multiple-choice catechism of propriety:

ENDING: Happy / Unhappy / Moral
TREATMENT OF LIQUOR: None Shown or Consumed / Shown Only / Shown and Consumed
FATE OF CRIMINALS: Killed / Death by Accident / Punished by

Law / Suicide / Reform / Mental Suffering / Other / No
Punishment
VIOLENCE: Yes / No
IF YES, IN WHICH FORMS: Shooting / Knifing / Swordplay /
Strangling / Torture / Punch / Fistfight / Flogging / War
/ Other (Bouncing-Kick-Clunks)

In addition to the industry strictures, there was the Legion of Decency—the Catholic Church's powerful pressure group—which rated movies from A (Okay) to the dreaded C (Condemned). At Paramount, even Betty Hutton's smash hit *The Greatest Show on Earth* had been rated B—"morally objectionable for all," mostly because of the "suggestive costuming" worn by Gloria Grahame, the elephant girl. De Mille was so aggravated by that rationale that he wrote to the Legion: "I suppose that there are a few individuals out there so morbidly prurient that looking at someone dressed in a circus costume might constitute a moral danger for them. Such unfortunate persons should go to see a psychiatrist rather than *The Greatest Show on Earth.*"

At five o'clock in the morning, the streetlamps still glowed along Dressing Room Row on the Paramount lot, giving a misty dimension to the small town look. The dressing rooms were decorated to suit the star—Dietrich's had been furnished with sleek Art Deco fittings, a white satin chaise longue and crimson carpet. My dressing room was bright and wide—ten feet by thirty feet—with sheer panels over the windows and smooth surfaces of blond wood everywhere. Besides the main living space, complete with wet bar, there was a curtained sleeping alcove.

I was treated like a star, and I acted like one. I thought I needed more glamorous surroundings. Jackie and I moved to the Beverly Hills Hotel for a while, then to a house on Bedford Drive. I liked spacious houses with lawns and pools; when I heard that Judy Garland was giving up her house on Maple Drive, I told Shribman that I wanted to move in. On the day her rental was up, she wasn't ready to move out. I waited some more. When he assured me it was ready, I showed up at the door.

"I have children!" She was shouting at me from inside the house, without opening the door. "You should know that when a woman has children, she can't just leave on the spur of the moment!" It was anything but spur of the moment, but I backed away. Judy was acting like a star, too. While I waited to move in, I rented an apartment on Doheny Drive, near the corner of Cynthia and Doheny, where Marilyn Monroe kept a place; my apartment was furnished with expensive upholstered pieces, including a navy-blue velvet armchair, and there was a fish pond in the courtyard.

I strolled the Paramount lot with my 150-pound Great Dane, Cuddles, on a rhinestone-studded leash. I was dressed by Paramount's top designer, Edith Head. She came up with the Clooney look: turned-down collar, nipped waist, full, swirling skirts, and padded hips—I was so thin below the waist that I needed to be lined with ultra-thin foam. I wore tight pants and a bright red baseball cap as captain of a Paramount softball team, opposite a team headed by choreographer Nick Castle. I took special notice of a dark-haired, long-legged outfielder on that team, the dancer who was assigned to give me lessons for my next picture, *Here Come the Girls*.

Dante DiPaolo was only two years older than I, but he'd been in show business since he was six. His family came from Consano, a tiny town in the Abruzzi region of central Italy in the Apennines. His father had emigrated to Colorado, where he worked in a coal mine for six dollars a day, living with his wife and children and assorted family members in a little house in the mining camp. "I remember sleeping in a bed with four of my uncles," Dante recalled merrily, "everybody's feet touching." Like me, he had clear memories of his grandmother. "She used to hang her washing outside, even in the snow. And she'd bake bread in the brick oven outside. When I die, if I see a line of clean washing blowing on a clothesline in the snow and smell bread baking, I'll know I'm in the right place."

He'd begun tap dancing as a toddler, just jigging around the porch, doing what came naturally. His mother found a dance class in a town twelve miles away, sewed him a pair of black velvet bell-bottoms with white pearl buttons, because she thought that was the way dancers had to dress, even for practice. His white satin blouse had puffed sleeves, so when he did the buck and wing, he seemed to be very high-flying. He won so many amateur contests that when he was nine, his mother brought him to

Hollywood on a Greyhound bus. The friend they stayed with—a typesetter for the *Los Angeles Times*—introduced them to his circle, including a man who took Dante to strip joints downtown; with his sailor suit on, Dante would dance and use his hat to pick up the money people tossed. He'd met Bing Crosby before I did, when Dante was thirteen, with a dancing part in Crosby's film *The Starmaker*. By that time, he already had a scrapbook of clippings. "They called me 'The Whirlwind of Colorado,'" he bragged.

In *Here Come the Girls,* Bob Hope played Stanley Snodgrass, a hapless hoofer; I was Daisy Crockett, his dance partner and his girl. It was such a flimsy picture that even Dolores Hope, surely the most forgiving wife in the world, didn't want to see it. But it was a carefree time for me. Dante found me a straw hat and a blazer, and we began practice sessions in a rehearsal studio. Our rehearsal pianist, Ian Bernard, was a friend of Dante's; along with Bea Allen, one of the dance coaches, we began going out together, just as a frolicsome foursome. Like a number of musicians I'd worked with, Ian had a background that included both jazz and classical training; he'd landed the Paramount job, his first studio job as a pianist, through a guy he met in a bar. We were all around the same age; working and playing together was like being on a college campus. After work we'd often go across the street to Lucy's, the restaurant with curtained booths where Paramount people, along with folks from neighboring Columbia and RKO, ate and drank and fell in love: Janet Leigh and Tony Curtis instantly, and—gradually—Dante and I.

"I'll call you Rosella," he decided. "That's what we'd call you in Abruzzi." Dante talked nonstop; he remembered everything that had ever happened to him and loved telling about it. He was proud of being a friend of Fred Astaire, whom he'd met—and impressed—while filming *Easter Parade.* "I had a routine I did to 'Jealousy,' tango-tap, a little ballet, a little matador—hell of a number," Dante said. "Fred loved it. When we took a break on the set, he'd say, 'Dante, get up and hoof a little bit!'" After a stint in the infantry in World War II, Dante had worked with Nick Castle on a Broadway show, *Heaven on Earth.* He liked quoting a line from one of the reviews: "'If this is heaven on earth, where do the sinners go?'"

When Nicky came to visit, just after his high school graduation, he took to Dante at once. One night at Lucy's we were just finishing dessert when I took a spoonful of water and idly flicked it at Dante. He laughed,

I laughed, Nicky laughed. Then Dante idly flicked a spoonful of water back at me. Then it was two spoonfuls, then the water in a half-filled glass, then a full glass.

Nicky and I escaped from the restaurant first, Dante following in his Buick, honking the horn all the way. At the house, Nicky scooped up water from the fish pond; while Dante was wiping goldfish off his face, Nicky and I scrambled inside. Nicky settled into the armchair; I jumped onto his lap. I figured that Dante wouldn't pour water over blue velvet. When Dante went into the bathroom and emerged with a spilling-over pail, I knew I'd figured wrong.

I think it was that water fight that always symbolized, for me, the wonderful lighthearted quality of our time together.

Sometimes the four of us—Bea and Ian and Dante and I—would drive out to Pacific Ocean Park and ride the Ferris wheel. I hadn't done that kind of thing since Cincinnati, when Betty and I played Moonlite Gardens. We had our pictures taken with our heads sticking out of the cutout holes under outsized Mexican sombreros. One night we kept riding the carousel, laughing and singing, until the operator told us we had to get off.

By the time we met, Dante's father had quit the coal mines and come to California, working first at Warner's, then at Paramount, where he became foreman for the set-moving department. Dante was close to his parents, still living at home with them. When I invited him to my dressing room, the door was open, but he knocked anyway.

"Hi, Rosella," he said.

"Come in," I said.

He came in. "Close the door," I said.

He closed the door. I winked. He laughed.

"Lock the door, Whirlwind," I said.

Since "Come On," I'd been splashed over magazine covers and trade papers; on the cover of *Cash Box*, I promoted a new phonograph. I'd even gotten to record the death-defying love song I'd aspired to: in November 1951, Percy Faith conducted six violins, two violas, a cello, and me in

"Tenderly." Now, in Hollywood, the Paramount publicity machine was grinding full time on my behalf. Though I hadn't finished high school, one publicity piece said my favorite author was Camus. Rosemary Clooney paper dolls and coloring books flooded the newsstands. I was photographed every unlikely place I could be posed: perched on Frankie Laine's shoulders, talking on the phone while he drank coffee. In a bathing suit, one foot dipping into the water, holding a telephone, over the caption COME ON-A MY POOL. In elbow-length gloves, nibbling popcorn from a bag held by Liberace. Putting on foot cream, hand cream, nail polish, makeup, eyeliner, perfume. Poised over a bowlful of pasta, my fork halfway to my mouth, Miss Pastafazoola of 1952. In a baby-doll nightgown, considered so sexy at the time that I beat out Betty Grable as pin-up girl for Carlson's Raiders, a bunch of Marines at Parris Island. I was named Woman of the Year in Music in an AP poll.

I made my first major purchase, a full-length fur coat. Joe Shribman took me to a furrier whom Jackie recommended; when he heard the price—$8,000—he was speechless. He finally managed to ask, "Is it warm?" I liked the coat, and I liked knowing I could have it. But the money part of my success never seemed real to me. I never saw any money coming in or out—never held it in my hand—so it meant nothing to me. Checks went to my lawyer, or to my accountant, or to my manager. I didn't question it then; I was in a heady new world and I just assumed someone else would take care of all that.

I'd been presented to Louella Parsons, one of the two reigning gossip queens. The choice had to be made between Parsons and her fractious rival, Hedda Hopper. I wasn't told why Paramount chose Parsons to be my advocate, and I didn't ask, though I heard that in general Louella got along better with women, while Hedda preferred leading men. Louella, called "Lolly" by her intimates, lived with a personal assistant, two cocker spaniels—Jimmy and Woody—two secretaries, and three phone lines in a house with a red door on Maple Drive. Her daily column appeared daily in a dozen Hearst papers and was syndicated in over a thousand others; her house was a magnet for flowers and gifts. She liked to see and be seen, including at Good Shepherd, the Catholic church in Beverly Hills where the movie elite turned out; she was Mia Farrow's godmother.

"I want to be the first to know," she told me in her high-pitched voice.

Dark-haired, petite, a little chunky, she didn't look the part of a Hollywood terrorist. But she was. "I *must* be the first to know. And I must be the first to tell it." If Louella wasn't the first, her displeasure fell heavily on the studio publicity people. So Herb Steinberg, publicity chief at Paramount, impressed on me the importance of giving Louella the scoop. His office was at Paramount's corporate headquarters in New York, but he often came to Hollywood to handle important meetings, pressing matters. He was extremely professional, but a somehow comforting figure, too— Grace Kelly called him Uncle Herb. He'd handled publicity for Hitchcock films, supervised forty people who spent their time arranging interviews and photo shoots and patrolling personal traffic through certain active dressing rooms, especially Danny Kaye's, Bob Hope's, and Jerry Lewis's.

The publicity people's first move, as soon as a contract was signed, was to customize the biography. Janet Leigh had been signed at MGM because her father, a hotel clerk, had kept her photo on the front desk. Norma Shearer had spotted the picture and taken a copy; at Chasen's restaurant one night, she had shown the photo to Lew Wasserman, the powerful MCA head, and, over dinner, a star was born. Janet's publicity people were delighted. They told her it was a wonderful story, as good or better than any they could have dreamed up—but just for their own information, she must tell them how it *really* happened.

"We cover up everything," Herb Steinberg assured me. "We'll protect you—absolutely. Don't worry about a thing." The names in my little black book only indicated, it seemed to me, how popular I was; I didn't think I had anything to be covered up, or worried about, or protected from. Then I saw one of the newspaper stories about me, based on a Paramount press release. In this airbrushed version of my family history, my Aunt Ann hadn't died of a drug overdose on the floor of a public hospital. She had simply "died, very suddenly, at the age of twenty-four, while listening to the Andrews Sisters on the radio."

But nobody tried to change the way I looked, because I'd been brought in as "the girl next door" who sang, and people knew what I was supposed to look like. Girls who hadn't been known before coming to town weren't so lucky; their faces could be altered as readily as their biographies. Even Ava Gardner, who was perfection, had mortician's wax stuffed into her dimples. Eyebrows were either shaved off or, ouch, plucked out and replaced on the naked face with a pencil-thin line. Ann Rutherford had seen Rita Hayworth sobbing with pain in a makeup chair; Rita's natural hairline was very low, and she was being given a new, much higher hairline with pots of steaming wax. It was Ann's opinion about eyebrows, in fact, that had ignited her career. She'd been traveling on a train with her mother when she'd spotted David Selznick in the vestibule of the dining car. "I don't know what possessed me," she recalled, "but I hurled myself at him and said, 'Mr. Selznick! You must promise me! When you make *Gone With the Wind*, you must tell your makeup men to throw their tweezers away! You must remember that wonderful passage in the book when Margaret Mitchell describes Scarlett with her wonderful raven's-wings eyebrows.'" Selznick not only took the teenager's advice, but cast her as Carreen, Scarlett's youngest sister.

Dante got a terrific dancing role, as leader of the town boys in *Seven Brides for Seven Brothers*. Part of the film was shot on location in Sun Valley, Idaho, so he couldn't be in my next picture. But I was glad to be working with Guy Mitchell, my old friend from Columbia Records. Guy was one of the most joyful people I'd ever known. He refused to ever be downhearted—when he was turned down for the role of Li'l Abner, the notably tall cartoon character, he grinned and said, "Couldn't you just get a shorter Daisy Mae?" He'd started in radio, too, then had traveled as boy singer with the Carmen Cavallero band. "Sixty one-nighters coast to coast," he said, "and I have fifty-eight hotel towels to prove it." He'd gone from his five-dollars-a-week furnished room in New York to a three-million record with "My Heart Cries for You," one of the songs Sinatra had turned down. As a kid in northern California, Guy had worked on a ranch, roping steers; he kept saying he wanted to go back home and be a cowboy. With our new picture, he came close.

Paramount filmed its Westerns in Wyoming, but *Red Garters* was a Western only in the broadest sense. It was a stylized take on the genre, set in the town of Paradise Lost in Limbo County. A new imagistic technique replaced ordinary scenery: On a floor of burnished-orange sand, painted cutouts formed the backdrop of a town, suggesting the outline of a door here, a hitching post there, in the manner of classical Greek theater. And the film was a pointed spoof, with men tipping their hats whenever anyone mentioned "the code of the West," with characters straight out of cartoons—the black hat, the white hat, the dancer at the Red Dog Saloon—and with classically stilted lines: "Brave men will die in the morning." Dietrich came by the set to show me how to roll a cigarette.

But I was glad when the picture was finished. My costar Gene Barry didn't like me—he'd been promised top billing, which had gone to me instead. I didn't like him—he constantly upstaged me. Once, when he was carrying me, he dropped me. He sprained his ankle. Dancers pulled muscles; a wardrobe finisher ran a sewing machine needle through her finger. Everybody was more than ready for the wrap party, where Guy's relatives roasted lambs on a spit and served homemade Yugoslavian wine. Guy invited everybody on the lot, from cops and janitors to Cecil B. De Mille, who actually showed up. George Marshall, the director, looked suspiciously at the big chunk of roasted meat on his plate. "Where's Rosemary's dog?" he asked. "I'm not taking one bite until I see Cuddles." Guy's family sang as they cooked. "My family always sings," he explained. "They sing when they feel good, and when they don't feel good, they sing to make themselves feel better."

As soon as *Red Garters* was finished, I went to Maysville for the world premiere of *The Stars Are Singing* in January 1953. Paramount publicity people always looked for the hook; they opened Bing Crosby's *Here Comes the Groom* in Elko, Nevada. Even though Bing's ranch was eighty miles from town, Elko was, by publicity standards, his hometown.

I felt like a woman on the run, crouched down in the backseat of a bright red Cadillac convertible, pulling a nondescript raincoat over my new Aleutian mink as we crossed the city limits into Maysville. The parade in my honor wasn't until late afternoon, and the premiere not until evening, but I was being smuggled in early, like contraband. Grandma Guilfoyle had come home to Maysville to live, and I wanted to see her first. I was hiding so I wouldn't be seen around town and spoil the effect of my grand entrance.

From my position, all I could see was the cornice of an occasional building, the limb of an occasional tree against the winter sky. I tugged at Jackie's sleeve to make her look down at me. "What do you see?"

"Looks like the main street," she said. "My God, what a backwater town."

"Stay down, Rosie," Herb Steinberg called from the front seat. "We're almost there."

The home of my childhood was rented to someone else now. Grandma was living in a modest house without a view of the river. She met us at the door, dressed in her best, and hugged me. "Your coat feels so nice."

The table in the dining room was spread with a lace cloth and set with refreshments: three cut-crystal glasses, a bottle of Manischewitz wine. I thought I saw Herb and Jackie exchange glances.

But we all raised glasses in a toast: to the film, to homecomings. Herb sipped the sweet purple wine without flinching and, bless his heart, made sure Grandma was part of the conversation. "Yes, ma'am, that's what I do," he said. "I send out notices to the newspapers, telling them things about the stars." He smiled disarmingly. "Can you keep a secret? Nine times out of ten they're made up. We say to the actor, 'This is what we're sending out—don't you believe it.' Do you read Walter Winchell's column?" He didn't wait for an answer. "I used to make up stock tips and send them in to him."

Herb was putting her at ease, and I was grateful. "I think your friends are enjoying themselves," she said as we got ready to leave. She put on her black cloth coat and her little black hat with the artificial violets in front, right over her forehead, and we set out together.

Our open car became a motorcade. I rode with Grandma, with our mayor—Rebekah Hord, the only woman mayor in the state, with spots of rouge high on her cheekbones and an excited gleam in her eye—and with Blanchie Mae Chambers; I'd refused to ride without her. "You're my best friend," I reminded her when she protested that a black person in the car would upset townspeople, especially my snobbish Aunt Olivette. It was Blanche's idea, then, to tell the press that she was riding with me as my personal maid. Eleven cars drove ahead of us: Herb and Jackie, lots of press, a Paramount newsreel crew. A police car with lights and siren headed the line of floats—the Lions Club, the Maysville Tobacco Board of Trade—and the marching bands.

I knew Herb and Paramount had spread the word; Grandma had told me that folks were excited. But I was in no way prepared for what I was seeing now. Thousands of people filled the streets, standing on stoops and cars to get a view. Someone said there were 20,000 people—four times the population of our town—and that they'd been waiting since early morning. They leaned out of windows, cheering and calling and waving to me. Blanchie Mae nudged me. "Wave back!"

I waved and smiled, then turned to the other side of the street and smiled and waved some more. We passed under a grandstand, and I gave the people my biggest, most heartfelt smile yet as it began to sink in that this was all for me. I saw Aunt Chris, Aunt Rose, Uncle William and Uncle Chick, Uncle Neal and his wife Mary. Mama, divorced from her sailor, had come with Gail. Nick was in the Army; Betty was working—so she and Uncle George, her manager, weren't there.

In the window of Magee's Bakery, I saw a huge poster with my picture and the slogan: ROSEMARY, YOU TAKE THE CAKE! At a tobacco warehouse, I auctioned off 15,000 pounds of tobacco; at the corner of Second Street and Lower, I took up a bottle of Kentucky limestone water and broke it over a new street sign, instantly renaming the steep, narrow street that ran down to the river Rosemary Clooney Street.

I remembered the Maysville *Public Ledger* as a thin packet of claustrophobically personal news. Sometimes a whole page would be taken up with sale announcements: *Because my husband's health forces him to quit farming, we will offer at auction the following . . . one Jersey cow . . . sixty Austrian hens, laying . . . dishes of all kinds.*

But in the edition that reported on my premiere, the "Colored News" and the auction lists were swamped in Clooney coverage. A banner headline proclaimed:

CINDERELLA COMES BACK IN A CADILLAC!

At the Russell Theater, I would have liked to sit back and enjoy the movie, but I was hustled onstage to sing. I didn't sing "Come On" or any other song people might expect. I chose songs in honor of my grandparents. For Grandma Guilfoyle, in a prime aisle seat, I sang "Moonlight and Roses." For Papa Clooney, I sang "Home on the Range," the song I'd sung at his Rotary lunch when I was five years old. Afterward, I was swept along to Mayor Hord's house, which was stuffed full of flowers and food, for a reception in my honor. I glimpsed Mama making her way from group to group, working the room. I found Jackie and pulled her out onto the porch for a cigarette.

From the porch, the Ohio was just visible in the moonlight, its surface an opaque, faintly luminous gray that could signal stormy weather. I told Jackie about the time Betty and I went down to the river in our traveling dresses to wait for our ship to come in, the time she almost drowned.

Jackie frowned. "It looks awfully dirty," she said.

When Jackie went back inside, I stayed on the porch. The river didn't look dirty to me. It looked swollen with early winter rain and the leaves and earth the rain had washed away, but that was the river's nature. It still looked like a route to possibility more than peril. And to me, it still looked navigable.

From Maysville, I embarked on a breakneck tour, promoting *Stars* in cities from Cincinnati to D.C., showing up onstage at the movie houses where it was playing, and meeting the exhibitors. Always a luncheon; always a wide expanse of white tablecloth; always a group photo. In Atlanta, Herb Steinberg and I were almost hidden behind an enormous floral center-piece.

That night, after I'd appeared at a downtown movie house, we ate at an all-night grill. I was finishing my mushroom omelette, skimming the morning paper, when I came upon Dorothy Kilgallen's column. I read that the noted actor José Ferrer of classical and contemporary theater was stepping out with Tempest Storm.

"Who the hell is that?" I yelled, shoving the paper at Herb.

"Stripper du jour," he said. "It's just gossip. Don't give it a thought."

But I was already halfway to the pay phone, where I got Joe on the line and told that noted actor exactly what I thought of him—in copious and vivid detail.

Later on, the people I was with that night told me I'd scared them by reacting so violently. "You melted the wires," Herb said half-admiringly. But in truth, blowing up that way scared me a little, too. I knew I had the family temper, like Nick, but I tried hard to keep those reactions in, and until then I'd thought I was doing all right. I determined to keep the lid on tighter in the future. It didn't occur to me that if I kept it on too tight, like volatile gas in a closed chamber, an explosive pressure would build inside.

Joe had been writing to me in French—at least the beginning of his letters, what the nuns in grammar school had taught me was the "salutation." I didn't know French, but I assumed that *ma très chère* was very loving, and when I saw him in New York, he assured me I was right.

I believed him when he laughed off gossip like the item about Tempest Storm. And I believed him when he said his separation from his wife was permanent and they'd soon be divorced. So on the night of the Academy Awards—March 19, 1953—we went out in public together to the NBC International Theater in New York.

Moulin Rouge had opened at the end of 1952 to be eligible for that year's awards. John Huston was nominated for Best Director, the film for Best Picture, and Joe for Best Actor. He expected to win, having immersed himself in the role of the diminutive painter Henri de Toulouse-Lautrec, with what was, even for Joe, exceptional intensity. Because Joe was five-foot-ten, playing a man only four-foot-eight, he'd had himself fitted with a pair of short artificial legs which he had strapped to his knees. His own lower legs stuck out in back, out of camera range. To ease the pain from the loss of circulation that the straps and the pressure on his knees caused, he'd gone to a yoga teacher to learn to control his breathing and jackknife his body into improbable positions.

That night was the first time the Academy Awards were televised on both coasts, with Bob Hope as the emcee in Hollywood and Conrad Nagel as the emcee in New York. Joe and I were seated on the aisle, with the camera crews right there at our elbows, waiting to catch our expressions. Earlier in the day, a doctor friend of mine had given me a couple of tranquilizers for Joe, in case he got nervous. I wasn't taking pills then, but in those days Miltowns and other tranquilizers were passed around like popcorn. Joe said he didn't want one. But just as the envelope was being opened, he leaned over to me and said, "Is it too late to take that pill now?"

As Gary Cooper was being announced as Best Actor for *High Noon,* the television camera caught us bending over, laughing our fool heads off. John Huston didn't win either, and the picture lost out to *The Greatest Show on Earth*. De Mille hadn't made any headway with the Legion of Decency, but he'd won his first Best Picture Oscar.

I was disappointed for Joe, but I had my own reason to celebrate. On February 23, 1953, my face was on the cover of *Time* magazine.

For weeks, we'd sat on pins and needles, because if anything major happened—if somebody famous died, or got married, or was put in jail—my face would be replaced. Boris Chaliapin did the cover, so it was a very big deal. A lot of people were responsible for that cover, especially Walter Murphy at Columbia Records and Jackie, who had a friend who worked for Clare Booth Luce, who was married to Henry Luce, who could make or unmake a *Time* cover with a press of the buzzer on his desk. I wanted the cover so badly that I even appeared at a Republican gala in honor of Richard Nixon, because Henry Luce was there. "Your grandfather must be turning over in his grave," Jackie teased.

Years later, an article in *GQ* said of me, regarding that *Time* cover: "She was the ideal creation for the time, fabricated from whole blonde cloth." Fabricated is a tough word, but it suited. I was still trying to be what people expected of me and doing it well. But that insight was long in coming. In 1953, I didn't have time for such introspection—in less than two years, I'd gone from unknown to public property, to a salable commodity in constant demand. And even if I'd had the time, I wouldn't have had the perception.

Even on a less serious level, there was something of an identity crisis. I auditioned for a show Jackie Cooper was doing—a Garson Kanin work—but they said I sounded too naïve. "Much too innocent for this part." Then I tried out for the role of Sarah, the Salvation Army girl, in *Guys and Dolls*. Frank Loesser said I sounded too knowing. "Much too seductive for this part. There's no way in the world an audience is going to believe you're a virgin when you sing."

I was relieved when I didn't get either part; I'd already been told I had more of a microphone voice than a stage voice, and I never wanted a stage role, which meant doing the same thing day after day. I'd auditioned because other people wanted me to: my manager, my MCA agent, and Joe.

And Paramount had plans for me. I was so high on their priority list that I was a bridesmaid for Judy Balaban, the boss's daughter, when she married Jay Kanter, an agent at MCA. Geographically, the wedding was a New York event—at the Plaza—but at heart it was a Hollywood production. Grace Kelly, one of Judy's seven attendants, didn't even meet the bride until that day. But Grace was a Paramount player and an MCA client. Marlon Brando, the best man, was not only a close friend of Jay's, he was an MCA client, too. So was I. I wasn't just *invited* to be a member of the wedding; in a way, I was assigned.

The next project the studio had lined up for me with Bing Crosby—a film that genuinely deserved the label "major motion picture"—was scheduled to start filming that fall of 1953. In the meantime, partly because Jackie and Joe didn't get along and partly because I liked California so much and had movies to make, I was rarely at the Hampshire House anymore. I'd moved into the Beverly Hills house I'd been waiting for, Judy Garland's place on Maple Drive, roomy and elegant. Joe called me often from Dallas, where he was appearing in *Kiss Me Kate* at the Texas State Fair. But now Dante was back from the *Seven Brides* location in Sun Valley, Idaho.

I loved them both, in ways as different as they were different themselves. I was impressed by Joe's fame, excited by the attention we drew when we were together. He was still waiting for Phyllis Hill to agree to a divorce. But he'd given me a ring from Victor Hammer's chic Manhattan gallery: an exquisite circlet of Russian gold and enamelwork, with a little note he'd written tucked inside: *I LOVE YOU.* The very fact that he wanted me thrilled me; how could it not? And being with someone so much older, so literate, so cultured, was a challenge I expected myself to meet. It was difficult sometimes, but it felt like a necessary kind of development.

Being with Dante, on the other hand, didn't take any effort at all. Everything was easy and delightful: with his wonderful sense of humor, he kept everyone around him laughing. I knew he was a compassionate and faithful man; I knew he would do all he could to make me happy. He had his own bright career ahead of him. When he danced Bill Bailey with Ann Miller on the "Hollywood Palace" television show, she called him out in front of the cameras and introduced him: "This is Dante DiPaolo, and he's going to be a very big star."

And Dante fit in beautifully with my family. When Nicky came to visit again that summer, the two of them spent whole afternoons splashing in the pool. I was sitting on the patio, watching, when Dante climbed out of the pool, poised on the edge, then jumped onto a rubber raft. Nicky tried to do the same thing, but he missed the raft and disappeared underwater.

When Dante saw bubbles on the surface, he dived under, grabbed Nicky around the waist, and pulled him up and over to the side of the pool. I ran over to them. Dante was gasping, but he waved at me. "It's okay, Rosella, we're fine. Nicky's fine." That evening Dante cooked spaghetti, with tomatoes and basil from his mother's garden; we drank his father's homemade wine, laughed, and talked like a family. "You saved my life, Dante," Nicky said earnestly. "I'm going to get you a present." And he did—a Zippo cigarette lighter with an alligator band around it.

The next afternoon they were back in the pool. I could see them from the window of my room, where I was packing my suitcase on the bed. Joe had phoned: Phyllis was getting a quickie divorce in Mexico.

I watched Nicky and Dante as long as I could, with a divided heart. I knew Dante thought we'd get married someday—he'd telephoned my grandmother and talked about it. Now, for a wild moment, I thought I'd stop packing. I'd run out and join him by the pool, dip my hands in the water and splash him.

With Dante, I wouldn't have to change. I could act my age; I could be myself.

But I didn't find myself very interesting.

⌒

I married José Ferrer on July 13, 1953, in Durant, Oklahoma, the nearest town to Dallas that didn't require a waiting period. It was a ten-minute ceremony in a judge's office, with only Joe's agent and my manager present. We had to leave right away, because Joe had a performance that night. But first I had to make a phone call.

I called Louella Parsons.

SIX

~

*P*ink blossoms, the color of cotton candy, lay thickly on the front lawn. The crepe myrtle was in brilliant bloom; we called it "the August tree." I was waiting at the front door when Joe's car turned into the driveway. He hurried to me along the veranda, laughing. We kissed and went inside. Under the chandelier in the marble entrance hall, we kissed again. "Welcome home," I said. He took my hand and we walked up the wide circular staircase to our bedroom. Except for the butler, the cook, the housekeeper, the upstairs maid, the laundress, the secretary, the gardener, and the pool man, we were alone.

~

I hadn't seen the house before Joe bought it for us, but he was sure I'd agree it was perfect. I loved the rambling Spanish-style house on sight. A front veranda led to the dark wood front door. White wrought-iron gates closed off the driveway, which led back to the guest house, the swimming pool and pool house, the tennis court. In the center of the spacious back lawn, an olive tree grew in austere majesty, encircled by a narrow stone path. To me, the olive tree, the oldest kind of tree on earth, symbolized the forever quality of our love and marriage.

I'd flown back to Beverly Hills the day after we were married, while Joe stayed in Dallas, finishing his work. I called Betty with my news, then Grandma. "José Ferrer?" Grandma repeated. She gave a kind of huffing sound. "Never heard of him. Where's Dante?"

I didn't call Dante. The news of our marriage had been carried on the wire services. *The New York Times* had run an edgy piece that described Joe as "the forty-one-year-old divorced actor," and as for me, "It was the first marriage for Miss Clooney, who gave her age as twenty-five." I really was twenty-five; it was the first time I'd seen how casually cynical the press could be. In any case, I knew Dante would have seen Louella's column with its optimistic headline:

FERRER WEATHER WITH A ROSY FUTURE

Joe had bought the house from Ginny Simms, who'd been a band singer on radio and with the Kay Kyser band. Before that, the house had been rented by George and Ira Gershwin. Just to the left of the entrance hall, the step-down living room stretched for what seemed half a block. One wall had a set of lighted cabinets; Joe began collecting striking black Wedgwood to display there. In the far corner of the room, near a big square window, the Gershwins had placed their piano. My favorite Gershwin song, "Love Is Here to Stay," had been written right there in my living room.

George had died in 1937, but Ira and his wife, Leonore, still lived next door. Ira was a darling, with round glasses and a serious gaze, like a little

Buddha. He thought his mission in life was to protect his brother's music. When he talked, he was just reminiscing, but I was hearing history. He recalled the night George had gone out to dinner and had come home late. Ira was sitting in the living room, reading, when George rushed in and dropped his hat and coat on a chair. "TOWN!" he called out, in a triumphant, I've-got-it tone. "Not just London—" He was at the piano, fingering the notes. "A foggy day in London *town.*"

I was delighted when Ira came over to chat, but after a while, he stopped coming. He was reminded too much of George; he got depressed. He remembered so many happy times in the house. He showed us a home movie of a particularly gala party, with tables set up all over the back lawn. Lillian Hellman was there, and Harold Arlen, and Paulette Goddard, who table-hopped with George, draped over his arm.

When I recorded an album in 1989, *Rosemary Clooney Sings the Lyrics of Ira Gershwin,* I wanted Ira to write the liner notes. He was reluctant to praise his own work. "But I loved every word," he said wryly to Michael Feinstein, who was working with him on his archives, so that's what we used.

Besides its musical spirit, the house held a musical ghost. In 1934, the singer Russ Columbo—considered a worthy rival to Bing Crosby, especially noted for "Prisoner of Love"—was killed in a freak accident in the den. He'd been visiting a friend whose family owned the house then, and he was inspecting an antique dueling pistol when it suddenly fired. The ball ricocheted off the wall and into his brain. In all the time Bing Crosby came to the house, more than twenty years, he avoided that room. When we began taping a radio show for CBS—a twenty-minute slice of song and chatter, informal and easygoing—we sometimes worked at the studio, sometimes at my house. Bing always insisted that the engineers set up their microphones, amplifiers, mixers, and assorted equipment in the living room, never in the den.

Joe bought a gleaming Steinway, signed 1939, and placed it in the Gershwin spot. At Princeton he'd organized a band, the Pied Pipers; he'd taken singing lessons for years. As soon as we started going out together in New York, he'd confided that his dearest wish was to play George M. Cohan; he was trying to buy film rights to *Musical Comedy Man,* and he intended me to play Mary. The fact that he was not a singer—the reviews of

Kiss Me Kate in Dallas said so—never deterred him. He'd always been determined to sing and dance. I thought that might be because it was what he did least well—he'd been panned for *No No Nanette* in St. Louis and as a three-week replacement for Danny Kaye in *Let's Face It.* When he decided to take on *Carousel,* he asked Ian Bernard, my Paramount friend, to coach him. "You are the worst singer in the history of the world," Ian informed Joe. "You cannot keep on key. You bellow. It hurts my ears to hear you." Joe just laughed and kept trying. "Can't" was a four-letter word to him. There was nothing—no sport, no art, no discipline—he felt he couldn't master with the proper training. He intended to sing opera one day.

"Sometimes I think you married me to boost your singing career," I teased him. I knew that people were speculating wildly on what was seen as the Marriage Most Unlikely to Succeed. So many of Joe's chess-playing, Shakespeare-quoting friends thought of our union as just one of Joe's flings, not to be taken seriously, that I was especially grateful to the Logans. Josh Logan had been one of Joe's friends at Princeton; he and his wife Nedda were the first of Joe's circle to treat me as though I belonged. "I'm so glad you're with Joe," Nedda told me. "How wonderful for Joe." That made me feel so good; she was looking beyond the surface and seeing me as a person. Many other people saw our marriage in clearly contrasting terms: Joe was enormously successful, but I was more popular. So they applied the well-worn Ginger Rogers–Fred Astaire rationale: She gave him sex appeal, he gave her class.

In our Beverly Hills neighborhood, we had noteworthy neighbors: Lucille Ball across the street, next to Jack Benny, Jimmy Stewart at the corner. Sigmund Romberg had lived just past Ira's house, not far from Larry Hart, Jerome Kern, Oscar Levant.

Joe bought the house for a good price, $150,000, because he was able to pay cash, thanks to *Moulin Rouge.* Early on, he'd bought the rights to the main book on which the film was based. So when John Huston went looking for the rights, he got a leading man as well.

But I paid the bills: phone, utilities, household staff. "Rosemary's work is in California, while Joe's is in New York," his people told my people. He had an accountant, a manager, an agent, a lawyer or two, and so did I. "He votes in New York and pays New York taxes, so he'll pay all the expenses there. She'll pay all the expenses here." It didn't occur to me then that the New York expenses were minimal: the maintenance charge for his apartment on West 57th Street and the upkeep on the country house in Ossining, New York, where I never even visited—too many ghosts of former wives drifting around. I didn't pay attention to the bills, or to taxes. If I was told to write a check, I wrote it; if a check came for me to endorse, I signed it. All I knew was there seemed to be plenty of money and I liked spending it. As for the accounting and the paperwork, I didn't care.

What I cared about was being Mrs. José Ferrer. I'd always lived in someone else's house, from my grandparents' in Maysville to the series of rentals in Beverly Hills. Now I walked around my own house in a happy daze, trying to keep track of all the rooms. On the second floor were three bedrooms with baths, along with a huge room, windows on three sides, that Joe planned to use as his art studio. Our bedroom, which had been George Gershwin's, was directly to the right at the top of the winding stairs, with a fireplace and two dressing rooms with baths, each of them almost as large as my Hampshire House studio. The smoked mirror over the fireplace had to go; Joe had a silvered, mirrored dressing table made for me at Universal. "Always do your own makeup when you can," he said. "Nobody knows your face as well as you do." For movies and TV, I had makeup people, but for my single acts, I always did my own makeup, and I still do.

Downstairs, a small room opened off the living room, with sliding glass doors opening onto the back lawn. "This little room would be perfect for ladies to play cards," Joe suggested. I laughed; it became our secretary's office. The formal dining room had a butler's pantry almost as fully equipped as the main kitchen. Beyond the kitchen, an entire wing stretched, with several small rooms and baths for live-in help.

I was not unaccustomed to being waited on; I'd stayed in first-rate hotels, and considered "room service" two of the most compelling words in the English language. But I wasn't used to a butler hovering, holding the door open for me, closing it softly. I wasn't sure we needed a butler, but he'd worked for Ginny Simms; he came with the territory. Our secretary, Lynn Westbrook, hired the rest of the staff.

And I certainly wasn't accustomed to a stern-faced woman emerging from somewhere at the back of my house to consult with me on the menu. I just looked at her. "What should Cook prepare for you and Mr. Ferrer for dinner?" she asked. I said the first thing that popped into my head. "Mushroom omelettes." She nodded without laughing, which gave me confidence. "And a salad and some fruit," I said firmly.

It took no time at all for me to become smugly accustomed to this lifestyle. I enjoyed being pampered, thanks partly to my tender treatment at Paramount. Once upon an insecure time, I'd have gotten down on my knees for an Ed Sullivan spot; now, when I found myself booked onto that show just a few weeks after my marriage, I was annoyed. I hadn't learned to say no, but I could complain to my manager, hoping he'd say no for me. I didn't want to leave home and fly to New York just to sing on television; he convinced me that I couldn't afford to pass and promised that he'd get Paramount to send my hairdresser and my makeup person with me. God forbid I'd have to depend on strangers to brush my hair and powder my nose.

Joe and I were soon to be separated, anyway. He was going to New York to work on not one, not two, not three, but four major productions in eight weeks at the City Center—producing one, directing another, starring in all four. *Richard III, The Shrike, Cyrano de Bergerac, Charley's Aunt:* One critic called it the Ferrer Festival. And I had another picture to make; our honeymoon would have to be delayed.

How about a dame called Rosemary Clooney? Sings a good song—and is purportedly personable. Bing Crosby wrote that in a letter to a Paramount producer in the summer of 1951, when *White Christmas* was still in the talking stage. A little over two years later, in the late summer of 1953, he'd apparently decided this dame was personable enough to appear in the picture with him, along with Danny Kaye and Vera-Ellen. The picture was Paramount's big splurge for the year—$4 million budget—its first release in Vista Vision, score by Irving Berlin.

I was enough at ease by then to call the composer by his first name, even though he'd been on his way to legendary status as the composer of "Alexander's Ragtime Band" when my mother was a toddler. Like Cole Porter, he wrote both the music and the words to a long list of American classics: "God Bless America," "Blue Skies," "Cheek to Cheek." Just a couple of years before we met, he'd had an enormous smash with "Annie Get Your Gun."

He was friendly with me—sometimes he'd stand next to me and, while watching intently what was going on in front of the camera, just take my hand and hold it. But he looked serious and dressed formally, in a suit and tie, white shirt, with black-rimmed glasses that gave him a vaguely forbidding look. He was given an office on the Paramount lot, where he stayed while the dramatic scenes were being filmed; he wasn't interested in the drama, not that there was much drama to be interested in. But he was always a concerned presence for the musical numbers, including rehearsals. One day when he looked especially tense, Bing put an arm around his shoulder. "Don't worry, Irving," Bing said. "we can't do anything to hurt your picture. It's already a hit." *White Christmas* was a partial remake of *Holiday Inn,* which Bing had made with Fred Astaire ten years earlier. "White Christmas," Berlin's song, had won the Oscar; within the decade, it had sold some 14 million records, 9 million of them by Bing. Paramount was now paying the composer $300,000, plus a percentage, to use his music in the remake. I couldn't imagine what Irving had to worry about.

Unless it was my dancing. I'd never liked to dance, not even ballroom dancing. Now I not only had to dance a lot, I was teamed with Vera-Ellen, one of the most accomplished dancers ever. Most of the steps and routines were so easy for her that she'd work with me a little, then get bored, so Bea Allen was called in. With Dante, I could have learned them in no time, but he'd left town, I was told, gone to live and work in Vegas. I missed him.

Bob Alton, the choreographer, came from Metro; he was probably the most famous then, after Busby Berkeley. He had a modern sensibility and a sense of humor about it: One production number lampooned modern dance, with Danny Kaye in black turtleneck and beret, surrounded by women with long hair and leotards, striking weird angular poses to the dissonant sounds of horns. Danny, who'd taken the Fred Astaire part, wasn't a dancer either, but he was so limber and agile that he looked like one. But it took me forever to learn the dance steps, simple as they were, for the number that Vera and I did together, "Sisters." Maybe the words, not the steps, were the problem. My name in the film was Betty, and in one scene,

Vera-Ellen says to Betty, "We always knew that one day we'd break up the act." I promised myself I'd record "Sisters" with my own Betty one day.

As the shooting progressed, I relaxed. I loved watching Bing and Danny film the nightclub scene in which they did a takeoff on the "Sisters" number, using big blue feather fans and simpering smiles. As family-friendly as the picture was, with an A rating from the Legion of Decency, the Production Code people could never let well enough alone. A letter from the Breen office, the enforcers, warned us that there should be nothing to "lend a flavor of a 'pansy' routine to this bit of business." Still, Danny whapped Bing with his folded fan and enjoyed it so much that he kept whapping him on the beat, even when it didn't fit the lyrics.

I learned some tricks of the trade, too. When a scene called for us to be eating, I started spooning up my soup as soon as the cameras rolled. But they needed a master shot, then a shot from Bing's point of view, then from Vera's. Finally I said, "I can't *eat* any more!" My soup bowl was empty; everyone else's was full. "You're supposed to play with it," Bing explained to me, "not eat it all!" He called me "the Buffet Bandit of Bourbon County."

The picture was a wonderful medley of showbiz and holiday spirit, with sleigh bells and saxophones, red satin Santa suits with white fur muffs. It was an absolute joy to sit by the fire in that Vermont lodge and sing "Count Your Blessings" with Bing. Never mind that it wasn't really a Vermont lodge; most of the picture was filmed on four Paramount sound stages. Singing together came as naturally to each of us as breathing. We had the same range: Mine was an octave and five notes, while Bing's was probably larger, but at least that. That meant we could do the duet dramatically, the way that fit the story best. Bing would sing a line, and because my next line would be in exactly the same range of notes, I could sing whatever lyrics it made sense for me to sing to him. We didn't have to make any concessions to accommodate our voices. Bing smiled as he sang—not always a broad grin you could see, but enough to shape his mouth inside. I tried to match that, and the blend was beautiful.

The memorable Berlin score included ballads, quartets in close harmony—"Snow" for Bing and Danny and Vera and me—and uptempo comic numbers, like "Gee, I Wish I Was Back in the Army." And he wrote a new song for the picture, "Love, You Didn't Do Right by Me," whose lyrics had an inside joke for me: *to send me a Joe who had winter and snow in his heart . . . wasn't smart!*

Our director was Mike Curtiz, who called Bing "Binkie" and who often talked to me in words that, even though they were English, I couldn't understand. In one scene, I had to climb through a window; I was half in, half out, when he cut and walked over to me. "When we start the scene," he said, "could you give me a little off from balance?"

Even though Curtiz was a celebrated director—*Casablanca*—and even though Danny Kaye had his own agenda and a very strong ego, Bing was always in charge. Sometimes he'd just disappear. He'd say, "I'm going over the wall." Nobody would know where he went, and nobody would ask. We'd already shot the finale of the picture, a lavish production number done on two stages, but on the day the king and queen of Greece came by, Curtiz announced that we'd do it again. "We will not film it, but Binkie and Danny and Vera and Rosemary will pretend to film it for their majesties, the king and queen of Greece."

Bing leaned over to me. "Cover for me. I'm going over the wall." So we did the scene without him, lip-synching to the playback, trying to pretend that Bing wasn't supposed to appear in the number, even though his voice, singing "White Christmas," was coming out of my mouth.

Bing had a hard time being direct with people; if he wanted to pay a compliment, he'd do it by going "around the horn," saying it to someone else. Even when he tried to make a joke of it, he'd do it second-hand. The minstrel show number contained this bit of banter for me and Danny:

"Mr. Bones, Mr. Bones, how do you feel, Mr. Bones?"

"Rattling!"

"Mr. Bones feels rattling! Ah, that's a good one!" The move was for me to put my hand over my left breast. Then all the dancers behind us burst out laughing; Bing had stage-whispered to them, "And the other one's not bad, either."

I know that Bing could be very aloof, his eyes not sky-blue, but steel-blue. He had a way of appearing friendly—"Hiya, pardner," he'd say, but then he'd just keep moving. Dinah Shore once told me that Bing lived behind a "privacy curtain," and I couldn't see behind it, as close as he and I were. "Nothing that takes place in this house is ever to go outside this house," Bing's wife had told their sons. I didn't know that the curtain concealed a family burdened by alcoholism and Bing's harsh methods of discipline. Later, when he more or less apologized to the boys for his abusive treatment of them, it was indirectly, in a newspaper interview.

Judy Balaban, the boss's daughter, had become a good friend of Grace Kelly, who played Bing's wife in *The Country Girl,* one of his 1954 hits. I know Judy said that Bing and Gracie were just friends. But one evening when I was invited to his house, it was dinner in the dining room, silver and china, the boys in neckties. When I arrived, Grace was already there, sitting in the library, knitting. Knitting! She was wearing low-heeled shoes—Bing wasn't tall—and a skirt and sweater, and she looked amazingly domestic. I thought, *What the hell is this? Is she auditioning? Is this some kind of test?*

Then Grace met her prince—Judy Balaban was a bridesmaid at that royal wedding—and Bing eventually married Kathryn Grant, the young contract player he met at Paramount when we were making *White Christmas.* Bing was thirty years older than Kathryn, and people said she wasn't right for him. But she *was* right for him. He made the decisions; she made the concessions. When they were married, I still went over sometimes to watch the fights, and of course Kathryn joined us. But when she'd make a comment, he'd say, "Just shut up. You don't know anything about it." Then he'd point to the screen: "Rosie, look—did you see *that?*" I kept trying to bring her into the conversation, but he kept cutting her off.

It wasn't easy for me and Kathryn to become friends, but as time went on, we did—and I became friends with Bing's second family, his two boys and a girl with Kathryn. I continued to visit them, though Bing never visited us much. Kathryn said he was jealous, didn't think Joe was good enough for me. I think it was because Joe tried to force Bing's friendship. With Bing, you had to lay back—he didn't want to be told how wonderful he was, and that was something Joe could never understand.

I was paid $5,000 a week for my part in *White Christmas,* double my previous movies' salary. But in prestige and publicity power, it was priceless. Paramount was delighted and announced more pictures being planned for me. Everybody said *White Christmas* was only the beginning of my brilliant career. As it happened, everybody was wrong, but I made some good friends then. Janet Leigh was making *Living It Up* with Dean Martin and Jerry Lewis; we had a lot in common, having watched movies all day on Saturdays as kids, and we were both newly married. Janet was very much like me—cast in the same wholesome image.

Audrey Hepburn, though, was one of a kind, wide-eyed yet elegant, with an unaffected grace. She was making *Sabrina* on the lot with William Holden and Humphrey Bogart when we met; I was lonesome without Joe, so I invited her to dinner. We ate on trays in the den. I felt a little ridiculous with all the staff bustling about, but dinner for the two of us in the elaborate dining room seemed even more ridiculous. We were chatting easily, so when she asked, "What do you think of Mel Ferrer?" I answered just as casually, "Oh, I can't stand him. He's so pompous, isn't he? Considers himself such a fine actor, when he really isn't very good at all."

Audrey didn't say much after that. She left earlier than I'd expected, and when Joe called me that night, I told him about her visit. He told me that Audrey and Mel were going to do *Ondine* together on Broadway, that they would be not only living together, but living together in Joe's house in Ossining, because they didn't want the press to catch on. Joe was doing them a favor because he liked Audrey, with whom he shared an agent, Kurt Frings; he hadn't told me, he said, because he was afraid I'd let it slip at Paramount. "You made me slip up right here at home," I retorted. The usual misunderstanding was that Mel and Joe were related—Ferrer was a common Latin name, like Smith, and their families were acquainted but not connected—but this misunderstanding was deeper, and it was a while before Audrey and I could laugh about it.

Joe called late every night, from his backstage dressing room. I'd be curled up in bed, wanting him; we had long, loving conversations. I couldn't wait to be with him; we'd be spending our first Christmas together at his apartment—*our* apartment now—in New York City. Then we'd fly away on our belated honeymoon, to England and Ireland, then France. Before Christmas, we'd make a record together. I'd worked hard to arrange it, and it was gratifying for me to do something for Joe—to have our positions reversed, so that I was the one with experience to share. Mitch Miller agreed to the plan, on the condition that Joe and I sing together. He had his doubts about Joe as recording artist, but a duet with star power and a novelty twist appealed to the gimmick lover in him.

The night before I left for New York I sat under the olive tree, feeling as secure in my marriage as in a fortified kingdom: safe, protected, nestled.

I cherish the memory of that time, when happiness had come to me like grace: freely given, unquestioned, even if undeserved. I actually thought about my happiness; I felt it in a tangible way, something I could objectively observe. *Look at me, I'm so happy here.*

"Rosie, he's terrible," Mitch groaned. "He has no pitch!" He'd drawn me to the side during a break in the recording session. We were doing two sides under Norman Leyden's baton: "Man (Uh-Huh) Woman (Uh-Huh)" from *Red Garters* and my solo, "You Make Me Feel So Young." The look on Mitch's face while we ran through the first song showed that whatever he had expected, this was worse.

"He's trying hard," I pointed out. Maybe love was deaf as well as blind; to me, Joe sounded all right.

"He sounds like a bull seal in heat and you can tell him I said so."

I didn't think that was a good idea. There was always some friction between Joe and Mitch; I just wanted to finish the record. I knew Mitch had wanted me to stay in New York, and he hadn't bothered to spare my feelings when it came to my films. "They stink. Not a hit song in any of them."

I don't know if Joe noticed my white knuckles gripping the music when I joined him at the mike. "Let's wrap this up," I whispered.

The apartment still seemed more Joe's than mine. It matched his vision of life; his carriage, his voice, and his manner showed well against its background. "It's so bohemian," Janet Leigh said when she visited. "But in an erudite manner," she added. She was right: The living room, done in oyster gray with a black marble fireplace, full of antiques and old posters elegantly framed, was like a rich man's dream of a garret. "I feel so New Yorkish here," she said. "So *in.*"

I'd refused to set foot in the apartment when Joe was still married, and now I was struggling to feel at home. The man was mine, but all the things felt like hers, especially the bedroom set. Dietrich told me where to go for a new one. "Pick it out," she said, "and they'll have it in place by tomorrow, because I'll call and tell them."

Dietrich had advice for every situation. When I had trouble sleeping, she brought me some sleeping pills in suppository form from Paris. "You don't have to worry about overdosing with these," she pointed out, "because you won't stay awake long enough to keep shoving them up your ass." The pills were called Hypnotiques, but she and Noel Coward called them "Lamases," because Noel thought Fernando Lamas could put anybody to sleep.

And she had advice for Joe, whose reputation for philandering she knew. "Don't make any mistakes here," she warned him. "Rosemary's important to me. She's important to a lot of people. Don't break her heart."

"Which side does the sun come up on?" Joe asked as we settled into the first-class cabin on the plane.

I could swear the steward almost bowed. "Whichever side you prefer, sir." He turned to me. "Madam, your berth is on this side."

Joe winked. "Don't be surprised if you find us together in one berth," he said.

It was a time of airborne luxury, of deference so absolute it defied logic. All the way across the Atlantic, caviar mounded and champagne flowed until I stepped out onto European ground for the first time.

London town was a little foggy. Joe had fallen in love with the city during his student days, when he brought his Pied Pipers over on tour; he felt so at home there, and was such a natural linguist, that a British accent crept into his speech before we even got off the plane. He showed me not just the tourist treasures, but his personal picks: cocktails in the Claridge's lounge, "Twelfth Night" at the Old Vic.

Joe's friends and colleagues on this side of the Atlantic were theater royalty; I couldn't imagine what I'd find to talk about with John Gielgud, Laurence Olivier, Vivien Leigh. But they accepted me at once.

Joe and I didn't record together in London, but he came with me one day to hear "While We're Young," and "Love Is a Beautiful Stranger," which Joe cowrote. England was a new world to me, but the Conway Hall recording studio in Red Lion Square was an island of familiarity. We drank tea instead of coffee in the breaks; the boys in Wally Stott's band called each other "old man" instead of "pal," called me "luv" instead of "baby." But once the music started, I was at home.

We spent a weekend at Notley Abbey, the country home of the Oliviers. Garson Kanin was there with Ruth Gordon. We were shown to our suite; Joe went into the bathroom and came out looking dismayed— the pipes were frozen. He clattered down the thirteenth-century stairs. "Larry, old man, could I have a word with you?"

Vivien called for tea, and we chatted while two of the greatest actors in the English-speaking world worked on the toilet tank. "Notley Abbey was founded during the reign of Henry II and endowed by Henry V," she told me. "Now you see why the plumbing doesn't work."

She put me completely at ease, talking about the house, and her work, and people we knew. She'd played Blanche DuBois opposite Brando in the film version of *Streetcar* in 1951, and she asked after him. "Does he still play the bongos? How's his raccoon?"

Red Garters had previewed in the United States on January 25, 1954, opening the following week to mixed reviews; I remembered the good ones, especially *Newsweek*'s "brisk and beautiful spoofing." Peter Finch escorted me to a private showing at Paramount's London screening room. I'd seen the rushes on the set, but it was something else to watch it unfold on the big screen, with the text that had been added in editing: *Many people have said, "The movies should be more like life," but a wise man answered, "Life should be more like the movies."* Fade to black, and then the scene emerged—just the outline of a town, a wall, a tree, a door. And here came Guy Mitchell, all in pale beige, wearing a white hat and riding a horse to match: light palomino, white mane. I had to laugh at the sight of myself performing the tamest strip-tease ever seen on any stage, thanks to the Production Code. *Red garters on a dancing girl, now that's what I call art!*

On our last night in England, Joe took me to dinner in an authentic pub. Just as we were raising our pints in a toast, the barmaid came up to our table. "There's a phone call for you, Mrs. Ferrer."

When I came back, Joe had finished his pint and started on a new one. "That was Mama," I told him. She'd tracked me down. "Now that she's divorced, she wants to go on the road with Betty and put Gail in a boarding school. She wants us to help find a place."

"Gail's only nine," Joe said. "That's too young for boarding school. Why does she need to go away?"

"Well, Mama can't be around all the time," I began. Then I realized how unconvincing that sounded and how familiar. She'd always made other arrangements for Betty, Nicky, and me when it didn't suit her to stay. I wished I could think of a way to justify what she was asking—and interrupting us on our honeymoon to ask it—but I didn't try.

Joe reached across the table and took my hand. "Why don't we have Gail come and live with us?" he said. "We should have so many children around our house that we have to push them out of the way."

John Huston was still promoting *Moulin Rouge,* more than a year after its release; the invitation to his country house in Ireland was part social, part publicity. When we landed at Dublin airport and the Aer Lingus stewardess bent over our seats—"Mr. and Mrs. Ferrer, would you please go out last? They're wanting to take your picture"—I figured he'd drummed up a nice welcome for Joe.

As we came down the stairs, flashbulbs popped and questions flew.

"Miss Clooney, what part of Ireland is your family from?"

"What's your next record going to be?"

"Sing us a song, Rosie!"

I managed a few one-word answers, all the while trying to stay in the background so I wouldn't eclipse Joe. He'd already been miffed when a newspaper in England made my helpful husband sound like my valet: "He fetches and he draws baths." So I wanted to be very careful of our profile. The publicity machine never took a vacation, not even a honeymoon; I'd had to phone L.A. columnist Sheilah Graham from Claridge's for a gushy article: ROSEMARY CLOONEY THINKS HER HUSBAND, JOSÉ FERRER, PERFECT.

Even in the car on the way to Huston's house, I couldn't relax; he'd invited the press along. In the Great Room at Courtown—an imposing pile of stone on three hundred acres in County Kildare—the reporters started in again.

"Sing us some Irish songs, Rosie!"

"I don't know any Irish songs," I muttered.

"Well then," one young man called out, "we'll sing some for you!"

I pulled John's wife aside. "What is your husband *doing?*"

She laughed. "He's publicizing his picture, Rosemary. That's what he's doing."

Ricki Huston was beautiful—a former ballerina who'd been on the cover of *Life* before she gave up her career to become John's fourth wife. But even though they had young children—Tony was almost four, Anjelica just two—John made no attempt to conceal his infidelity. His romance with Suzanne Flon, from the cast of *Moulin Rouge,* was the most recent, and the only one I was privy to. Ricki told me she was thinking of divorce, even though her stepmother had pointed out that when she married a man with a history of other women, she should have known she wouldn't be able to change him.

Joe didn't seem to mind the attention to me, so I began to relax. He and John were laughing, reminiscing about the picture. They had a lot in common—both painted and knew the power of color. Huston had wanted his film to look like a Toulouse-Lautrec poster, so he'd used softly colored gels—I remembered Shubert Pink—for a mellow misty effect. Both men had enormous egos and a commanding presence. Anything one could do, the other determined to do better. On this Irish estate, John had begun riding to hounds, so Joe acquired boots, hacking jacket, hard hat and crop, and began taking lessons. Back home, when a friend of mine saw Joe in the outfit, he thought Joe was in costume.

John presented me with my first glass of eau-de-vie. "In the seventeenth century, an Alsatian monk boiled fermented cherries to make an elixir," he said. "He hoped it would provide a cure for cholera." As I sipped, feeling the explosion of fruit flavor, it seemed to me the drink would cure anything.

Then John took up his position in front of the blazing peat fire, one arm resting on the mantle, glass in hand, and began telling a story. *Hamlet* was running in the West End, so he told that story. With flourishes and embellishments, he led up to Hamlet seeing the ghost of his father, who tells him that Hamlet's uncle is his murderer. Then he waved his pipe in a sweeping gesture. "Isn't that a grand story, now?" Everybody laughed and applauded.

*G*lamorous and sophisticated in the early 1950s.

*T*he Clooney Sisters...

in a Universal short subject made while the band
was at the Palladium in Hollywood

singing together

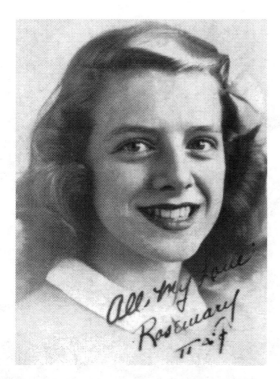

Me as a sophomore
in high school

singing with the band

$\mathcal{W}$hen Frank and I were both very young.

*A*unt Ann at
her most
glamorous

and Uncle George,
looking handsome
in his uniform

_R_iding in the Cadillac at my homecoming celebration with Grandma next to me in the backseat.

_D_edicating Rosemary Clooney Street. That's Mayor Rebekah Hord on my right.

_A_t the Mayor's house with Blanche Chambers. Dad is smoking in the background.

*W*ith Mitch Miller, and Dietrich as critic.

*O*n the radio with Tony Bennett   and singing with Joe

Exiting the courthouse in Durant, Oklahoma, on the day of my marriage to Joe

and under the olive tree at Roxbury Drive

When Joe and I got to our room, I turned to him. "That's not the end of the story, is it?" I protested. "Doesn't Hamlet say, 'I've got a problem here, now I've got to kill my uncle?'" Joe laughed and said I was right; John just thought it made a better story his way.

I started to talk about Ricki's unhappiness, but Joe changed the subject. "Let's have a bedtime story," he said. We snuggled under the quilts as Joe read aloud from *French for the Traveler*, with me repeating each momentous question after him. "Where is the nearest café?" "What time does the ferry depart?" "Where is it that one may buy shoes?"

The nearest café was just down the block from our hotel, at the end of the Avenue Kléber, where it met the Champs-Élysées. Over sweet vermouth on the rocks, Joe and I laughed and touched hands like the honeymooners we were.

I thought Paris was the most beautiful place I'd ever seen. Every vista was magical, right out of an Impressionist painting. I was surprisingly moved by the sight of the Arc de Triomphe, looming almost tall enough to cast its shadow over our table. I thought of history, of struggles, of victories. I thought of my uncles; it had been less than a decade since the Allies marched in to liberate the city. I was so carried away by this enchanting place that I felt I could even converse in its language. Joe and I went to see Yves Montand's show; at the interval, we were outside, smoking, when an elegantly dressed woman approached and asked if I spoke French. I meant to say *petit peu*—a little bit—but as I tossed my head airily and smiled, it came out *petits pois*—little peas.

Our room at the Hotel Raphael, complete with velvet-draped bathroom suite, opened onto a wrought-iron balcony. Inside, we sipped Pernod, reclining on chaises of gilt and damask; on the balcony, wrapped in the hotel's soft robes, we sipped café crème and watched the city awaken.

I didn't find out what time the ferry left or where to buy shoes; I didn't even learn much French. But I did find an antique cradle of smooth old wood in an artisan's studio on the Left Bank and shipped it home so I'd be ready. I discovered the city's delights, with Joe at my side in the

Louvre and the Grand Palais to put his own gloss on the Old Masters. I discovered that when you order shrimp in a restaurant in France, they arrive intact on a plate: heads and all, black eyes staring. And I discovered just what a serious business this eating thing really was.

Sitting in the Café aux Deux Magots, Joe plotted our course for Riviera, using a map and the *Guide Michelin*. There were several restaurants with a four-star rating on the way down. On a cloudy early spring day, we set out in a rented French Ford to connect-the-restaurants on our way to the sea.

We took our time, enjoyed the road, each other—and the food. In a small town about halfway down, we stopped at a place called Chez Pic: a hotel with ten rooms, thick comforters, *bains* down the hall, and an excellent restaurant, all run by a very fat man who sat on a swivel chair in a square niche. To check us in, he swiveled to one side of the enclosure; to make our dinner reservation, he swiveled to the other; to talk with someone on the staff, he swiveled to the back.

Joe found the soup of his dreams at Chez Pic. I came down the stairs on our last day to find him leaning on the fat man's counter, conversing earnestly in French. He was smiling broadly when he came out to the car.

"Dig this—I got the recipe!" he said triumphantly. "I told him I was a writer for a food magazine."

In Paris a chill had lingered in the air, but on the Côte d'Azur it was already spring, the air soft and scented with mimosa. Joe had a friend who owned a villalike hotel in the little town of Beaulieu, just a few miles from Monte Carlo and the Italian border beyond. In the other direction, Joe and I spent an afternoon in Villefranche-sur-Mer, whose fourteenth-century fortress defended a stunning natural harbor. We walked the steep cobbled streets of the old town, exploring the dungeonlike depths of its one covered street, the Rue Obscure. From Villefranche, we drove along the Lower Corniche to Nice, with its quayside promenade lined with palms and magnificent hotels all in a row.

Beaulieu was a quieter town, impossibly picturesque, with houses scattered up the seaward slope of the Alpes-Maritimes, like a burst of foam cast up from the surf. We stayed in the hotel owner's quarters, an old-fashioned bungalow with living room downstairs and a single bedroom above, connected by an open curving staircase. With no doors to close between the rooms, we felt the breeze from the sea all through the house.

The sea was still too cold to swim in, so we waded in the turquoise water on a beach that was covered in smooth stones. "Why isn't there any sand?" I asked Joe.

"There's sand at Cannes," he said. "Until then, it's all like this. People lie down on it to sunbathe anyway." He gave me a wink. "Lots of the ladies sunbathe *sans* tops."

That night, sitting in the living room of the bungalow, I fingered a stone I'd picked up on the beach. It was translucent, a smooth, flattened oval. Joe had run into a friend of his—Jan de Hartog, the writer of *The Four Poster*, which Joe had directed—and I didn't have much to contribute to their conversation, since they frequently spoke in French. I felt left out as they laughed about shared experiences and friends in the theater. Before long I excused myself and went up to bed.

I could still hear them talk, because of the way the house was laid out. I put the stone on the bedside table and settled down to read. Their words drifted up to me. At some point they lapsed back into English. I heard Joe say "she" and "her." He wasn't talking about me.

As I lay there listening, my husband treated his friend to the raw details of a sexual episode in his dressing room in New York, the very room he'd been calling me from every night, while I was rushing to finish my movie so I could join him.

I didn't hear every word; I heard enough. I sat there, holding my book, looking at the same line over and over.

When I heard Joe come upstairs, I kept staring at that line. "How's the book?" he said.

When I didn't answer, he started toward me. I dropped the book and looked at him.

"I heard you," I said. "I heard everything." As soon as the words were out, I started to sob.

With all my heart, I wanted him to come to me, to comfort me, to say it wasn't true. But he just stood at the foot of the bed, watching me cry. "I'll call Shribman," he said at last. "He'll arrange to get you home."

So my marriage would end almost as soon as it had begun. I was not the kind of wife Joe wanted; I was not strong enough to handle what I'd heard. If our marriage failed now, it would be my failure.

"I'm sorry," I heard myself say. "Don't call him."

A few minutes ago it had seemed so clear that I was the one being wronged. Now there was so much disappointment, so much distaste in his eyes, that I was crying out of humiliation, and out of desperation: He was going to send me away.

Joe came and sat on the edge of the bed. He picked up my translucent stone and held it to the light. Then he looked at me.

"Are you going to be all right?" he asked.

I knew there was only one possible answer.

"Yes," I said.

SEVEN

⁓

*N*obody gives parties on Monday night," Joe said, "so we will." The cook and the butler were delighted; I suspected that the butler, at least, was often bored. By now I'd mastered the art of composing a menu—most of the time. With Marcel Marceau in Paris, Joe had had confit of duck. *What the hell part of a duck is the confit?* I wondered. I didn't want the cook to know I didn't know, so I called Jackie at the Hampshire House. I wasn't close to her anymore, now that Joe had taken over, but she was always available to tell me how something should be done.

After cocktails in the den, we'd move into the dining room, with its carved Spanish oak table and high-backed chairs, one wall mirrored, the others lined with satin brocade. The room was awash in candlelight: more than a hundred candles, in sconces along the walls, in pillar candle stands that Joe had found in antique shops, in brass and pewter candlesticks all along the table. Always pale ivory candles for the most elegant effect.

My experience with Joe in Beaulieu had marked me, though I didn't let him see. I couldn't acknowledge my anger; all I could do was put on a resolutely carefree face for the rest of the trip. We never mentioned that night again. But I was more determined than ever to make our marriage work, even as I realized how much work that would take. I was sure that Joe wouldn't have affairs, that everything would be perfect if I did everything well enough.

So I tried to make our Monday night dinners flawless. I arranged a mix of friends, Joe's and mine: Janet Leigh and Tony Curtis, Nat and Maria Cole, Stanley and Marion Donen were regulars. Tony admired Joe for his patrician manner; Joe welcomed the admiration, and the two of them tried to outdo one another in their sartorial elegance. Tony always aspired to be Baron von Curtis, Janet said, so Joe was the perfect mentor.

As the table was being cleared, Nat would stand up and stretch. "How about a little music for dessert?" In his loose, athletic stride, he'd amble the length of the living room and settle down at the piano, cigarette in hand. I have a very clear, very precious memory of sitting at the table as the candles burned down, people murmuring softly, Nat's velvet voice drifting toward us: *Mona Lisa, Mona Lisa, men have named you* . . .

I'd met Nat and Maria shortly after I left Tony Pastor, when I was appearing at an auto show in Washington, D.C. When I heard that Nat Cole was appearing at a club there, Jackie and I went to his show, then we finagled our way backstage. Maria Cole opened the dressing room door. "I'm Rosemary Clooney," I said, "and I'm one of Mr. Cole's biggest fans." She laughed. "I know who you are," she said, "because I'm one of *your* biggest fans."

Nat's speaking voice was as soft as his singing voice. "I was going to do 'You Started Something,' " he told me, "but when I heard your recording, there was no reason for me to do it again." I told him that *he'd* started something, that Betty and I had sung his "Straighten Up and Fly Right" when we auditioned for the WLW job. He said the title was based on a sermon his father, a Baptist minister, had preached. Nat had sold the song for just $50, no royalties, when he was hard up; it had become a million-seller for Capitol.

There was no racial crisis in the country when I met Nat Cole. It was worse than that: Segregation was woven into the fabric of American life. When I made a record with Duke Ellington, we could not be photographed together for the cover; a small photo of me, resting my cheek against my hand as though pondering the silliness of it all, was set into the corner of the cover, with its large photo of Duke. Once, when a black entertainer dipped his foot into a hotel pool in Vegas, the pool was drained. A black entertainer could perform at a first-rate hotel but couldn't stay there. Guests at the Hotel Lincoln in New York City complained when Billie Holiday, who was performing in the Blue Room, got on the elevator with them; the hotel's owner told Billie she would have to use the service elevator. When Nat Cole was given his own TV show, it was a network first. Although a long list of celebrities, starting with Sinatra, volunteered their time, the show died because it couldn't attract a national sponsor. The reasoning seemed clear, if cynical: "Madison Avenue is afraid of the dark."

Nat's success hadn't made him any more acceptable to the bigoted Hollywood rich. The Coles moved into a spacious Tudor house in Hancock Park; they put in a rose garden, a pool, a playhouse built of seventeenth-century wood imported from England. Then stones were thrown through their windows; a sign was stuck into their lawn: NIGGER HEAVEN. Their dog was poisoned. Yet I never saw Nat angry, any more than people ever saw me angry. Whenever he sang, in that caressing voice, he made you feel that everything was going to be all right.

And for a magical time, it was. At that juncture in our social history, romance met reality and smoothly merged. At night, as the hills above our house turned indigo, fantasy became exotic fact. Canaries fluttered behind the long glass wall at the Mocambo; at the Luau, we reached our table across a footbridge over a counterfeit creek. The Beachcomber's tin roof was rained on every ten minutes. Dancing at Ciro's, in a space deliberately kept tiny so that dancers would "bump posteriors." Vodka gimlets and tent parties, ladies in floppy-legged beach pajamas and hair in a pompadour, lily of the valley cologne, the tent stretching from patio to pool, with a dance floor laid over the pool and an orchestra playing in the poolhouse shell: *No, no, they can't take that away from me.* At Romanoff's, daytime drinkers—Bogart, Herbert Marshall—sat in shadow, lighting cigarettes from matchbooks embossed with the distinctive double R. A compartment on the Super Chief, linen and china, camellias and mimosa, and the assumption—unexamined because it was unconscious—that it would last forever.

Hollywood was a town of fight fans—Sinatra would invite his pals to dinner at Romanoff's, then convey everybody down to the Legion Stadium in limos. Prizefights in those days were a true sport, not a bloody brawl; Joe and I even backed a boxer, Vince Martinez. We invited Bob and Dolores Hope to come with us one night to watch our wonderful welterweight. Vince just danced around the ring, an embarrassing exhibition. When Joe lit into him afterward, Vince explained, "I didn't want to get hit when Bob Hope was watching."

Some nights we'd drop in at the Cocoanut Grove in the Ambassador Hotel, where Merv Griffin became famous singing "I've Got a Lovely Bunch of Coconuts." Joe liked its big dance floor; most clubs, like Ciro's, had tiny patches of parquet. But mostly when we went out, we went to dinner—often at a family-owned Italian place on Little Santa Monica, La Dolce Vita. Not long after we were back from Europe, we were having dinner at Chasen's when I felt a foot nudging my shoulder, followed by an oddly familiar voice. "José! Is this your new wife?" It was Henry Fonda, climbing over the back of the banquette to say hello. Joe knew and loved fine food—at one point, he bought a dozen cookbooks and became a superb, self-taught cook. When he'd conquered that, he moved on to something else. "Anybody can learn anything in fifteen minutes," he insisted, "as long as they concentrate."

We liked being home together, so we turned down a lot of invitations, though never to one of Gary and Rocky Cooper's dinner parties. At home, Joe invited people to play tennis, including Rita Hayworth, who'd appeared with him in *Miss Sadie Thompson,* the musical remake of Somerset Maugham's *Rain.* When we gave a big party, it was for professional reasons. Joe had worked with Al Morgan in adapting Morgan's novel, *The Great Man,* for the screen; then he both directed and starred in it. Everyone knew that this tough, behind-the-scenes look at a beloved television star was based on the life of Arthur Godfrey, so when we gave a cocktail party for Morgan, our guest list was carefully chronicled in the columns— Jack and Mary Benny; George Burns and Gracie Allen; the Edgar Bergens; Tony and Janet; Betty Comden and Adolph Green; Agnes Moorehead; Bacall and Bogart—I loved it when Bogart called me "Miss Clownie." Edith Head, my Paramount designer, dark-haired and petite, wore dark glasses and a necklace made of Chinese gaming chips, mother-of-pearl, every day of her life. We'd become friends at the studio—she knew I hated hats, so she'd wait until the end of the workday, then order a pitcher of martinis and start having me try on hats. She knew that after a couple of martinis, I'd say yes to anything.

When Cole Porter gave dinner parties at his house in Brentwood, he'd insist that everybody sit down and watch "The $64,000 Question." When the Gershwins gave parties, Ira would stay in a quiet corner; somebody might play the piano, but mostly it was conversation. We saw Judy Garland there often. Ira had been best man when she married Vincente Minnelli in 1945; even when she had another husband, Sid Luft, she'd stayed close to the Gershwins. One night we were visiting when, in a momentary silence, we heard Sid saying, "Culturally speaking . . ." Bogart cut in: "What right do you have to say, 'culturally speaking'? You weren't really exposed to much culture as a young man, were you?" Sid just stared as Bogart went on. "Now I lived on Park Avenue, my father was a doctor, my mother was an artist, so if I say, 'culturally speaking,' people will take it to be the truth. But you, Sid?" He pushed and pushed until Sid was furious. "That does it," Sid said. "Let's take this outside!" Whereupon Bogart whipped his glasses out of his pocket and put them on. "You wouldn't hit an old man with glasses, would you?" Sid looked chagrined. "Oh, okay, Bogie, I'm sorry." And Bogie grinned. "But seriously, Sid, why *would* you say, 'culturally speaking'?"

Joe and I were rarely alone anymore, even at home, now that my mother had sent Gail to us. She was only nine; she needed a mother as much as she needed a big sister, so I tried to be both. I fixed up a room for her opposite ours at the top of the stairs, shopped for clothes, and enrolled her in school.

It was a tense time for Joe, who was having difficulty getting work. He'd had a wood floor and a barre installed in the garage so he could prepare for a television role in *Pal Joey*. Then his part vanished. He'd expected to be cast in the MGM musical *The Bandwagon*, and when that part vanished, too, he blamed the blacklist.

Until I married Joe, I hadn't been especially affected by the frenzy spilling out from Washington and soiling the whole country, especially Hollywood. In 1950, when the spooky paperback *Red Channels: The Report of Communist Influence in Radio and Television* was published, I was mostly influenced by the need to pay my rent. Joe was named in *Red Channels*, along with 150 others on a list that read like a kind of honor roll—Orson Welles, Arthur Miller, Leonard Bernstein—but for some spelled heartache and disaster. Next to the names were lists of suspicious organizations with which they were involved or were said to have been involved; the actress Jean Muir lost her television series because, as a student of the Stanislavski acting method, she'd sent a cable of congratulations to the Moscow Art Theatre when it celebrated its fiftieth anniversary. Among Joe's citations was "Veterans of the Abraham Lincoln Brigade"—one of his uncles had been killed in the Spanish Civil War. That the substance of the citations might be totally irrelevant didn't matter; what mattered was the listing itself, which made an actor controversial and thus unemployable.

In 1943, Joe had been signed to play Iago in *Othello* on Broadway, then to go on tour, with Paul Robeson as Othello. The FBI had a phone tap on Robeson, so that meant guilt by association. Moreover, Uta Hagen had played Desdemona; offstage, she'd been Joe's wife then and Paul's lover, so Joe might have been presumed guilty on the transitive principle.

There was more. Before John Huston directed Joe in *Moulin Rouge*, John had opposed a loyalty oath for members of the Screen Directors Guild. The loyalty oath had been voted down, but John had gone on to help organize the Committee for the First Amendment to protest the mushrooming hysteria. A columnist had labeled him "the brains of the Communist Party" in Hollywood—so when a splinter group of the American Legion picketed the West Coast opening of *Moulin Rouge*, it was presumably a way of killing two birds with one ultra-patriotic stone.

In May 1951, Joe was subpoenaed to testify at the hearings on Communist Infiltration of the Hollywood Motion Picture Industry. He spoke in an unusually low voice, so that more than once he was instructed to please speak louder. "Righto," Joe said, going on to plead innocence, ignorance. "Time and time and time again, I have relied on the names of other people, the names of organizations in whom I had faith, to guide me in letting my name be used."

Joe's testimony took nearly two days as the questions were hurled. Didn't he have his picture taken with Charles Collins, a black candidate for the Senate on the American Labor Party ticket? "Yes, in Cyrano costume, for publicity." Didn't he attend a birthday gala for Paul Robeson in 1945, and hadn't Robeson supported Benjamin Davis, a candidate for the New York City Council on the Communist Party ticket? "Yes, and yes, but I didn't know he was a Communist." And wasn't Joe a close personal friend of Robeson? Joe said he hadn't spoken to Paul Robeson in six years, and while that was true, the implication—which he didn't correct—was that he hadn't spoken to Robeson because the guy was a Communist.

Joe swore that he himself was not. He didn't name names, but he promised the Committee he'd sure try to come up with some names, and if he did, he'd let them know. He was represented by two lawyers—Arthur Friend of Friend and Reiskind, whose nameplate Betty and I had seen in the office building directory along with José Ferrer Productions, and Abe Fortas, who went on to be a Supreme Court Justice. Three decades later, in one of the ironies to which the entertainment industry seems especially susceptible, Joe played Fortas in a television film, *Gideon's Trumpet,* about the Miranda ruling, protecting the rights of the accused.

In 1954, Joe's movie career was reenergized by his friend Stanley Donen, who cast him in *Deep in My Heart.* It wasn't a particularly significant picture, but it got Joe back in front of the cameras. He played Sigmund Romberg, and I had a cameo role—the only time Joe and I appeared in a movie together.

Stanley came by to play chess almost every night, while his wife and I watched Charlie Chan movies. "Another exciting night in Hollywood," Marion groaned. Stanley would stare at the chessboard for what seemed like hours. "Why can't I see it?" he'd exclaim, exasperated. "There are sixty-four squares and thirty-two pieces—I ought to be able to figure it out!"

Joe couldn't stand not being the best. When Bobby Fischer, the chess prodigy, became well known, Joe brought him into the house as live-in tutor, a tedious month for me. I remember Bobby Fischer as a rude little guy who kept following me around. Joe always wanted to learn and to teach, and I wanted to be taught. I'd always loved learning, and Joe with his energy and enthusiasm, made everything interesting except, maybe, for Dickens. "We're going to read *The Pickwick Papers,*" he announced one night as he climbed into bed. I felt the smoothness of his silk pajamas as he began reading; next thing I knew, he was nudging me. "Sweetie, don't fall asleep, I'm just starting." He'd get through another paragraph or two before I drifted off again.

I never felt that Joe was being condescending when he read to me—no Professor Higgins to my Eliza Doolittle. I'd been reading myself to sleep since I was seven years old. Indeed, I've never stopped the reading habit. I still read at least a book a week, usually more. Even if I've watched a late movie on television, I still have to read two or three pages before I'm ready to go to sleep.

What I didn't like about Hollywood parties was the way the men congregated together, apart from the women. "Men have men friends, men don't have women friends," Stanley Donen said with a shrug. "That's just the way life is."

To me, it was a little more complicated—and a lot more distressing. It was a man's world, according to a popular lyric:

> A fella needs a girl to sit by his side
> At the end of a weary day,
> To sit by his side, and listen to him talk,
> And agree with the things he'll say . . .

At least, when sung by Perry Como, those words had a cocoa-and-bedroom-slippers feeling, which you couldn't say of Cole Porter's "Without Love":

> Without love, what is a woman?
> A pleasure unemployed.

Without love, what is a woman?
A zero in a void . . .

But with love, what is a woman?
Serene contentment, the perfect wife.
For a woman to a man is just a woman
But a man to a woman is her life.

I had always done what was expected of me, what I had come to expect of myself, even if my expectations had been formed by others. What was expected of me now was to be the perfect Fifties Wife. And I wanted to be that. I wanted to be married, to have babies. Mrs. José Ferrer wanted to sit by his side and listen to him talk, even though Rosemary Clooney was paying the bills.

Nobody knew that, of course. It didn't fit the image the publicity people worked so hard to maintain. "I think a girl's most important job is to be a good wife and mother," I told a reporter, "and I certainly wouldn't want my outside job to interfere with our home." A long article appeared in a magazine under my byline: "How You Can Win Your Man." My publicists sent articles for syndication around the country. The headlines, composed at each newspaper, were different:

LIFE IS ROSY FOR ROSIE AND JOE

HOW I MAKE CAREERS AND MARRIAGE MIX

THE MERGER THAT FOOLED 'EM

But the message was the same: I made careers and marriage mix by praising my husband—"José has helped me to weed out nonessentials and has stimulated my curiosity and expanded my interests"—and, if necessary, by making myself look foolish: "The reason he can accomplish so much is that he has such powers of concentration. I'm trying to learn this, but I'm an awful scatterbrain."

Publicity began not just to reflect but subtly to impact our lives. Besides the publicity machines at the film studio and the recording studio, I'd acquired my personal publicists, the high-priced, high-profile firm of

Rogers & Cowan. When Joe was in New York, he came across a newspaper piece about us. He didn't send it to me but to the Beverly Hills office of Rogers & Cowan, where Warren Cowan forwarded it to me—addressed, as I'd asked, to Mrs. José Ferrer—with a little note: DEAR ROSIE, JOSÉ WANTED YOU TO SEE THIS. So of course my pregnancy was a press release, issued on our first anniversary, carried on the wires worldwide.

I'd wanted a baby so desperately that when I didn't become pregnant immediately, I'd gone to see an endocrinologist about my problem. "What problem?" Dr. Cavanaugh asked. "You're young and healthy, just married. What's the rush?"

When I said it was a matter of expectations, he laughed, thinking I was making a pun. But I was serious. Having a baby was an indispensable piece of the plan for my life. It wasn't just a wish—*Wouldn't it be nice?*—it was a blueprint. The Fifties Wife was expected to be a mother, within a suitably discreet time. And for me, there was a compelling need.

Remembering the comfort that Betty and Nicky and I always found in one another, I wanted my children—I expected more than one—to have that kind of closeness, that emotional safety net. And now, since the shock of the night at Beaulieu, I expected a baby would be a safety net for me, too. Surely a baby would keep Joe content with hearth and home. It was a role that appealed to him: patriarchal, benevolent, baronial.

Long before I needed to, I began wearing maternity clothes. One day, when I went over to the Gershwins', Bogart was there. "My God, look at Miss Clownie, she's in maternity clothes!" he said. "What do you want to have, Miss Clownie?" "A boy," I said, "to look like Joe." "I've never won a bet with a pregnant woman in my life," he said, "so I'll bet you have a girl, and that way you'll win. Fifty bucks."

Paramount would have to write me out of my next picture, but I'd just be taking a hiatus. "Of course I'll not give up my career," I told a show-biz columnist, "but I know I can mix it with motherhood." I wanted to concentrate on the baby anyway. I convinced the doctor to give me hormone injections as a precaution. Having this baby was such a consuming priority that I had the nerve to turn down Mitch Miller when he asked me to come to New York and cut a few sides. No way would I consider traveling in this early, risky stage of my pregnancy.

True to form, he wouldn't take no for an answer. "Then I'm coming out there," he said. "I'll send an ambulance for you and you can record in a wheelchair if you need to—but you are going to make these platters."

So I did. Mitch made a flying trip from New York, and I went into the Radio Recorders studio on Santa Monica—on foot, under my own power—to record a raft of singles. On the first day, "Too Young"; my favorite from *White Christmas*, "Love, You Didn't Do Right by Me"; and a sentimental favorite from 1947, "Grieving for You," which had brought me to Mitch's attention in the first place. On the second, "Hey There" from *The Pajama Game*, and a folksy number, "This Ole House." Johnnie Ray, among others, had recorded "Hey There" without significant success. Mitch seemed to think our version would be a smash, and I gave it my best shot. *Hey there, you with the stars in your eyes!* I was swept up in the swingy melody. *He has you dancing on a string—break it and he won't care. Or are you not seeing things too clear? Are you too much in love to hear?*

The record sold 2 million copies—from studio to platinum in six weeks. "See!" Mitch said triumphantly. "I told you you could do it!"

Obviously I could sing and be pregnant at the same time; Dr. Cavanaugh assured me it hadn't hurt the baby, and it certainly hadn't hurt me. Jo Stafford had told me once, "You'll never sing better than when you're pregnant," and I did think my voice on that record had a little more warmth, a little more depth. I recorded all through my pregnancy; only in the last month was there a little shortness of breath. I couldn't believe how easy it was turning out to be: I really could do everything I wanted, all at once.

I recorded a little of everything: ballads, show tunes, novelties. I just couldn't lose that fake accent; Mitch gave me a broad, rollicking number called "Mambo Italiano." He even wanted me to record a French version, so Joe coached me on how to sing with a fake Italian accent in French; mercifully, that track never got done. Joe and I recorded together: "Mr. and Mrs.," then a number he and Nicky had written, "Young Man, Young Man." When I did a set of children's songs, I thought of my own baby and sang for him. I even made a recording with Gail, a sweet Sunday school number, "The Lord Is Counting on You." The pace kept up through my ninth month, when I asked the musical, no longer rhetorical question, "Where Will the Dimple Be?"

That Sunday night I sat propped up in bed, watching "The Ed Sullivan Show." I tried to concentrate, but it was hard because Joe and Stanley Donen had moved their chess game into my room, followed by everybody who'd filled the house during the day—cartoonist George Baker, songwriter Henry Nemo, and a handful of others who'd come to play tennis and stayed. I was distracted by their comments on the chess game and the show, as well as by the labor pains that were coming closer and closer together.

As the closing credits rolled, I said quietly to Joe, "I think it's time to go to the hospital."

Joe looked amazed. "Right!" he exclaimed. But he didn't move.

"I think it's time to *go,*" I explained.

"Right!" He jumped up from the chessboard and swept me and my prepacked bag into the car. Then he ran back inside and grabbed his own things—the chessboard, the chess pieces and four thick books. There was hardly room in the Jaguar two-seater for everything.

We peeled out of the driveway. When I glanced in the mirror, I saw a line of cars peeling out behind us, one after the other. "Do we need all these people?" I asked rhetorically. A motorcade worthy of a Hollywood premiere trailed us to St. John's Hospital.

Miguel José Ferrer, seven pounds nine ounces, was born at 1:33 A.M. on Monday, February 7, 1955. The doctor showed him to me upside down, but I could tell he was a duplicate of Joe. As they wheeled me back to my room, I glimpsed Joe in the waiting room. "It's a boy!" I called to him. "How happy can you get?"

Soon my room was jammed with cards and flowers. Lew Wasserman, the head of MCA, and his wife Edie sent dinner from Chasen's, with a waiter to serve it. But the first to arrive was an enormous armful of coral roses with a $50 bill and a note: *YOU WIN. BOGIE.*

Religious practices had long been displaced from my life by more tangible concerns, but I never considered leaving my baby unbaptized. I remembered Grandma's Bible verse; if someone didn't do right by a child, "it were better for him that a millstone were hanged about his neck, and that he were drowned in the depths of the sea." I hadn't stopped believing in God; I'd just stopped thinking about it. I didn't have time. Blanchie Mae Chambers had always said that the church was a hospital for sick people—and I'd never felt better in my life.

We dressed Miguel in a long lace gown and carried him down to Good Shepherd. Monsignor Concannon looked at me. "What is the child's name, Rosemary?"

"Miguel José," I said.

Monsignor Concannon stiffened and glared at Joe. "I baptize this child Michael Joseph," he said firmly.

Betty flew out for the christening to be Miguel's godmother. Thankfully, she was her usual buoyant self. I knew that sometimes she endured dark spells, once so severe that she'd spent a few days in the hospital. It frightened me, reminding me of Aunt Ann's swings from hilarity to despair and back.

Professionally, hers was a seesaw career. She'd recorded on the Coral label, nothing distinguished; "An Onion and You" was a gimmick written by a grocery clerk. She'd incorporated bits of "Come On-a My House" into her act and been criticized for it by a reviewer.

But then she'd been booked at the Starlight Roof of the Waldorf-Astoria in New York and signed as a regular on Jack Paar's "Morning Show" on CBS. We'd recorded "Sisters" for Columbia, its release timed to the opening of *White Christmas*. That wasn't just a sentimental notion; I couldn't record songs from the film with the other players because we recorded on different labels. Bing, under Decca contract, recorded with Peggy Lee.

With a national network show, Betty had settled with Mama into an apartment at the Westmore on West 57th Street, a few blocks from our Manhattan place. She was a delight on morning television, a beaming wake-up call. Jack Paar thought a lot of her, and so did the audience. Nick went into the Army when he was twenty; when he wrote her a letter from basic training, complaining about the bitter cold and describing the nifty handwarmer one lucky guy used on bivouac, Betty talked about it on the air. Within weeks, every man in Nick's outfit had a couple of those gadgets.

For a while, she'd dated Gary Crosby, Bing's oldest. When Gary filled in on his father's radio show, Betty joined him in a duet; their ranges matched and their voices blended as perfectly as Bing's and mine—and Gary fell in love. But he was a troubled young man, full of anger at his father, deep into drink and drugs. When he flew to New York for Betty's Waldorf show, he'd gone into an irrational rage and ripped a sink right out of her bathroom wall. That was enough for Betty.

The bandleader on "The Morning Show" was a suave Latin drummer named Pupi Campo. "His real name is Jacinto," Betty explained, "which sounds fine until you realize it means hyacinth." Pupi was not only handsome but funny; Betty loved anyone who could make her laugh.

But he was more than twenty years older than Betty, already in his mid-forties when they met, already married to a dancer whom Joe had worked with in *Miss Sadie Thompson*. Joe called Pupi "a second-rate talent, always the relief band. You'd go to see Xavier Cugat and you'd hear Pupi's band at intermission."

When Pupi had a falling-out with Paar and was fired, Betty was fired, too. On the record, Paar said he'd let Pupi go because the man had no talent, and Betty because he'd found a more versatile girl in Edie Adams. But I was sure that Betty's involvement with Pupi was her undoing. She had more status on the show than Pupi; he must have thought he would gain some leverage from that. I thought he was using her—and not just professionally. I thought he was using the breakup of his marriage as a way to keep Betty tied to him. His divorce was quick and messy, with conflicts over money; *I'm doing this all for you* was the guilt-inducing implication.

Uncle George had stayed with Betty as manager through all these ups and downs—until Pupi. Then he moved back to Maysville to go into partnership with a buddy on a small horse farm. My own rift with him had lasted a couple of years; we were on speaking terms again, a little more warmly each time, reaching a peace that was still tentative but important to me.

Even though Betty's stint at CBS had ended unhappily, she'd gained experience and recognition there, and she had another job lined up with my old friend Robert Q. Lewis. She was glad to be working again—and so was I.

⌒

"Come sing at the Sands," Sinatra said.

"Okay," I said.

That was the extent of our conversation: classic, clipped Sinatra. I was pleased for both of us. I'd been playing Vegas at least once a year, because that's where the money was—$20,000 a week by now—but this would be my first time at the Sands. Sinatra had a financial interest in the hotel and was making it a singer's showcase; he'd won an Oscar in 1953 for the role of the tragic Maggio in *From Here to Eternity*, a part he'd begged for, would have done for nothing—and, at $8,000, almost did. Altogether, Sinatra had achieved what *Variety* called "the greatest come-back in theater history." Joe and I had been visiting Peter Ustinov and his wife one night in a bungalow complex on Wilshire. We were walking along the path, past an open door, when I heard Sinatra's voice: "Rose, come in for a minute, I want you to hear something." Frank had taken a little apartment there; he played a record he'd just done, and it was marvelous. He was singing beautifully, better than he'd sung in years; the arrangement was stunning, done by a man I'd heard of but never met, Nelson Riddle.

I was glad to have the Sands booking—and not just for the salary or the status: It gave me more motivation to get back in shape. I wanted to trim down as quickly as possible; just six weeks after Miguel arrived, I was slated to sing one of the nominated songs at the Academy Awards. Dietrich sent me a masseuse, Louise Long, who had hands of iron. Thanks to Louise, and to a personal trainer—a boxer, Terry Hunt—I was pressed and pounded and punched back into my tight-belted waistline so quickly and successfully that I followed the same plan after each of my babies was born. I never had a weight problem, not until much later.

I was on the Paramount lot the day of the Oscars, March 30, to have my hair done. Grace Kelly was having her hair done, too; she'd been nominated for *The Country Girl*, along with Bing, who was up against Brando in *On the Waterfront*. With our regular hairdresser on the lot, Leonore

Weaver, away on assignment, Gracie and I were turned over to a new stylist.

My hair just fell into place naturally, and there wasn't much anyone could do to hurt it. But Gracie had her heart set on a very special hairdo to go with a very special dress. What she got was less than special. As we walked out, she started to cry.

I hurried her over to Saks for a salvage operation. And when she stepped up onstage to accept her award for Best Actress, she wore her hair swept back simply, just the way they'd fixed it at the store.

With a new person on the payroll, a baby nurse, I left eleven-week-old Miguel at home when I went to the Sands. Joe was in Lisbon, making *Cockleshell Heroes*—I teased him that it was "cockamamie," but we were thrilled that he was working again. I took Gail with me.

We were at the pool—Gail splashing, me dozing—when I heard him. "Rosella."

I sat up quickly in the lounge chair. He was standing in front of me, casting a tall shadow. "Dante," I said.

He sat down on the end of my chair. "I caught your show last night. You're sensational."

I couldn't say a thing.

"I was shattered when you left," he said. "I was just shattered."

"Well, I didn't know *you* were leaving," I told him. "I had to find out through the grapevine that you were here."

He looked away, toward the pool where Gail was playing.

"I'm going to London," I said brightly to fill the silence. "I'm playing the Palladium." He looked at me but didn't say anything. "Well, what are *you* doing?" I asked.

To my relief and delight, he grinned, the same easy grin, spreading warmth. He was working at the Sahara, with Mae West and her muscle men—guys with the kind of bulging biceps you saw in magazine ads, who carried her onstage every night, like Cleopatra. Dante wasn't a muscle man, but one of the song-and-dance men. "I auditioned for the job at her penthouse in Hollywood," he said. "All white and gold, with nude statues of herself all over the place."

We laughed, then there was another silence. I couldn't think of anything else to say. "I'm really looking forward to the Palladium," I managed at last.

"You sound happy," Dante said. "Are you?"

I knew there was only one possible answer.

"Yes," I said. "Are you?"

My bare feet were almost touching him. He tapped each of my toes in turn, big toe to little toe, then back. "I'm proud of you, Rosella." He rested his hand, light and warm, on my ankle and looked up at me. "You were terrific on the Oscars. I loved that song. It should have won."

He leaned over and kissed me quickly, then stood up. "Bye, Rosella."

"Bye, Dante," I said as he turned to go.

I loved the song, too. It was from *A Star Is Born*, Judy Garland's most memorable number: "The Man That Got Away."

With twenty-two pieces of luggage and three hundred jars of baby food, Miguel and his nurse and I came down the gangway of the *Queen Elizabeth*. Joe stood on the dock, waving. "Wait till you see the house I found," he said as he hugged me.

First I'd play Glasgow, where the Empire Theater was sold out for two weeks. But I couldn't take all the credit for my popularity there. Nicky had made Clooney a household name with his DJ show on the Armed Forces Network. Broadcast on an open channel from Frankfurt, where he was stationed, the show won Highland hearts with three solid hours of American pop music a day, lots more than on the BBC, where individual records had limited play. In the States, Nicky had made the news when he enlisted because he was Rosemary Clooney's brother; in Glasgow, I was Nick Clooney's sister. At the stage door, a crowd pressed around: "Where's Nick? How can we get in touch with Nick?"

Waiting in the Empire wings, I watched a procession of performers worthy of the Olympia in Miami. A small black and tan dog named Susie opened the show by climbing a ladder blindfolded and barking out numbers on call. She was followed by a roller-skating pair, then a comic, then a juggling act. Finally Teddy Foster's orchestra started up with the intro to "Tenderly." A voice came over the speakers: "For the first time on any British stage, we have pleasure in presenting Rosemary Clooney."

In the middle of a ballad, I heard a voice from the gallery. I tried to sing over it, but it called again. "Rosemary!" The r's rumbled through the music: "RRROSEMARY!"

I stopped singing and the band stopped playing. "What do you want?" I called.

" 'Come On-a My House!' "

Applause erupted all around the voice. I'd been saving the number for a finale—but you can't fight a happy hall.

At the London Palladium, I was more than a little nervous. I was prepared, but it was a world-renowned showplace, a very big deal for a girl singer just four years into her success. I'd never appeared at a place where ushers actually came onto the stage and handed you bouquets of flowers; I'd seen that only in the movies. I played two shows a night, the 6 P.M. show for people on their way home from work, a later show for the aristocracy, genuine or otherwise. I thought that the early show, on my opening night, would be an easy time to get used to this famous theater—then, right in the middle of the third row, surrounded by men carrying lunch pails, two people in black tie were smiling at me: Dietrich and Noel Coward.

"Good evening, ladies and gentlemen," I said. "When I first started in the singing business, people told me I had to work hard on my diction—to be a success, I had to sing very clearly and perfectly. I have spent several years working on that, and now I think I've perfected it. Like this." I tumbled my words sloppily over one another in my cheesiest accent: "Come on-a my house-a, my house—botcha me!" The audience roared. When I bantered with Buddy Cole, my accompanist, they loved it. Just like my first night at the Steel Pier, they were with me. So were the critics. The *New Musical Express* praised "a clever Clooney showing an audience how they can be nursed, coaxed, humoured, and sent home contented."

Only Noel Coward wasn't entirely content. When Dietrich brought him to my dressing room to introduce us, he scolded: "You're giving too much attention to your musicians. Keep that for yourself!" But he liked what I did. "I saw you in Vegas," he told me. "You were charming."

Noel Coward was the ultimate dandy, wickedly smooth and delightfully bitchy. He and Dietrich and I sat around in my dressing room, dishing. He'd just played the Desert Inn, his first trip to Las Vegas. "What a fabulous, extraordinary madhouse. The gangsters who run the place are all urbane and charming." Sinatra had brought in his cronies—Bogart, Bacall, Garland—on a chartered plane, and *Life* magazine had photographed Coward in a dinner jacket, 118 degrees in the parched desert. *Mad dogs and Englishmen go out in the midday sun.* He'd been paid an extraordinary amount for the engagement, even by Vegas standards— $160,000 in salary and British tax offsets—although he wasn't playing to his usual café society crowd, but to what he called "Nescafé society."

If I'd taken Noel's advice and cut the patter out of my act, I could have saved myself a substantial embarrassment at the Palladium another night. But when I was held up by a traffic jam, I felt I owed the audience an explanation. "I'm so sorry," I said. "I got blocked in traffic." The audience practically fell on the floor, laughing. "Oh, Miss Clooney," the stage manager said, suppressing a giggle. "Over here, 'blocked' means the same as 'screwed.'"

Again I was living on a river, the possibilities still limitless. Our house in Harefield, Black Jack's Mill, was a rambling spread of weathered stone, with interesting angles and secret corners, five bedrooms, and—remarkably—central heating. River traffic on the Colne passed by outside our leaded windows. On our back lawn, graceful footbridges spanned a meandering brook that ran into a lake where we swam and fished or just lay in hammocks, looking up at the clear sky.

Joe was in his element, playing the country squire, ascot and cap and walking stick. He rode every chance he got, taking lessons at a stable outside Maidenhead. He insisted I be fitted for the riding habit, boots, hard hat, jodhpurs. But I was happiest on the riverbank, playing with Miguel, watching him discover leaves and grass and earthworms. When Dietrich came to visit, I watched with fascination as she baited her fishing hook. "Now this isn't going to hurt," she explained to the wriggling worm. "Just think how nice it's going to be when a big fish sees you and ends up on the table. Won't that be marvelous?"

On my opening night at the Palladium, a great bouquet of roses had arrived backstage: HAVE A GREAT SUCCESS, LARRY AND VIVIEN. So the Oliviers came to spend a few days with us, by our old mill stream. And I was delighted to see Janet Leigh and her mother. Janet was shooting part of a film in England, before going to Kenya to finish it. She thought our house was right out of a storybook. "Too much," she cried as they climbed out of the car. "Just too much!"

Late in the summer, when everything was at its fullest and greenest and ripest, just before the slow turn into autumn, I had a phone call. Joe was reading to Miguel, who was asleep in his crib.

"That was Mama," I told Joe. She'd tracked me down again. I suddenly felt very tired. "Betty's marrying Pupi, and she told Mama she couldn't live with her anymore. Mama doesn't have anyplace to go."

"He doesn't deserve your sister," Joe said.

"In the Lady Chapel at St. Patrick's Cathedral, can you beat that? Mama didn't sound happy about it." *Goddamn, I wish I could stop her. But he kissed off his wife for her and now she thinks she has an obligation.*

If there was one area in which Joe was unfailingly gracious, it was with family; the lord of the manor could act no other way. Of course Mama would come to live with us.

Clearly it wasn't true that she had no place to go. She was still in her forties, hardly a charity case. Her own mother was living in Maysville. But my mother had always wanted to break out, to be somebody. She hadn't managed that on her own; now, through her famous daughter, she had a chance.

If anyone were to object to her coming to us, it should have been me. She hadn't been there for me when I was a child; why should I be there for her now? Maybe for that very reason: Because she hadn't been there for me, I was needy enough to want her back. There was a chance she might like me.

On our way home from England, we spent a little time in New York before going back to the West Coast for Christmas. The first snow was falling the night we gave a small party, and we lit a fire in the black marble fireplace. Marlon was playing his drums—he walked around with his bongo drums all the time, ready to play them at the drop of a hat. John Huston came in with Marilyn Monroe, whom I'd met once before; she hadn't said much to me, and I figured she was just cool to ladies. But tonight she came up to me and said, "Where's the baby?"

"Upstairs," I said.

She went straight upstairs, with snow on her fur coat and in her hair, and picked Miguel up right out of his crib. The nurse just watched while she held him, walked with him, laid down on the bed, and played with him.

After about an hour, John Huston finally asked, "What the hell is she doing up there?"

"She's playing with the baby," I said.

Joe was dancing with Betty Bacall. When they dipped, she tossed her head back and laughed. I felt a jolt of envy—not because she was dancing with my husband, but because of her gaiety. I was cloaked, that Christmas Eve, in a sadness I couldn't shake because I couldn't find its source.

The Bogarts' traditional Christmas Eve party at their house on Mapleton Drive was a whirl of music and laughter. Every famous face I'd ever seen at the Russell Theater seemed to be there. I was wearing an exquisite new dress of aqua chiffon that Edith Head had copied for me from a film. But I was miserable. I walked over to one side of the room and stood apart, looking out the window.

What in God's name did I have to be unhappy about? I was having one success after another. My life was a series of bravos. I'd been named in a nationwide poll of DJs, along with Sinatra, as Best Vocalist, with "Hey There" the most requested record. In a survey of movie exhibitors, I'd come in second as Best Female Musical Performer, just behind Judy Garland. I had a famous husband, a bouncing baby boy, a future as dazzling as the Christmas lights reflected in the picture window.

There was a face in the window, too, coming toward me. I kept looking out as Spencer Tracy came and stood beside me.

We'd met, but I didn't know him well; I still knew him mostly from the movies. I'd always admired his thoughtful way of looking down as he walked slowly across wherever he was walking—a hallway, a courtroom, a street. Then he'd stop and look up, and when he spoke, it seemed as though he'd been pondering something wise to say. Now that I knew something about Hollywood, I knew that his slow, thoughtful walk was his way of finding his mark, to be sure he stopped when he was supposed to.

"What's the matter?" he asked.

"I don't know," I said. Then I thought that sounded silly. "I've never been to a party on Christmas Eve," I said. "I guess I'm just homesick." That sounded even sillier. I lived just blocks away.

He kept looking out the window. His voice was strong, but not unkind. "Get used to it," he said.

It would be a long time—nearly twenty years—before I knew that the reason for my sadness that Christmas Eve was both very subtle and very simple. I was trying to keep out of reach of the girl I'd left behind.

EIGHT

*B*illie Holiday held out her glass. I filled it from the pitcher of gin and orange juice—mostly gin—then filled my own.

Until that afternoon in my den, we'd met only in passing, and I never thought she liked me very much. Then Joe and I went with Dinah Shore and her husband, George Montgomery, to hear Billie at a little club on Hollywood Boulevard. She'd stopped by our table, and now the two of us were sitting together, drinking in a blue haze of smoke in our own little den of iniquity.

"To girl singers," she said. "Especially us Irish singers."

I looked surprised; she laughed. "Yes, Irish. One-eighth, anyway. My great-grandmother was a slave in Virginia and my great-grandfather was the master, Charles Fagan."

It was only the first of the surprising things I had in common with this strange, elegant, troubled woman. When Billie was born, her mother was only thirteen years old. Her fifteen-year-old father wasn't around any more than mine was. Like me, she was shuffled among relatives when her parents couldn't care for her; like me, she was raised mostly by her grandmother. Her mother promised to send for her when she was able; unlike my mother, she actually did. When Billie's grandmother put her on a train to New York, she handed her her suitcase and a basket of fried chicken for the trip.

I knew she had been jailed for prostitution, had wrestled with a heroin addiction in the midst of her success—"I had the white gowns, the white gardenias, and the white junk"—and I knew her life had none of the security I enjoyed in mine: When she performed at the club, I'd heard the pain in her voice, a raw sound just beneath the smooth surface of the melodic line, sometimes showing through before she shaped it into laughter. She was thirteen years older than I. But for a few hours, while we sat and talked—about men, music, life—looking at her through the curling smoky air was like looking at an opaque reflection of myself.

Like me, she started singing professionally not as much out of love as out of need, as I'd sung at WLW. In the direst of straits—facing eviction from her Harlem railroad flat—she pounded the pavement, club to club, looking for a job, any job. At Pod's and Jerry's on 133rd Street, she tried out as a dancer. "I was terrible." Then someone chanced to ask if she could sing, and the place went quiet as everyone listened.

"The first time I played the Apollo, I went to the bathroom eighteen times before I went on," she told me. "I had to go again, but someone shoved me out onstage. My knees were shaking so badly that one broad in the front row called out, 'She's dancing and singing at the same time!'"

I told her how I'd listened to her records as a teenager—Aunt Ann's "Strange Fruit" and the well-worn "Gloomy Sunday"—and I told her about Aunt Ann. "I knew that song was about suicide, even then," I said. "I don't know how I knew."

"You just felt it," she said. "Young kids always ask me what my style is derived from and how it evolved and all that. But if you find a tune and it's got something to do with you, you don't have to evolve anything. You just feel it, and when you sing it, other people can feel something, too."

Billie poured herself another glassful. "I heard my first jazz records on a Victrola in a whorehouse parlor," she said. "Louis Armstrong and Bessie Smith. 'West End Blues' used to gas me. It was the first time I ever heard anybody sing without using any words. I didn't know he was singing whatever came into his head when he forgot the lyrics. *Ba-ba-ba-ba-ba-ba-ba* and the rest of it had plenty of meaning for me. But the meaning used to change, depending on how I felt."

"I know what you mean," I said. "The same thing happens when I sing."

"I joined Count Basie's band to make a little money and see the world," she reminisced. "For almost two years, I didn't see anything but the inside of a Blue Goose bus. At the Fox Theater in Detroit, the management didn't like black men on stage with white women, so they gave the chorus girls black masks and mammy dresses. Then they put greasepaint on me to make me darker, because somebody might think I was white if the light didn't hit me just right. But the next time I went West, it was with sixteen white cats, Artie Shaw, and a Rolls-Royce." She looked at me thoughtfully. "You're from Kentucky, aren't you?"

"Yes," I said. "Maysville, right on the river."

"I had some experiences in that state. One place we played, the sheriff tugged on Artie's pants cuff while he was conducting, pointed at me and said, 'Hey you, what's Blackie going to sing?'" She laughed. "Then they couldn't find a hotel to rent me a room. So Artie put eight of the boys around me and marched me into the lobby of the biggest hotel in town, like the *Queen Mary* surrounded by tugboats. The clerk couldn't imagine that a black woman would walk in like that with white men. He thought I was Spanish or something," Billie said, "so I got a nice room."

"Tony Pastor used to talk about you a lot," I told her.

"Did he tell you this story?" she asked. "One time we were eating at a dirty little hole-in-the-wall, and this blonde bitch waitress ignored me like I wasn't even there. Tony got real sore. 'This is Lady Day,' he hollered. 'Now you feed her.'" She smiled. "If you've got one of those Italian boys like Tony in your corner, they'll go to hell for you and die for you."

Billie's early days were played out in Prohibition joints: Basement Brownies, the Yea Man, the Next, the Clam House, the Morocco, the Spider Web. At the Log Cabin, Benny Goodman came in with Mildred Bailey, "the Rocking Chair Lady." Then he asked her to make a record with him, her first. "I was scared of the big old microphone," she said. "Someone finally told me I didn't have to sing into it or even look at it, I just had to stand near it."

He and Billie used to meet at late-night jam sessions, after the bands had finished their sets. I got the feeling there had been a kind of romance, though she didn't say so to me. "My mother didn't want me running around with white boys, and his sister didn't want him being seen with a black chick" was all she said. "But we used to outwit them. He was a nice cat, never a drag."

"I just met him last fall," I said. "We did three records together. We even sang a duet on 'It's Bad for Me.' "

"He can't sing," Billie said.

"No," I agreed. "But he really threw himself into it. He took it all very seriously. I was having trouble with the top note in 'Memories of You,' and do you know what he said to me? 'You're the big female star at Columbia, and you can't pick that note out of the air?' "

"Did he give you The Ray?"

I laughed. She meant the trademark Goodman glare. "I didn't get it, but my little boy did."

I told Billie how I'd met Benny Goodman in New York in November 1955, when we got together at my apartment for our first rehearsal on what happened to be the baby nurse's day off. Benny was the first one there; while we waited for the rest of the sextet, he put his clarinet together and I put Miguel in the playpen. "He'll just play quietly," I said to Benny. "He won't be any trouble." Then Benny did a run up and down. Miguel's face crumpled and he started to cry loudly. He'd never heard a sound like that before.

Benny stopped. "He doesn't like the way I play," he said. I laughed. But he didn't. He was serious.

"He hasn't had much experience listening," I explained. "He doesn't realize you're the best." I knew Benny was a perfectionist, but I couldn't believe he really thought my nine-month-old baby was making a comment on his technique.

"Benny was a very intense fellow," Billie agreed. "He talked a lot about having his own band one day." She looked thoughtfully out at the olive tree. I emptied the pitcher into our glasses.

"Know what my dream is?" she said quietly. "To have a big place of my own out in the country someplace, where I could take care of stray dogs and orphan kids. We'd have a big kitchen with a chartreuse stove, and I'd supervise all the cooking and baking. And I'd always be around to teach them my kind of teaching." She gave me a long, level look. "Not the kind that tells them how to spell Mississippi, but how to be glad to be who you are and what you are."

"That's a hard thing to learn," I said.

Billie reached out and put her hand on my belly. "I want to be this one's godmother," she said with a smile that started out warm, then turned savvy and sly. "It takes a *baaaad* woman to be a good godmother."

I was as pleased by my pregnancy as other people seemed surprised. I'd always said I could mix marriage and a family with a busy career, and now I was proving it. Miguel was just nine months old when I became pregnant again. "I plan to have six children," I told a reporter. "A nice in-between number. Three more than my mother, three less than my grandmother." On Mother's Day, 1956, Joe presented me with a beautiful oil painting. Noel Coward had a Vlaminck, Bing Crosby had two, and I'd always admired them. Now I had my own Vlaminck, bigger than Bing's: a winding street in a little French town, houses, a church, a man in the lower left corner, his back turned, peeing. In the background, the sky was darkening, but in the foreground the sky was lighter. When we hung the painting over the fireplace in the living room, I kissed Joe and vowed never to part with it.

Janet Leigh was expecting a baby, too. Lew and Edie Wasserman gave us the most glamorous baby shower imaginable. Not the typical girls-only affair, but a party, with music and dancing, a celebrity coed crowd, and party food, centered around an enormous ice sculpture stork. Since the typical '50s mother-to-be didn't snack on caviar at splashy parties, in the *Silver Screen* photo layout that Janet and I posed for, I was showing her how to fold diapers.

I'd signed the contract for a television series before my pregnancy was announced, so there was no backing out, even as my condition became a visual challenge. Lucille Ball had gotten away with her on-screen pregnancy because everybody really did love Lucy, the laughing clown, one-of-a-kind. I was just a singer getting bulgier by the week, so I was filmed sitting, with a pair of Scotties in my lap, or standing behind a stove or a soda fountain or a wheelbarrow filled with flowers—the flowers growing taller, the wheelbarrow more brimming, as the months went by.

"The Rosemary Clooney Show" was syndicated by MCA, thirty-nine filmed half hours in black-and-white. The show opened with a profile of me in silhouette, under my theme song, "Tenderly." I made sure Joe was a guest on my first show; we did a duet on "Love and Marriage." Gail and I sat on the porch of the Maysville Arms, wearing sunbonnets, singing "The Lord Is Counting on You." I felt very lucky when the Hi-Lo's, the most talented quartet of our time—to my way of thinking, of any time—joined our musical cast, which was led by conductor-arranger Nelson Riddle.

I'd asked for Les Brown to be our music director, but MCA had Nelson under contract, and he had a sterling reputation. He'd worked with Nat Cole and had saved Sinatra from musical limbo, beginning with Frank's comeback hit, "Young at Heart." With Frank, he'd pioneered the art of the "concept" album when new recording technology made LPs an alternative to singles. He was wry and funny in a self-deprecating, sardonic way. And he was amazingly shy, hated being on-camera. He'd had a hit record, "Lisbon Antigua," so I lured him in front of the camera to talk about it. And he couldn't. He just couldn't talk about it. I teased him, winking at the audience. "Isn't he just the cutest thing you ever saw?" He ducked his head in an abashed little-boy way—but he *was* cute, with dark curly hair, dark eyes, a slow smile. He could do remarkable things with music. I remember a skit with Buster Keaton alone in his apartment when the phone started ringing. He couldn't find it. The skit ran about five minutes—no talking, only music—and it was brilliant.

Our comedy skits were touchingly innocent. "The Baker's Wife Needs Dough"; Tony Curtis with his magic tricks—a dancing handkerchief, a vanishing cigarette. Still, throughout my radio and television career, the censors found things to blue-pencil. When I sang Frank Loesser's "Pet Me Poppa," the lyrics had to be scoured, from *If you want me home by the fire, especially when it's time to retire* to *If you want me home by the fire, please don't phone, please don't wire.* All TV variety shows went through this: In a Carol Burnett sketch, when a reporter asked how folks in a nudist colony danced, the punch line couldn't be "Very carefully." The Smothers Brothers weren't allowed to say, "Ronald Reagan is a known heterosexual."

But it was the music, under Nelson's command, that distinguished my show. Hearing a smooth, superbly put-together orchestra play, it's easy to forget that it didn't get that way by itself—that someone has given a great deal of thought to what parts each instrument should play, and when, and how, and most importantly, why. I've heard a wonderful arrangement of "Get Happy" with each line in a different key—*Hallelujah, come on, get happy,* going up and up, higher and happier. A good arranger reads the words and knows exactly what the song should convey; he knows which words the orchestration should support, what mood it should create. And a very good arranger knows the style and the strengths of the singer he's writing for, so he can write to complement the singer's particular sense of rhythm and phrasing.

I work differently with different arrangers. Peter Matz and I sit at the piano, find a key I'm comfortable with, figure out what the top should be, how low we should go, what tempo works best. We map out the song—how many choruses we'll do, verse or no verse, any extra bars—and we run through it two or three times, until he begins to understand how I feel about the song. Then he knows how to approach the scoring. Stan Freeman, from my "Come On" days, likes to work on arrangements all by himself at the piano in a quiet environment; Peter likes to have people singing and dancing around him when he's working, or—best of all—a baseball game on the radio. Bob Thompson has no illusions about the chaos arrangers have to turn into order. "You sit down and make parts for every player who's sitting there, and hopefully out of that mess will come something pleasing."

Bob sees arranging as a dying art, because so much music is made electronically these days, created on synthesizers by people he calls musical illiterates who can't tell one note from another on paper. But in Nelson's day, the art was the essence of good music, and Nelson was truly an artist. He didn't overpower a lyric or a melody; he used the different colors of the instruments in the orchestra expertly, but subtly and sparingly, to wonderful effect. He was considered a very sparse writer, because he was careful never to cover the singer up with too many horns or too many of anything. His chief concern was always to complement and support the singer. He knew my limitations, and he knew how to cushion me in places where I might have difficulty. If I had a high C—my top note—that I had to hold for a long time, he would build a phrase underneath me, so I could just float on top. With a bad arranger, I'm just an average singer. But with a very good arranger, I can be a very good singer.

Nelson had rigorous standards for himself and for everyone he worked with. "I can tell by the way a man unpacks his horn what kind of musician he is," he said. I welcomed the challenge; I was pleased to do work that required me to stretch a little. When I had the chance to do an album with Duke Ellington, I was thrilled, because Duke was one of the most respected jazzmen around, with a cool, sophisticated sound and a stellar history. In the early '30s, he'd become famous broadcasting from the Cotton Club in Harlem; it was the one place where downtown society ventured uptown. Some people said Duke had compromised his art to make it in the white establishment, but I didn't believe it—his music was intelligent, rich in harmony, pure enough yet complex enough to define an era: "It Don't Mean a Thing If It Ain't Got That Swing."

Like Mitch Miller, Duke had a talent for making records, though he put it to a very different use. In the late '20s and early '30s, he experimented with platter speeds and widths—twelve-inch versus ten-inch, 33 1/3 versus 78 rpm—and made the bass more prominent than it had ever been on a record, "probably by shoving it closer to the microphone," one critic pointed out. When he and I got together to do an album, his inventiveness was called on again—for the simple reason that we didn't get *together* at all.

Duke was in New York, playing Café Society, and I was pregnant in Beverly Hills. So Billy Strayhorn, a terrific young arranger and composer with Duke's outfit, came out to California and worked with me to prepare the songs for the album. Billy was a delight to be around, gentle and sweet—and brilliant. He'd written "Take the 'A' Train," Ellington's theme and a universal classic. Listening to the haunting "Lush Life," which he'd written in his teens, I wondered at his talent—and wondered what he'd been through, at such an age, to write a song like that and make it ring true.

We became friends. He had a key to my back door; he'd come in and bring me soda crackers from the kitchen when I was having morning sickness. Once he brought an apple pie and carried it straight up to my room. We sat on the bed and dug right in, ate the whole thing while we looked over the music, picking songs and laughing. Eventually we went downstairs to the piano for more focused work on the tunes: standards like "I Let a Song Go Out of My Heart" and "Mood Indigo"; striking new arrangements of "I Got It Bad" and "Sophisticated Lady"; and a new number Billy wrote especially for me, an instrumental he called "Blue Rose." I had no lyrics to sing, just vocalized along with the melody. "I want you to imagine you're living in New York and you've got a really hot date and you're getting ready to go out," Billy said, looking at me through his big square glasses. "You're a beautiful woman, looking into the mirror and combing your hair, and there's no Duke Ellington and there's no band. The radio is playing the record, and you just sing along with the orchestra, and we overhear it."

Then we did something that would have been impossible just a few years earlier. Billy went back to New York with the songs we'd chosen, and Duke and his orchestra recorded the instrumental tracks at Columbia's East 30th Street studio. When Billy brought the masters back to California, I did the vocals at Radio Recorders on Santa Monica, listening to the orchestra on headphones. We never laid eyes on each other the whole time. But I felt like I was right in the middle of that band. I was too caught up in the excitement and challenge of the project to notice a new singer who appeared on Tommy Dorsey's television show on January 28, 1956, the day after Duke finished the *Blue Rose* instrumentals: a former truck driver named Elvis Presley.

When a singer pays for an arrangement, it belongs to that singer exclusively. Nelson did a fabulous, exciting arrangement for me of "Come Rain or Come Shine." He had me sing rather slowly, against a double-time background with a kind of bongo rhythm. Then, on an album, Judy Garland did the song using that arrangement. My arrangement! I gave Nelson hell about it, and he admitted that he'd been pressed for time.

When Judy played the Palace in New York, Joe and I went to see her then went backstage. She was sitting at her dressing table, taking off her makeup. She stared at me in the mirror as I stood in the doorway: "Just what the hell do you and Mitch Miller think you're doing, lifting my record?"

I walked to the telephone by her dressing table. "I didn't steal your arrangement, Judy," I told her. "That was *my* arrangement Nelson gave to you. And I'm going to get him on the phone and settle it right now." As I picked up the phone, she sighed, smiled into the mirror. "Don't bother," she said. Then she stood up and hugged me. "Darling, how *are* you?"

I couldn't help hugging back. Judy had a gift for involving you with her. At a party at the Gershwin's once, she was talking about the time her baby Joey was born. He was very small, and she wasn't able to hold him at first. She had to stand outside the nursery, looking at him through the window, telling him, "Come on, baby—come on, Joey, you've got to make it—you've got to live, Joey—you've got to live for me! I need you, baby . . ." I found myself weeping uncontrollably as she told that story; she could capture you so, could get so far inside your heart. She could do it on a stage, and she could do it in somebody's living room. It seemed to me that she was very much like Billie Holiday in that way. I never forgot that afternoon in my den, even though I never saw Billie again—she died three years later, only forty-four years old. But when my daughter, Maria Providencia, was baptized in the summer of 1956, I made sure that Billie was officially recorded as her godmother.

Billie said it wasn't work to do a song she could feel—the only kind of song she would do—and I felt "Blue Rose" and all the songs on that album in a way I could never feel "Come On-a My House." When I recorded "Come On," I wasn't in a position to choose my material, and if I had been, I might not have had the confidence to do it. Now I did.

I was growing more and more impatient with the novelty music that was woven into Mitch Miller's career plan for me. I couldn't deny that the plan had worked, as far as it went; Benny Goodman wouldn't have been playing scales in my living room if I'd never done "Come On." But Mitch had never stopped trying to replicate the formula of that particular success, and while some of the novelties that resulted were respectable hits, some—like "Cheegah Choonem (I Haven't Got It)"—flopped. Mitch's commercial instinct was on the money most of the time, but it was fallible. Now it seemed limiting as well, and I didn't want limits; I wanted horizons.

A review of "Cheegah Choonem" called my performance "Rosie in her less intimate, less convincing style," but that wasn't the Rosie I wanted to be; I wanted, like Billie, to make a listener feel something in my songs. I wanted to sing my best, to use my instrument, my talent, in the best possible way. And now I wondered whether Mitch was the one to show me that way. The last recording session he led for me, in the summer of 1956, included a perfect illustration: "Sailor Boys Have Talk to Me in English" was a quintessential gimmick in pidgin English, with all the novelty content of "Come On-a My House" but none of the fun. I'd record on the Columbia label for a couple more years, but Mitch would never again conduct while I recorded; he wouldn't pick my songs, either, or manage the business end.

We'd begun to grow distant from each other almost as soon as I married Joe; I regretted that distance, because Mitch had been a mentor when I needed one. But he had let me know he resented my marriage; he had let me know he thought Joe was all wrong for me. Then he let everyone know it, in *The Saturday Evening Post.*

Joe came into the den with the magazine in his hand. "What is this guy up to? What makes him think he can go around talking like this?"

I put down my glass of wine. "It's nothing to get upset about," I told him.

Joe brandished the magazine, quoting. " 'Then she married this José Ferrer, and suddenly she's with the books. She's got culture and she's got him. If she loses him, she's gonna ask, "What did I do wrong? I read the books, didn't I?" ' "

I just looked at him.

"I don't want you working with him anymore," Joe went on. "You should be doing better things."

I had been thinking the same thing, but hearing it from Joe had a curious effect: I suddenly resented him instead of Mitch. "I don't need you to tell me what I should be doing," I informed him.

"I think you do," he said. "You're wasting your time and your talent with this joker. If you were smart, you'd see that for yourself."

"So I'm wasting my time now?"

"He has you running around, coast to coast, always something," Joe said. "It doesn't matter what you have going on at home, does the baby need you, do I need you—all he has to do is say the word."

"That's not fair," I said, because it wasn't; Joe did as much running as I did. Just a couple of months before, he'd taken off on a lengthy tour to promote *The Shrike*. "I dropped everything so Miguel and I could come along on your trip," I reminded him.

He actually sneered at me. "You went on every DJ show at every radio station we came near. You didn't go on that trip for me; you went for you."

I was trying to keep my temper; that was what I always did. Cora, our laundress, who emptied the pockets of Joe's trousers before she sent them to the dry cleaner, had been finding slips of paper with phone numbers and girls' names. When she handed them to me without comment, I felt a weakness spreading through my chest, then over my entire body—a hot feeling, like an instant high fever. I'd been putting the slips of paper under the liner in my bureau drawer.

But Joe kept pushing. "You think Miller's such a prince, always has your best interests at heart, but he doesn't. He never did."

"Yes, he did," I burst out. "He warned me I shouldn't trust *you!*"

Joe stood still and looked at me. "What does *that* mean?"

When Joe got angry, it could be frightening. I wished I'd kept my mouth shut. But drinking made it harder not to let my anger show.

"What does that mean?" he asked again, dangerously quiet.

"He knew Uta Hagen," I began. Probably the best way out was to tell him part of the truth. "He told me you had troubles with her." That was the vaguest understatement I could hope to get by with.

Mitch hadn't been vague at all. He'd told me about the Christmas Eve Uta spent with Paul Robeson while she was still married to Joe. They were sitting in the living room—a totally uncompromising position—when she heard a noise in the foyer and found Joe standing there, a photographer and a lawyer at hand. Paul just looked at him. *"Oh, Joe, no"* was all he could say. When Joe and Uta divorced, he got all the property, the apartment on 57th Street, the house in Ossining. She was left with nothing.

Joe looked at me strangely. "What do you mean, 'troubles'?"

"Oh, Joe," I said, just like Paul. "I don't want to talk about it."

"Damn it, we're going to talk about it!"

"Don't shout at me," I said.

"Tell me what he told you!"

"He told me you blackmailed Uta." I backed away as Joe started toward me. "He said I should have property in my own name so you couldn't take it away from me. He said—"

"Son of a bitch!" Joe picked up my glass and flung it against the wall. The wine ran in red rivulets down to the baseboard. "Beautiful," I muttered as he stormed out.

Mama looked around the marble entrance hall. "Beautiful," she pronounced. "Perfectly beautiful." When the butler carried her bags up the circular staircase, she followed him with her head held high. As a convenience—perhaps as an escape hatch—I'd rented a small apartment for her in Beverly Hills, five minutes from our house. As it turned out, she rarely used the place. She settled into the big room upstairs that Joe had planned for his art studio, before the house began filling up.

I was ambivalent about my mother coming. I'd been a footnote to her life for twenty-seven years, and I resented that. Yet I welcomed the chance to establish the bond we'd never had, and I wanted my children to know her and be secured by her presence, as I had been with Grandma Guilfoyle. I felt comfortable leaving her in charge when I was on the road—I was away as much as I was at home. I could hire a lot of people, but I couldn't hold them finally responsible for my children's welfare. When my mother was there, I trusted she would keep close watch, though the irony wasn't lost on me: She took far better care of my children than she ever had of her own.

I felt a family link was missing without Betty and Nicky. Our special closeness was being fragmented, partly by necessity: Nicky was in the Army, I was on the road a lot. But partly by carelessness: Betty hadn't let

Nicky know she was getting married; she wrote him a note after the fact. I'd been too busy to write. So when Nicky finished his Army stint in 1956, I pleaded with him to come to California. He'd turned me down the first time I asked, after high school, when Joe and I wanted him to come live with us so we could send him to college; this time he agreed. He was twenty-two years old, insisting that I drop the childish *y* from his name. So it was Nick who came to California to try for the acting career he didn't particularly want, but I wanted for him.

He'd already had an accidental screen test. When I was making *White Christmas,* he was visiting the set, strolling along one of the Paramount streets when Cecil B. himself spotted Nick from the backseat of his limo. The very next day, my kid brother was doing a scene from *Golden Boy.* Nick never met De Mille, who watched with his minions from behind a dark window, the way witnesses pick out suspects in a police lineup. But he recognized De Mille's voice from having heard it on the radio: "Mr. Clooney, we like the way you look and we like the way you sound. However, we do not like the two together. You look like a twenty-year-old boy. But you sound like a forty-year-old man."

Nick had always had a resonant voice, a splendid broadcasting voice. As a high school senior, he worked part-time at radio station WFTM ("World's Finest Tobacco Market") in Maysville. For fifty cents an hour, he worked the Sunday morning shift, signing on at seven o'clock. On those Sunday mornings, following rambunctious small town Saturday nights, fundamentalist preachers bought airtime, a dollar a minute. With Nick in the control booth their only visible audience, they tended to focus their fire and brimstone on him. Nick was just seventeen. "I spent many a Sunday morning repenting for sins I hadn't gotten around to yet," he said.

Nick arrived just before Christmas, which turned into a family reunion. My cousin Phyllis and her husband were living in Westwood, twenty minutes away. Aunt Rose had never forgiven nor forgotten the intolerance of her Catholic Church toward her marriage to Isadore Middleman, so when Phyllis married Sherman Holvey, a Jewish doctor, Aunt Rose was delighted. Aunt Jeanne and Uncle Roy had moved to San Bernardino, so we were able to see them often, too.

On Christmas Eve, we were standing around the gorgeous Douglas fir, fifteen feet tall, that we'd put up in our entrance hall, when we heard caroling on the front lawn. Bing and his boys were making the rounds. Janet and Tony came by with their daughter Kelly, born just six weeks before Maria. The *Los Angeles Times* reported that I would be appearing with Tony in his new movie, *Sweet Smell of Success*. But shortly after Christmas I was pregnant again.

The tempo of my life was speeding up. Joe signed for the lead in *I Accuse!*, the story of Alfred Dreyfus's treason trial with a script by Gore Vidal; they couldn't film in France, because France refused to let the film company shoot a story about Dreyfus, so Joe and I made another trip to England. We left Maria at home with my mother, but Miguel and his nurse came along. We took him to the set on the day they shot the degredation scene. Joe, as Dreyfus, had the buttons torn from his jacket, epaulets ripped off, his sword broken; two-year-old Miguel knew only that something bad was happening to his father, and he was upset for days.

Again I loved England; Joe took an elegant, moody picture of me in the spring, standing in a field in Maidenhead, wearing a long-sleeved maternity smock, casting a sidelong look at an uninterested swan. My baby wasn't due until October, but even my pregnancy was hurried; Gabriel Vicente arrived two months early, weighing just four pounds, and had to be kept at St. John's Hospital for a month. The hospital had only two Isolettes then; Joe was so grateful that his son's life had been saved that he donated another Isolette.

Dietrich came to the hospital to see me and the baby, carrying a big jar of caviar. She buttonholed the nurse in my room. "Where do you keep your penicillin?" Dietrich demanded. She smiled at me. "The temperature at which one keeps penicillin is the perfect temperature for caviar, darling."

She had just finished making *Witness for the Prosecution* and, as usual when she was in Hollywood, she came by the house often. When I had a cold or a touch of the flu, she'd sweep in and take over, like a vigilant *hausfrau*. "Take the day off," she'd say with a wave of her hand, dismissing the help. She'd put on an apron—she liked big white ones with wide bands and square pockets that she bought at the Lighthouse for the Blind.

She made mushroom broth for me, and beef tea; when I felt better, a bowl of buttermilk soup, with diced ham, chopped shrimp, bits of hard-cooked egg, all scented with dill. She loved housework—washing dishes, scouring bathroom tile. If the floor wasn't scrubbed to her satisfaction, she'd get down on hands and knees and scrub it again.

Joe admired Marlene, but he wasn't happy when she came by, because she paid absolutely no attention to him. She'd bring a tray up to my room, indicating to Joe that he was welcome to have a bowl of soup in the kitchen. She brought me trash to read. "You cannot concentrate when you're unwell, darling," she'd say. "The only thing one feels like reading when one is sick is something like this." And she'd hand me the latest issue of the scandal sheet of that time, *Confidential*. Joe was upset when that kind of reading material got scattered around our bedroom, and he may have been upset because he thought we were talking about him. We weren't. Even though Marlene had warned him, "Don't break her heart," I didn't tell her about the pieces of paper with phone numbers I'd hidden under the liner in my bureau drawer. I didn't tell her about the reports of his backstage activities in New York that were filtering back to me.

Even if I'd chosen to unburden myself to a friend, it wouldn't have been Dietrich. Her list of lovers was almost legendary by then, including one who was rarely talked about. Sinatra was half in the bag one night, and he whispered to me, "Isn't it interesting that nobody knows about me and Dietrich?" Their affair wasn't long, but it was very intense. At its height, she'd called me from Vegas. "Come up here so we can talk," she said. "I can't talk to all these people he surrounds himself with." I had to laugh. It seemed I was always being summoned to have talks with people in Vegas. Almost always when I was appearing there, I'd get a message: "Mr. Tracy is waiting in the lounge." So I'd join Spencer Tracy, and we'd talk—mostly about what it was like to be married to an actor, about the complexities of being Catholic.

Joe and I went up, along with Sammy Goldwyn, Jr., and his wife Jennifer. We were all sitting around a big table when Frank offered me a cigarette from a staggeringly beautiful case. "That's gorgeous," I told him. "Let me see." Dietrich made a motion to me: *Don't let on that you've seen it before.* It was gold, with a little Van Cleef sapphire and an inscription in French that I couldn't read and was too embarrassed to ask about. She'd given that same cigarette case to at least one other lover, I knew. I handed it back to Frank and laughed. I was reminded of Betty: Whenever she broke up with a guy, she'd give him a St. Christopher medal for safe travel through life. I once told Betty she should buy those medals by the gross—I wondered how many cigarette cases Dietrich had handed out.

"Frank's gonna blow it," Bing said to me. "He's gonna blow it, and you and I are gonna have to bail him out." Bing and I were rehearsing for a Ford television special, to air on October 13, 1957; Frank hadn't bothered to show up. There was a difficult chord change in a medley we were doing, and we knew that if he didn't rehearse with us, he wouldn't get it.

I loved doing that show. Sinatra smoked a cigarette while he sang "Birth of the Blues" with Louis Armstrong and his jazzmen. I wasn't pregnant that month, so I wore a sparkly dress with a wasp waist and a full, swirling skirt as I sang "Tenderly." Bing and I did a duet, a fast, jazzy version of "Don't Fence Me In." Dean Martin dropped in; he and Bing and Frank did a "Robin Hood" sketch. Bing and Kathryn Crosby sang "Dream," as Betty and I had sung for our WLW audition. Bob Hope sang the song from "Road to Morocco" with Bing: *Like Webster's dictionary, we're Morocco-bound!* Then Bing and Frank and I did our long medley—maybe fifteen minutes—with me standing in the middle. When Frank started in with "Blues in the Night" a cappella, it sounded fine for about a bar, until the band came in with a chord in a totally different key. Bing had been right—Frank blew it. But it didn't matter, because Frank shrugged and laughed at himself—"The note's *somewhere* in there"—and the audience loved it. Bing and I just looked at one another. The Voice could get away with anything.

It was a terrific show for me and, apparently, for the viewers: *Look* magazine gave it their Best Musical Show award. The sponsor didn't do so well, though. The show was built around the newest Ford offering, the 1958 Edsel. *A new vista of motoring pleasure, unlike any other car you've ever seen.* The only Edsel I ever saw was the one they gave me to drive while I was rehearsing. I came out of the CBS Building, up those little steps to the street where my purple Edsel was waiting, like the *Normandie* in drydock.

Mr. Ford was right behind me, heading for his Edsel. I opened the door of my car and the handle came off. I turned to him, holding it out to him. "About your car . . ."

Gabri was seven weeks old, home from the hospital and thriving, when Joe had to go back to London for some last-minute work on *I Accuse!* I went with him. I made a record while I was there: at the Phillips Studio on Stanhope Place, I cut four sides, including "A Foggy Day in London Town." But mostly I went just to be with Joe. I still thought I could do it all. I would continue to be the perfect wife: unquestioning, uncomplaining. I would sign for another television series. I would become pregnant again. I *would* do it all. But now I knew I would have to do it with an armored heart.

NINE

⁓

hiny Miss Friendly Face," a reviewer called me. "An outgoing, eager-to-please quality so thick you can slice it."

Pleasing people had always been my major virtue. Now, with my new television series, just one season after my first, I acquired a network to please and a sponsor, as well as an audience. And I kept trying to please Joe. He was working in a play, *Oh Captain,* in New York, so I arranged a frenzied schedule that meant I would be with him every weekend.

Rehearsals for my show ran Monday to Thursday. After the show was broadcast live on Thursday night, I'd go directly to the airport for the all-night flight, arriving in time for lunch with Joe on Friday. We then had one full day together before I flew back on Sunday in time to kiss my babies goodnight and be ready to show up at NBC, bright-eyed and bubbling, on Monday morning. At rehearsal breaks, I'd drive over to CBS to cut tapes for my radio show with Bing.

My new TV show was well received, but I was beginning to resent my success because it intruded so on my personal life. "We're glad you had your baby early, so it didn't interfere with the start of the show," a network man confided. I thought of Gabri, born prematurely, so fragile that he'd been listed in "guarded condition" lying in his Isolette, and stifled my anger at that casually insensitive remark. I made it a point to be with my children as much as I possibly could, even though it could cause delays and complications. Miguel was two and a half when I took him into the recording booth with me, holding my music in my left hand, reaching down to pat his head with my right hand as he tugged at my skirt.

Even in a town overflowing with celebrities, I was in demand. I wore long white gloves and a generous smile as I wielded the ceremonial shovel at the 1957 groundbreaking ceremony for the new Mount Sinai Hospital: "Where the sick shall be healed without regard as to race, creed or color, or their ability to pay." When Aunt Jeanne drove over from San Bernardino to visit with Mama and meet our new baby, she was amazed at my comings and goings. "What a hectic world you've been thrown into," she said. But I hadn't been thrown into this lifestyle; I'd stepped into it voluntarily. Nobody ever told me I had to do it all; I expected it of myself. I didn't know then that by trying to please everybody I was straining myself to a breaking point. I didn't know that I could decide for myself when it was time to cut back or just stop. I thought someone else had to decide that for me. That sounds ridiculous now, but at the time, I didn't think to question it.

"LIVE FROM HOLLYWOOD IN LIVING COLOR, IT'S 'THE LUX SHOW STARRING ROSEMARY CLOONEY!'" This new show was basically the same as my first variety show, with a little more polish and a lot more money, thanks to our national sponsor. "Good evening, ladies and gentlemen," I trilled. "Welcome to 'The Lux Show' on behalf of Lux Soap, Lux Liquid, and Rinso Blue." We were able to attract top-notch guests: Carol Channing, Charles Laughton, Nelson Eddy, Mel Tormé. Twelve-year-old Gail became a sunny fixture on the show, joining me in duets. Betty flew in from New York at Thanksgiving, so the four of us— Betty, Nick, Gail, and I—did a family sketch. Nick was supposed to put a leaf in the dining table; when someone set down a floral centerpiece, it crashed to the floor. No leaf. Nick looked chagrined. "Shoulda put more starch in the tablecloth." As in my first TV series, all our sketches were that innocent. The naughtiest line I can recall is when Nick became exasperated with Betty and me. "You women make about as much sense as hip pockets on a girdle!" We gave "Sisters" our own spin on a lyric: *always united . . . we never fighted.* The homemade line reminded me of Uncle George spicing up "The Sheik of Araby" for us, a long, long time ago.

Nick went back to Kentucky after that show. He'd landed a bit contract with Metro, meaning he could speak a certain number of lines on-camera, which an extra couldn't do. He'd appeared in four movies, though he was never sure of the titles, because they used shooting scripts and he was never around when the picture was finished. He'd loved talking with actors—Thomas Mitchell and Walter Abel, especially—but he'd had to do a dog food commercial to make money. I know he could have made it in movies—he was twenty-four, dark-eyed, honey-voiced, and handsome—but his heart was in broadcasting.

He was too young and inexperienced for L.A., a major market. When he was offered a newsman's job in Indio, California, a small town in the desert, he felt he could do just as well back home, so he spent the last of his savings on a one-way train ticket on the El Capitan. He got a job at WLAP radio in Lexington and, within the year, moved to television with the Coca-Cola Bottling Company's "Teen Bandstand." He tried to racially integrate the show, but the sponsor got nervous. When Coca-Cola dumped it, the station did, too. Nick revived it with the idea of focusing on schools, a different one each week. He had the schools send integrated groups to dance on the show; it worked so well that he became the production director and the weekend news anchor at the station.

As I neared the end of the TV season, I was noticeably pregnant. When the wheelbarrow was dragged out again, I tried to joke about it. On one of our last shows, in June of 1958, Joe and I did a "Nursery Rhyme

Love Song." "There was an old woman who lived in a shoe. She had so many children she didn't know what to do." I paused and looked at the audience, deadpan. "Welcome to the club."

My show was not renewed because I was expecting another baby, and my Paramount option wasn't picked up for the same reason—nobody was writing parts for pregnant ladies. But onstage, yards of fabric—taffeta, anything with bulk of its own—could camouflage a lot, so I didn't stop working. On the last day of shooting my TV show, Joe and I, with three babies and two nurses, took the train to San Francisco, where we changed to a train for Reno. I played Tahoe, then we drove to Vegas, where I played the Sands. I was determined that we all be together, so we went next to La Jolla, where Joe was trying out a new play, *Edwin Booth*. My mother and Gail joined us there, so we had to rent two apartments. We must have looked like a pack of overdressed Gypsies.

And I didn't stop recording. In July 1958, six months pregnant, I made my favorite album with Bing. *Fancy Meeting You Here* had a lighthearted travel theme, dreamed up by Sammy Cahn and Jimmy Van Heusen, that linked witty arrangements of "Hindustan," "Brazil," "Calcutta," and "Isle of Capri." Frank Loesser's "On a Slow Boat to China" gave Bing and me intertwined parts, melody and countermelody; the counterpoint yielded interesting juxtapositions of lyrics and unexpected harmonies. We cha-cha'd our way through "It Happened in Monterey" and blended our voices, so closely matched in timbre, on the smoky standard "I Can't Get Started," which Bob Hope and Eve Arden had sung in the Ziegfeld Follies of 1936.

It was always a joy to record with Bing, even though when he was unhappy about something, he could do outrageous things. He hated small talk, didn't like to be around strangers. Some visitors came into the recording booth that day, and Bing just turned his chair so he was facing the wall—just sat there, silent, stone-faced. I walked over to him. "What's the matter?" I whispered. "Do you want a break? Do you want a sandwich?" He kept staring at the wall. "I want those people out of the control room, and *then* I want a sandwich."

When Monsita Teresa was born that October, I'd had four children in three and a half years. "Vatican roulette," Bob Hope joked. But I wasn't having a baby a year because I opposed birth control. I'd always wanted a big family, and, against continuing evidence, I was still relying on my babies to keep my husband satisfied with hearth and home. Betty was doing the same thing. She'd married a man whose extracurricular activities were even more flagrant than Joe's, and she had three children in three years, though she took a brief intermission before the fourth. Nick married Nina Warren, Miss Lexington, whom he'd met while judging a beauty contest, in 1959. They had a baby girl, Ada Frances, in 1960, then George Timothy in 1961. Nick's theory is that even without thinking about it, we all assumed we should have kids close together; the best relationship we'd ever known, as kids, was the sibling relationship. That was the one that stuck.

I tried to please Joe by doing anything he wanted to do. Some Sundays we'd meet at the house of Betsy and Alfred Bloomingdale, with Nancy and Ronald Reagan and a few other couples, and drive into the country to go "hilltopping"—a chase with the scent of a fox, not a real fox, to get the hounds running. I hated it. Still, it kept me close to Joe, which seemed more and more urgent.

But I didn't have to pretend to be interested in Joe's work. He loved to talk about acting, and I loved to listen. I remember Warren Beatty coming to the house to read for Joe. He didn't get the part, but he walked out as cockily as he'd come in—very much like Charlton Heston, whom Joe called "Chuckles." When Joe worked with Kim Stanley in *The Chase,* she asked him very seriously, "Shall I relate to the window?" Joe had never had an acting lesson in his life, let alone studied the Method. So he raised an impatient eyebrow. "Miss Stanley, by 'relating to the window,' do you mean turn your back to it? Throw a stone through it? Or do you mean, jump out of it?"

But no matter how successful he became, he remained terribly insecure. If a week or ten days went by after he'd finished a project, he'd think his career was over. In this business, a lot of things are planned but don't come together; when that happened, he'd feel rejected. Most evenings when we were at home, he'd want his dinner served on a tray in the den, where he sat in his wide burgundy leather chair next to the phone so that he could answer it quickly.

He could be insecure in other contexts, too. We were in an elevator once when a man got in after me. He didn't say a word to me, but Joe got suspicious and smashed his briefcase against the elevator wall. "What the hell do you mean, flirting with my wife?" Joe yelled at the astonished man. "I didn't do anything," he said. When we got off the elevator, I tried to calm Joe down. "He didn't do anything." Maybe because Joe was so active with other women, he thought all other men were, too.

Joe's reputation as a Latin lady-killer had never been much of a secret. Sometimes when I'd answer the phone, there'd be a pause, then a hang-up. Sometimes she didn't even hang up. "This is Stephanie," a voice said sweetly one time. "May I please speak to Joe?" "No, Stephanie," I told her. "I think you should do this when I'm not here." I didn't slam the phone down, just hung up gently. I didn't confront her; I'd already realized I couldn't confront Joe. I just wanted her to know I knew.

I talked freely to very few people about my faltering marriage. My sister sympathized, because that was her generous nature, and empathized, because she knew the pain firsthand. But Nick was outraged. He admired Joe the professional, but Joe the husband he despised for his calculated betrayal of me. "There isn't anybody in the world who can't make a mistake in a relationship," Nick said, "but to endemically assume that you have the right to philander when you've made a commitment—that's bullshit. Did he ever say to you, 'I want to have an open marriage?' Did he ever say those words to you?" "Of course not," I told Nick. "Then he's a cheat and a liar!"

Kathryn Crosby took a more practical view. "You have to be realistic," she told me—gently but frankly. "You have to realize you married a Latin man."

It sounded just like Ricki Huston's stepmother telling her she couldn't expect John to change. I bristled. "He has to realize he married an Irish Catholic girl!"

I knew all too well that my marriage was in trouble, but generally women didn't talk to one another about those things then. My friend Janet Leigh had her second baby, Jamie Lee, just a month after my Monsita. Her husband was straying, too, divorce looming, when they gave an extravagant party—250 guests, a dance floor built over the pool—to celebrate their tenth wedding anniversary. "I was never so miserable in my life," Janet said. But she said it years later. In the fabricated '50s, our smiling faces were on magazine covers: *Time*, *Photoplay*, *TV Guide*. Didn't that prove we were happy? I was the girl next door; I couldn't let people down. My *TV Guide* piece saw to it that I didn't: "I have made it a firm rule to make the concessions, if any concessions have to be made, in order for us to be together. If Joe said, 'I'd rather you not work anymore,' I'd stop right now. He's *allowing* me to work."

It had occurred to me that I might fight fire with fire. But when I flirted with a young man at a party and knew at once that I could have all the action I wanted, I didn't want it. I didn't want another man. I wanted a solid marriage with a contented, faithful husband. For some time, Joe had wanted us to move to New York; when he asked me again, I didn't object.

Maybe Nick's phone call on New Year's Day, 1959, had something to do with it. Grandma Guilfoyle had died the night before from complications of diabetes. Nick was with her at the hospital, holding her hand. The obituary in the Maysville paper was written in its customary florid style: "Hers had been a full, busy, useful life that had known both the fullness of joy and the heartbreak of disaster." Heartbreak included my grandfather's early death, then Aunt Ann's; for the joy, there was devotion to her abundant family—twenty-two grandchildren, a dozen great-grandchildren. As a grandchild, I'd known that devotion first-hand—strawberry shortcake on the fireplace grate. I wouldn't call it a resolution, exactly, but I began the New Year remembering her commitment to keeping the family together. And I agreed to move to New York in the spring.

Not without some regrets. California was wonderful for the children. My household was running smoothly. Now, besides the baby nurse for Gabri and Monsita, we had a governess for Miguel and Maria, with my mother in residence to supervise. Her room became command central, with a crib, a playpen, three or four twin beds, books, and a phone. A back stairway ran down to the kitchen, so people could live in that big room almost unnoticed.

Still, some time in New York with Joe might help our marriage, without our mother's shadow over it. She didn't want to make the move, and I wasn't sorry. I'd tried to establish a good relationship with her. Knowing that she'd always wanted to "be somebody," I'd arranged for her to appear on a game show, "The Name's the Same." The celebrity panel was to guess who this woman was related to. Mama relished that half hour; she looked imposing, even imperious, wearing a fur stole and a haughty smile.

But she always refused to have a serious discussion with me. I longed to talk about the past, to figure out what had gone wrong, and why, and how we could overcome it now. I wanted to know why she hadn't been with us, why we'd been shunted around so, growing up in other people's houses. I'd been too young to discuss it with Grandma Guilfoyle when I lived with her.

I'd pretty much lost touch with my dad. He'd married again, to a woman only three years older than I. She called him "sir" or "Daddy." They had three children in three years, so just about the time I was starting my family, Daddy was starting his second and was as sadly unequipped to deal with it as he had been with us. He didn't drink much—for a while—but one day he went out to get a haircut and got a beer instead. He fell, one of his ribs pierced a lung, and he spent four months in intensive care.

I wanted specifically to know why my mother hadn't brought Betty and me to California as she'd promised. I think I'd have been satisfied with almost any explanation except the one she finally gave me, in an exasperated why-are-you-bringing-this-up-again tone. "I wanted to bring you out to California, but your father wouldn't let you girls go." I didn't believe that for a second; the last thing my father wanted was the responsibility for two teenaged girls. Clearly I couldn't trust my mother to tell me the truth, so I stopped asking, stopped trying to make her my friend. As time went on, we got an intercom system, so my mother could communicate with me without either of us needing to leave our rooms.

An advantage for me in moving to New York was that Joe would be paying the bills. I wasn't worried about money—there seemed to be an abundance—but why not let him support us for a change? I never kept track of my earnings, but I knew I was making a lot. I played Vegas and Reno every year, the Paramount or the Waldorf or the Americana in New York every year, and places in between. I liked living well; I liked knowing I could buy anything I wanted.

I bought myself a seven-and-a-half-carat yellow diamond ring. At the Americana, I cleaned the diamond and wrapped it in a Kleenex after I'd finished my makeup. When Bessie, my maid, tidied the dressing table, she scooped up all the tissues and flushed them down the toilet. "Aren't there traps in your drain someplace?" I demanded of the manager. "People drop things, you know." There were no traps. My diamond had gone directly from one of the top floors of the Americana Hotel to the Atlantic Ocean. Twenty minutes later, I went onstage, and that was the end of it. When I told that story to Kay Starr, she said, "Well, if you didn't care enough about it to watch it and take care of it, then you didn't deserve it." And she was right: I didn't care that much.

I should have cared a lot more. When I played the Kentucky State Fair in the summer of 1959, this was the newspaper headline:

FABIAN, NEW TO MUSIC, HELPS STIR INTEREST
IN FAIR'S CLOONEY SHOW

I'd never expected to need a teen sensation to attract people to my show. I sang the hits people expected to hear: "Come On-a My House," "Botcha Me," "This Ole House," and, for balance, "Tenderly" and "Hey There." The audience applauded warmly. But when sixteen-year-old Fabian took the mike, fans ran screaming down the aisles to the stage.

Fabian was cast, almost literally, in the teen idol mold: a critic called him "the star who was made, not born," a "musical Frankenstein" created by showbiz hustlers to pander to the tastes of teenage girls. Noted for his youth and his looks, he was a lightweight piece of photogenic flotsam. But he was carried along on a powerful turning tide, and I was caught in the undertow.

There had always been various currents flowing through American pop music: "race" music and "hillbilly" music—politely recast as "rhythm & blues" and "country and western"—as well as the conventional pop that I'd come of age with. But beneath the glassy, placid surface of the '50s, it all began to come together in a turbulent stream of beat, sound, and national mood. The timing was right as never before: A new generation of teenagers with a whole new kind of influence was coming along. When I was a kid, we listened to grown-up music and bought grown-up records, the only records there were. But unlike my generation or those before me, these kids had their own money to spend. That meant they had their own market, for the first time in popular music. And they weren't interested in standards or TV variety shows; they had their own taste, and promoters, producers, and DJs had to play to it or be washed right off the scene. Alan Freed, a Cleveland DJ, was one of the first to understand what was at stake. For his radio show aimed at the new youth market, he wanted a title without a racial inflection—R&B clearly meant black music—so he settled on "Rock 'n' Roll House Party" and gave the tide a name.

Some saw the new music as purely generational; some as a phenomenon of technology overtaking live artistry; some as a battle between BMI and ASCAP. In the fall of 1959, the House Special Subcommittee on Legislative Oversight held hearings on the connection between broadcasters and music publishers. Among the famous names they questioned was squeaky-clean Dick Clark, who had an interest in a record company and played some of its songs on his "American Band stand." He was cleared of wrongdoing, and the hearings eventually fizzled out, perhaps having been less important for their investigative power than for the attitudes they revealed. Testimony referred to "Elvis Presley and his animal posturings" and depicted the new breed of popular singers as "a set of untalented twitchers and twisters whose appeal is largely to the zootsuiter and the juvenile delinquent." The tide and the emotions ran high.

It's tempting to mark that time as the smooth end of an era. Tommy Dorsey died in late 1956, just months after he stood back and let Elvis Presley—the answer to the race issue, a white singer who sang like a black one—take the spotlight on his show. Tony Pastor gave up his big band in 1957. Manie Sachs died in 1958; Billie Holiday, godmother to my Maria and a generation of girl singers, in 1959. But it wasn't a linear progression, and it didn't happen overnight: While I was headlining at the Sands and the London Palladium, with "Hey There" topping the charts, Chuck Berry and Little Richard were already stirring things up with songs like "Johnny B. Goode" and "Tutti-Frutti," sounding a frenetic, oversexed call to arms. *Wop-bop-a-loo-bop-a-wop-bam-BOOM!*

Among singers of my ilk, there was a substantial backlash. Nat Cole got a standing ovation at the Copa for a number that said it all: "Mr. Cole Won't Rock and Roll." I didn't like the new music, either; it made me nervous. I had tremendous respect for good musicians, but I never came across more than a handful of rock 'n' roll singers who could really sing. My friend and conductor Bob Thompson didn't beat around the bush. "It's wiped out music as we know it," he told me. "I saw Elvis Presley in the studio—a tough-looking kid with a bunch of bandits!" When I listened, I could hardly understand the lyrics, and that made no sense to me. It did the music a disservice, too, because the words might just be worth hearing. "I never understood the Beatles' lyrics," a musician friend told me years later. "Not a word. Then I saw some of them written out, and I realized those guys were poets!"

I knew only one way to sing a song: The words had to mean something, and you had to be sure you knew what they meant before you started to sing. Then you had to hit the note and hit it true. As a singer, I couldn't have been less like Fabian if I had tried. The review of the Kentucky State Fair show called my performance "everything that rock 'n' roll is not."

That was meant as a compliment, but it also spelled a certain kind of doom—because the rock wave was cresting, about to break, and when it did, it would wash *my* kind of music right out of the mainstream. Within a decade, nobody would be able to get a contract to record the kind of music I understood and loved: not Frank, who'd take a six-year hiatus; not Bing, who'd sign with a British label because he couldn't find one stateside. Not long after I shared the stage with Fabian, an industry poll named me Female Vocalist of the Year in radio, but my Columbia contract had already come to an end, for different reasons. Goddard Lieberson, the Columbia president, had tried to salvage my relationship with Mitch Miller; he'd taken Miller to task for his indiscreet *Post* interview, and Miller had denied saying anything untoward. "You know how concerned

I am about the situation as it now exists between you and us, and how anxious I am to find a satisfactory solution," Lieberson wrote. "It does seem silly to go on this way wasting month after month." I agreed; once I'd broken with Columbia, no more time was wasted. But I didn't have a contract anymore, and a contract was the base of a career.

So I made some freelance records for MGM, RCA, and Coral. I also did commercial work. For Bank of America, holding a bankbook: "Here's where I record my favorite numbers." For the Remington Roll-a-Matic shaver: "Buy one and get a free record, 'Music to Shave By.'" For fiberglass panels, posing with Joe and Miguel. I had plenty of smaller projects to work on.

And a big one: my marriage.

Mama, my zipper got stuck!

Mama, Miggie pushed me!

Mama, I'm hot!

Mama—

"BE QUIET!"

Four faces turned up to me, blankly; the shock of my loud voice cleared away petty tensions. Monsita, who was just beginning to walk, dropped to the hall floor with a thump and started to cry. The others seemed about to join in.

"Joe!" I called. "Joe, I need you. Where's Nanny?"

There he was, coming out of the library. "Joe," I said loudly, "Monsita's crying. The children are crying."

With a funny look on his face that I couldn't interpret, he knelt on the terrazzo floor and wiped Monsita's little red face, got Miguel's snowsuit zipped, got Gabri's mittens clipped on, and tied the drawstring on Maria's tiny hood. He kissed each one on the forehead. He got them all in a line as the nanny came running. Then he went back into the library without a word to me. The apartment, with its echoing rooms that flowed into one another and opened in unexpected corners, was quiet, and I was alone.

I stood at the window, pressing my forehead against the cold glass. Down below, Central Park was draped elegantly in snow like a dowager in a cloak of ermine. In a minute, I would see the children come out of the building and cross Central Park West. There they were, the nanny carrying Monsita, with Gabri holding on to her free hand and Maria holding on to his. Miguel trailed behind them, pulling his sled across the pavement.

I lost them behind the trees for a minute, but then they came out into an open area where I could watch them: colorful patches on the snow. Miguel sat on his sled and skidded down a little incline. The others trooped behind the nanny, who walked without looking back. Then Gabri stopped and turned around. He was holding one leg up in a funny way, and even from this height I could tell that my little boy was crying. Sunk in the snow behind him was a dark spot—one of his boots.

He looked at the boot, then he looked at the nanny walking away. Why didn't she turn around? Gabri looked up, and I thought he could see me, even though I knew I was too far away. Then he put his bootless foot down in the snow and trudged on after the nanny.

We were living at the Dakota on West 72nd Street, a massive old building with turrets and gables and a wrought-iron balcony encircling the top story. I was six months pregnant; my fifth child was due in March.

When the Dakota was built, in 1884, it was an expensive, ornate outpost, named because it was as far from the fashionable downtown life of the city as the Dakotas were from the East Coast: a vigorously defended frontier. Later, it would become indelibly famous as the deathplace of John Lennon.

As splendid as the apartment was—ten rooms, seventeen-foot ceilings—there was something disquieting in the air. Something unsettling about the shadows that clung to the crown moldings, the way steps echoed and whispery sounds brooded in the corners, and me with my big pregnant belly, sunk in a soft chair. It was not a felicitous time. Miguel crashed his sled into a tree. Three-year-old Maria—dangerously allergic to chocolate—invented a system for swiping the Christmas candies set out on a hall table; she needed emergency treatment for hives on her skin and in her throat. When Joe's friend Ira Levin came by one evening to talk about a project, he thought the place seemed eerie, something strange about it. When his book came out, then the film—*This house has a high incidence of unpleasant happenings*—we all recognized *Rosemary's Baby*.

So I could have blamed the apartment itself when, surrounded by everything I could ever want, looking out the window at my children in Central Park, faraway figures in swirling snow, right off a Christmas card, I was unhappy. Instead, I blamed myself. I still thought there must be something I wasn't doing, something I could still figure out to do that would make our lives right. Some way I could fortify the frontier of our happiness against attacks in the night. I was hoping the new baby would make a difference.

I'd be going back to California for our baby's birth, with the doctor I knew so well. Dr. Shulman had become a friend—my general doctor as well as my obstetrician, because whenever I had a cold or some minor ailment, I was generally also pregnant, so I'd just pop in to see him for anything. He'd given me a camellia bush before my first pregnancy as a kind of good-luck charm, just because I'd mentioned that I liked camellias. Joe agreed that I go back to Dr. Shulman; he assumed we'd return to the Dakota afterward. I think I knew then, with a bleak knowing as unmistakable as it was unwelcome, that I wouldn't.

We celebrated the New Year, and the new decade, with a month of gala parties and dinners. My friend and former roommate Jackie Sherman was married; her husband, Bob Rose, was very much like Joe—an expert at most things he contemplated, including chess—so her marriage had brought us together again. Victor Hammer, the jeweler who'd made my enamel ring, joined us for a splendid dinner at the Forum of the Twelve Caesars, then we went back to his apartment to drink vodka and sing Russian songs. Three days before we all left New York, we gave a cocktail party for sixty people, followed by supper for thirty, with waiters in black tie swooping in and out among the guests, balancing trays of champagne glasses—laughter and glitter and dancing in the dark.

Rafael Francisco was born on March 23, 1960, named for Joe's father. All my children are named for members of the Ferrer family—not because Joe asked it, but because I wanted it. It seemed to me that his aristocratic family name should be so honored. His father had been a renowned criminal lawyer; the family included an architect, a doctor, a sculptor. He'd lost touch with them, and I wanted to bring them closer.

His sister Elvira, who lived in Mexico City, began coming to visit us with her children; I always felt good about bringing them together.

During that political spring and summer, I became active in John Kennedy's campaign. I'd been intrigued by politics since Blanchie Mae Chambers and I sang at the corner of Second and Market streets in Maysville when Papa Clooney was running for mayor. We sang "Home on the Range," because that was President Roosevelt's favorite song, and Papa Clooney was an FDR Democrat through and through. When Alben Barkley, the Vice President, came through town once, he stopped by to talk with my grandfather. I'd fallen asleep, but Betty stayed awake, and the Vice President of the United States kissed her hand. I never quite forgave her for that.

I wasn't just a Kennedy Democrat; Papa Clooney had bequeathed me a deep regard for and belief in the Democratic Party's priorities and ideas. I'd voted for Adlai Stevenson in 1952, my first presidential vote. I'd met Patricia Kennedy and her husband, Peter Lawford, at a rally at Janet Leigh's house. Sometimes the Kennedy people asked me to sing at a benefit, or just do a drop-in, maybe a few remarks. I was invited to lunch at Hickory Hill, where I was charmed by Bobby Kennedy and his Irish wit. Ethel Kennedy kept the conversation lighthearted, wanting to know who in Hollywood I had a crush on. "Not anybody?" she asked, incredulous. "Don't you have a crush on *anybody?*"

Joe's dream came true that summer: he sang Puccini's one-act *Gianni Schicchi*, at the Santa Fe Opera. I determined that all the baritone's family, including newborn and nannies, would be in the audience, so we made the trek by train. I was enormously proud of my husband. Even Miguel, age five, hummed on the train home: *O mio babbino caro!*

Igor Stravinsky was in Santa Fe then, conducting his *Oedipus*. When I was his dinner partner at the opening night ball, he was furious when I took out a cigarette. "I will not sit here and watch you hurt your voice!"

he declared. "If you must smoke, you must leave the table." I doubt that smoking ever hurt my voice; when I gave it up, finally, some thirty years later, it was because of my asthma.

At that time, I was singing as well as ever, maybe better. I played Harrah's, with a month-long booking at the Empire Room of the Waldorf coming in the fall. After a long dry spell, Joe finally had a film job, directing *Return to Peyton Place*. The two of us were signed for a Thanksgiving Day special with Carol Burnett and Dick Van Dyke. So I felt absolutely sure that now, with our work going well, if I had another child, my sixth, as I'd planned, we'd surely live happily ever after.

Dr. Shulman had advised me to wait at least a year before having another baby, but I couldn't wait that long to be happy. When Rafi was three months old, in the summer of 1960, I became pregnant again.

Was there ever such a textbook example of expectations overcoming reason? I began making notes in a journal. When I look at it now, I'm alarmed at the random jottings that chart my emotional disarray. I was soaring, I was leaning, I was plunging.

Joe talked on the phone to a friend, a conversation that sounded to me just like the one that had clouded my honeymoon. *I heard too much*, I wrote. But when he went to Denver a few days later, I watched the clock, waiting for his call: *8:20, no word. 8:35, no word. 9:00, no word. 9:15, HE CALLED I LOVE HIM*. Two weeks later: *Joe's not happy, what's to be*—followed by *SO HAPPY WITH EVERYTHING*. Clearly I was acting as I'd once said in my press release: I was a scatterbrain. But it wasn't at all lighthearted. I had an early miscarriage.

In midsummer, either my mother or Joe had arranged a birthday party for Maria and Gabri; I was resting in bed, recovering from my overnight at the hospital. I walked over to the window and watched them all frolicking for a while, then I took some pills so I could get some sleep.

I opened at the Waldorf in October. King Hussein of Jordan came to my show half a dozen times, accompanied by a tableful of bodyguards and State Department officials; later he wrote me a lovely letter telling me how much he'd enjoyed my performances. I wore a white ostrich-feather coat, like a tent, over a red satin Scaasi design. Betty and I had always said we'd wear ostrich feathers someday. Now I threw open my coat and laughed at the audience: "Bet that half of you were saying, 'My God, she's pregnant again!' I fooled you, didn't I?"

I fooled the television audience at Thanksgiving, when Joe and I laughed our way through the special, *There's No Place Like Home.* I fooled Louella when she quoted me in her column: "Our marriage is working just great, now that we have all the children." I fooled the readers of *Coronet* magazine in a homespun piece that detailed what the Ferrers needed to keep each week in their fridge: forty-two quarts of milk, fourteen quarts of orange juice, thirty pounds of fresh oranges, twelve dozen eggs.

I didn't fool myself, though. I knew my marriage was finished. I packed my maternity wardrobe away for good. I wouldn't be greeted at the Gershwins' as "Miss Clownie" anymore. Bogart was dead.

TEN

~

*F*lying home from Paris via the polar route took an eternity. Suspended over the desolate cap of the world, I had the time to arrange and rearrange the days ahead—to configure the rest of my life.

It was the summer of 1961. Once again my mother had tracked me down across an ocean and a couple of continents, from her upstairs room on Roxbury Drive to the ornate little bar of the Hotel Raphael. The desk man had tried my room, paged me, finally carried a phone to my corner table. When my mother heard my voice, she plunged right in. "Your daughter damn near died!"

I gripped the phone like a drowning woman as she related the frightening episode. Maria's throat had swollen, an attack of epiglottitis. Late at night, when her fever shot up, Mama had called the doctor, who'd come to the house and found my daughter in such straits that he'd driven her and Mama directly to the hospital, not waiting for an ambulance. "Your husband didn't call you because he was out when Maria got sick. He was out all night. He was out with a friend." The word "friend" didn't need emphasis.

Maria had come close to needing a tracheotomy, but thankfully, the swelling had subsided enough so that a tube could be glided down her throat. She'd spent a week in the hospital, Mama with her around the clock. Now they were home, and Maria was doing fine.

I wished she had given me that blessed bit of information right away, at the beginning of the call, to take the edge off the fear. Instead, she had saved it for last—Mama at her dramatic best, knowing that at those first terrifying words I would have one forsaken moment before the rest of her news brought me back to life.

I'd cancelled my bookings, appointments, everything. Sleepless, staring out the plane window into nothingness, I thought of how consistently I'd put aside the hurts Joe had inflicted on me, often using the same plausible logic: *He's a good father.* Now that logic was blasted clean away. Of course I had observed Joe being a good father. I knew the children adored him, and one incident didn't change all that history—but it changed me.

It isn't my fault.

I was staggered by the implications of that simple acknowledgment. On that hopeless night in Beaulieu, my straightforward anger had been skewed to craven anguish by the conviction that I was the one who had failed. In trying to make our fractured life whole, I assumed responsibility for all the ways in which it fell short. Joe's sins of commission became my sins of omission: I hadn't done enough, or hadn't done the right things.

It isn't my fault, and it never was.

I was shocked to see the time I'd wasted, the energy and the pain. But I knew I wouldn't waste any more. It was really over, and that was all right. It would be so freeing to shed the burden of someone else's blame.

⌒

For the first time in my life, I saw Joe at a loss for words. He stood in the entrance to the living room as I rushed up the stairs to Mama's room.

Miguel was asleep on one of the twin beds, Gabri on another. My heart in my throat, I shook Mama awake. "Mama, where is she? Where's Maria?"

"She's fine," Mama said sleepily. "She wanted to go back to her own room." Maria had claimed the bright corner room, opposite my bedroom, as her own; Monsita, not yet three, was in no position to argue.

I slipped into Maria's room and saw, by the dim glow of the nightlight, that she was sound asleep, one hand tucked under her cheek. When I touched her forehead, she didn't stir. I watched her for a minute, as my warm surge of relief turned to chill anger.

Mama was waiting outside the door. "You know he sees other women," she said. "Sometimes when you're gone, he brings them here."

Joe followed me into our bedroom. "I need to talk with you," I said. He made a move to embrace me, but I turned away. "I want you out of the house tonight."

"I don't understand," Joe said.

"You are not going to step over my dead body, or the bodies of my children, to get what you want. You didn't tell me about Maria being in the hospital—you've just been having a very good time."

"I'm curious," he said. "Have you had me followed?"

"I didn't need to. You're not very discreet about what you do."

"Oh, Rose," he said impatiently. "You knew before you married me the kind of man I am. I can't change."

"I want you out of the house," I said again. "Tonight."

"Right." He turned and walked out. It must have seemed abrupt to him; I don't think he knew I'd been keeping score.

I heard voices below, then the sound of the front door closing hard. Less than an hour after I'd stormed in, jet-lagged but determined as never before, my husband was gone.

I couldn't relax. I raged through the house, pulling his things out of drawers and off shelves. I dragged boxes into the middle of our bedroom and threw in everything I could lay my hands on: clothes, books, chess pieces. Miguel and Gabri, six and four years old, heard me; they followed me wide-eyed until I turned to my mother. "Put them back to bed, please." I couldn't stand to see the looks of mixed wonder and fear on their faces.

My mother pulled out the telephone book and found the number for Bekins movers. The answering service suggested I call back in the morning. "No, I want to do this *now,* "I said. I didn't know where Joe had gone, so I shipped everything to his lawyer in New York, C.O.D.

The fallout was swift and deadly. In the space of less than two weeks, I filed for divorce; Louella broke the news in her column; and the sponsors of "The Bell Telephone Hour" called a meeting.

I was scheduled to appear on the season premiere on September 27; fourteen minutes of the hour-long show would be devoted to my seven numbers. But wait: I was slated to sing love songs! The sponsors got the jitters. My divorce was news; if I got up in front of the cameras and sang "Just Imagine" and "If Love Were All," would I appear to be flip? Or bitter? Or would it just make people squirm? Oddly, it was all right for me to open the set by singing "Fine and Dandy." But those ballads would have to go.

"I'll drop 'Just Imagine,'" I said, "but not the other." I didn't want to lose Noel Coward's wry, finely crafted lyric, although I had to agree that it resonated with my life now as never before. Surely I could sing the song as an artist, not as a woman with a personal life hopelessly tangled in my art. "It'll ruin the whole segment if we take it out," I insisted. When they held their ground, I walked out. The season premiere of "The Bell Telephone Hour" would go on without Noel's too-true chagrin: *I believe the more you love a man, the more you give your trust, the more you're bound to lose.*

Nelson Riddle and I had become friends when we worked together on my first TV show. And for a long time it was just that, a friendship based on our respect and concern for the music. "I think you are the best singer who ever lived!" I once told him, "because you know just what to do on any given word or any particular note. What you write conveys exactly what I'm feeling. Exactly!" Nelson didn't embellish a lyric or even enhance it. He ennobled it.

When we discovered that our birthdays were just one week apart— mine on May 23, his on June 1—we began celebrating them together, first in a group, then just the two of us.

I loved to try to make him laugh. He had a wry, sardonic sense of humor, but beneath it was an intense sadness—Julie Andrews called him Eeyore, the forlorn. The fact that he didn't know where the sadness came from made it all the more poignant, I thought.

Joe and I hadn't talked that much about ourselves—too busy, too distant. We'd never discussed his two earlier marriages, why they'd failed and what we might have learned from that. Instead, we talked about our work. Perhaps we were too seduced by success to probe for potential failings; perhaps, amid the clamor of our bustling household, we could hardly hear one another's voices. Or if we heard, we didn't listen.

Nelson and I talked very little about music; we talked about our lives. I was warmed by his interest in me: he wanted to know where I'd been, what I'd done, who I was. I told him everything. When I told him about Sy Berger, the trombone player with Tony Pastor's band whom I'd loved so much—a story significant to me that I'd never told anyone—he touched my hand and smiled. When we made a theme album, *Love*, he took a song I'd recorded when Sy and I were together—"You Started Something"—and scored it for all trombones.

By the time I knew my marriage was over, at least emotionally, I also knew that I was in love with this caring man. He was one of the two men in my life who loved me just for myself, as a person. Like Dante DiPaolo, he didn't just appreciate my strengths and overlook my weaknesses; if anything, it was the other way around. He loved me for just one reason. The reason was Rosemary.

But we were both legally married, so when he went to London to score the film version of *Lolita*, I wrote to him undercover, putting my letter inside an envelope addressed to Stella Magee, the woman from the secretarial pool who worked for him there. His secretary at home, Naomi, knew about us: She made bookings for us at the Plaza in New York. I'd already filed for divorce; Nelson said he was waiting for the right time to tell his wife. That would be difficult, we knew; his wife was desperately insecure, her life totally given to his career.

When we recorded *Love* on RCA Victor, we were at the height of our feelings for one another. Tears ran down my face as I stood at the microphone. I blinked, trying to focus on his conducting; he swam in a watery blur. Every time he caught my eye over the heads of the orchestra, my heart leapt. Each song was more pointed and poignant than the last, many of them elegaic in tone—"How Will I Remember You?"—and all of them laden with yearning, with regret lurking just around the corner. *I wish it so . . . what I wish I still don't know . . . but it's bound to come, though so long to wait.*

My friend Ian Bernard had written "Find the Way," a rich arrangement with a melody that was like a cry, and he'd come to the studio to hear us record it. *Find the way to love me, find the way to tell me that I'm for you.* I tried to smile at Ian. *Tell me now and dry my tears.* My visible emotion was a great ego boost for Ian, who didn't know then about the love between Nelson and me. "I'm watching you singing my song, tears coming down," he told me, laughing, once he knew. "I thought, 'I am one of the greatest songwriters in the history of the world!' "

Tears in court made very good copy:

> Weeping uncontrollably on the witness stand, singer Rosemary Clooney, thirty-three, today accused her husband, actor José Ferrer, forty-nine, who fathered her five children, of "having affairs with other women since the beginning of our marriage" and "violent acts of temper . . ."

Yet my divorce trial in the spring of 1962 wasn't about lovers: his many, my one. It wasn't about tempers, not even about custody of the children. In the grubbiest of soap opera scenes, Joe and I, with our teams of lawyers, had come to Santa Monica Superior Court to fight about money.

I was asking for the house and $8,000 a month. Joe's response was that I was "an extravagant housewife." I agreed that the $7,558 a month it cost to run the house was a lot, but "that figure could be reduced considerably if I could have been home more to check on things. I was away more than half the time, working to pay bills." I wasn't astonished when I was told how much I'd been spending to run the house. I wasn't stupid, and I knew it had to cost a lot. I just wasn't paying attention.

Joe testified that he was "financially insolvent." He also testified that he didn't know how much money he made, or how much he owed; he said he signed his income tax returns without reading them. He said he didn't know how much money he had in bank accounts in Los Angeles, New York, Switzerland, London, and San Juan. He said he didn't know how many houses or how many acres of sugarcane he owned in Puerto Rico.

Joe had just been paid $25,000 for one week's work in *Lawrence of Arabia*. Unfortunately for me, I'd just come off a job paying $20,000 a week, with more bookings scheduled. So the judge decided that the children and I could manage nicely on $1,500 a month from Joe: $300 a month for each child. I got the piano, the Vlaminck, and the hi-fi equipment; Joe got other paintings, books, athletic gear. The house was mine to live in until I remarried or until all the children turned twenty-one; then it would belong to them, in equal shares.

That was a long way off. At this wrenching time of my life, my children were just two, three, four, five, and seven. So I kept my explanation simple: Daddy wouldn't be living with us anymore, but they would still see him often; hardly anything would change. Joe was always away from home as much as he was there, anyway. The children saw us on the news, coming out of the courtroom separately, talking to reporters, and the older ones knew something was wrong. But I told myself I didn't have to explain; they were used to seeing us on TV. And not even the oldest could understand the screaming headline:

STAY OUTTA MY HOUSE

It was always fascinating to me that the people who'd wondered when we married: *How could such an unlikely marriage last?* now wondered: *How could such a wonderful marriage possibly break up?* One reporter wrote of me as though I had emerged from a Gothic novel. "Her worn and weary countenance makes her look as if fate had whacked her right in the face.

She appears repulsed by the past, disdainful of the present, confused about the future." He was wrong about the future, though, as I assured a reporter outside the courtroom: "It's going to be great. I'll be able to do so many things again. You know, I've been mostly having babies for a long, long time now."

That May, when Nelson and I met at the Plaza for our birthday weekend, I felt lighthearted, almost buoyant, in a way I hadn't felt for years. I told him about Kentucky, how his kids and mine were sure to become friends, how we'd send them all down to Uncle George in the summers where they could muck out stalls and run barefoot and jump into haystacks and do all the country things they couldn't do in Beverly Hills.

At dinner in a dusky, romantic bistro on a side street near the Plaza, I kept trying to make him laugh. I told him what I'd said to a reporter who'd caught me just as I was getting into my car after the trial. She'd seen my mother in court; now she asked about my father.

"He lives in Ohio," I told her. "He's a painter."

"An artist in the family!" she gushed. "How wonderful. What does he paint?"

"Houses, mostly," I said, deadpan. "Sometimes a garage."

After dinner, we walked along Central Park South in the sweet spring night, holding hands. Near the entrance to the Plaza, on one side of the fountain where F. Scott Fitzgerald had playfully splashed, we kissed. "Champagne's waiting upstairs," I reminded him.

And, along with the champagne, a message: From the way he sat on the edge of the bed, his shoulders hunched, I knew who'd called. "My wife," he confirmed in a subdued, pained voice. "To wish me a happy birthday."

I walked to the window and looked down at the fountain. A woman in a yellow hat was feeding a roll to the pigeons, bit by bit. I thought of the times I'd called Joe when he was away from home, never suspecting that someone might be in the room with him, waiting for him to hang up. Then I thought of the times Phyllis had tried to reach him while they were still married and he was with me. It made me heartsick that again I was the other woman. "I don't think we can keep this up," I said.

It was a step I never meant to take. But I couldn't take it back. I would have to take the next step, and the next, and hope they didn't lead me too far astray. I looked at Nelson to see what he was going to say. He didn't answer, just waited for me to go on.

"I don't think we should see each other like this anymore," I said. I wanted him to say that I was right—that he'd leave his wife and marry me.

"I think you're right, Rosemary," he said finally. The woman in the yellow hat got up and walked away from the pigeons. I waited for him to say the rest. But he never did.

The next day we sat together in the bar at the airport, saying our goodbyes before I flew back to California. I'd made a mistake, one I didn't know how to fix. Dimly, I thought that if I kept repeating what I'd said, eventually it would bring the right response. So while we sat at our little table in the semidark, I rehearsed all over again the reasons why we couldn't be lovers anymore. "We just can't keep on like this." I said it over and over again, but he never took the cue.

That summer, when my life was shattered, I turned with pleasure and relief to something that was bright and intact. I'd kept in touch with the Kennedys, and I was delighted to be asked to sing at a benefit at the Mayflower Hotel in Washington. At a cocktail reception before the concert, I was introduced to Harry Truman.

"Hello, Mr. President," I began. He shook my hand, but didn't say hello. "You know, I wrote that letter to the music critic myself," he said briskly. "I put a stamp on it and then I just walked out of the White House and went down to the corner mail box and mailed it." I was taken aback; it took me a moment to realize he was talking about the time a music critic had lambasted Margaret Truman for her singing. Apparently when President Truman met someone, he immediately associated that person with something in his life. I was a singer, so he'd immediately thought I'd want to know about his daughter's singing. I hoped he hadn't seen the piece in the *New York Herald Tribune* when Miss Truman had appeared on "The Milton Berle Show": "As a singer, she is not now nor ever will be a Rosemary Clooney."

My grandfather's old friend from Maysville, Stanley Reed, now a justice on the Supreme Court, lived at the Mayflower. When we met for a drink at the hotel bar, he pulled out a watch that my grandfather had made for him: A. CLOONEY, MAYSVILLE, KY on its face. "You know that I respected your grandfather a great deal," Justice Reed told me. "And I'm convinced that if he had had his way politically, you and your entire family would be living in Soviet Russia now." Remembering Papa Clooney's conviction that water should be free and how we'd had to haul buckets across the street from the New Central Hotel, I laughed. I didn't talk issues of the day, which probably was just as well—in 1954, Justice Reed had been the last holdout on the Supreme Court in *Brown* v. *Board of Education*. The landmark ruling would have come down without him, but Earl Warren so much wanted a unanimous decision that he'd leaned on Reed without mercy. Papa Clooney and Stanley Reed—the best of friends, strangest of bedfellows.

After the benefit, nearly midnight, I was lying in bed in my suite, listening to the radio, when my phone rang. It was Stephen Smith, the President's brother-in-law. "Could you come over to the White House for a cup of coffee or a drink?"

I was out of bed like a flash, back into the long white lace dress with a little off-the-shoulder jacket that Edith Head had made. Steve Smith came by for me, and when we got to the White House, everything was dark. We drove through the main gate, I think—I remember somebody saluting. But we used a side entrance, then we got into a little elevator, up to the residential floor.

The first thing I saw was the back of a rocking chair, and suspenders. I'd met President Kennedy in a group before, but this was the first time up close. He got up from his rocking chair and shook my hand. "You were wonderful tonight, and I want to thank you," he said. "Jackie enjoyed it a lot."

"Well, thank *you*, Mr. President," I said. He asked me to sit down, so I sat on the couch where Peter Lawford was sitting. "Hi, Rose," he said casually. He had his shoes off, wearing red socks.

President Kennedy sat next to me on the sofa and we just chatted—small talk. He asked where I'd be working next; I told him I'd be doing some one-nighters in and around London. When he was talking to some-one else, I scanned the room quickly, hoping to see Jackie. She wasn't there; there were several men milling around, and a woman to whom I wasn't introduced, someone on the periphery.

Then the President stood up suddenly. "Who wants scrambled eggs?"

"Sounds good," Lawford said. Steve Smith agreed, and everybody else seemed to agree, so I did, too. The President went into an adjoining room and I heard the sound of rattling pans. I couldn't stand it. "Steve, could I please make a phone call?"

He led me into a small room with a desk and a phone and closed the door behind him. I got the operator and asked to put through a call to Lexington, Kentucky. *Please let him be home, please, please!* When the phone was answered, I tried to keep my voice low. "Nicky! Nicky! At this very moment I am in the White House and the President of the United States is scrambling eggs for me! Oh, Nicky—it's a hell of a long way from Maysville, Kentucky!"

When I hung up the phone, I took some deep breaths to compose myself, then sauntered back into the main room. I sat down on the couch again. People were eating scrambled eggs; someone handed me my plate. I started eating and *Oh my God*, a forkful of eggs dropped onto the carpet. Nobody seemed to notice, but I didn't want to bend over and pick them up; my dress was very low-cut, and that, I thought, would make people notice. "Peter," I hissed. "Would you please pick up my eggs off the floor?"

It was an odd little visit—the President didn't have anything particular to say to me, just wanted to have me around. And that was nice. I'd campaigned for him; I was getting to know Bobby and Ethel Kennedy better, and later on, I became friends with Ted Kennedy. This night at the White House I didn't stay very long; it was already very late when I got there. As the little group began to break up, the President shook my hand again.

"I just have one question for you," he said. He grinned and gestured to my jacket. "What keeps that jacket on your shoulders?"

"Oh," I said. "Oh. Oh, well, it's very simple, Mr. President. It has snaps. See?" I reached inside the jacket and unsnapped it; the jacket came off that shoulder. "It has snaps," I said again. I didn't know what else to say, so I just smiled at him, and he smiled back.

In spite of what I'd told the newspapers, life wasn't great after the divorce. It was dismal. The house had a listless feeling, even with plenty of people around. And wherever I turned, there was my mother.

I was glad she was there to take charge, because I felt stretched to my limit. I had trouble sleeping—nothing new, only now the pills my doctor had given me weren't helping anymore. So I tried another kind. There were any number of medications that could help you sleep: Miltown, Equanil, Seconal, Nembutal, Tuinal. Sometimes I took more than one kind at a time.

In the morning, I'd sometimes hear her up and about early, calling the children, getting them dressed and ready for the day. But a lot of the time I was sleeping so heavily I didn't even hear. By the time I did get up, my mother would have done it all. Wherever the children needed to be—school, dentist, playground—she made sure they got there. At Halloween, she dressed them up and took them trick-or-treating around the neighborhood; down the street, Lucille Ball handed out silver dollars. It bothered me a little to see my children turning more and more to my mother when something had to be done or decided. But mostly it was a relief.

We still saw Joe often. Some days he would come by and drive the children to school or pick them up in the afternoon and bring them home. I didn't stop him, because I knew how much they missed him. When Joe was expected, Miguel would stand in the driveway for hours, watching for him.

I missed Joe, too. No rose-colored filter had dropped between me and the past—I hadn't forgotten our troubles, or his wrongs—but loving him was a powerful, seductive habit. When he was in the house, I found myself talking to him the way I always had, even kissing him hello and good-bye—sometimes just kissing him for the kiss's sake. I knew he had wanted us to stay together from the first—he'd said so in court—and I knew he wanted to be reconciled now. Something shifted subtly when he was in the house: The children were happy, the picture was complete. Maybe the

ideal I'd nurtured so painstakingly for so long still had a hold on me. Or
maybe I was reacting to more practical concerns. I didn't know a thing
about handling money, but I did know that there was more of it when Joe
was in the picture. I think that was the reason my mother, who had relished her role in the drama of our breakup, now stood by without object-
ing as we circled each other, considering whether—and how—to mend
the break. She didn't know any more about money than I did, though she
pretended to, but she realized our lives were easier with Joe in them.

I was lonely without Nelson, unhappy in my hectic home, and, most
of all, confused. I hadn't picked up my final divorce decree, and the year
allowed under California law had run out. Now I wasn't even divorced
anymore. When Joe called, I felt myself slipping.

He asked if Maria needed the book she'd left in his car. I took a deep
breath. "Joe," I said, "why don't you come home?"

Our marriage had been a wire story, and so had our divorce; now the
news of our reconciliation traveled the world on UPI. Joe moved back to
Roxbury Drive with little ceremony. It felt as though he'd hardly been
gone, and that made me wonder what the pain of the last year had been
for.

To say that loving him was a habit is to trivialize the emotion
involved. Better to say that it was a way of being to which I'd grown
accustomed, a deep groove worn in my impressionable heart. One night
after he was in bed, I sat out in the yard under the olive tree. I truly
believed I could get back the happiness that had once overwhelmed me
there. It wouldn't come to me like grace this time, freely given, even if
undeserved. Now I'd worked for my happiness; it would be well deserved
and hard-won.

When Joe went to Germany to work that winter, he stayed in touch,
playing a scaled-down version of the game I'd played all our marriage
long—reaching out from far away, defying distance and scheduling to
hold the family together. He insisted on joining me in Monaco when I sang
at a Red Cross benefit at Princess Grace's invitation. Of course, I was still
playing the game, too. I'd never stopped. On Rafi's third birthday, I was
booked in San Francisco, playing the Venetian Room at the Fairmont
Hotel. But instead of missing the occasion—or celebrating it later when I
got home—I brought all five children, and their nannies, and Mama to

join me at the Fairmont. Waiters wheeled a birthday cake full of sparklers into my suite; I turned off the lights, and everybody sang.

My kids didn't think a birthday party in a hotel room was unusual; they'd known how to order room service before they could spell their names. Even a backyard birthday party wasn't all that ordinary; at Miguel's third birthday, Morgan Mason, age three—son of James and Pamela Mason—had smoked a cigarette, which his mother lighted for him. And now, when the phone rang in our suite, nobody thought it strange that Daddy was calling from across the ocean to wish his littlest boy a happy day. It was like being a family again. Except I was still in love with someone else.

That November Joe took the male lead in Noel Coward's musical *The Girl Who Came to Supper*, a role both Rex Harrison and Christopher Plummer had turned down. Noel had had doubts about Joe from the beginning. "Those evil fairies at his Puerto Rican christening bestowed on him short legs, a too large nose, small eyes, and a toneless singing voice," he wrote of Joe in his diaries, which happily weren't public at the time.

The show played in Philadelphia, prior to opening on Broadway. I was at the Ziegfeld Theater in New York, appearing with Dorothy Loudon on "The Garry Moore Show" on November 22, 1963, when in the middle of a song, the monitors suddenly cut away from what was happening onstage. In place of the Garry Moore set, Walter Cronkite appeared, solemn and shaky, saying there had been a shooting in Dallas.

Everyone stopped right where they were, standing or sitting, onstage or off. Horrified, transfixed, we watched as the news came in. Dorothy Loudon grasped my hand and held it tight. An Irish cameraman wept.

The show couldn't go on, not now. Everyone wandered out onto the dazed city streets. Dorothy and I sat and drank at the Plaza's Oak Bar. "I'm just devastated," she kept saying. But I could still hear him: *I want to thank you . . . scrambled eggs . . . thank you . . . what keeps that jacket on your shoulders?*

I had to be with Joe to get through this. When I couldn't get a seat on a plane, I hired a car and driver to take me down to Philadelphia. He was at his hotel when I got there; *Girl* was cancelled for the night, too. In his sympathetic embrace, I could succumb to a luxury of grief—for Jackie and the family, for the orphaned country, for myself. I threw myself into his arms. The reality was starting to sink in, and sobs clogged my throat. "Joe, what's going to happen?"

But Joe's embrace wasn't that sympathetic. He stroked my hair a moment, but he didn't encourage me to pour out my feelings. We watched television, like everyone else—the open car, the jerk of the head, over and over—but it wasn't the only thing that held his attention. Joe was upset over Noel's criticism. "He says I have all the signs of being a good comedian," Joe told me. "But my sense of timing is defective. He says I don't judge effects right, that I talk through the laughs."

With an effort, I responded. "Didn't he say you were improving?"

"That's not the point," Joe said angrily. "I don't need him to tell me I'm *improving.*"

Exhausted with pain and nerves, I didn't have anything left for him. Tears welled up and rolled down my cheeks. "Joe," I sighed. "I can't talk about this now."

"For God's sake, Rosemary," he said. I thought he was going to berate me for overreacting; I wouldn't even care. But he didn't. He stayed next to me on the couch, though we didn't talk much more.

Girl was set to open on Broadway in mid-December; Joe wouldn't be able to come home to us for Christmas. So I decided we would all go to him—me, Mama, and all the children. I booked a raft of rooms at the Plaza—six rooms on the park side, all in a row—and a flotilla of house seats for the opening: a packed house right out of *Who's Who*, a glittering party afterward at a Hawaiian-themed club on Broadway. Noel sailed in with Lena Horne and Joan Sutherland on his arm, followed by the Lunts, Mary Martin, Claudette Colbert, Otto Preminger, Edna Ferber, the Richard Rodgerses, Cyril Ritchard, and Richard Halliday. "I had a small weeny doubt about José," Noel whispered to me behind a fake palm tree. "But tonight he was better than he's ever been."

Caught up in the whirl of celebration, I thought everything was better than it had ever been. My husband was happy; my family was together, the children tucked into their Plaza beds; a fabulous Christmas tree for our suite was on order from F.A.O. Schwarz. My head felt swimmingly light with the goodness of things.

A shaft of sunlight pierced the drapes on Christmas morning, making a little hot spot on the pillow around my head. I could hear the children in the adjoining room; I guessed they were being bathed and dressed.

In the bathroom, I sat on the edge of the tub and pulled my cosmetic bag onto my lap, starting to feel anxious. Usually it was the easiest thing in the world to pick up downers on the road; all I had to do was call the hotel doctor. *The time change bothers me, I've forgotten my medication, could you give me two or three pills so I can get some sleep tonight?* Instead, the doctor would give me fifty, or a hundred, figuring no one who was addicted would ask for just two or three. But on Christmas Day, I might not be able to get the doctor at all. I rooted around for my little bottle. At least a dozen Miltown and a few Equanil: That would do it for tonight.

The Girl Who Came to Supper closed in eleven weeks. "I tried to wishful-think myself into believing that José would be good, but I knew in my heart from the very beginning that he was miscast," Noel Coward wrote in his diaries.

At home, things were more strained than ever. Joe realized I was getting into trouble with drugs, but communications had collapsed so completely that he didn't bring it up with me. He told his lawyer. His lawyer told my lawyer. My lawyer told my manager. My manager told my doctor. My doctor told me.

And I realized all over again how precarious an actor's existence was. After years of success, awards, and honors, "You're the Top," Joe was still waiting for the phone to ring, still insisting we eat dinner on trays in the den so he wouldn't miss a call. *What a thankless damn profession*, I thought. *Please, God, don't let any of my children become actors.*

Sometimes days went by without a call. That was the nature of the business, and Joe knew it, but it still made him nervous. Sometimes when he got nervous, he drank. Sometimes when he drank, he drank gin, and that made him hostile. "It's like a poison in my body," he once said. "I need to get the poison out, and once it's out, all is well."

But when it was working in him, he didn't reflect on the process. He just lashed out at anything that got in his way. He never touched me or the children, only things. Miguel's drums were thrown against a wall, one of the children's bikes hurled at the swimming pool fence. One night when he was sitting in the den, drinking, I tried to jolly him out of his mood. "Joe, Joe!" I teased. "Why the long face? One of these days, you'll get your big break." I came around his chair and perched on his lap. "You'll see!"

" 'You'll see!' " he mimicked. "Things always come easy for you."

"No, they don't," I said. "That isn't true, Joe."

"You can't understand that I have to work for everything we have," he said harshly.

"Hey, I'm the one who works damn hard," I said. "It's my work that pays the bills, remember?"

He pushed me aside and stood up, glaring. Now I was angry, too, and I didn't want the children to hear me yelling. I walked out of the den, and as I went up the stairs to my bedroom, I heard him. "Work? Is this what you call your work?" I heard the sound of the cabinet door being pulled open, a record being smashed against the wall. Then another and another. I put my hands over my ears and ran into the bedroom. I locked the door and threw myself onto the bed, screaming into the pillow.

Our attempt at reconciliation was a doomed charade. We separated in April 1966; on August 17, I filed for divorce again, and now that the children were old enough to understand—from seven to twelve—I supplied the drama. I had my mother line them up outside my bedroom door, then they were admitted, one by one, so that I could tell them the news. Miguel remembers that as each child got the message, the ones left waiting, as though in line for the scaffold, heard crying and wondered what was so terrible in Mama's room.

Nelson and I drifted back together, and for a while my hopes were high. Naomi, his secretary, rented a pretty little apartment for us, high in the Hollywood hills, above the Capitol Records Building on Vine Street.

She kept it stocked with lovers' needs: champagne, candles, perfume for me, always the wrong fragrance. Nelson worked himself impossibly hard; I think he had something of Joe's feeling that success was precarious and work precious. Still, we made time for each other—and there were some lovely times. Except for the birth of my children, my time with Nelson was the happiest of my life.

But I wanted more—I was ready for more—and I was frustrated at the difficulties. Nelson's wife knew about us, but she'd taken the news so hard that he felt he couldn't go through with the divorce right away. He felt too guilty. He kept stalling, and finally I did what I never thought I would do: I called Sinatra. "I need to have a talk with you," I said.

Frank took me to dinner at LaRue's, the first and last time I'd been to that restaurant, the first and last time I was with Frank, alone. He was still in touch with Ava, who was living in Spain. "She wants me to send her some kitchen appliances," he told me. "She wants a stove and a refrigerator in avocado green, and she can't get that color over there."

"I need your help," I told Frank. "You're close to Nelson. I need you to persuade him to get a divorce."

His face darkened. "No," he said. "It won't work, Rose. You have five kids, Nelson has six. That makes eleven kids."

"I can count," I said edgily. "I know how many kids there are."

"You can't break up families with so many kids," he said. "Nelson can't get a divorce."

"Mine is already broken up," I told him. "And I want to marry Nelson."

He studied me carefully. "Tell me about the pills you're taking."

"That's pretty much under control," I told him stiffly. Then I hesitated. "I think so, anyway. I'm not sure."

"The pills will hurt your voice," he said. "In fact, Rose, they are already hurting your voice."

$\smile$

Frank was both right and wrong.

He was right about the pills hurting my voice. On an album of show tunes I made with him in the summer of 1963, I sounded as though I were underwater.

But he was wrong about Nelson. Nelson did get a divorce. He married Naomi. And Joe Ferrer married Stella Magee, the secretary who'd worked for Nelson in London when I was writing him love letters.

Just another of those secretarial-pool jokes God likes to play.

ELEVEN

*T*hat slum of a decade" is what the writer Russell Baker called the 1960s. The country was cracking up: assassinations, Vietnam, fire hoses turned on people with pressure strong enough to strip the bark off trees. And I was living in my own slum, a place of brokenness, impoverished, littered with smashed hopes.

I began missing whole days of my life, either because I registered nothing or because I couldn't get out of bed at all. Sometimes I would be fuzzily awake enough to realize what was happening, and I would buzz my mother on the intercom. "I'm slipping," I would mumble. "The lights are going out." Then she'd go into full alert mode, make coffee, try to walk me around. Often she would make one of the children do it, because she herself was frail and increasingly unwell. She spent much of the day lying on the floor in her big room, phone and cigarettes within reach, an afghan over her legs. Because of her emphysema and asthma, lying flat was her most comfortable position; but it was a strange sight. Some of the children's friends got scared when they saw her, because they thought she had no legs.

Monsita became the worker bee, whom Mama would wake earlier than the others to go down to the kitchen to make a pot of tea and then try to wake me up. Being sent in to wake me from my drugged state was like being given the death penalty, walking the last mile. Sometimes Mama sent Rafi, knowing that he was my baby, so I probably wouldn't throw things at him or hit him. But if I wasn't asleep, it could be worse. "Your mother's on the warpath," my mother would warn, a phrase they didn't understand at first but all too quickly grasped. Stay out of Mama's way.

Nobody could predict how I would act from one day to the next, or even one hour to the next; I might go into a room smiling and come out yelling. At one extreme, I carried a tray of my fine jewelry downstairs so that visitors could take whatever they wanted. Maria, who was eleven then, watched while I did this; later, she scooped it up and carried it back to my room. At the other extreme, I stayed in my room with the door closed all day; I kept my TV set on day and night, though I paid little attention. When my mother sent one of the children into my room to rouse me, I'd open my eyes to a blinding headachy light with the child inside it. Then I'd scream something at it. The next time I opened my eyes, the child would be gone.

One of the most hurtful things for me to remember now is that my children were often afraid of me. When they were able to get out of the house, on their way to school, they felt safe; they'd escaped. "If I can only make it past the driveway, I'll be okay." School was a haven, even though they couldn't confide in anyone; my mother had drilled into them the need for secrecy. "What happens in this house stays in this house," she lectured. I was too deadened to recognize that sad refrain from the Crosby household, where the image of Bing's happy boys had to be maintained at all costs.

One of the children's teachers knew. Rae Bernson, a former Dominican nun who ruled with an iron hand—and was capable of wielding the ruler itself, especially on the boys—came to know my mother, through school meetings, by seeing her at Sunday Mass, then by coming to the house. Once, to give the kids a break, she took them with her to San Francisco to a teachers' convention. "I'll make sure they get to Mass," she told me, and I said, "They'd better!" Even though I didn't go to church anymore, it was important to me that my children stay in touch.

Monsignor Concannon, the rigid pastor who'd baptized my babies in the Irish versions of their names, had left the parish. Father Peter O'Reilly, the new associate pastor, made it a point to come around the neighborhood and visit his flock at home. All my sons were altar boys, beginning in the fifth grade. Sometimes Father O'Reilly came by to give Communion to my mother as she lay on her mat on the floor.

When he first came by, I was on the defensive. I thought he'd yell at me for not coming to church, for not even having been married in the church. But he was completely nonjudgmental, with a wry Irish take on things. "I deal with people as they are," he told me simply. "And I admire you for your effort to keep your family together." He hesitated, then told me kindly that he'd heard I was having money problems. "Maybe it would be better if you got a smaller place."

"If I leave here, nobody will want to talk to me anymore," I explained. "I have to have this address on Roxbury Drive. Beverly Hills is where I have to live." Father O'Reilly looked puzzled. His previous parish post had been in a bleak neighborhood where the Watts riots of August 1965 resonated tragically. He'd watched the jeeps going up and down Crenshaw in front of his church, men with machine guns. Directly across from his church, he'd seen a policeman shoot a man, who fell facedown on the street. Beverly Hills was a world apart, although Father O'Reilly found a certain bleakness there, too. In his own assessment: "The bigger the house, the emptier the heart."

With me, Father O'Reilly was understanding to what I thought was an astonishing degree. Of course, I shouldn't have been astonished. "Who is God? God is love," I'd recited in second grade from the Baltimore Catechism. Yet the God I'd been taught then had more to do with fear and punishment than with love. Now I was beginning to realize that love was the real test, the basis of our faith. Did you love unsparingly, as Christ did? If you were arrested for being a Christian, would there be enough evidence to convict you?

Father O'Reilly talked about the woman whom Jesus had met at the well. "She was burdened with a tremendous amount of guilt, on the defensive. How many husbands did she have? Five? And now she's living with a man who's not her husband. But you know, the search for God is not just one-way. Jesus dealt with the woman at the well in the situation she was in then, and he healed her. The interesting thing is that she was the very first person, then, to go out and preach him to others. She went back to the village and began to tell what had happened to her. So out of that encounter came truth."

But he didn't preach to me. We just talked. His family came from Ireland, halfway between Dublin and Galway. I told him about Papa Clooney. And we talked optimistically about Bobby Kennedy, who we hoped would run for President. Father O'Reilly told me one of Bobby's favorite quotes, from Aeschylus: "Life for him was an adventure perilous indeed, but men are not made for safe havens."

Somehow I kept working, because I had to. Joe Shribman was gone, unable to deal with my problems, but I had some bookings made ahead, and I found a new manager who continued to get me jobs, warning me that I had to be careful with money. I'd already fired most of the staff, except for the gardener and a cleaning woman who did some cooking. I still didn't have firsthand knowledge of my financial status, never having paid attention, but in 1953, a trade paper estimated my annual income at $500,000. I was still a rising star then, so at some point, I guess I became a millionaire. According to my first divorce papers, I was then in "a solvent financial position." But by the time I filed for divorce again in 1966, my annual income had plummeted to $18,750. My personal debts came to $49,282.82. After one concert in Reno, having paid the musicians and taken care of the other expenses that were my responsibility, I came home with $47.

I had no clearer idea of where the money went than I had of where it came from. Shopping sprees—drugs—and how about the seven-and-a-half-carat diamond that got flushed down the toilet? And I had no one checking up on my behalf: When I got a record royalty check for $342.10, I didn't question the accounting.

All I knew for sure was that I'd saved more when I was on the road with Tony Pastor, sending money home to Grandma, than when I was into six figures. All I knew was that I'd had a lot of money, and I didn't have it anymore.

I'd trusted too many people. Like Joe, I signed income tax returns without reading them. I'd given my mother power of attorney, because I was away so much; I found out later that both she and my manager were spending my money freely, often improperly. I knew I needed to work at the money places, yet I didn't feel right about it. I gave a weird interview saying that I was going to do only one show a year. "It's too much of a drain. I believe that no woman can be happy unless she puts her family first and everything falls into line after that."

The only way I could really put my family first was to stay home. Since I couldn't afford to do that, and since the children were settled in school and couldn't go on the road with me anymore, I did what seemed logical to me but obviously looked odd to others. When I appeared at the Royal Box at the Americana Hotel in New York, I used seven-foot-tall blowups of their pictures as a backdrop. "More homey than swinging," one reviewer wrote. "She trots out gigantic photos of her five children . . ."

Anyway, I wasn't singing well. *The New York Times* was blunt: "Her voice is a shadow of what it was."

When I played the Three Rivers Inn in Syracuse, New York, my old friend Ron Shaw from the Olympia in Miami came to see me. He'd given up show business for the corporate world, but we'd kept in touch until suddenly I'd stopped writing. That night, he told me later, I sang like a robot. "It was spooky, seeing you like that. You looked programmed. You just stared at the audience and you sang automatically, with no life in it." Backstage, I greeted him blankly, hugged him, then closed the door, leaving him outside. I have no memory of that. I'm told that in the spring of 1967, I invited the seniors from St. Patrick's High School in Maysville, who were in New York on their class trip, to my show at the Empire Room at the Waldorf. I have no memory of that, either. When I see pictures from that time, I'm dismayed at the way I looked: thin and tense, my face rigid with anxiety.

Because drugs had taken over. It no longer occurred to me to ask whether I needed them to sleep. The question was no longer relevant. I didn't ask it when I went into the bathroom at someone's house, opened the medicine cabinet, and just scooped up whatever I found. All I asked was my first question to myself in the morning: *How many pills have I got?*

How's my stash? As soon as I woke up, I had to make sure that I'd be all right for that night. I loved seeing the colors of the pills, like a bouquet in the palm of my hand: Percodan, Seconal, Miltown, Tuinal, sunshine and lipstick and snowdrifts. *Red white yellows see the pretty fellows down the hatch . . .*

But I have an all-too-clear memory of a love affair I had with a young drummer. He was fifteen years younger than I, just about the age span there'd been between Joe and me. So this time I was the smart one, the worldly one. I was the mentor and experienced lover. The fact that he was newly married made no difference to me. In the distorted state of my mind and soul, I believed that because I didn't know his wife, I wasn't a part of her life, so she wasn't a part of mine, so nothing I did could possibly affect her.

I never intended to marry him. I just needed desperately to feel that someone loved me. He lived in San Diego, so we'd meet halfway, at the Beach and Tennis Club in La Jolla. I'd reserve a suite, then I'd cook dinner, we'd walk on the beach, spend an indulgent night. The idyll was illusory, but my happiness was real.

Early in 1968, when I was nearly forty and he was twenty-five, he was scheduled to go with me on a long overseas tour: Japan, Thailand, Vietnam, then Germany, Spain, England, Brazil, Canada. He'd never been to any of those places—I couldn't wait to be his guide, to open the world to him as Joe had opened it to me. I told him all about the times I'd been there, told him the wonderful places we'd see, where we'd stay. I told him about Claridge's, with its white-gloved doormen, and drives in the English countryside. I told him about the Naserhof Hotel in Weisbaden— flaky apple strudel, claw-foot bathtubs, featherbeds.

He told me he wasn't going.

"I have to get my life together," he told me. "I'm going into therapy."

I responded scornfully. "Anybody who needs that kind of help, who can't get things together in his own mind, with his own self-will, is a very weak person." Then I changed my approach; I wheedled. "I need you— please, you can't leave me." And he said the same thing my mother had always said: "You're strong, Rose. You'll be all right." How could I be strong when my last hope for love was gone? How could I be all right?

When Bob Thompson came by my house to go over some music, he was so concerned that he sat me down in my living room for a talk. "I know it's not my business to talk to you like this, Rose," he said seriously. "But you're taking this thing way out of proportion. You're agonizing over your break with this young guy, and it just isn't worth it. I think you're in danger, I really do."

I'd always liked Bob and his wife Paula, who was coming along on the trip. When Dante had danced at the Sahara with Mae West and her muscle men, Bob conducted her band. Paula laughed when she remembered what a tyrant Mae West had been, how she would not allow any of the musicians' wives in the audience at the show, not even in the back row. If they came into the theater, they had to sit through the entire performance in the ladies' room.

I tried to pay attention to what Bob was saying. He was a top-notch musician who had studied music theory, the art of arranging. I knew he cared about my career; he'd been urging me to work with a combo, a more up-to-date setup, while I still felt I needed the energy and dynamic of a big band.

But as he talked, my eyes drifted up to the Vlaminck over the mantel, and finally I couldn't keep it in any longer. "Look at that painting!" I told him. "Isn't it beautiful? Isn't it superb? My husband bought it for me on Mother's Day."

When Bob left, I stood by the fireplace, looking up at the Vlaminck. It helped me position myself. It reminded me where I was.

Tokyo was a sleepless nightmare. The Seconals I took at night—half a dozen at least, a dangerous amount—worked in reverse, leaving me agitated and paranoid. This bounce-back effect isn't common, I was later told, but it can happen—and it happened to me. I was restless, but I couldn't leave my hotel room, the only place I felt safe; I stayed there until it was time to be driven to the theater. I was astonished when Paula Thompson went out and took a sight-seeing bus tour. "You went all by yourself in this strange city?" I asked her. I found that shocking. It was an absolutely foreign, unimaginable idea to me, that anyone could do that kind of thing on her own. I'd traveled the world, but I'd always depended on someone else to smooth the way.

I found fault with everything. I wrote an eleven-page letter to the concert manager—a sweet man, a friend—complaining about everything and everybody who crossed my path. When he came to my suite, mystified and upset, I tried to explain my problem. But I rambled so unintelligibly that he left me as puzzled as when he'd arrived.

What I'd tried to explain was that I was invisible. Nobody could see me, I was convinced, except when I was onstage singing. Nobody could hear me. I was walking around, looking at people, but feeling completely frustrated because I could see them, but they could see me only when I was performing. And if that was the only way I could get their attention, then I didn't want it. Goddamn it! I didn't want it! All my life I'd put everything I had into my singing, yet everything had gone hopelessly wrong. I'd been scheduled to go to Vietnam to entertain, but when I was told I couldn't go because of the Tet Offensive, I took it personally. The Tet Offensive was a plot to persecute me. I planned to discuss it with Bobby Kennedy when I got home. Bobby would straighten it out.

And who had the right to deprive me of my children? The very idea made me furious. But when I called them and heard their voices—*Everything's fine, Mama, we're all fine*—I felt worse. They didn't need me. My mother had stolen them from me. Maybe the house would be empty when I got back. Everybody would be gone. Maybe I would be gone by then, too.

In Bangkok, young boys sprayed perfume in my path as I walked down the hotel hallway. Silks, exotic fruits, a fairyland. I shopped constantly, spent money as fast as I earned it, buying anything and everything—from dresses to diamonds.

I still wasn't sleeping when I got to Clark Field in the Philippines, where I went through a hospital for Vietnam casualties. Young men—boys, really—missing arms and legs, one missing most of his face. "When you say you can't take any more, we'll stop," the nurse said.

"I want to go through the whole place," I told her, and I did, but it was hell. When I sang softly to one young man, he just stared at me, eyes empty of everything but pain. *When I get home*, I promised myself, *I'll take my boys away somewhere, anywhere, so they'll never have to be in a war.*

YOU ARE MY LAST HOPE, I cabled to Bobby Kennedy when Martin Luther King, Jr., was murdered. I'LL BE BACK IN TIME TO WORK FOR YOU IN THE CALIFORNIA PRIMARY. LOVE TO ETHEL. I cried as I sent that cable from Germany. I cried in my hotel room, I cried on the street. I cried at a corner table at The Star, a pub in London where the Irish hung out, where I'd once gone with Joe. And when I'd been drinking all evening, I decided to stir things up by standing up and roaring, "Fuck the Irish!" Paddy Kennedy, the owner, was quick on his feet and hustled me into a cab.

I didn't cry in Rio, where the colors, the excitement, and the glamour galvanized me. I stayed up all night, then hurried out into a strange dawn, shades of lavender and blue, looking for the man who sold cloth kites. I knew I couldn't leave until I bought five, in different colors, one for each of my children. But when I got to New York and phoned them, I cried again. I met my friend Godfrey Cambridge, the actor, for dinner at the Plaza. "You've been working too hard," he told me. "This has been an uncommonly bad time for you. Now you really must take some time off." The idea that someone cared enough about me to say that made me so weepy that I couldn't finish the meal.

I deliberately missed the plane from New York to Edmonton; I vaguely thought that then I wouldn't have to do my Canadian concerts. But my lawyer chartered a Learjet to get me there. Bob Thompson had finished his portion of the tour, and Paul Moer had taken over as my pianist and conductor. At the airport leaving Canada, I reached into my handbag and came up with a fistful of bills—a few hundred dollars, I think. "This is all I have to show for my long tour," I told Paul. I owed him all of it, but that was all right. I was loaded with gifts for my children, and that was the important thing.

On May 23, 1968—my fortieth birthday—I spent the afternoon looking for evidence of myself. I scoured my bedroom, my desk drawers, the little office off the living room that Joe had suggested be the ladies' card room. I found a picture of me holding one of my babies—I don't know which one—as we left the hospital; I was in a wheelchair, looking down at my baby and grinning.

When I found a picture with Joe in it, I took a black marker and put a big black X through his face.

I found a picture of me with Blanchie Mae Chambers, my best friend, with my dad sitting behind us, smoking a cigarette.

I found a picture of myself in braids, four years old, taken at Murphy's dime store in Maysville, where my half-brother Andy Clooney once worked. Until he walked into a step-off in the Ohio River and drowned. I wondered how many people knew about that dangerous current. Poor Andy.

Pictures with Bing, with Bob, with Sinatra on the Edsel show. I should have a picture of the Edsel. *Oh, Mr. Ford, about your car . . .*

I found a picture of Betty and me, just sitting on the couch in my New York apartment. A big picture of me in a straw hat, my arms outstretched, belting a song at Harrah's Club in Tahoe. Betty wasn't in that picture.

I arranged the pictures all around the room, then I stepped back and looked at each one very, very closely. Sad pictures, moody pictures, happy ones. Then I walked over to the piano and tried very hard to figure out how I had fit into George Gershwin's life.

—————

"Maria, will you hang on to my coat for me, please?" Bobby Kennedy asked my daughter. He had such a winning way with children—my daughter hugged his coat on her lap all the way home.

We were on our way back from San Diego, where I'd sung at a Kennedy rally. In this secure context, I felt settled and aligned; I felt like myself again. On the way from the hotel to the airport, Maria and I sat with Ethel Kennedy in the backseat of the open car, Bobby in front, with star athletes riding on the fenders: Rafer Johnson, the Olympic decathlon champion, and Roosevelt "Rosie" Grier, from the Los Angeles Rams' defensive line. It wasn't a victory motorcade—San Diego was Republican territory, and this was the day before the primary election—but it felt like one. I believed in my heart that Bobby Kennedy would win the Democratic nomination for President and go on to be elected in the fall.

Once, when I was working for John Kennedy, Bobby had come to hear me at a club where I was appearing. People recognized him and applauded when I introduced him. So he came up and sang a song with me—or tried to. When Bobby was elected senator from New York, I'd sent congratulations, and he'd wired back: YOU'RE JUST GLAD I GOT ELECTED, SO YOU DON'T HAVE TO SING WITH ME ANYMORE. But in fact, I did. I'd been singing "When Irish Eyes Are Smiling" at a pre-primary rally in Oakland when he and John Glenn joined in. John Glenn was okay, but Bobby Kennedy was dreadful. "You're absolutely tone-deaf," I said, hugging him. "But I'm voting for you anyway."

On the plane, Maria and I sat with Bobby and Ethel and their dog Freckles in the front compartment. Bobby catnapped most of the way. At the airport, I was saying goodbye to Ethel when I felt a quick kiss on the back of my neck. I turned—Bobby grinned at me. "Thanks, Rosemary. See you tomorrow night."

The Kennedys spent June 4, 1968, at John Frankenheimer's place in Malibu; Ethel was pregnant, and I hoped she was relaxing, maybe walking on the beach. I'd be with them that night at campaign headquarters, the Ambassador Hotel, as election returns came in.

Maria and Miguel were old enough, I felt, to appreciate the importance of involvement, of backing a candidate who cared about people and their problems, who wanted to make a difference in the world. So I took them with me. We met Paula and Bob Thompson at the hotel, along with Pat Morita, the comedian. I wore a new kelly green suit with green shoes, the inside of my jacket covered with Kennedy buttons. I was a flasher, throwing open the jacket to show off my buttons every few minutes. Ethel was wearing green, too, a green silk dress. I didn't try to talk to either of them—we'd be going upstairs to their fifth-floor suite afterward.

"Hold still!" somebody called out. Rosie Grier put his arm around me; a man with a camera wanted a picture of "the two Rosies" together. A kid started singing "This Land Is Your Land" and I joined in. Then other people joined in. It was a jubilant mêlée—balloons and banners, shouts and keyed-up laughter. "We won! He won!" somebody cried.

I don't remember his speech that night. I do remember telling somebody it was a wonderful speech. And it was: I have the clipping. He said he wanted to repair the country's brokenness—"the division, the violence, the disenchantment with our society, whether it's between blacks and whites, between the poor and the more affluent, between age groups, or in the war in Vietnam. We are a great country, an unselfish country, and a compassionate country . . ."

The plan was that, after the speech, he would come to the side of the hall where I was sitting with the children and the Thompsons to take us up to his suite. For a while, Bob Thompson had left our little group; he'd gone out to the foyer for a drink at the bar. Security was so loose that when he tried to get back into the hall and they wouldn't let him, he went to the press desk, bought a press badge for five dollars, then walked right back in.

Rosie Grier had been keeping an eye on Maria. "When things get finished," he'd told her, "just get to where I am, and I'll hold on to you. There'll be a lot of people pushing, but I'm a big guy, so you'll know where I am."

Applause swept over our heads as Bobby finished speaking and turned away from the microphone. There was a large bank of TV screens to the right of the stage; Maria remembers seeing a man on the screen, just walking by, who looked different from the rest of the crowd, not as well dressed, short and stocky, with black curly hair. It was Sirhan Sirhan.

Maria thought the noises were flashbulbs breaking. Somebody else thought firecrackers. Bob knew they were gunshots. "Get under the table!" he yelled. I saw a woman running toward us from the pantry, her bloodied hands over her face. I pushed Maria and Miguel down, under the table, and crawled in with them. In the midst of the screaming, I heard a shout: "Someone pray!" I clutched my children and began reciting the rosary out loud. Then Bob was pulling us out. "We've got to get out of here! Rose, come on!"

With Bob leading us, Paula and I and the children pushed our way down the stairway to a side exit with double doors chained shut. "Sorry, no one can leave," a policeman said. "I'm Rosemary Clooney and I've got to get out of here!" I told him. "Sorry," he began, and I grabbed his arm. "Look at me! You know who I am! I'm Rosemary Clooney!" I screamed. "Look at my children! See how young they are? We've got to get out of here!" When he opened the doors for us, a lot of other people pushed their way out, too.

Outside, we watched Bobby Kennedy being put in the ambulance, and we watched his wife watching him. Maria wanted to look for Rosie Grier, because she'd promised she'd get to wherever he was. Somebody said Rosie was inside. He'd grabbed the shooter's arm and smashed it against a stainless-steel table until the gun flew out of his hand. In the car on the way home, Maria cried; I had salty tear marks on my green suit for a long time. Miguel kept saying, "I'm all right if you're all right, Mama." I felt numb. I felt turned to stone. "I'm all right, honey," I told him. Closing my eyes, I made a deal with God. If Bobby lived, I'd go back to church.

At home, after long ghastly hours of television, the announcement came that Robert Kennedy was dead. But I didn't cry. I laughed. The man who'd shot him was a Jordanian subject. I still had the letter from King Hussein of Jordan, written six years earlier, when I'd sung at the Waldorf. The letter was clear evidence of a hoax.

I showed the letter to Father O'Reilly; I called my friend Carol Burnett; I even called Ethel Kennedy to tell her what I knew. "Rosie," she said gently. "Just remember that he was really happy because he got to spend the day before he died with you." That's when it hit me. I was the only person in the world who knew Bobby was still alive.

"Wear something patriotic," my manager said. "You'll be there over the Fourth."

I'd completely forgotten that I had a booking at Harold's Club in Reno in July. Now it made perfect sense. Of course Bobby Kennedy wouldn't be hanging around Los Angeles; he knew my work, so he'd be waiting somewhere around the club.

Until it was time to leave, I mostly stayed shut up in my room, with the television set on constantly. I loved the sound of sitcom laughter. I didn't want to talk to anybody about Bobby. This was something personal, something meant for me alone. Some kind of lesson for me, and then perhaps for me to teach the American people. I'd find out about it when the time was right.

In or out of my room, I yelled a lot. For the first time, I noticed that my mother flinched when I screamed at her. She called my doctor, who came to the house several times to give me Demerol shots. But nothing could quiet me; my system just wasn't accepting sedation anymore.

My mother had called her sister to help keep an eye on me, so Aunt Jeanne drove with me to Reno. Because it was summertime, I took Miguel and Rafi and two of their friends, along with Rae Bernson, their teacher from Beverly Hills Catholic.

We were booked into a lovely hotel near the casino, but I couldn't stay still. I rented another place as well, a small house in Tahoe. Now I had two places to stay, which gave me a good reason to be on the move, driving back and forth.

My show went badly from the opening night. I entered from the rear of the room, but instead of entrance music, there was clunky silence—I had to wait, stage-side, in front of the closed curtain, while the orchestra set up. There were problems with mikes and lights; the drummer lagged the beat and the conductor miscued. As for me, the July 2 review in *Variety* said I had "obvious throat problems."

Throat problems were the least of my worries. After my show, I'd roam around the hotel, looking for something in the kitchen, or in the pantry, or in the hallway. I wasn't sure what I was looking for, but I knew if I looked long enough and seriously enough, I'd find it.

Late one night, after a show in which I thought people hadn't been paying enough attention to me, I took a handful of Seconals, made the rounds of the hotel again, and, at three in the morning, phoned my manager.

"I want to hold a press conference at six A.M.," I informed him, "and I want Frank Sinatra in attendance!"

There was a long silence.

"That's three hours from now, Rose," he said sleepily. "Is there something in particular you want to announce?"

"You're goddamn right there's something in particular I want to announce!" I shouted. Since I didn't want to tell him what it was, I hung up quickly. The next morning he was gone, back to L.A. on the early plane. I cornered the hotel publicity woman and demanded that she set up a press conference at noon.

$\mathcal{W}$ith some of my friends...

rehearsing for "The Edsel Show" with Frank and Bing

with William Holden at Paramount

with Bob Hope in a scene from *Here Come the Girls*

with Tony Curtis at home on Roxbury Drive

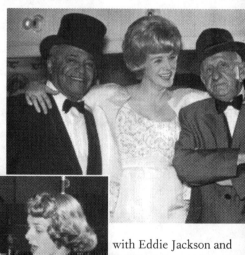

with Eddie Jackson and Jimmy Durante

and again with Bing

$\mathcal{W}$ith some of my TV guests...

my sister Gail

Jerry Colonna

Lassie

and Joe

$\mathcal{M}$y children provided many a photo op...

left to right: Maria, Gabri, Miguel,
Monsita (in front), and Rafi (in Joe's arms)

left to right: Miguel, Monsita,
Maria, and Gabri

left to right: Miguel, me,
Maria, and Gabri

left to right: Gabri, Monsita, Rafi,
Maria, and Miguel

*W*ith my mother.

*W*ith Dad in Los Angeles.

*W*ith my brother, Nick,
at his daughter
Ada's wedding.

A rare photo of me and Nelson Riddle.

*O*nstage with
Dante

and cutting the cake—
from Magee's Bakery—at
our wedding

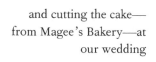

*W*ith seven of my nine grandchildren. Front row, left to right: Dustin Ferrer,
Harry Botwick, me, Tessa Ferrer. Back row, left to right: Gabi Ferrer
(Gabi and Dustin are twins), Jordan Ferrer, Nathaniel and Theo Botwick.
Dustin, Tessa, Gabi, and Jordan are Gabri and Debbie's children; Harry, Nathaniel,
and Theo are the children of Monsita and Terry Botwick.

*L*ukas, age six (left), and Rafael Ferrer, age three,
the children of Miguel and Leilani.

Nick and Nina Clooney

left to right behind me: Maria, Rafael,
Gabriel, Monsita, Dante, and Miguel

Jackie Sherman Rose with her
two daughters, Kathy (left) and Susie

singing with Bing's son
Harry Crosby

smooching with Carol Burnett

Still singing—with Michael Feinstein,
Bob and Dolores Hope.

Four reporters actually showed up. "I am announcing my retirement," I said firmly. "I do not have enough time to be a mother and also a full-time performer. Thank you."

A reporter from *Time* approached me. "You seem very unhappy," he said quietly. "Is something wrong?"

I remembered being on the cover of *Time*, but when? It didn't matter; *Time* had been nice to me. I could talk to this man. "It's Robert Kennedy's death," I said, and I began to cry. Loud, rending sobs. "I'm sorry," he said, backing away. For one fleeting moment, I'd stood on the threshold of the real world—I'd used the word "death" in connection with Bobby. But it was a very brief encounter with sanity. I saw demons everywhere, and by the time I was to go onstage that night, I was sure I needed a disguise. I put on a trenchcoat. Miguel and his friend were standing in the wings; just as I went on, I grabbed his friend's big horn-rimmed glasses and put them on my face. I glared at the audience.

"Why are you here?" I demanded. "I'm sick of singing for you jerks."

There was a silence, then pockets of uneasy laughter. Clooney was surely joking, starting her act in an unusual new way.

But the laughter made me furious. "I'm not something to laugh at," I screamed. "I'm not a monkey in a cage! I'm a person!"

"Hey, Rosemary," someone called, trying to get me back on track. "Give us 'Come On-a My House'!"

"You see how stupid you all are?" I screeched. "You ask a dumb question about a silly song. You don't deserve to hear me sing."

Nobody was laughing now. "You want to hear 'Come On-a My House'? You want to hear how it sounds without my voice on it?" I took the handheld microphone and hurled it at the band. "Play it, gentlemen." As I strode offstage, the band was playing "Come On-a My House."

In my dressing room, I sat, fuming. When the stage manager showed up at my door with a doctor, I knew he was part of the plot. I darted past him. Barefoot, I ran down the up escalator and jumped into a cab. Back at my hotel, I trashed the place—curtains, blinds, pictures came crashing down in my hands. I grabbed my evening gowns from the closet and began ripping them apart.

People were crowding into the room; I escaped again. Grabbing my car keys, I jumped into my long white Cadillac, pressed my bare foot to the gas, and took off up the old mountain road to Tahoe. I would put God to the test. I would drive all the way on the wrong side of the road. *If you really love me, you won't let me die.*

Headlights coming toward me on the twisting, narrow road seemed like shooting stars that veered away at the last possible moment. "That's one for you, God!" I yelled every time.

Rafi, my youngest son, just eight, had stayed at the Tahoe house that night with his friend and Rae Bernson. I screeched to a halt at the house, disheveled and wild-eyed. Rae clasped my hand tightly and began saying a prayer. But I couldn't follow along; My mind was filled with other voices. *If I stay with you, I'll always be small-time . . . Peach and-a pear. I love-a your hair . . .*

Somebody called my friend Shecky Greene, the comedian, who was appearing at Harvey's Resort Hotel in Tahoe. When he came to my room, he gave Rafi the key to his suite and hustled him out. "You and your friend go over to my place," he said. "Order room service, watch the ball game, and just stay there until I come back for you." When they left, he turned with an angry motion and swept the bottles of pills off my bedside table. "I just wish I could slap you in the face and say, 'Come out of it!'" he said. "I'm not Catholic, Rose, but my kids go to Beverly Hills Catholic, and I thank God I'm here to help you. We can't lose you. Losing you would be a terrible, terrible loss." Then he sat down and held my hand tightly. "I know you're unhappy, Rose," he kept saying. "I know you feel trapped. But you're going to be all right."

I felt calmer with Shecky there, but when they put me in the ambulance, I panicked. "Rafi!" I screamed.

"He's fine, Rose," Shecky said. "Rafi's fine."

Rae Bernson rode with me to the hospital. I was strapped down at the elbows, but I could reach my wallet in my purse, which I had clutched to my stomach. "Help me," I said to the paramedic. "I can't breathe. Open the window." When he opened the small sliding panel, I flung my wallet out the window. Somebody was bound to find it and realize that Rosemary Clooney had been kidnapped.

At the hospital, I was given an injection that left me with a multicolored bruise about five inches across. When I woke up, I studied it as though it were a relief map. I was alone, with no restraints, so I went out and walked down the hall until I found myself in front of the nursery. *Babies!* I pressed my face up against the glass, peering at the tiny people. I had to get in. I had to get in and pick up a baby. I opened the first door I found, but I'd been tricked—it was only the nursery stockroom. Diapers, piles and piles of them. Screaming, I grabbed the diapers and began hurling them out into the hall. *Where are the babies?*

When I woke up again, I was in another hospital, this time a familiar one—St. John's in Santa Monica, where my babies had been born. That got me thinking: *What can I tell the doctor to make him let me go? What does he want to hear?* "Doctor, I've got to go home," I said humbly. "My children need me. There's nothing you can do for me here that can't be done at home."

As a condition of my release, I had a nurse with me at home. Even though she wore a starched white uniform, I knew she wasn't really a nurse; she was a jailer, and I was still a prisoner. But I did have power—I could tell by the fear I saw in my mother's eyes. I gloated when I saw how she tried to keep out of my way. And as long as I played along, didn't make a fuss, I would find Bobby, sooner or later. A doctor came to the house every day or two, and I assumed Bobby would come in his place one day.

When he didn't appear, I realized he couldn't find the house. I would have to light the way.

I hurried down to the dining room and gathered all the candles. I dragged the pillar candle stands up the stairs, placing them along the wall, one on each step. At the top of the stairs I arranged the brass and pewter candlesticks, then I brought more candles from my bedroom. With the candlelight licking against the stairs, in the wash of candlelight at the top, I folded my hands and began to sing.

My children were huddled at the bottom of the stairs, with my mother behind them, clasping them tight. When my cousin the doctor arrived—Sherman Holvey, Phyllis's husband—he looked up the stairs at me, then took my mother and the children into the den and closed the door.

Then it was Father O'Reilly coming up the stairs. I knelt down quickly. "Bless me, Father," I began. He made the sign of the cross over me, placed both his hands gently on my head. "Rosemary, you need to go to the hospital," he said.

"I don't want to go back to the hospital," I argued. "Why should I go back to the hospital? Just give me one good reason!"

"Because God wants you to go."

At Mount Sinai, the nurse gave me a form. "What's that?" I demanded.

"Sign here," she said. "You're committing yourself."

"Fuck that!" I snapped. "I can't write!" Grabbing the pen, I made a huge black X over the dotted line.

And so it came to pass that in the summer of 1968, Rosemary Clooney, girl singer, age forty, was locked up in the psychiatric unit of the hospital for which, not so long before, she'd smiled and broken ground.

The clinical term was "drug-induced psychosis."

Nick's term, just as accurate but prettier, was "overload and disconnect."

My kids said it the most clearly: "Mama went nuts."

TWELVE

As soon as I looked out the window of my room, I understood. The giant billboard said that PATTI PAGE was appearing at the FREMONT HOTEL, LAS VEGAS. She was hundreds of miles away from my hospital room, but she must be part of the plot.

Of course! I should have caught on sooner. Patti had come onto the pop music scene just about the time I did, with her cornball "Tennessee Waltz," which sold six million copies. I'd hated it when people mistook her for me—or was it the other way around? Sometimes they even thought I was the one who'd recorded that silly ditty, "How Much Is That Doggie in the Window?"

Why was I worrying about Patti Page? She was yesterday. I was now. I'd pasted tiny flower decals all over my long white Cadillac. People stared as I drove around Beverly Hills in my flowery car, which proved I was contemporary. I know people had once thought of Patti Page and me as rivals, but I never did. I thought I was better.

Six fucking million! I pounded on the wall. I ran out of the room and down the hall, yelling. I heard voices around me, behind me, coming toward me. "Who's that?" someone called out. I hollered over my shoulder, "Well, it ain't Patti Page!"

When I woke up, everything was quiet. The room was quiet, with no windows, a door with only a small window, like a square porthole. I was quiet, too—stretched out on a bed, looking up at the ceiling. I didn't know how long I'd been in the isolation room. Six hours, somebody said later. Long enough, anyway.

She suffered a psychotic reaction with severe depressive and paranoid features. Her symptoms included hallucinations, fear, depression, violently aggressive behavior, and an inability to distinguish between the real and the unreal.

In the treatment room—a small room without windows, a small table with a chair on either side, just like in the movies—I stood with my back against the wall. "I want out," I told the psychiatrist. "I don't want to be here."

To my amazement, he agreed with me. He said he understood that I didn't want to be there. So I was able to relax a little. "I'm Dr. Monke," he said. *If you're a monk, where's your hood?* "I'm looking forward to working with you." My cousin Sherman had convinced him—begged him, more accurately—to take me on as a patient. Dr. J. Victor Monke had helped establish the psychiatric ward at Mount Sinai; he rarely took new patients anymore.

We talked for just a few minutes that day, a little longer the next. Then I was able to sit still for twenty minutes. Then thirty. In my private sessions with Dr. Monke and in the group sessions, I found it strange at first, then exciting, then exhilarating, to be able to say anything I wanted. To anybody! To just blurt out whatever was on my mind! My heart would pound as I got ready to speak. Truth without consequences!

All the people in group were graduates of private analysis with the doctor. It's an interesting process: In group, you put to work what you've worked through with him. He sees how you act toward people you're facing every day. In group, there was a young man, chasing around, though he was married; I was against him immediately. One woman was a mother figure. One young girl, very much like my sister, was high on drugs; I felt very protective toward her.

It felt good to be in such a structured place. No decisions, no responsibility. Wake-up at seven-thirty, breakfast cafeteria style, medication call every four hours. Chores, too: I was in a four-bed room with a kitchenette for snacks, and we took turns cleaning up, including scrubbing the floor. Calisthenics in the morning; crafts sessions; a nap in the afternoon, and a daily walk with our keepers that took us past Chasen's. I wouldn't walk by the door, because I might see people I knew; I thought I'd be safe on the other side of the street. But one day I saw Richard Burton walking his dog. "How are you?" he said. "Fine," I said as I kept walking, hoping like hell he wouldn't notice that I was walking in a line of people.

It felt so good, in fact, that after a month, when Dr. Monke said it was time to leave, I wanted to stay. I didn't want to rejoin the hurtling world I'd lived in, that demanding world. But Dr. Monke told me I wouldn't have to. "You may never have such an acute psychotic episode again," he said. "But it would be very useful for you to explore the reasons for this one. It will be time-consuming, difficult, expensive. It's your decision." He said my breakdown was only partly due to the drugs, that other elements, other strains in my life were surely involved. I was sane enough to know that I would do anything to keep that disorienting terror from overcoming me again. Of course I would go into therapy. I remembered ruefully how I'd told my lover that only weak people needed therapy. Just the opposite: You had to be strong to delve into yourself that deeply.

So from the day I left Mount Sinai, I saw Dr. Monke every other day, three times a week without fail. Sherman arranged for me to pay $35 an hour, about half the usual rate; even so, I'd have to pay on the installment plan.

In group therapy, I made new friends, including a woman who came to spend the night. When she decided she wasn't getting enough attention from me, she slashed her wrists in my kitchen. Fortunately, I'd never paid much attention to the knives, so the blade was too dull to even pierce the skin. But I was furious that she'd done that with my children in the house.

I still got angry, especially when I'd been drinking, only now I'd learned to let the anger out. One night I grabbed a baseball bat, intending to smash the windshield on Miguel's friend's car. But once I got out to the driveway, it occurred to me that this might not be the best way to let the anger out.

Clearly, I had to concentrate harder on analyzing myself and the forces that had derailed me. I began to understand—or thought I did—how my life had spun out of control: It had been out of *my* control. Under the doctor's guidance, I could see the patterns of influence, from earliest childhood, when I took pains to make myself the Rosemary grown-ups wanted me to be, to my marriage, when I burned myself up in the quest to be and do all that was expected. I'd been hostage to that most relentless of captors: myself.

I had given up crucial ties to my own life, and I had to take them back. Sounds simple, but of course it wasn't. Among other things, I had to be careful, in therapy, not to tell the doctor what I thought *he* wanted me to say.

My mother came down the circular stairs slowly, gripping the rail with one hand, a cigarette in the other. She was so skinny she looked gaunt. Her gray hair hung in a long straight line down her back, almost to her waist. She looked like a fragile Tennessee Williams character, maybe Amanda in *The Glass Menagerie.*

But her voice was as forceful as ever as we faced one another in the marble hall. "What did you talk about today?" she asked. "Did you talk about me again?"

"Oh, Mama," I said, "I can't tell you what we talked about. That's not how therapy works."

"Oh, really? How does it work?"

I took a deep breath. "You and I have to come to a better understanding, Mama. I know you have taken wonderful care of my children, and they will always love you for it. Now I want to talk about why you couldn't take care of me."

She ground out her cigarette and lit another. "That's not important."

"I'm sorry, Mama, but it *is* important," I said. "I have to get it all straight."

She raised her eyebrows. "Is that what Dr. Monke told you? Is that what you're paying him all that money to find out?"

I tried to keep my voice even. "I'll tell you exactly what he told me, Mama. He told me I have to take charge of my life. I have to make the decisions and pay the bills. I have to be the head of this house. You are welcome to stay. You know that."

"Actually, I don't know that," she said curtly. She turned and began to make her way back upstairs. When she was almost to the top, she looked back at me. "Try telling the children you're fit to take charge."

In fact, my children were not as traumatized by my breakdown as I might have expected. I'd been behaving so irrationally for so long that the complete flip-out and hospitalization just seemed part of a bizarre pattern. All through my lost years, they'd lived their separate lives, relying on a few constants: their school, their church, their friends, and especially their grandmother. As difficult as she was with me, my mother never criticized me to my children. "Don't you ever blame your mother," Monsita remembers her saying. "When she has to go out on the road and work, she's doing it for you." She never spoke to them in negative terms about Joe, either. He had remained a strong support: They'd spent summers with him in Puerto Rico or at his country place in Ossining. When he made a picture in South Africa, they went on location with him, living on a game preserve for six weeks. Only thirteen-year-old Miguel had great difficulty in coming to terms with my breakdown. Angry and hurt, he withdrew, both emotionally and physically—he moved his things into the guest house.

I needed to let them know they could rely on their mother now. I called a meeting in the living room. "It's been real rough on all of us," I told them. "I know that. I promise you now that I'm going to do my best for you. I don't know how to be a good mother, but I'm going to try and find out."

They looked at me, then at one another. The silence stretched just to the brink of discomfort. Then Gabri said, "Okay, Mama." The others chimed in. "Okay." Then they looked around again, as if wondering, *Now what?* "Okay!" I said.

I began to cook more, and I did it well. I began to do the laundry, which I did not do well. Two of Maria's expensive woolen ski sweaters went into the washing machine full-sized and came out doll-sized. I was better at crafts. Artwork was considered therapeutically sound, in the hospital, so at home, I turned into Craft Woman. I clipped photos and articles from magazines and used them to decoupage everything in sight: Kleenex boxes, bathroom walls. The children joked to one another, "If you hold still long enough, she'll decoupage *you.*"

***

"This is the single finest day of my life," Nick said. He beamed at the studio audience. Backstage, Betty and I beamed with pride: Our little brother had his own TV variety show on WCPO in Cincinnati.

It had been less than a year since I turned my back on the audience in Reno, less than a year since that terrifying darkness loomed and I lost myself in it. I'd gone back to work all too soon after Mount Sinai—about six months later, around Christmastime of 1968. But I had to put food on the table; a lot of people were depending on me. I'd already been booked at the Tropicana in Vegas, so I appeared there, the last place I should have begun. I was singing by rote, almost automatically. The joy of singing was gone. After each show, I'd cross off that performance and count how many I had left to do.

I'd begun to gain weight, so much that I didn't really look like myself anymore. And most of the time, my indifference to my singing showed all too clearly. When you don't give a damn, word gets around just as quickly as it does when you're falling down from booze or drugs, and the word was getting around about me. *She doesn't care.*

But there were bright spots, like this shining day for Nick. At WCPO, he could hire cohosts and pay them $750 for three days, plus expenses. I'd tried to help him when I was able to; I knew he was glad that he was in a position to help me now. Under the bright lights on the set of my little brother's show, I was a guest of honor.

Nick was in top form, smooth and relaxed; by contrast, his first guest, the mayor of Cincinnati, looked positively wooden, even when Jerry Conrad's band played "Stout-Hearted Men" to usher him off the set. Sitting on my high stool between Nick and Betty, passing the microphone back and forth while we chatted and joked, I felt strong and well. We sang in unison. Then Betty and Nick stood back and I took the mike alone. The Conrad band played the intro to "Tenderly." I took a deep breath, and then I sang. I knew I didn't look like the girl singer people remembered from "Come On" days, but I looked right at the audience, ladies in bee-hives and men in shadow plaid, and they looked back at me, encouraging, enjoying the music.

They roared at Nick's early songwriting efforts, *Jesus, Jesus, I'm so lonely* and a morbidly patriotic march he'd written a year later, at age seven: *Our Army, Navy and Marines / Are on the job, no matter what it means / Death or freedom, slave or freed / Killed in action or bleed*. It made me happier than I can say to see him doing well. At one time, I'd wished he'd stayed in Los Angeles and pursued the acting career I was sure he could build. But now I could see he'd made the right choice. Broadcasting was what he loved, and in front of the cameras, he was in his element.

Off the set, things were going well for him, too. He and Nina had moved to a farm outside Mason, Ohio. Ada was nine years old, a wonder-fully bright girl with dark hair and sparkling eyes; George, an eight-year-old rascal, already looked uncannily like Nick—with a little of his namesake, our Uncle George, mixed in. At night, after the children were in bed, we sat together on the porch and talked in the soft night air.

Nick hadn't known about my breakdown while it was happening. Mama hadn't called him, which didn't surprise me; I knew she'd wished the whole thing would just go away. It had fallen to Betty to let him know. "I wish I'd been there for you," he said. "You should have told me you were in trouble."

"I'm sorry, Nicky," I said. "But you know, when you're having a breakdown, you don't exactly send out announcements. You don't say to yourself, 'Whom should I inform of my crackup?'" Some good friends—Janet Leigh, Carol Burnett—wished they'd known, so they could have helped me; others, I suspected, were only too glad to keep their distance.

He and Betty laughed, and I laughed, too. I thought that was a good sign: If I could laugh at myself, I must be getting well.

On the show, when it was Betty's turn to do a solo, she'd chosen "Put on a Happy Face." And she did put on a happy face, moving through the audience with a warm smile, shaking hands. But it wasn't a happy time for her. She and Pupi were living in Miami, but soon they would be moving to Las Vegas; I think Betty imagined—such an easy hope to fall into—that in a new place, their life would be made new, all the wrong things made right. I knew it wasn't that simple. In Las Vegas, Pupi would still be a mediocre musician, still the lounge act; he would still be a hurtful, unfaithful husband.

Betty's children were her solace and delight. The eldest—born on my birthday and named for me, but called Cari—was thirteen now; Cathi was twelve, Carlos eleven, and Cristina seven. "You two were in some kind of marathon, practically one child a year," Nick said, laughing. But neither Betty nor I regretted the way our families had arranged themselves. Like my children, her four knew an irreplaceable closeness, the very kind that had sustained the three of us in our hardest times.

In the midst of her dismal marriage, Betty did all she could to make home a sunny place for her children. When she packed their lunches for school, she wrote little notes to each of them on the brown bags, small messages of love, encouragement, fun. On the way home from school, they'd argue about who would get to sit with Mom first and tell her about the day.

Betty had never gone back to school, she'd never gone farther than the ninth grade. But she loved knowledge, just as I did, for its own sake, for the intrinsic interest and excitement of it. She had studied the classics on her own, and Nabokov, and the Bible; she spoke fluent Spanish, which she had taught herself. She had a remarkable mind. She read to her children with expressive flair, books like *Robinson Crusoe*, and she was delighted when they took to reading with the same enthusiasm—they even enjoyed encyclopedias. But she had never gone on with her career. To Nick and me, it seemed as if Pupi was draining the energy she needed for herself, and we feared for her.

Betty had left her cheating husband a couple of times, but it had always turned out to be temporary. She'd come to stay with Nick and Nina; I'd done that once, too. Our baby brother had become our big brother, a sturdy male shoulder to cry on. "Come here for a while. We'll talk. You can get away from it," he always said when one of us phoned. Nobody had to explain what "it" meant.

As clouded as my marriage had been, though, Betty's was worse. Joe genuinely liked women and considered them equals, at least as much as he could consider anyone his equal. Pupi Campo seemed to me just a classless lecher, whose attitude toward women was simple and gross: Use 'em, then lose 'em.

So Nick had worked strenuously to help her get away from Pupi and back to work. The last time she visited, he'd managed to get her a job offer at WCPO, a show of her own, doing what she did best: talking, laughing, singing, winning people over with her unaffected, loving charm. At first, Betty had agreed it was an offer she couldn't refuse, but then she'd changed her mind. She told Nick she'd decided to go back to Pupi because the kids wanted to. "If you want to stay, then it would be better for the kids if you stayed," Nick protested. "Kids don't want anything to change— and that's not their fault. It's just what kids do. Sometimes you have to make a command decision." When Betty left, Nick felt she was making a serious, even life-threatening mistake. He knew the stress that life with Pupi subjected her to and worried that it might jeopardize not only her emotional, but also her physical health.

Now we tried again to tell her it wasn't too late. "You know you can come to Nina and me," Nick said.

"Or to Beverly Hills," I chimed in.

"You don't understand," Betty said. "It's not that easy."

"I most certainly *do* understand," I told her. "I understand, because I went through it with Joe. It was hell, but I'm so glad I did it."

Betty just looked at me with her deep, thoughtful eyes. I knew she believed the choices she'd made—to be a mother instead of a performer, to focus on her family's cohesion instead of her own ambition—were irrevocable, and I knew she believed those choices were right. Part of me envied her that certainty, maybe even envied the path she'd chosen. She was the center of her children's lives, as they were of hers, while my children sometimes looked at me now as if I were a friendly, slightly unpredictable stranger, and in many ways they were strangers to me, too.

"You're stronger than I am, then," Betty said. "You can do what you need to do, even when it's hard. Even when it hurts people."

Did she mean the way I'd broken up the act, leaving her and Uncle George to go out on my own? Certainly that first definitive choice had led inevitably to all the choices I'd made since then. And not all the choices I'd made had been right for me. Betty had made the opposite choices, and they hadn't all been right for her, either.

Maybe Nick thought I was going to defend myself, even explode. "Leaving may seem like hurting your kids, but kids don't always know what's best for them," he said quickly. Then he turned to me. "How's Mama doing?"

"She drives me crazy," I said. "Maybe I should rephrase that. Anyway, she keeps wanting to know what Dr. Monke and I talk about. She thinks we talk about her."

"Do you?" Nick asked.

"Well, of course," I said. "You know how manipulative Mama has always been."

"Come on, Rose," he said. "She's the worst manipulator I've ever seen. The 'East Lynne' syndrome—oh, poor me. We used to laugh about that, remember?"

"No, I don't remember," I said.

"There was a time when you and Betty felt the same way about Mama as I do—that she's a terrific lady, trying to make something of her life. I think you're wrong about her now, and remember, I spent more time with her than either you or Betty did."

I tried to keep my voice gentle. "Can you possibly think I don't remember, Nick? Do you think it's slipped my mind that you're the one she took with her to California?"

"I think your Dr. Monke is using Mom to shift the guilt," Nick retorted.

"And what do you think I have to feel guilty about?" I asked as calmly as I could.

"Well, for one thing, bringing kids into the world and not being there for them. There was a long period when you were very self-indulgent, Rose. You've said so yourself. I think Dr. Monke sees that you are being eaten up by guilt, and he's using Mom as the target. And who knows? Maybe he's right to do that."

"And maybe I should start coming to you for my therapy," I said. "Would you give me a family discount?"

Nick flushed. He was about to strike back when Betty put an arm around each of us. "I want to talk about our trip," she said lightly. "None of us getting any younger, as Grandma would say. When are we going to Venice? Or to Raffles, to sit under the ceiling fan and drink Singapore Slings?"

Nick and I looked at one another, and we both seemed to be thinking the same thing. *Don't take this any further. Don't say anything you'll regret.*

"Soon as I get my kids through school and orthodontists," he said.

"Soon as I do the same with mine, only I've got five, remember," I said.

"Okay then," Betty said. "I can wait, as long as you promise we'll go—sometime. Promise?"

"Promise," we said together. We all stood up and did a kind of awkward group hug. "I did think Mama was going to bring you both out to California," Nick murmured into my shoulder. "All the way out there I sang 'Close to You.' I missed you so much."

Betty and I stayed with Nick and Nina a week, making several appearances on his show. My brother and I kept finding reasons to bring up the subject of Betty's career, hoping she'd think seriously about resuming it. We could see that she was exhilarated to be performing again; she came alive in front of the audience, and the audience, as always, responded with enthusiasm and warmth. We thought we were getting somewhere until she got the phone call backstage. Cristina had fallen out of a tree onto the concrete. She was seriously hurt, and Betty was scared.

It was the first time she had left her children to perform anywhere. "I never should have come," she said. "This never would have happened if I'd been there." "You know that's not true!" I said, hoping she believed me. Nick called for a car, and she left in the middle of the show. He and I went back in front of the cameras, but all I could think about was Betty. I hoped to God she wouldn't be overwhelmed by the impossible guilt that had brought me down. I hoped she'd come to me, and within a year, she did.

⁓

I heard the station wagon in the driveway. By the time I got outside, the kids were piling out, with a white German shepherd somewhere among them. "This is absolutely the right thing for you to do," I told Betty. "You know that, don't you?" I hugged her tight.

The kids fanned out into other kids' rooms. Carlos went into the guest house with Miguel and whichever of Miguel's friends happened to be staying there at the time. For years, young people drifted in and out of the house, some staying for a few days, some for many months. My cousin Michael, son of Aunt Jeanne and Uncle Roy, stayed for six months. My nephew Rafael, Joe's sister's son, lived with us for a while. I was fond of Joe's sister Elvira and saw no reason why my divorce from Joe should mean separation from them.

Mama stayed out of our way. Betty went to the big room to talk with her, but we didn't spend any time together, the three of us. I knew Betty would have liked to be closer to her. But Betty's marriage had effectively ruled that out. Pupi made it clear that her mother couldn't live with them, and Mama had never made a secret of her dislike for him. Betty didn't have any illusions about our history with Mama; she'd been left behind, along with me. In the life she'd built for her own family, in the passionate energy she poured into her role as mother, Betty was building on a tradition that had never really existed, trying to regain something she'd never had.

I didn't want to talk about Mama, anyway. I just wanted to enjoy my sister. I'd forgotten how good it felt to see her every day. How could I ever have gotten along without her? Happily, I would no longer have to; she was serious about divorcing Pupi and resuming her career.

She enrolled her three oldest children in Beverly Hills High School; Cristina, whom everybody called "the baby," went to Beverly Hills Catholic with Rafi. Betty's son Carlos had his heart set on an acting career; he enjoyed poking around in the basement, where Joe had left some of his theatrical costumes, some recreations of stage sets.

My kids were crazy about their Aunt Betty. She had a way of connecting with people that made you feel as though you were more important than anyone else. When the girls were little, she'd bend down to their level and whisper, "Do you like Arpège?" When she gave them a dab on the wrist, they felt very special. Even now, Monsita followed Betty around so noticeably that I felt a flash of envy. She always tried to sit next to Betty; when Betty got up and went into another room, so did Monsita.

"I loved being on Nick's show," Betty said wistfully. "When I finish a show, I feel so good about myself."

"You should feel good about yourself all the time," I told her. "Not just when you're on Nick's show. All the time!"

Betty had head shots taken, an audition tape made. It occurred to me that, for all my vaunted success, I was pretty much in the same position she was. If anything, she was in a somewhat better position. I was not merely unemployed and in financial difficulties; I was high-risk, with a hell of a lot to live down.

She and the children hadn't been with me long—a matter of weeks—when the doorbell rang. I was upstairs in my room, but my door was open, so I could hear Betty. "Hello, Pupi," she said, and my heart dropped. She went with him into the living room and closed the louvered doors. Some of her kids tried to peek in to see what was going on; all they could see through the louvers was that Betty and her husband were standing at the end of the long room, by the piano, facing one another. Her kids knew that Betty usually called her husband "honey" or "sweetheart." This time she'd called him by his name, and that meant she was serious.

So was he. I'd always felt he'd lured Betty into marriage by making her feel responsible for him. And the rationale worked again; now he made Betty believe that, for the children's sake, she should come back to him.

I watched helplessly as she packed. Nothing I could say made any difference. "Just until the kids are grown up and out of high school," she said. "Just a few more years."

Pupi had made all sorts of pledges and promises: to be a better father, to be a better husband. As they drove away back to Las Vegas, I felt a sick certainty that nothing he'd promised would come to be. At least Joe had told me straight out he couldn't change.

⌒

For a singer who'd called her audience "stupid" and stormed off the stage, the road back was bound to be long and painful. No more limos, no more hotel suites with flowers and fruit and a gushy note of welcome from the management. Now it was waiting in line to board the plane and find my coach-class seat, then waiting in line again to rent a midsize car. But I had a dependable traveling companion. Gavin de Becker was a friend of Miguel's from Beverly Hills High. He'd grown up on food stamps and welfare in a tough neighborhood, but his grandfather had rented a one-room apartment in Beverly Hills so Gavin would be eligible to attend its excellent high school. One morning Miguel came into my room very early; Gavin had found his mother dead on the floor, an overdose. He was standing in the street, dazed; I held him and told him he was coming to live with us. We moved a bed into the little office off the living room, and when he finished high school, Gavin became my seventeen-year-old executive assistant and road manager. "I know I'm low-experience," he told me, "but I'm very high-energy."

I wasn't even considered for the big theaters, the top clubs; I had to scramble for jobs at county fairs and suburban Holiday Inns, my name looking slightly crooked and a little lonely in the block letters on roadside marquees. One night after a show, a woman from the audience came up to me. "Rosemary Clooney," she said. "I've always been a fan of yours. What are you doing in a dump like this?"

But I didn't mind playing downscale venues. I didn't mind singing to audiences that were sparse or distracted. I didn't even mind singing "Come On-a My House." I was lucky to be working. Even if I had been at the top of my form, with my reputation unblemished, I doubt I could have played the big theaters or the top clubs. They simply weren't showcasing singers like me anymore; they were bringing in rock 'n' roll acts, *popular* acts.

What did that mean for me? I couldn't afford to stop working; I was having trouble making ends meet as it was. And I didn't want my career to end. I would have to start over somehow. I would have to reinvent myself as a performer, find a new way to be.

In my earliest sessions with Dr. Monke, I had told him how wonderfully free I felt, now that I no longer had to mold myself to anyone's expectations, including my own. And he'd agreed. All the pressure is off now, he told me. Like water seeking its own level, you can flow back into your natural, essential self. You don't have to be anything or anybody except yourself. *Just who you are.*

Terrifying words, paralyzing freedom. I didn't know who that was. My natural, essential self had been molded for so long by outside forces that it had lost its original form. I could seek my own level, but I wouldn't find it, because there was nothing left to mark where it had been.

Would I have to reinvent myself not just as a performer, but as a person? Would I have to start over not just on stage, but in my soul?

I tried. In Dr. Monke's office and at home in my room, I thought very hard about myself and my life, searching for a baseline, seeking my level. But understanding myself was tiring; sometimes the very fact that any of this had happened made me sad and resentful. The issues that therapy brought up were hurtful and hard to confront: the fact that I'd never felt in control, whether of my money or my career; my relationship with my mother; my long-submerged anger—when I threw the microphone and stalked off the stage in Reno, everyone at whom I'd ever felt anger was in that audience.

At night, I lay awake, listening to the soft sounds of the house, like regretful echoes of the life I'd planned to live there. Laid over those sounds was the tense buzz of the life I lived now: my children wary, my mother anxious and intrusive. *Try telling the children you're fit to take charge.* I opened my eyes to a dark, empty room. Was this what it felt like to be well?

I got up and went downstairs, hoping I could find a way to relax, to rest my mind. Outside, in the gentle night, I sat under the olive tree, looking up through its silvered leaves at the somber sky. I tried to remember the way this place had once made me feel. But that time was impossibly long ago, that serene self a distant stranger.

An aspirin would help my head. Back in my room, I pulled my cosmetic bag onto my lap and rooted in it.

red white yellows

One or two to help me sleep. No more than that. Just for tonight.

see the pretty fellows down the hatch

⌣

When I was booked at the Lookout House in Fort Wright, Kentucky, near Cincinnati, it was a chance to stay with my brother and his family and to sing on his show again. Since my regular audiences wanted to hear "Come On-a My House" and not much else, his show gave me a valuable chance to get new arrangements done, to try new material. On the set, he smiled at me as warmly as he had the first time, when he'd announced Betty and me so proudly as we came out of the wings. At home with Nina and the children, I thought I caught something strange in his glance, but I didn't focus on it.

Then I heard his voice, as if it were drifting down to me through dark water. Rose . . . Rose . . .

He was shaking me. I batted his hand away. "What?" I snapped. "I was sound asleep."

"I couldn't tell if you were breathing." He bent close over me. "Are you all right?"

"Go back to bed," I told him. But when I opened my eyes again, I saw that he was stretched on the floor beside my bed.

The next time I opened my eyes, gray light was coming in the window and my door was open. I heard low voices outside it. I padded out into the hallway.

Nick and Nina were standing in the bathroom with my cosmetic bag open on the sink. Nick emptied a bottle into the toilet and flushed it down.

"Those are vitamins," I said loudly. I grabbed for my bag and held it to me. "And these are cold tablets, and these are aspirin. You didn't have to throw them away."

"Not all of those pills are vitamins," Nick said hotly. "During the night, you were breathing so shallowly I thought you were dead. I won't let you do this to yourself again."

"If you have so little trust in me, I won't stay in your house." I swept back into my room with my cosmetic bag and locked the door behind me. I didn't want to leave my brother's house, and I wished I hadn't raised the stakes that high, but now it was too late. I packed in a hurry so I wouldn't have to think about it, and then I drove to a hotel in Cincinnati to finish out my booking.

There's a great loneliness in a woman getting ready to go on the stage. You're sitting alone in a dressing room, looking at a face that you know all too well. There's a great loneliness, and sometimes the only friend you have is a pill, or a glass of booze, that doesn't talk back. You're hearing all the noise outside—a hum of anticipation, stagehands getting ready, musicians tuning up. Everybody is in it together, except that you're absolutely apart. You listen to all that, and you're not a part of it at all. Until you set foot on the stage.

Then you are.

⁓

Monsita was thirteen the summer of 1972, when I played Tivoli Gardens in Copenhagen. I wanted to get to know my children again and to spend time with each of them, so I took her with me. Then we'd go on to Paris. I wanted it to be an unforgettable experience for her, and it was.

"Here's the list of things I need," I said to her the first morning at our hotel. Basic things: hair curlers, safety pins, a record or two. "And don't come back until you have everything on that list!"

Tivoli was unforgettable for me, too. Every tiny white light in the gardens was twinkling for me. The thrill of singing surged over me. My joy was so intense it frightened me.

The siren frightened me, too. Back at the hotel, late at night, I heard that unmistakable sound: *woo-EE, woo-EE* . . . "They're coming for me," I told Monsita casually.

Joe phoned the next morning. "I've got a wonderful idea," he said. "I'm going to join you. We'll show Monsita around Paris together." We took a suite at the Raphael with a balcony; Monsita told me she wanted to sleep in her father's room. The other children were already in Puerto Rico for the summer; when we left Paris, Joe took Monsita there, too, and I went home alone.

Later I found out that Monsita was so frightened of me in Tivoli that she'd called her father, phoning from the train station so I wouldn't see the charge on the hotel bill. For me, however, Tivoli was a joyous breakthrough. "Something's happened," I told Dr. Monke. "Something's changed, as far as my work is concerned. I'm feeling very excited—but I'm a little scared, too."

We talked about the process of healing. It's not always linear or predictable, he explained. You don't turn it on and off like a lightbulb. Sometimes it flickers—like a bulb that hasn't been screwed in quite all the way.

It occurred to me that my whole life was like that—flickering in and out of order, in and out of my control. My mother had never accepted the fact that I was taking charge, and the children, long accustomed to her authority, had not acknowledged any change of command. When Dr. Monke told me I had to make it clear to my mother, I asked for his help; I couldn't do it alone. "For you, I'll make a house call," he said.

"What did you talk about?" I asked my mother when he was gone.

"Oh, Rosemary," she said. "I can't tell you what we talked about. That's not how therapy works. Remember?"

Basically, what Dr. Monke had told her was that it was important for me to be in charge now. I had to take control. Mama couldn't accept that, so she left. She stayed with Betty, very briefly, then she went to Nick's, then to her sister Chris. No arrangement worked, so within a year of her leaving me, she took an apartment in Cincinnati.

She was only sixty-four when she died of emphysema, just before Christmas, 1973. I didn't feel much right away. My first thought centered on how I could afford to take all the children to her funeral. I called Joe, but he declined to loan me money for plane fares. "They spent a lot of time with their grandmother," he pointed out. "Years and years. A funeral is a pointless ritual. It's not necessary for them all to fly across the country for that."

So I passed the hat among my more prosperous relatives. I felt it was important that we all go to the funeral. My mother had been my children's mainstay during my lost years, their shelter from the emotional storm that had lashed and lacerated me. When they came back from Puerto Rico with their father, that Tivoli summer, I know they'd been alarmed to find her gone. "What if Mama flips again?" "Who's going to protect us from her then?" "How will we know if it's time for her to go back to the hospital?"

The Ashby-Porter mortuary was thick with the sweet, perfumey smell of funeral flowers. I twined a rosary through my mother's thin, ice-cold fingers. Her hands were crossed on her breast; her gray hair, normally pulled back in a bun, stood out in puffs around her face. Her narrow mouth was a vivid pink, her cheeks rouged with two round spots in that same rosy hue. Maria winced when she saw the open casket. But I made each of the children kneel with me for a few moments, in turn, on the prie-dieu that had been placed just in front of it. I still didn't feel great remorse or regret, just the normal sadness one feels at a funeral. I prayed that Mama was in a place where she'd found some understanding. I'd come to understand her some, through professional help. But that was a luxury my mother never had. I guess if you crack up, people pay more attention to your problems. Whatever my mother felt and thought and worried about, whatever made her need to be so in control, was to be buried with her.

Daddy didn't come to the funeral. He lived not far away, in Milford, Ohio, but he was too sick to travel. Betty and Nick brought their children to the funeral Mass at St. Patrick's, the church that was such a significant part of our family history.

Betty took Mama's death very, very hard. When she'd gotten the phone call, she'd doubled over crying, clutching her stomach. She told Cathi she was devastated at the thought that she'd never really known her mother. She'd written out the lyrics to the song "The Way We Were." At the funeral home on the morning of the Mass, just before the casket lid was closed, she put the slip of paper under Mama's hands: WHAT'S TOO PAINFUL TO REMEMBER WE SIMPLY CHOOSE TO FORGET.

What was painful for me was knowing that so much had been left unresolved between my mother and me. I'd been caught up in the bustle of the funeral rituals—casseroles and baked hams and layer cakes brought to the house, people sitting on folding chairs at the funeral home, showing wallet-size photos of new babies, catching up on lives. The reality of loss didn't sink in until I was back home, sitting in Dr. Monke's office, suddenly crying. My mother was dead. Mama was gone. I would never have another chance to talk with her, to finally get to the bottom of our relationship and heal what needed healing.

"There's so much I wanted to say to her," I said to Dr. Monke, sobbing. "And I think there's so much she would have explained to me, if I'd just known how to go about it. If I'd just had more time." I couldn't stop crying. "Sixty-four isn't old enough to die. She should have had more time. She left too many loose ends. She was only sixty-four."

"Welcome to the real world, Rosemary," Dr. Monke said, not unkindly. "Life is all about loose ends. And that's not an easy thing to accept. You're going to have some lonely times."

I still felt sad as I drove home, though talking with Dr. Monke always made me feel better. I didn't have to put up a front with him; I didn't have to pretend anything. On this visit, I hadn't even bothered to dress particularly well. I'd tied up my hair, which needed a shampoo, in a scarf, no makeup. My eyes were swollen from crying. When I stopped at a red light at the corner of Canon Drive and Little Santa Monica, I reached for a tissue.

It was the end of the afternoon—rush hour—so I paid no attention when a white Thunderbird with the top down drew up alongside me in the next lane. I was in my old blue Corvette, its top down, too, but I didn't turn my head until I heard the other driver call out.

"Rosella!"

A term of endearment, Abruzzi-style. Only one man in the world had ever called me that.

THIRTEEN

〜

*I*n the dining room, the mirrored wall reflected dancing candlelight and a long table beautifully set: china and crystal, linen and Cartier silver. And it reflected five teenagers sitting in various degrees of slump in their straight-backed chairs, all of them staring at the same person also reflected in the mirror: tall and dark and under scrutiny.

Dante had taken down my phone number while we were stopped at the traffic light. With no paper handy, he'd traced it with his index finger in the dust on the T-Bird's dash. Then he'd called me so quickly that I figured he must have gone straight from the car to the phone. I hadn't been home more than an hour when he called. I invited him to dinner the very next evening.

I tried to imagine how I would seem to him. He'd known me as a single swinging star, buoyant and carefree; now I was a woman in the grip of middle age, harnessed to an uncomfortable history, settled in a home I'd shared for years with another man whose presence had shaped my life. Not only did I have five children, I had five almost-grown children—not babies and toddlers to cluck and coo over, but individuals with personalities to reckon with.

And I tried to imagine how they would seem to him. Would they seem like spoiled Beverly Hills brats? I hoped they wouldn't, because I didn't think they were. True, I'd sent them to the Beverly Hills Cotillion, along with Nat and Maria Cole's kids, to learn to waltz and bow and which fork to use when. But I was pretty sure they'd grown up unconscious of distinctions in class and race. On a train once, Maria had seen a black porter with a nametag: KENNEDY. "Hi, Mr. Kennedy," she said enthusiastically. "My mother knows your relatives."

It occurred to me that Dante probably didn't even know how many children I had. Miguel was just eleven weeks old when I'd seen Dante at the Sands. Now my oldest son, almost nineteen, was an eerie replica of Joe. Phyllis Hill, Joe's former wife, had never met Miguel. When she saw him one time at a drugstore in the Valley, she said, "You're Joe Ferrer's son, aren't you? Please don't come any closer. You're scaring me."

Maria took after Joe, too, but in her lovely face, her father's features were somehow transmuted into fine-edged beauty. I didn't know how God had managed that. Monsita and Rafi looked like me: fair-haired and apple-cheeked. Monsita's beauty was of the wholesome "girl next door" type, the image I'd been labeled with early on. Gabri, my middle child, straddled the genetic line most evenly, blending my looks and Joe's in a handsome, thoughtful face.

I hadn't built up Dante's visit, no elaborate guess-who's-coming-to-dinner game. "Just an old friend," I said casually. "I met him at Paramount twenty years ago."

But at the table, the decades dissolved. Dante was still slim and lanky, with melting brown eyes, the same easygoing, endearing guy. As I served sole Veronique—I was putting serious food on the table these days—he was talking about the homemade wine he'd brought. "My father makes it, right here at home, just the way they made it back in Italy."

"Does he stomp the grapes himself?" Rafi piped up.

I tensed. Was he making fun of Dante?

"Sure," Dante said seriously. "That's where it gets the distinctive bouquet." All the kids laughed. I needn't have felt so protective, and I needn't have worried they would be unkind to my friend. They weren't even that much on the alert; Dante wasn't the first guy I'd brought to dinner, and they had no reason to think he would be the last.

Anyway, Dante put them all at ease, telling good-natured stories of the life he'd been living. Not long after I sat by the pool at the Sands with the sun in my eyes, watching him walk away, he'd married a Tropicana showgirl and they'd gone to Europe. They were living in Rome when an acquaintance of hers called, a man who worked in movie production; Dante answered the phone in Italian, and the next thing he knew, he was in a movie.

"I made twelve pictures in four years," Dante said. "One of them was completely in Italian." He made Bible pictures, spaghetti Westerns, films with titles like *Blood and Black Lace;* he had to use his eyebrows a lot. He played supporting roles, second-lead roles. "In *Pontius Pilate*, I was Simon the Pharisee. Basil Rathbone was Caiaphas, and John Barrymore, Jr., played Judas and Christ."

"How could the same person play both?" Monsita asked.

"Because for Christ, they just used his eyes."

I sat back, sipping the wine, listening. "I made a film called *The Land of Cyclops,*" Dante said. "They put me in a loincloth and really dark makeup. I would lower people into a pit. And I did *Joseph and His Brethren.*"

"The coat of many colors," Gabri said.

"Right," Dante said. "I was the brother sent by the devil. I did Joseph in."

"What did you do to him?" The kids were really interested.

"I hit him with a rock and threw him in a pit." Dante laughed. "I guess I threw everybody in a pit."

He'd expected to be in *The Agony and the Ecstasy,* but there was a rule that there could be only one American passport on an Italian film and another actor beat him to it. Then, after seven years of marriage, no children, he and his wife split, and Dante came back to L.A. to live with his parents. He kept his film career going, appearing in *Sweet Charity* with Shirley Maclaine. His doctor had an office in the same building as Dr. Monke. "I went in and out of that building a lot," he told the kids. "I bet

I just missed your mother a dozen times." He smiled at me, a smile more crinkly around the eyes but as warm and infectious as ever, and lifted his glass to me.

Rafi wanted to hear more about the movies. "What did you do to Joseph then?" he asked.

Dante looked up at the ceiling. "After I threw him in the pit? Let me think . . . I remember I sold him down the river. I bartered with the guys who bought him." Then he leaned forward, elbows on the table. "Now it's your turn to tell me about you."

The kids very intently stared down at their plates.

Dante looked at me questioningly. I smiled. I was proud of my children, with their richly varied talents and temperaments, and glad that, with all the turmoil in our household, they were turning out to be absolutely typical teenagers. Which meant, among other things, that Gabriel and Miguel had once tried to dry marijuana in the oven, then forgotten about it. The scent permeated all the rooms until the entire house was a contact high. Which meant that they were perfectly capable of turning sullen and silent with Dante now.

Then Gabri broke the silence. "For a while, I wanted to be a priest," he said. "Then I realized priests can't go on dates."

"I told Gabri that if he still wanted to be a priest when he finished high school, I'd give my permission," I explained. "I thought just out of eighth grade was way too early. Now he's taking home ec, because that's where the girls are."

Everybody laughed. The awkward silence was past. "I used to think dogs were boys and cats were girls," Maria said. Everybody laughed again.

"I'm a very good friend of Ira Gershwin," Rafi boasted. "He lives next door. I was practicing my flute in the driveway"—he glared around the table—"I had to practice in the driveway because my wonderful brothers and sisters kicked me out of every room in the house—and Mr. Gershwin saw me. He said, 'Do you know what a person who plays the flute is called?' I said, 'A flutist?' 'That's right,' he said, 'but also a *flautist*.' And Mr. Gershwin has a pinball machine that he and I play sometimes."

"Monsita has the best voice, but she doesn't want to be a singer," I said. "Maria's very interested in design. Gabri plays the piano, and he's a wonderful artist. So is Miguel." I didn't mention that Joe had arranged for Miguel's artwork to be exhibited at a San Francisco gallery when Miguel was just twelve. His pieces had been listed in the catalog, including *"Trip Time,* crayon, 1966" and *"Green Monster,* tempera, 1962," done when Miguel was seven, without a trace of irony.

My oldest son and I had made a cautious peace. His anger at me had turned him, for a while, to hard drugs and drinking. Now he was forgiving me, little by little, for my breakdown. He'd started to travel with me as part of my band, playing the drums. I still felt the sting of his rejection and welcomed every sign of acceptance in him, so it was gratifying when he stayed at the table that night, smoking a cigar with Dante, after the other kids drifted away.

I drained another glass of the fruity wine, feeling more and more lightheaded. Through clouds of fragrant smoke, I heard them saying they were going for a ride in the Porsche. "Sean Cassidy is playing, Mama," Miguel said. "Want to come along?"

"Your father got that Porsche for playing in a movie," I said vaguely. *"Ship of Fools,* I think. It wasn't a major role, so he had to be persuaded with a new car."

Dante smiled. "So are you coming with us?"

"I don't think so." I got up, a little unsteady. "I'm going to bed. You kids have fun."

Dante walked me to the foot of the stairs. "You have a terrific family," he said. He kissed me very softly. "Good night, Rosella."

I woke up with smoke in my nostrils, clogging my throat. I heard doors opening, the children coughing and calling out, as I rushed downstairs. Smoke was pouring from the dining room; the candles were still lit on the table, and the table was on fire.

"They left the candles burning!" I shouted as I tore through the sideboard drawers. I whipped out a tablecloth and flung it over the burning table.

"Don't fan it!" Monsita cried from the doorway.

"I'm not," I said. "I'm smothering it." I staggered out into the marble hall and collapsed on a step. "They left the damn candles burning," I said again, and suddenly it seemed like the funniest thing that had happened in our house in a very long time. The girls sank down on the stairs beside me, and we laughed until our eyes watered with smoke and silliness.

"You like him a lot, don't you, Mama?" Maria said.

"Yes," I said. "Yes, I do."

When my father remarried, his wife said that her goal in life was to put all the pieces of his life back together. It was an impossible task—when he died in August 1974, just eight months after Mama, he was a hopelessly broken man. Not because of the length of his life—he was seventy-two—but because of its weight. His daughter Bridget said he was one of the saddest men in the world, burdened with melancholy and regrets. "He kept all your 78s in a big stack by his chair," she told me at his funeral. "He listened to them all day. His favorite song of yours was 'Did Anyone Call?' So I sang that for him sometimes."

Betty had called him two months earlier, on Father's Day. "My mama's gone, and now I want to talk to you, Daddy," she said, crying. When he died, she didn't come to his funeral. "I can't take it, so soon after Mama," she told me on the phone. She sent a blanket of white roses.

Besides Bridget, Daddy had two other children from his second family, Joe and Celeste. Nick kept in touch with them; I had grown so far apart that I scarcely knew them. I asked Nick to put the rosary in Daddy's hands. "I did it for Mama," I told him. All I could think about was my own regret, that I'd known my father so little, when there had surely been things worth knowing. How had this Kentucky boy come to sit around singing Cole Porter instead of country? I couldn't begin to piece his story together; none of us knew enough. Betty's children had never even met him, though he kept pictures of them all on his mantel. A couple of my kids had met him on visits to the Midwest, but only in passing.

It only made me sadder when Bridget told me that he had wanted just as much to know us. His second family had accepted this nostalgia, even encouraged it; his wife would arrange for him to talk on the phone to Mama, and Bridget made it a point to ask him about us. But the only result was that he was never fully present in anyone's life. "Daddy was a holo-gram," Bridget said.

Dante went with me to the funeral at St. Andrew's Church in Milford, Ohio. He hadn't intended to be a pallbearer, but most of Daddy's drink-ing buddies weren't in good enough shape to carry his coffin. So Dante was pressed into service. He took the job seriously, though not without his self-deprecating good humor. "I didn't know him when he was alive," he murmured to me. "I hope I don't drop him now that he's dead."

At the cemetery, as we stood quietly around, Uncle George came over to Bridget. "Your father was a prince among men," he told her. We always remembered that, because so few people ever had anything good to say about Daddy.

I was still working sporadically, in the suburbs, but I didn't mind—that semiobscurity suited me fine. My old friend Merv Griffin had heard about my breakdown and had been inviting me on his TV talk show, but I kept declining. I was scared. I still sounded like a '50s jukebox, though I knew I couldn't coast along forever doing "Come On" and "This Ole House," not even at Holiday Inns. I had fun with what I called my "revenge med-ley": "I Cried for You," "Who's Sorry Now," and "Goody Goody." But as much as the audiences seemed to enjoy it, that bit had a short shelf life. There'd come a time when people wouldn't remember, let alone care, who I was being vengeful about.

But my act was enhanced by my spiffy new road manager. Dante DiPaolo had slipped back into my life as fluidly as he danced. The twenty years since I'd left him in the swimming pool on Maple Drive while I went off to marry another man might have been a fleeting dream—he was still my loving, lovable "Whirlwind." We began seeing one another so often—nearly every day—after that first dinner that within a few months, I sug-gested he move in. And he did.

Not that I intended to marry him. I made sure he knew that. "Once is enough," I told him. "I have no intention of marrying again—*ever.*" He didn't argue the point. In fact, he didn't argue about anything—at first. I would lose my temper over something trivial, scream at him, and he'd just let me rage on, because he didn't want to make me more upset. Slowly but surely, he learned to stand up for himself, to give as good as he got; my children began to call it "The Rose and Dante Show."

I began to wonder how I'd ever been content without him—without his unselfish love. And I wondered how I'd managed without him around the house. He did the kinds of things my mother had done, only better: If we had a plumbing problem, Mama would have called a plumber. Dante would just put on old clothes and fix whatever needed fixing. My friend Ann Rutherford appreciated his practical mix of charms: "He looks great in a tux—and he can cook!" His specialty was spaghetti sauce, which he could whip up in the most makeshift kitchenette in the most downscale motel when we were on the road.

With only a shred of a career left, there wasn't much to guide; I went through a series of managers, some more well-meaning than others. In a misguided attempt to keep current, I was persuaded to make a handful of demo records for Motown, so embarrassing that my friend Michael Feinstein keeps them locked up now, safely out of hearing. Yet even those seem like gems compared with my punk-era video: Wearing big square glasses, I sang "Come On-a My House" while young people in orange mohawk haircuts and black clothing wriggled and writhed around me. All this was seen from the viewpoint of a wino sitting on a curb, looking down between his legs through a sewer grating, watching what he said was a "Party in My Pants."

Maybe that's what made me more receptive when Merv Griffin called again. "I'm not giving up on you," he warned. "I'm not going to let you sit around on your rear end. Why are you hiding out? Get over here and do my show!"

So I went on Merv's show. We chatted about my kids, about being on the road. And as we talked, Merv, God love him, made my breakdown sound like just one of those things. "It's not a brand-new story, is it?" he said casually. "It's happened to the biggest names in the business." When I sang, I got a standing ovation. As people whistled and cheered, I felt very much as I had when I'd stood on the stage at the Steel Pier in Atlantic City, listening to the applause: amazed and delighted and a little dazed. Back then, I'd sung the standards; now, on Merv's show, I sang a new song written by Marilyn and Alan Bergman, more than a little symbolic: "What Are You Doing the Rest of Your Life?"

Merv was a wonderful friend in need. He had me on his show more times than may have been good for his ratings, because he wanted to keep me in view, and because by appearing on TV periodically, I was able to keep up my AFTRA health insurance. Being on Merv's show was a significant step. People saw that I was interested in new material and that I could handle it. It helped me believe I could still have a satisfying life as a performer, making a good living by doing the work I loved. I didn't expect to be a headliner again—I'd plunged too far down for that. But I was confident I could make it again. And I was beginning to think that maybe—just maybe—Betty and I could make it together.

"Dante is a treasure," Betty said. "You know that, don't you?"

"Of course I know that, and don't get any ideas," I warned her. "He's mine. I lost him for twenty years and I'm not about to lose him again."

We were having dinner at Villa Capri, Sinatra's old hangout, just the two of us. Betty had driven down for a Christmas visit that year, 1975, with her daughter Cathi, who'd graduated high school and was intent on a singing career. That left just two kids in high school; I reminded Betty of her promise to leave her husband and start that happy new life. "By the time Cristi's out of school, I'll be back on my feet again," I told her. "Then you and I can really get moving."

I took a sip of my wine. "Bing called me. He asked me to do a benefit with him next March." Bing never talked to me about my breakdown. He was extremely uncomfortable with the idea of mental illness, didn't understand it. Bob Thompson had tried to find Bing when I was in the hospital and had been told Bing was on safari. Then I'd had a three-page letter from Bing in which he said he would pray for me and if there was anything he could do, to let him know. "No big deal, just a St. Patrick's Day bash," I told Betty, "but it'll be good to be onstage with him again. It'll give me some confidence."

"You'll be great," Betty said. "No question." She gave me a steady look. "Drug-free, right?"

"Never again," I said. I meant it. My relapse, if that's what it was, hadn't been deep or prolonged. That was part of the unsettled past now. "Nothing that would interfere with the Clooney Sisters' comeback," I went on. "We can still do it, the way we always planned."

"Well, not quite," she said. "We've had a few detours along the way." If there was a strained note in her voice, I chose not to notice. "Of course, we'll sell out Carnegie Hall," Betty said, laughing.

"Well, maybe not Carnegie," I admitted. "And certainly not with ostrich feathers." I had no more illusions about Carnegie Hall. But I was pretty sure Betty and I could make a decent living, a happy living, singing together in midlevel venues. We'd just need the right manager, some time to tune up, and a little bit of luck. "Maybe we can put the kids in our act," I said.

"Carlos wants to be an actor," Betty said. "He's applying to Carnegie-Mellon. I'm helping him with his dramatic monologue. Pray he gets in."

"I'm hoping none of my kids will want to be actors," I said. "It's just one rejection after another. Now with me—I mean, with us—we can just take our work with us anywhere—put it under our hats and go."

It was pouring rain when we left the restaurant, but we were determined to stop by the Vine Lodge, where we'd stayed with the Tony Pastor band.

The past thirty years had been no kinder to the Vine Lodge than they'd been to me: Its pink stucco walls were chipped and grimy, its little lobby turned shabby.

"Hello, Miss Clooney," the desk clerk said to me in a surprised voice. "Are you sure you're in the right place?"

I told him we'd stayed there once, and I introduced Betty. We took a quick look into the courtyard, where we'd waited to see June Christy in her suede trenchcoat. "It was raining that night, too," Betty said. I wondered if she was thinking what I was thinking: *If I had made other decisions, the clerk would have recognized her, too.*

Driving home, I thought of bringing that up—of talking the whole thing out. Then I decided to let it go for now. In a few years, she'd be coming down from Vegas to be with me for good; we'd have the luxury of time to talk, to heal what needed healing.

"Don't forget," I told her as she and Cathi were leaving.

She laughed. "See you onstage." She drove off with her signature phrase ringing in my ears: "I love you."

———

The *Los Angeles Times* ran a big ad for Bing's concert, and the vast Dorothy Chandler Pavilion sold out. And when I stood in the wings, peeking out at the 3,000-plus crowd, I knew for sure I wouldn't be able to slip in unnoticed amid a parade of singers doing a number or two apiece. I only wished I'd known it sooner, while there was still time to say no.

We were there to celebrate Bing's landmark anniversary, the kickoff of his fiftieth year in show business, and it was so much more than I could handle, I was terrified. I clutched my music in sweaty hands, trying to cram the lyrics into my seething brain. When I felt Bing's hand on my shoulder, I whirled around.

"I don't know this," I hissed. What I really meant was *I don't want to do this,* but my fear focused on the more immediate concern.

"If you're that worried," he said, "take it with you."

I stared. *Take it* with *me?* "I can't do that," I said.

"Why not?" he asked. "Why can't you?" In the midst of the hubbub backstage, minutes to curtain, he was looking into my eyes, genuinely wanting to know my answer.

"I just can't."

He clasped my hands, holding the music, in his own. "You can," he told me. "You can take the piece of paper out there with you." Then he smiled at me and walked past me out onto the stage.

I stood where he'd left me, transfixed by fear tinged with an uneasy hope. A singer was expected to know the music. I couldn't take it onstage with me.

Why can't you?

Why couldn't I? I'd been struggling so long to unlearn my expectations and inhabit a new unconstrained self. The idea that I had to know the music belonged to someone else—to that performer named Rosemary Clooney, whom I had created and who wasn't me at all. The new Rosemary—my real, honest self, freed from outworn expectations—

could take the music onstage, and would, and did. With my music held lightly and easily in my hands, I stepped out of the wings and onto the stage. I smiled. I sang.

Bing's invitation to work with him was a breakthrough both personal and professional, like an apostolic blessing. Once I appeared with him, under his imprimatur, in his major venues, the world began to open up to me again. I'd had good reviews from the anniversary benefit; I began getting offers for more and better work, and I accepted them with confidence. So when Bing asked me to join him on tour that same spring, I was ready for the challenge and the exposure.

We played Vegas, San Francisco, New York—then we crossed the Atlantic to play the London Palladium. I felt that the pieces of my life were shifting and locking into place: Dante was at my side, Miguel was the drummer in my band, doors were opening in my work that I'd feared might be sealed for good. I brought all the children along, except Gabri, on an art scholarship at Pepperdine, who had exams he couldn't miss. At night, when Bing and Kathryn called it a day—they just had corn flakes and went to bed—Dante and I took all the kids out for big spaghetti dinners.

One evening before our show, we were all invited to a small party at Buckingham Palace, where Prince Philip seemed happy to meet us. "It's wonderful that you have your son working here and you have all your children," he said. "It's a very good thing to do. We should talk that over in our family."

Then I saw the Queen of England making her way toward us. *Shake hands and curtsy,* I thought automatically, but both my gloved hands were full: sherry in one hand, purse in the other. At the very last moment I thrust my glass onto a passing waiter's tray and managed a very unstable, totally unrehearsed curtsy.

The Queen was as approachable and amiable as her husband. She and Kathryn and I stood and chatted for a full twenty minutes about our families, our children. Our concerns weren't identical—I worried about my children's choice of career, while the Queen's were born to theirs—but underneath, they were very much alike.

Backstage at the Palladium, I gave myself a moment to remember—not quite regret—the life I'd been living the first time I was here: Dietrich and Coward gossiping in my dressing room, Joe and baby Miguel waiting for me at Harefield on the Colne River. I was a long way from that life now, and yet I couldn't think of it as another life entirely; somehow, by a complex chain of happenings and feelings, that had led to this.

Onstage, I opened my arms and thanked the audience for welcoming me back. Then I introduced the musicians. "The first time I sang here, I was a proud new mother," I said. "My son was three months old, and he missed most of my shows. Tonight Miguel Ferrer is on the drums." I felt a surge of pride and pleasure as the audience cheered.

Just as I'd been remembering Dietrich in my Palladium dressing room, she phoned me in Bing's dressing room. "This is Miss Marlene Dietrich's maid," she said in a low conspiratorial voice. "I must speak to Rosemary Clooney." We hadn't been in touch for years, but I recognized her voice instantly. "Marlene, I know it's you, it's not the maid."

She sounded distraught. "My husband has had a stroke. He is in California. I want you to see that he is being taken care of."

"Marlene, I can't do that," I said. "I'm on tour. I'm appearing with Bing at the Palladium." Still, she called several times, always identifying herself as the maid. In a final call, she told me that her husband had died; she wanted me to fly to California to make sure the burial arrangements were suitable. I didn't try to explain to her how impossible that was. She'd reached a point where that kind of rational discussion wouldn't work. I'd always think of her as my glamorous friend from those promising early days. But she'd gone into seclusion, and we never spoke again.

On the first of August, I opened in Virginia Beach, booked into the Moonraker. When I appeared someplace on my own, Dante sometimes got into the act. "I want to put my irons on," he told me. So he hoofed a little, sang a little, as an opener. Our first night there, he and Miguel and I walked on the beach. I told them about the time Betty and I had played Virginia Beach with Tony Pastor's band. "At the end of the last show," I said, "the boys marched off the bandstand and right into the water."

"They must have been high," Miguel said.

I laughed. Something besides drugs had been at work that night—straight-ahead high spirits, in an almost-forgotten time when spirits could run that high.

"Did you girls walk into the water, too?" Dante asked.

"We did," I said. I didn't tell him that that had been our last night as the Clooney Sisters or that I'd known then I would take the next step on my own. I just told him how Betty and I had held hands and waded into the icy water.

Miguel was the one who got the call two days later. "Mama, Sherman called," he said when I came in. "He wants you to call him back as soon as you can."

When you know something is wrong, your mind runs on ahead, much faster than conscious thought, checking for possibilities, weak points. Even as I dialed Sherman's number, my mind was with the children—especially Maria and Monsita, who were due back that day from a trip to the Soviet Union, Monsita's graduation present. *Dear God, something has happened.*

I didn't want to hear whatever Sherman had to say. But I couldn't have imagined how profoundly it would shock me. "Rosemary," he said, "Betty's had a stroke."

Not Maria, not Monsita—but Betty? The realignment was so sudden and violent that I could hardly grasp it. "What does that mean?" I asked.

It meant a cerebral hemorrhage. It meant she was in danger; in the hospital, being closely monitored. It meant, Sherman said, that maybe I should think about coming to Las Vegas.

But every time I pictured myself getting on a plane, or even leaving the room where the phone was, my stomach lurched with dread. Something might happen to Betty while I was up there, out of reach, out of touch. She might—I knew what lurked under Sherman's careful report—she might die. I wanted someone to tell me what I should do, but no one did. So I stayed where I was, paralyzed by the possibilities. I couldn't risk not knowing whatever there was to know.

More calls, in a melancholy sequence.

To my house, where the girls had just come back from their trip; they would leave again, right away, to be with Betty.

To the Moonraker manager, explaining that I couldn't work that night; I couldn't do anything.

To the hospital, where I grasped at any information I could.

"They're going to operate in the morning to try to relieve the pressure," I told Dante when I hung up.

"Did you find out what happened?"

"She just dropped over," I said, because it really had been that sudden. Betty had been getting ready for her daughter Cari's wedding Saturday, only two days away. She had gone down to the pool to visit with Cari's fiancé's parents, the Learys, just arrived from Oregon. Sitting on a lounge chair with a towel wrapped around her head, talking to Mrs. Leary, she had paused. *Just a minute, Violet. I see a dark cloud passing over my head. I think I'm going to die. Can you get my son Carlos?*

By the time he got to her—and it took just seconds—she had fallen off her chair onto the pool deck, eyes rolled back in her head. *Take care of the baby.*

That night was an agony of waiting, praying for the phone to ring. Lying on the living room floor, with Dante holding me tightly, because the bedroom was too far from the telephone.

In the early morning, a call from Gail. Betty was in surgery. "I'll call you the minute I know anything else."

More waiting, then another call. "There's no point," Gail said in a raw voice. "They couldn't do much, because there were two aneurysms. Betty will probably live another forty-five minutes."

Now the balance had shifted. I wanted the phone gone from my sight; I prayed for it not to ring. Every time I looked at the clock, its hands seemed to be moving faster, ratcheting my sister's life away. I saw the two of us on the riverbank, trailing Aunt Olivette's long dresses in the mud. *We're going on a long trip, and we have to wait by the river till the boat comes. I'll never leave you behind.*

Gail's last call.

Now there was nothing to keep me on the ground. Dante arranged for me to get the next flight out. Once I was on my way, it hit me that if I'd done this a day earlier, I could have seen her alive one more time. Now I never would. As that knowledge began to seep in, I ordered a drink, then another and another, hoping—vainly—to keep it at bay.

Nicky met me at the airport. We didn't speak until we were in the car, driving down the Strip, a gauntlet of neon excess in the glaring light of the cold white desert sun. "My God," he said, "what a ridiculous place to die."

I felt like a woman turned to stone. Later, I wished I had tried harder to help Betty's children, to respond to their grief, but I was too lost in my own. Most of the time, I kept my dark glasses on, as if that thin shield could keep the pain away.

Nick, though, needed to remember Betty actively, aloud. At one point, he found Cathi in her room, just looking out the window. "Oh, come on now," he cried, "have a drink and we'll talk about her! That's what the Irish do."

I heard Carlos say that Betty had called him into her bedroom, about four months before, to tell him she knew she was going to die. "I need you to be strong," she'd said as he wept. "No, I don't want to know this," he protested. "This can't be true."

How had Betty known? Even though her daughter's wedding was just days away, she hadn't bought a dress. When Cari said to her, "Mom, come on. We've got to get your dress," Betty said, "I don't need to get one just now."

"She knew she wasn't going to be here much longer," Cathi said. "She was ready to go." When Cathi was in Beverly Hills the summer before, Gabri had talked to her about recommitting her life to the Lord; when she came home, she told Betty how exciting that was, the idea of having a personal relationship with God. Betty had started going to a charismatic Mass. "It really transformed her life," Cathi said. Before, the bleak periods of depression Betty always fought had overwhelmed her sunny times. "She cried all the time," Nick said. "All the time." But the last year of her life had been incredibly serene. "It was like a garment of heaviness she'd had on was completely removed," Cathi said. "She told me, 'I'm going to go home and be with the Lord.'"

Saturday, meant for Cari's wedding, was Betty's funeral. All the children sang "Going Home." I slipped out halfway through, heading back to the Moonraker for my two shows that night; I'd taken two nights off, and I didn't want the manager, who'd been so understanding, to lose his Saturday night business. It was a step I knew I had to take—the first step of my life without Betty.

I didn't know how I'd ever get used to that. I kept picking up the phone to call her, then realizing she wasn't going to be there. Nick and I were on our own now. I loved him, but I didn't always understand him too well, and he didn't always understand me. Betty had been our conduit, helping us know one another, keeping things smooth. "She's not here to straighten us out anymore," Nick said to me as the hard reality sank in. "We have to do it for each other."

"We'll take those trips," Nick and I promised each other. "A vacation together every year. We won't let anything else get in the way." Betty had left us so suddenly that I could only hope she'd known how important she was to me. With Nick, I made up my mind to do more than hope.

I would be lonely without Betty, I would miss her desperately—I already did—but I would be all right. When Dante and Miguel and I hovered by the phone, just before the end, I had sensed a layer of anxiety beneath their fear for Betty: Would this loss send me spinning into madness again? But my time with Dr. Monke, my years of self-scrutiny and hard, hard work, had strengthened me. I never deluded myself; I never imagined my sister wasn't gone. I grieved for her, but it was normal, rational grief, with a small hard core of acceptance. Less than a month after she died, the *Cincinnati Enquirer* ran a short piece about me under a headline of resilient promise:

CLOONEY AGAIN SINGING
LEARNING HOW TO COPE

I sang. I coped. I taped a television special with Bing in the spring of 1977 at the Ambassador Theater in Pasadena. As we were rehearsing, I thought it seemed like a strange setup: The middle part of the stage could be lowered for the sets to be changed. We went through all the rehearsals; the only thing we didn't rehearse was Bing's last medley. He'd done it so often, he didn't need to run through it—all the songs he'd been associated with, so many hits.

When I finished my part, I took his kids in my car, heading for Patsy D'Amore's restaurant, where we were to meet Kathryn and Bing. We had the radio on when the announcer cut in to say there had been an accident at the Ambassador. Bing Crosby had fallen on the stage. Bing had been rehearsing the close of the medley, saying good night at the apron of the stage. Then he'd turned to walk off; he didn't see that the center part of the stage had been lowered. He just stepped out of the light into the dark.

He spent weeks in the hospital, because he'd fallen twenty feet and ruptured discs. I don't know the full extent of the damage because he wouldn't talk about it. He had a hard time walking, and when we got to England that fall to play the Palladium again, he had to sit on a chair backstage between numbers.

But he'd been bound and determined to make the date. Having discovered the joy of being on the road, he didn't want to pass up any chance. This man who had sold an unbelievable 400 million records was just learning to have a rapport with the people who bought those records, and he was relishing it.

It was a terrific show, an all-family show—I considered myself family—except for a British comic, Ken Rogers, who was hilarious. Bing's only daughter, Mary Frances, did a solo dance. Kathryn sang. Harry played the guitar. I thought Nathaniel was getting short shrift, so I said to Bing, "Let me teach him 'How About You?' I did it with the Hi-Lo's." Bing was so much more relaxed with his second family than with his first, it was as though he had turned into another person. He made an announcement: "Miss Clooney is taking her life in her hands—her career in her hands—because she's going to do a duet with my youngest son, Nathaniel." As I came onstage, Nathaniel said to me, "Are you sure you want to go through with this?" I said yes. Then Nathaniel waved his father away. "Step aside!" he said grandly.

The evening was memorable, the music excellent. Bing and I did our own duet, "On a Slow Boat to China," with its difficult melody and countermelody, and it came off beautifully. Toward the end of the show, for his medley, Bing pared the band down to a small jazz combo, a fine bunch of guys; I got along especially well with the drummer, Jake Hanna. The audience gave Bing a standing ovation. I timed it: three minutes, and that's a long time. Bing didn't seem to know what to do. He'd always had a hard time acknowledging his feelings, even with family and friends. Now thousands of strangers were cheering him so enthusiastically that he had to respond somehow. He held out his arms in a tentative way, then drew them together as though he were folding them, enclosing the audience in his embrace. I saw him mouth the words: *I love you.*

It was a stunning moment. I applauded, too, with tears in my eyes, happy for him, hoping that from now on he could be more open with people, more accepting of them, and of himself.

We didn't talk about it as we went down in the elevator; it was too fragile to talk about. I was heading for my dressing room to change. He never changed at the theater because there'd be such a mass of people waiting backstage; he'd just run for the car. "I guess I won't see you for a while," I said.

"No, you won't," he said. "I'm going to Spain for some serious golf. When I'm home, we'll go to dinner and I'll pay!" He gave me a quick kiss and got off the elevator.

Before I left London, I dropped in to see Ava Gardner. She'd been living in La Moraleja, a suburb of Madrid, when Sinatra told me he was sending her an avocado-green stove and fridge. Then restlessness and tax trouble had brought her to Knightsbridge, where she lived in a spacious apartment overlooking gardens, a very quiet life. Every once in a while she'd see one of her old movies on television. "I think I look more interesting now," she said.

"When Ethel Merman did *Gypsy* on Broadway, I saw her at the Surrey Hotel," I said. "And she told me, 'Honey, don't ever look in a magnifying mirror after you've turned fifty.' "

Ava laughed. "I always wanted to be smart. People thought I was shy, but I was just afraid to open my mouth, because I thought I'd sound stupid. I always wanted to learn stuff."

"Me, too," I said. "That's one of the reasons I married Joe Ferrer."

"When I was married to Artie Shaw, he saw me reading *Forever*

Amber, " Ava said. "He grabbed it and threw it across the room and said he never wanted to see me reading rubbish. Then he married the gal who wrote that book."

I remembered Artie Shaw, too. I'd had one date with him, in my early years in New York; he kept quoting from books he told me I should have read. When I met Betty Kern, Jerome Kern's daughter and one of Artie's ex-wives, I told her that. "Well, I married him," she told me, "and I can assure you he only knew the quotations, not the books."

The afternoon passed in a happy haze as we meandered down a convoluted memory lane. Ava told me she'd been at the Hollywood Palladium when Betty and I sang there with Tony Pastor. Artie Shaw had always cut his own hair to save money; Bogart had been mean to Ava on the set of *The Barefoot Contessa*, but she had to admit he'd improved her acting.

Frank would always be her life's love, even though they couldn't stand to be near one another; they still talked on the phone a lot. Before she married Frank, he'd had a rousing affair with Lana Turner. When Lana ran into Ava in the ladies' room at a restaurant, Lana warned her that Frank had kept promising to divorce his wife and marry her. When he didn't get a divorce, Lana married Artie Shaw, and Ava married Frank.

After Ava and Frank divorced, he'd married Mia Farrow, whose father, John Farrow, had once had an affair with Ava. "My Grandmother Guilfoyle was born a Farrow," I said. "Maybe we're all related."

Bing died on October 14, 1977, the day I arrived home. Nick saw it on the newsroom wire and called me before I could hear it on the radio. Bing had died on the golf course at La Moraleja, which I'd just been talking about with Ava. He dropped dead with a heart attack, having just finished the last hole. He won by one stroke.

I couldn't sleep that night. The newspapers would be filled with essays and editorials about Bing's life and legacy; they wouldn't know, couldn't know, what he had meant to me. I had learned so much about singing from him, and now I owed him my resurrection.

He'd always been withdrawn, even icy, with most people, yet he'd been totally at ease with me, which had greatly aggravated Sinatra. "How can you be so relaxed with him?" he asked me once. "Isn't he so much a part of your life, before you knew him, that he's like a god to you? How can you work with him and talk with him as though he's anybody?" I remember Frank's asking that because it was one of the few times he paid attention to anything I said. "I just pretend he's not Bing Crosby," I answered, because that was how it worked.

My kids and I had blended beautifully with his family. We'd gone down to Baja California once; Gabri had jumped off Bing's cabin cruiser, the *True Love,* when the propeller was turning. He was copying Bing's son Harry, and he got every bit as tough a thrashing as Harry got.

I knew that Bing had been intolerant and judgmental, as reformed playboys and quasi-alcoholics often are. When we played Vegas, it wasn't in a hotel but in a concert hall. Still, there were slot machines in the foyer, which Bing demanded be removed or he'd cancel. "I will not be a shill for gambling," he announced piously. Mary Frances was warned that if she ever slept with a man who was not her husband, she would no longer be welcome at home. When Dante and I visited, he made a point of giving us separate bedrooms. Kathryn said that Bing wrote to Sinatra often, admonishing him for his scandalous behavior.

Sinatra didn't come to the funeral; I don't think he was invited. A great many people were not invited and were shocked that they weren't. But Bing had made it perfectly clear what he wanted. At his first wife's funeral in 1952, there had been an enormous crowd, outside the church and at the cemetery; people had thrown themselves at the grave and altogether her funeral had been horribly out of control. Bing's boys were distraught; Bing had promised, "Never again." He'd left specific instructions about his own funeral: a small service in a Catholic church, as early in the day as possible, as few people as possible.

So Bing's funeral Mass was not at Good Shepherd, but at St. Paul's Chapel in Westwood, at four o'clock in the morning, with only about twenty people. Bob Hope sat in a front row with Dolores, his head bowed, murmuring, "I wasn't ready for this. I had no preparation for this. I didn't know he would go this fast."

In the dimness of the chapel, I watched Kathryn greeting people softly, and I marveled at her strength. Years later, she proved that strength again when two of Bing's sons from his first marriage committed suicide within a year and a half of one another. Lindsay, who'd written me those letters from the set of *Little Boy Lost*, shot himself in the head in December 1989. I was on the road when Dennis shot himself in May 1991. When his funeral was held at Good Shepherd, a friend of his took the pulpit and denounced the woman whom he said had married Bing Crosby and put such a distance between him and his sons that, had it not been for her, Dennis would still be alive. Kathryn sat very still throughout the service. Then she drove to my house, a few blocks away, and only then, Monsita said, did she fall to pieces.

Jimmy Van Heusen once said that when he and his collaborator, Johnny Burke, were writing songs for Bing, they couldn't have a lyric say, overtly, "I love you." Bing couldn't handle that. But he could sing, "If I loved you . . ." Now I'd seen Bing standing on the stage as the Palladium audience cheered; I'd watched him open his arms. What made me especially sad, that morning, was knowing he had just begun to acknowledge his own heart.

Elvis Presley had died just a few weeks before, sparking a national outpouring of grief. Bing was mourned just as intensely and sincerely by his generation of fans, and columns were written about the impact each singer had had on the music scene. It's ironic, and saddening, that more than twenty years later, Elvis is still a presence in the American consciousness, while only aficionados still make an icon of Bing. But in his own way, in his own time, each had changed the face of popular music; on an even larger scale, their styles and personas had shaped popular culture. Each epitomized an era, and the contrast between them—critics said—defined the direction of our changing society. To me, the sheer amount of attention spoke of the power of music to capture the human imagination.

While I sat at Bing's predawn funeral, I was thinking of the work we'd done together, his flights over the wall, the wonderful *Fancy Meeting You Here* that would always be my favorite of all the recordings I'd made. I was greeting Bing's family and friends; I talked with Jake Hanna, the drummer from our tour. But underneath, an intrusive thought of my own future tugged at me. My career had just begun to right itself and move forward with Bing's help. What now? We got to Holy Cross Cemetery just as the sun was coming up. *When the blue of the night meets the gold of the day . . .*

Three days later, Jake Hanna called. "Do you want to make a record?"

Concord Jazz was a new label, a small label, started by a man who wasn't a musician, who just loved music and wanted it to be part of his life. Carl Jefferson, a friend of Jake's, ran a car dealership in Concord, in northern California. He'd been mostly responsible for building the Concord Pavilion, a wonderful venue set up in the hills; it was at the Concord Pavilion that Bing had made his last appearance on an American stage.

"You could really do almost anything you'd want to do," Jake said on the phone. "Just come up and do one record."

Concord was a label on a budget; a big band would be a bank-breaking expense. So I recorded with a small ensemble in a little studio on a side street, with Jake on the drums and Carl Jefferson listening in. It didn't seem strange to be making a record again; I'd recorded some of the pop music of the '70s—James Taylor, Randy Newman—as well as those Motown throwaways. But now I was singing Gershwin again—lyrics and music—and Arthur Freed, and Billy Rose; I sang "Hey There" and "As Time Goes By."

At the end of the session, Carl came over to me. "Would you like to do a record a year, maybe?"

I knew it was a risk—a new label, unproven, unknown—but Concord was taking a risk on me, too. I couldn't afford to be wary of new ventures; I'd run out of old ones. I was almost fifty years old. If I was going to reinvent myself, now was the time to do it, and this—I hoped—was a way to start.

Silently, I thanked Bing. *You stuck around long enough to see me on my way.* Then I shook Carl's hand; that was the only contract we'd ever have or need. "Sure," I said.

In my fiftieth year, Concord released the debut album of my new career: *Everything's Coming Up Rosie.* The cover was a drawing of me reclining in a wicker chaise, surrounded by roses almost as big as my head. Carl Jefferson asked Tony Bennett for a blurb to use in the liner notes. My friend may have overstated for old times' sake, but his one-word response gave me great hope for the future:

"Perfect."

FOURTEEN

*N*ever rub two girl singers together," Nelson Riddle once said, referring to the contretemps between Judy Garland and me over his arrangement of "Come Rain or Come Shine." I wondered whether Four Girls Four would mean double the trouble.

In the fall of 1977, I was invited to join a new act with a couple of singers, Margaret Whiting and Barbara McNair, and a singer-comedienne, Rose Marie. I wasn't delighted at the ad line—"A musical Mount Rushmore"—but I was intrigued at the idea: a quartet of women of a certain age strutting their stuff.

"We're stars, and we will dress like stars," Margaret declared. So we were sequined and beaded within an inch of our middle-aged lives. Barbara bowed out early, replaced by another singer from big-band days, Helen O'Connell. Our lineup settled into a comfortable rhythm, with the overture blending our signature tunes: Helen's "Tangerine," Margaret's "Moonlight in Vermont," "Rose-Marie" for Rose Marie, and "Come On-a My House" for me. Then the announcer called out: "Ladies and gentlemen, Miss Margaret Whiting!" Helen followed, surprising the audience with her unexpected edge of humor. After intermission, Rose Marie's comic turn kept the mood going; then, when the crowd was ready for someone who just sang, I stepped up to close. For a finale, we all burst onto the stage arm in arm, belting out "Side by Side." As our onstage rapport blossomed, so did our patter. Somebody would cock an eye at Margaret, who'd drifted over to flirt with the band, and crack, "Look at her! This is how she gets a date!"

I still felt tentative about performing, but the setup was perfect—it didn't lay too much responsibility on any one performer. There was a synergy at work, making up an energetic whole that really was more than the sum of its parts. Maybe people thought that with four for the price of one, they were getting a hell of a deal. Maybe they just wanted to hear our kind of music or take a look at us to see how the years had treated us. Maybe it was changing tastes or just nostalgia for a time and a way of life that we represented in our presence and in our songs. "If I'd known I was going to be part of an era," Helen said wryly, "I would have paid more attention."

For whatever reason—maybe all of the above—people paid attention now. On our opening night at the Beverly Doheny, a little movie house converted to live theater, the audience went wild, rushing up to the stage to reach out to us. We made the front page of the *Los Angeles Times*. When our week at the Beverly Doheny sold out, we played three weeks at the Huntington Hartford Theater in Hollywood, then went on the road: Dallas, Omaha, Salt Lake City, Chautauqua, the East Coast. Our reviews were heartwarming. "These are all contemporary performers," a critic wrote in *The New York Times*, "not just because their repertoires include contemporary songs, but because each one is singing better now than when she first made her name. The show has an immediacy that manages to make the past a relevant part of the present."

Recording for Concord, along with Four Girls Four, was a marvelous opportunity to keep up with the musical times while retaining the best of the past. I wanted my records to keep alive what was sparkling and sophisticated in the material of an earlier era, so I made a series of tribute albums in my early years with Concord: *Rosie Sings Bing;* a collection of Billie Holiday tunes on *Here's to My Lady; Rosemary Clooney Sings the Lyrics of Ira Gershwin,* with Ira's deadpan postscript to his liner note: "I loved every word!"

But when I recorded *With Love,* I blended songs by Billy Joel, Neil Sedaka, and Melissa Manchester with the Rodgers and Hammerstein, the Comden and Green; I sang "Tenderly," but also "Come in from the Rain" and "Just the Way You Are." In the late '50s, I'd made a snide, possibly defensive crack about the new phenomenon of rock 'n' roll: "I don't think much of the people—did I say people?—who sing to the kids these days—did I say sing?" But since then I'd been exposed to contemporary music in the most organic way possible: When my children played it on their record players while they were growing up, it blended with the ambient sounds of our everyday lives. Then, on tour with Bing, I'd brought in new material: Paul Simon's "Fifty Ways to Leave Your Lover," which always got a laugh from the audience. *Just drop off the key, Lee, and get yourself free.*

I'd met Margaret Whiting practically a lifetime ago, when we were both young singers plugging records in New York. Like me, she was a natural singer; unlike me, she came from a background of professional, not just occasional, music—a sophisticated, casually star-studded milieu. Her father was Richard Whiting, who'd worked with Chevalier and Hammerstein, written "Sleepytime Gal" and "Beyond the Blue Horizon." Their house was filled with music and musicians, from George Gershwin to Rachmaninoff, Stravinsky to Sigmund Romberg. She was eating linguine with Skitch Henderson, Sinatra, and Jimmy Van Heusen when Frank announced his plans to leave Tommy Dorsey and go out on his own. She was on a golf course with Johnny Mercer and Harold Arlen when Mercer said, "I've had this idea of starting a record company"—and Capitol was born.

Margaret cut one of the label's first singles, her father's "My Ideal"— her first record and her first million-seller. She introduced "Come Rain or Come Shine" and "It Might as Well Be Spring," and heard Walter Gross play "Tenderly" on the piano before it even had lyrics. She helped get it published, but she never recorded it. "I don't know why I let it get away from me," she said ruefully.

She was always upbeat, able to get a laugh when you'd least expect it. One night at intermission, we heard that a lady in the audience had had a heart attack. "God, isn't that awful," we were saying when Margaret chimed in, "At least she got to hear *me.*"

Rose Marie had been a child star with a woman's contralto; she had her own NBC radio show when she was five. "I had the same voice then that I do now, and people would write in and say, 'She's not a child; she's a midget,' " Rose Marie told us. "So NBC sent me on a fifty-two-week tour to prove I was a child." She laughed. "My father was arrested 138 times in Cleveland. After each show, they would arrest him because of the child labor laws, then they'd work something out and I'd do the second show, then they'd arrest him again."

By the time we joined up for Four Girls Four, she'd had a whole career in television: variety shows, game shows, sitcoms, three Emmy nominations as Sally Rogers on "The Dick Van Dyke Show." Her comic timing was dead-on, and her impression of Jimmy Durante brought down the house. By example and exhortation, she encouraged the rest of us to liven up our acts. "Don't just say, 'Now here's a song by Cole Porter, whom I love,' " she said. "Who cares? Tell a joke, or talk about your family, or something." To my surprise, I found it was easier than I'd expected; I was more and more relaxed onstage, less concerned with living up to anyone's image of me. I'd taken Bing's lesson to heart: When I sang "Just the Way You Are" on a cable TV special, I didn't panic when I forgot some of the words. I just sang what came into my head, the closest I could come. "Billy Joel never wrote that verse," I confided to the audience afterward. "I wrote that. Just now. Tonight!"

"We're like a circus family," Margaret would say of our tour. "Friends, children, lovers, agents—everybody passes through." Miguel played drums in our band for a while; Maria traveled with us briefly, and so did Monsita. Four Girls Four was flourishing. When we played the Midwest in the summer of 1982, we'd already had five successful years on the road. That summer, Nick's son George drove us from place to place. We called his maroon Monte Carlo "the Danger Car."

Dante was always with me. The other girls loved the way he'd pop up to help us all off the stage, even if it was just one step down. When Rose Marie needed medicine, he went out to get it in the middle of the night. When we traveled, sometimes by bus, more often in an RV with beds and couches, he'd schlep the big black trash bags we'd filled with ice—forty pounds—and bottles of beer. When I had a taste for spaghetti, he'd cook up a potful, toss a salad, and call everyone into our room to be fed. They asked me if I knew how lucky I was that I had someone so loving and funny in my life. I told them I knew.

Once in a while, Margaret and I went out by ourselves. Over martinis, we'd talk about work and life on the road; it was a little like traveling with Betty, sitting up late to talk over the show and our plans and dreams. Except Margaret and I often seemed to have more to say about what had been than about what might be. "Let's call Joe," I said to her more than once. "Let's just call him."

"What will we say?" she asked.

"We are two singers sitting here thinking of you."

Margaret and I never did call Joe during one of those sessions. But sometimes he called me at home. The children could always tell when I was talking to their father, they said, because of the way I sat and the way I sounded. I would be in his big leather chair in the den, my feet up on the ottoman, ankles crossed. "I can tell in a second," Monsita said. "You're so animated, laughing, like a little girl."

From the children, I gathered that Joe's wife resented the role I'd played in his life and the profound—if flawed—connection we'd forged. Joe and I never discussed that. Maria told me that once when she was visiting them, Joe had taken her aside. "He said to me, 'I need her,' " Maria told me. "He didn't say, 'I love her'; he said, 'I need her.' "

When Joe and his wife moved to Florida, he became artistic director of the Coconut Grove Playhouse. He named his price: a salary of one dollar a year, "because I'm going to do what I want to do." He didn't want the board to be able to say, "We're paying you all this money, now do things our way." Miguel and Rafi worked with him there from time to time. To my dismay, both of them had acting in their Ferrer blood. Miguel directed a production of *When You Comin' Back, Red Ryder?;* Rafi played Joe's son in *Life with Father,* with Kim Hunter playing his mother. They appeared together in one episode of "Miami Vice"—Rafi shot Miguel dead, which he found very cathartic. I figured that should save him several years of therapy.

To Nick's dismay, there was acting in the Clooney blood, too. His son George had worked with Joe, Miguel, and Rafi in *And They're Off,* an obscure movie shot in Lexington—so obscure that it was never released—and decided on an acting career. "Stay in school until you get a degree," Nick urged him. "Then you'll always have something to fall back on." Nick made no more headway with his son than I had with mine. "If I have something to fall back on, I may quit before I should," George told Nick. He drove the Danger Car to Beverly Hills with $300 in his pocket and settled into one of the back rooms in my house, having reasoned it out: "I can't sing like my Aunt Rosemary, and I'm not smart enough to be a journalist like my father, so I want something that doesn't take much talent or much smarts. Acting!"

From my earliest times with Joe, I'd seen how fickle a world the theater could be, especially the American theater. If Joe had been born in Europe, he would have earned the respect accorded there to fine actors, classical actors; here, he was vastly underappreciated. As time went on, he was forced to take on some projects that were sadly beneath him, cheap horror films like *Dracula's Dog*.

My relationship with Joe was on and off after we split for good, swinging from tension and bitterness to friendliness and fellowship, then back. When I appeared at Michael's Pub in New York in the spring of 1986, he booked a table for opening night. He didn't show up. But he was there another night, and we had our picture taken together. I was pleased to be able to introduce him from the stage: "I would like you to meet the father of my five children and the most brilliant actor in the world."

I was doing some brilliant acting of my own. Georgia-Pacific had polled shoppers in supermarkets across the country, giving them a list of fifteen familiar names and a question: *WHO WOULD YOU MOST BELIEVE? WHO WOULD YOU TRUST?* And the answer came back: *ROSEMARY CLOONEY*. So they put me in television spots for Coronet paper towels and bathroom tissue. Maria got her own Screen Actors Guild card so she could appear in them with me. Sometimes we filmed at the studio, sometimes at the house; at $100,000 a shoot, I was willing to be a little flexible. And for a number of years, Georgia-Pacific turned into a nice annuity. *Extra value is what you get when you buy Coronet!*

Trust had posed a knotty problem in my life at times and had caused me considerable pain. Maybe it was finally working itself out. Bing had helped me to see I could trust myself, my own instincts, as a performer; now it seemed I'd become a very figurehead of trust. But that wasn't such a stunning irony, after all. I'd been considered right for the Coronet commercials because I was someone consumers could understand, even identify with—I was the image of the girl next door. I wasn't that girl in the bloom of youth anymore; I'd been addicted to drugs, gotten a divorce, gained a lot of weight. All those things happen to the girl next door, too.

In the fall of 1953, Sheilah Graham noted in her column that in the two months since my marriage, I'd put on a few pounds. In 1998, a reviewer called me "dangerously overweight." So my weight has been a matter of public concern for nearly half a century.

My publicity people responded to Graham with a seven-day diet plan, sent to newspapers under my byline. The fabricated sermonizing, reminiscent of "How You Can Win Your Man," began: "My first year of marriage has taught me that the role of homemaker is far more complex than many people are willing to admit. The fact that I am continuing my singing and acting career does not, I believe, allow me to assume that I can overlook the major housewifely duties. So, although my life is a busy one, I consider it my responsibility to create a real home atmosphere."

That atmosphere was fed by two diets, one to prevent me from gaining, and one to keep Joe, with his overdrive energy, from losing. Breakfast for me was supposed to be ½ banana, ⅔ cup wheat flakes, 1 cup skim milk and coffee. For Joe, an entire banana, a whole cup of wheat flakes with milk and sugar, two waffles with butter and syrup. My midmorning snack was a cup of skim milk; his was eggnog. My bedtime snack was another cup of skim milk; his was a cup of chocolate milk and a piece of cake.

That 1,200-calorie diet—Joe's was three times as much—had nothing to do with real life. I'd kept trim without dieting throughout my married life. Then I'd begun to gain weight during therapy. At first, the excess weight was a kind of retreat for me, a cushion between me and the pressures of life and work. "I literally ate my way out of show business," I oversimplified to a magazine writer a few years after my breakdown. "I retired into that fat person. She was safe."

When I didn't need that cushion anymore, the rationale dissolved, but the weight stayed. I lost pounds, then they crept back. Cortisone injections for my throat exacerbated the problem. I became adjusted to my added weight, and I made some choices. I'd stopped smoking; I didn't want to start again. I just wanted to be comfortable. Other people may not be comfortable with my weight, and I'm not always comfortable with it, but most of the time I am.

When Four Girls Four was at its peak, we toured forty weeks out of fifty-two. Margaret had the grandest visions for us—she wrestled us into coordinating costumes, pushed for publicity, talked of television and even Broadway. I was mostly concerned with giving the audience the best possible performance of the music I knew they wanted to hear. When a reviewer wrote that he was sorry to see something in my performance he'd never known me to have, a slickness that reminded him of a Vegas act, I believed him. We had just come from three weeks at the Sands in Tahoe, playing to transient gambling audiences with none of the feeling of a city house. "You're absolutely right," I wrote to the reviewer. "I was doing easy things." I always make it a point to read reviews, even when I'm pretty sure they're going to be good, because I can always learn something from them.

I grew close to Rose Marie and to Margaret, even through the usual frictions of life on the road. Only Helen O'Connell rubbed me the wrong way, as I did her. Oddly, she and I had the most in common: She'd left high school without a diploma to sing with a big band and had spent four years on the road in Jimmy Dorsey's band bus. In the late '50s, she'd turned to television, as I had, appearing with my old flame Dave Garroway on "Today." She'd had her own bout with emotional problems. "I knew I should see a psychiatrist when I found myself walking very close to buildings and timing my steps to the corner so I'd be in synch with the traffic light," she said. We even had the same birthday. But though she was seven years older than I, she looked seven years younger; she'd always been extraordinarily beautiful.

She had a lot of anger—and I'd learned that anger was a perfectly valid human emotion. But she had a tendency to vent it on people who couldn't fight back: a wardrobe person or someone in the wings. Remembering how Dr. Monke had emphasized the importance of expressing my feelings—and knowing very well the danger of bottling them up—I told Helen how vicious I thought she was being. "I don't want to be part of this show if you're going to leave broken bodies along the way."

The other girls had problems with Helen, too, but she could be disarmingly apologetic when she knew she'd gone too far. She'd go over to Margaret or Rose Marie, then she'd take their hands in both of hers and say, "Let's start over. Let's take it from the top." I would warn them, "Don't do it. It's going to happen again!" But of course it was easier to keep the peace—or what passed for peace.

Not even the best will in the world could have kept Rose Marie and Margaret and me from clashing on occasion. Once, when we were playing Reno, we were asked to keep the show short, because the management didn't want to keep the audience away from gambling too long. Margaret and Helen timed themselves carefully to twenty minutes, but Rose Marie went on and on. I stood in the wings, fuming. *Doesn't she realize I'll have to cut my act short to make up for her overrun?* I knew she was notoriously hard to get off the stage, and I accepted her explanation: that her comic material, keyed to the audience's reactions, required a more flexible approach to timing than our straight music. But at that moment, I thought it was the height of rudeness. When she introduced me, I told her so, right onstage, in front of the band and a packed house. "You did twenty-eight minutes," I informed her.

She stared at me. "And they were great," she said. Then she walked off.

I felt bad when I realized how much I'd upset her. But that didn't keep me from blowing up again, for no real reason, at Margaret. "Why do you wrinkle up your nose when you're working with me?"

"I don't think I do," she said, baffled.

"Oh yes you do," I said.

"Then I'll try never to do it again," she promised.

Rose Marie thought she could shed some light on my inner workings, why I could get so angry so suddenly. "It's because you're a Gemini," she explained. "You're two people." She was a firm believer in astrology; one of her managers functioned as a kind of psychic adviser. I'd heard the same kind of instant analysis from Dietrich and her friends, where sometimes I thought that the line between astrology and superstition seemed blurred. Noel Coward insisted that when two nuns were traveling together, the plane was practically bound to crash on takeoff.

But when we got along, it was grand. We giggled like sorority sisters at a pajama party the night Margaret received a gift from her new beau, actor Jack Wrangler: he'd sent her an 8 x 10 glossy of himself, along with a big can of Magic Nuts. After a show, we'd go out in the small hours for what Rose Marie called "night lunch"; when our shows ran especially long, Margaret called it "dawn dinner."

Although we didn't have a complete band in our luggage, we had a terrific bandleader, Frankie Ortega, who was also Rose Marie's conductor. Since we didn't travel with a full complement of musicians, the bandleader would have to do the best he could with a strange band. Frankie was able to come into a town, take the players—part-timers, schoolteachers, whoever was available—and get them to play really well, beyond themselves.

I'd met Jerry White, the drummer who traveled with us, a few years earlier, and we'd become good friends. Sometimes he conducted the band and showed how capable he was at handling anything that came along. More than once he found himself with a piano player who didn't know his ass from third base, who'd just play a chord and leave me out there. But Jerry didn't explode over it, so I didn't, either. We just got together for cheeseburgers after the show and turned the air blue with our complaints about the guy.

Jerry had worked with Chet Atkins, whom I remembered as the early-morning country singer on WLW in Cincinnati. I didn't see any problem with Jerry's crossover; I'd made an album of Hank Williams songs, even had my own country hit with "Half as Much." To me, there's no difference between country music and any other kind. Good musicians are good musicians. So there's no change when you get south of the Mason-Dixon line. I've always liked the idea that my music can cut across genre lines.

More than one black musician has said to me, "We thought you were black because your records were played on black stations." And Jerry was a natural for Four Girls Four. He appreciated the way our different acts and contrary personalities sparked the show. "This is the best thing I ever did," he'd say. "It's a trip to work with four strong women who know how to sing."

Sometimes it was a trip; sometimes it was chaos. We had all the encumbrances of a performer on tour, multiplied several times—luggage, schedules, travel arrangements—and each of us had a manager to throw into the mix, ostensibly to organize it all. "This is like four managers four," Margaret complained. Rose Marie agreed. "We're going in like amateurs. We need a road manager." In typical take-charge fashion, she got us one.

Allen Sviridoff came highly recommended from a theater manager Rose Marie knew in New York. He was very bright, great at organization, terrific at lighting. So what if any one of us was old enough to be his mother? We flew him in to see our show in Phoenix, and afterward, I cooked shrimp in an electric skillet while everybody grilled Allen.

He'd gotten his start when he met the actress Mitzi Gaynor at a Connecticut theater where he was in a summer workshop. "All the other kids wanted to be on the stage—I wanted to put the program together and promote the show." Working his way up with Mitzi, from assistant production stage manager to sound engineer to production stage manager, he ended up with Ginger Roger's tour, eventually managing all her concert business.

Allen was a slight young man, with an intensity that gave him presence and made him seem older than he was. When Ginger somehow learned his age, she said, "I don't want a twenty-four-year-old child handling my business." Allen summoned his considerable, bespectacled dignity. "Ginger, I assure you, there is not a twenty-four-year-old *child* handling your business."

When he got our call, he was with Ginger in Buenos Aires. "I hated every minute of it," he said. "It's still military rule—guys on the streets with machine guns." A show scheduled for eight o'clock might not start until ten or midnight, or whenever the honchos who'd paid $150 a seat showed up. "A very different way of working," Allen said dryly. "The promoter said to us, 'I'd like you to stay another week.' I said we couldn't. Well, they were holding our passports and our airline tickets. So he said, 'I would LIKE you to stay another WEEK.'"

He had sat down with Ginger and explained the situation. "I think I should make a great deal, for a great deal more money, and if they're willing to pay it, we'll stay."

"I like this guy," Rose Marie said. "Let's keep him."

Allen laughed. "I had never done this kind of business transaction before," he said. "Argentina was charging a 100 percent tax on money leaving the country, so if they wired the money ahead for our bank to put in escrow, the way it's usually done, they'd essentially be paying double. So instead of paying us that way, the promoter sent the money to New York as shoes." We must have looked puzzled. "Shoes," Allen repeated. "He said, 'I'm sending $100,000 worth of shoes to New York.' And somehow, when it got to New York, it was turned into funds."

Allen started as our road manager a few weeks later in Lake Tahoe. The rest of us had been a little reluctant to take him on—another salary to pay—but Rose Marie was right: Now, with Allen in charge, we were going in like professionals. When we all met at the airport, he was there to take care of the luggage; when we landed, two limos met us at the curb. At the hotel, everything was seen to, bellboys tipped, our luggage brought to our rooms. It was something like the way of life, and the way of working, I'd been accustomed to; it was well worth the added expense, especially since we were splitting it. And we could afford it: our rate, about $20,000 a week for the four of us when we started, was close to $60,000 a week now.

My manager had a mantra: "Don't worry about it." That was his answer to most every question: logistical, artistic, financial. I'd been taking him at his word, as I'd always done with the people who handled my career. When you've got five kids, a show coming up, trying to get on the next plane, when do you have time to check on what the manager is doing?

But Allen had time. And he let me know it was time to start worrying. He told me that my manager, who sometimes handled the booking for all of us, had been double-contracting, writing one contract for the venue and one for the girls. If the venue contract said $15,000 and ours said $10,000, my manager kept the difference. He'd even taken deposits from venues that should have come straight to me, and he'd simply pocketed them. I was shocked at the gall and at the enormity of the betrayal.

So were the other girls. At the Westbury Music Fair, in a backstage blowup that wiped all our petty disagreements off the map, we raged and railed while the hapless house manager kept putting his head in. "Half an hour," he said hopefully.

"There will be no show tonight!" one of the girls exclaimed, full of righteous outrage.

Shortly he was back. "Fifteen minutes," he said doubtfully.

"Never!"

Then we heard the overture starting. Margaret rose majestically from her chair. "I am going out and *perform.*" She did her twenty minutes, wondering if any of us would follow her. When she finished, Helen was waiting in the wings. The show did go on.

Maybe my manager and I could have worked out our differences, but I didn't want to try. I'd had enough experience with broken trust. I asked Allen if he would be interested in handling my business. He was practically handling it already, taking care of nearly everything but the booking, and he'd grown close to me and my family, so he agreed. "But we have to be sure there's one thing that's a constant between us," he said. "That we're honest with each other. Because that's what will make the relationship work."

Rose Marie left in the summer of 1981, and Martha Raye took her place. Margaret peeled off not long afterward. I cried at her last performance, though she and I were booked for a show together only a few weeks later. "Hey, come on," she said, "it's not a long goodbye!"

Martha Raye didn't stick with us long. Singer-comedienne Kaye Ballard, who'd launched her career in New York shortly before I did at the Blue Angel, came in to replace her. Kay Starr, who'd been vocalist with Charlie Barnet's band, stepped in for Margaret. We played the last voyage of the *Rotterdam*, an eleven-day cruise, Los Angeles to Honolulu to Hong Kong, ten days of cruising and one day of work. In Hong Kong, we stayed on for a few days at the Regent Hotel, which was owned by a friend of Kay's husband: marble-and-glass suites at a rock-bottom rate, a stretch Mercedes to take us around town. The last time I'd been in the Far East, I was unraveling, about to fly to pieces; now I was delighted to go back, well and sane. And I fully appreciated the chance to do it in style. Rose Marie used to say, "Do you realize how lucky we are to have a show like this, success like this, at this stage of our lives?" It wasn't entirely luck; the early reviews had said we were all singing better now than when we started out. But I did realize my good fortune, and I enjoyed it.

I enjoyed it so much that in 1983, when Allen suggested I go out on my own, I hesitated. In six years, Four Girls Four had taken me from dreary clubs in the sticks to something resembling my early success, with all its luscious perks. True, the show seemed to be diminishing; in theaters where we'd once done a sold-out week, now we played one night to a partial house. But it was still a comfortable, reasonably profitable package. On my own, how much better could I realistically do? I had just one date booked on my own, for $7,500.

"I have something to confess, Rose," Allen told me. "When I came to work with Four Girls, I'd never heard of Rosemary Clooney. I didn't have a clue. Now I am absolutely convinced that within ten years, you could be in the legendary category—like Sinatra, like Ella." It had been a long time since anyone had had such boundless faith in me, including myself. So Allen Sviridoff became my personal manager. No paperwork, just a handshake. Allen got off to a fast start when he latched on to a music insider in New York, Hal Webman. Hal had been a critic at *Billboard*, a regular at Manie Sachs's gin games at the Hampshire House. He began digging on my behalf and began finding the money I'd been screwed out of. I was glad to have Hal on my side; he knew all there was to know about the intricacies of musical accounting and some things that people weren't supposed to know.

Through sheer persistence, Allen persuaded the agency that handled Tony Bennett to take me on as a client. Then I came under the guidance of Roger Vorce, who'd trained under Lew Wasserman at MCA. Lew's motto had been purely pragmatic: Don't judge 'em, book 'em. So very quickly, Roger booked me on a TV movie, *Sister Margaret and the Saturday Night Ladies*.

Perhaps not coincidentally, the characters I've played in the handful of TV movies I've made have been very angry. In an early piece, *The Losers*, with Lee Marvin and Keenan Wynn, I was truly angry at Marvin, who wouldn't take no for an answer offscreen. "You take one more step toward

me and I'll put this knife through you!" I screamed at him once. Sam Peckinpah used that anger for my role as Melissa, a girl badly scarred from an
accident. As harsh as the movie was, Sam was surprisingly gentle. I was
beginning to be interested in Nelson Riddle, so when Sam asked me out
for a drink, I declined. That Christmas Eve, he left a gift at my door: a
beautiful Mexican pottery dove, with a card: FOR MELISSA.

In *Sister Margaret,* I played Sarah Burlington, an ex-con who'd murdered her husband. I wasn't the star of that 1986 piece; in alphabetical
order, I was number four in a supporting cast of nine. I was paid just
$8,000 for the part, which is what Sinatra was paid for his comeback role
in *From Here to Eternity.* Not that my movie was up for any awards: Sarah
said things like "It never would have happened if I hadn't gotten sick."
But I was delighted to have the national exposure, to show the world that
I was vertical and breathing.

And even the eight grand came in handy. My days of letting other
people handle my affairs—of looking only at the backs of checks—were
coming back to haunt me. I'd always assumed somebody else would take
care of taxes for me, and when nobody did, the Feds began billing me for
back taxes, penalties, and interest—altogether, about $600,000.

When I confessed this to Allen, he had a ready solution. "Sell the
Vlaminck."

"Oh, I can't do that, Allen," I told him. I explained that Joe had given
me the painting for Mother's Day three decades ago, when I was pregnant
with Maria—that it was much more than a painting to me, it was a treasured symbol of my marriage, of my faith and my hopes.

"Sell the Vlaminck," Allen said.

I stood in my living room, looking up at the painting. I'd always loved
the way the darkened sky in the background changed in the foreground,
casting light on the houses and the people. I simply couldn't sell this tangible expression, this proof of an early love.

But I couldn't declare bankruptcy, either. A perfectly legal option, I'd
been told, but not an acceptable one for me. What would Papa Clooney
say? After I thought about it a while and cried about it a while longer, I
told Allen to call Sotheby's.

As difficult as it was to see the Vlaminck go, it was also liberating. It
freed me from unnecessary yearning, from the uselessness of outworn

sentiment. I still had all the good memories—and I still had all the black Wedgwood.

～

"You have a reputation for canceling shows, for making all kinds of excuses," Allen told me bluntly. "With Four Girls Four, you had the others depending on you, so you couldn't back out of things. It's very important, now that you're on your own, to prove that you're dependable all by yourself." He knew I couldn't fill big commercial venues, not yet. So he began booking me for charity events: no money, just goodwill. And it worked. The more we played a city, the more seats we filled, and the more producers saw how much the audiences liked me. But the most important event for me was an annual benefit we called "Singers' Salute to the Songwriter," with proceeds going to a charity very close to home: the Betty Clooney Foundation for Persons with Brain Injury.

My cousin Phyllis and her husband Sherman—who'd been my savior at the time of my great flip-out—were directly involved. Their beautiful young daughter Sandi was about to enroll in medical school when she was hurt in a waterskiing accident. We began to raise funds for a post-treatment facility, a daytime center for brain-injured people, who otherwise might just sit home and watch soap operas, even if they were capable of a great deal more. Not just busy work: The center has exercise classes, cooking classes, workshops to tune up communication skills, a remarkable garden, potting benches high enough to accommodate wheelchairs.

When people wondered how I persuaded high-priced performers—Linda Ronstadt, Melissa Manchester, Martin Short—to perform for free, I explained my formula: "I just go to them and beg." Beginning in 1986, I begged for eight years as we saluted writers from Jerome Kern to Barry Mann and Cynthia Weil, bringing together old and new friends and colleagues: Peter Matz, Beverly D'Angelo, Bob Hope, Lucie Arnaz. The Singers' Salutes to the Songwriter were amazingly successful—one year we raised half a million dollars at the packed Dorothy Chandler Pavilion. That year's Salute was a family affair, with Nick as master of ceremonies; my daughter-in-law Debby Boone sang, and so did my niece Cathi,

Betty's daughter. Cathi and I had great fun doing a number Betty and I used to sing together, "The Coffee Song."

The Betty Clooney Center in Long Beach, where Phyllis and Sherman live, opened on Betty's birthday, April 12, 1988. It was a way of distilling something worthwhile from her death, of keeping her name and spirit alive. I still think about my sister all the time—every day of my life. Nick and I have kept our promise to her, and to each other, to take the trips we always planned. Nick and Nina, Dante and I have made it a point to go someplace every year, starting when we really couldn't afford it. Sometimes Allen and his wife and other good friends—Roger Vorce; my Hampshire House roommate Jackie Sherman, now Jackie Rose, and her husband Bob—have gone with us.

We've gone to Singapore, checked in at Raffles, where Dante and I slept in the Somerset Maugham suite, Nick and Nina in the Rudyard Kipling. Under the ceiling fans in the bar, we drank Singapore Slings and nearly perished in the heat; as kids, we hadn't noticed that Singapore is only eighty-two miles from the equator.

We've taken the Orient Express from Paris to Venice, singing at the piano in the club car, seeing sunrise over the Alps. At the Bauer-Grunewald Hotel, elegant beyond our attic dreams—gilt and damask and inlaid wood—Nick and Nina and Dante and I each took a penthouse suite. "Nothing's too good for Betty," Nick declared.

We sat on the balcony on a soft June night, the moon shining down on the Grand Canal. "You went out and slew the dragons for us, Rose," Nick said. "Your daring and courage showed me I could stretch. Without you, I would have found a much easier way of going."

I looked at my brother. "Well, I thank you, Nicky," I said. "But I have to tell you, an easier way sounds pretty good to me now."

He didn't look at me. "The good news is, our dreams can come true," he said. "The bad news is, our dreams can come true."

FIFTEEN

$\mathscr{C}$arnegie Hall had always been one of those reachable stars. The dream that Betty and I had held so long came true on October 12, 1991. Only I was sixty-three years old, and I was a solo act.

"I'm always making a comeback," Billie Holiday once said. "But nobody ever tells me where I've been." I'd stood on the Carnegie stage before, taking part in tributes to other people; to help celebrate Irving Berlin's one-hundredth birthday, three years earlier, I'd sung "White Christmas" and "Count Your Blessings." Now, for the first time, I was there as a headliner. As I rode down to stage level in the enormous elevator built to hold a concert grand, I wasn't coming back from anywhere, except perhaps an interior exile.

I'd planned my program as a tribute to the talents behind the tunes: the arrangers. Nelson had helped me understand just how short their end of the stick could be; his son Chris played bass trombone with me that night. Arrangers, Nelson said, "devote their lives to ennobling the efforts of songwriters"—and get only a flat fee, no royalties, no nothing. In the early '40s, when he worked for Charlie Spivak, then Les Elgart, bandleaders known for their lead trumpets, his flat fee was $5.00 per arrangement, $7.50 if he copied out all the parts. Later, his rates rose; he was paid $4.00 a page for "Mona Lisa," which Nat Cole used so many times, Nelson figured it worked out to a penny a play.

I'd seen very little of Nelson in the past years. Our paths had crossed only rarely, in professional contexts. I knew his second marriage was not a happy one. In a three-hour interview on public radio in 1985, a retrospective of his extensive career, he'd sounded so forlorn, so resigned to a sadness I couldn't fathom, that I ached for him. He talked about me a little. "I still haven't lost the feeling for her," he said, knowing I would be listening. "I've lived two or three miles from her for decades, and I never make the trip, and I'm not about to. I remember; that's all that's important. We cannot help each other at this point." Whether he was right or wrong, we had no chance to find out. He died of cardiac and kidney failure not long after that interview, sixty-four years old, with all his children around him.

He had never stopped being appreciated—treasured, really—by the people who played and sang his work. But he had slipped out of the musical mainstream as times and tastes changed. At one low point, a twenty-six-year-old executive said to him—to *Nelson Riddle*—"So what have you done?" But then he'd won an Oscar for his score of the film *The Great Gatsby,* and a collaboration with Linda Ronstadt drew him back into public view. Their first album together sold more than three and a half million copies, making it the third-bestselling album of the year, and the second sold more than one and a half million. They had just finished work on the third when Nelson died.

I heard the news on the radio. I called Jonathan Schwartz, son of the composer Arthur Schwartz, because he'd been close to Nelson, and I wanted to talk. Talking crystallized what was most worth remembering, like the elegant way Jonathan summed up Nelson's gift for innovative orchestration. "He wrote music the way I thought it," Jonathan said, "as though he were putting down, in his language, what my inner life felt like. It was about the melody for the individual voice, the minority voice, the out-of-step voice being heard."

It comforted us both to know that Nelson, whose life had turned so bleak in middle age, had lived to see a renewal of admiration for his work. At a wonderful party Jonathan gave in Manhattan, friends and fans from every field—theater, television, music—had gathered to celebrate the renaissance. "I wanted faces that Nelson would recognize to pay tribute to him," Jonathan said. "I wanted him to see how widespread the devotion was." The stereo, with speakers wired to every room, pounded out Sinatra's live performance of "I've Got You Under My Skin," with his ad-lib opening: "Nelson Riddle's finest hour!" When it was over, all the famous faces turned and gave Nelson a standing ovation.

The whole point of a road is that it doesn't end. It stretches from a past we can't change to a future we don't know. Nick wrote that liner note for *Still on the Road.* Back when Allen Sviridoff laid out his ten-year plan for me, I knew he couldn't really see that far down the road; I was happy to concentrate on tomorrow, and maybe next week. But Allen had it right. A little less than ten years after he took up with a middle-aged girl singer with one $7,500 job lined up, I found myself booked into the very pinnacle of New York City glamour and prestige, high above the lights of midtown.

Rainbow and Stars—the brand-new supper club arm of the venerable Rainbow Room, sixty-five floors above Rockefeller Center—was full to its 120-person capacity for my opening in February 1990. My musicians had already squeezed their way among the tight-packed tables to the tiny stage, right up against a wall of windows. At the edge of the room, I waited in the near-dark, tense. Bismarck Irving, the maître d', creamy-black and devastatingly elegant, closed the door softly behind me. His John Lennon eyeglasses glinted as he smiled at me. There was no turning back now.

Ladies and gentlemen, Rosemary Clooney. Then the applause, filling the small space as Dante escorted me to the stage.

"I wish I could just start on the second night," I confided to the audience between songs. I meant it—and it got a laugh—but I knew this opening night was going well. I was relaxed enough to turn around while the guys were taking a chorus and enjoy the view: the dark park, the lights, framed by the two rivers converging at the northern tip of Manhattan, with a faint overlay of reflected faces from inside.

The audience was having fun, enjoying the Art Deco sheen of the place, the cigarette girl, the star-shaped spangles scattered over each table like fallout from a fantasy. The people were so close I could have touched them; singing to them was like talking to a handful of friends at home. I happen to think the mystique of the cabaret scene is overblown—cabaret just means you're singing in a small joint. But that can feel very, very nice. Singing at Rainbow did feel nice for nine years in a row. I was sorry when it closed in 1998. But I know that somewhere there must be another glittering rooftop with city lights and a starry-eyed girl singer.

And whether I'm appearing before 120 people in a small joint, or 17,000 at the Hollywood Bowl, singing has taken on once more the feeling of joy I had when I first started to sing, when I had no other responsibility except to sing well. It's wonderful to rediscover that heady experience of being in the middle of the music and doing what you want to do and having such a kick doing it.

I've just about talked Rafi into singing with me sometime. He lives in New York, and whenever I'm in town, we make a pasta pilgrimage to Patsy's, where Joey Scognamillo and his family run the place so successfully that their pasta sauces are now sold in upscale markets. We celebrated Dante's seventieth birthday there in 1996. I sang "My Funny Valentine" to him—and I was delighted to be in a position to pay my bill. Rafi's wife Heather was a criminal barrister in London when they met; Dante and I flew to Belfast for their wedding. Rafi's in great demand for voiceover work—his first big job was for Miller beer, then came DeBeers diamonds, a flu remedy, and, most recently, the voice of "Mr. Pencil" on HBO. Once, when he called me during the day, I asked why he wasn't working. "But I *am* working, Mama," he told me. "Just turn on television."

Like Rafi, Miguel was never deterred from acting by my misgivings. He's always made a good living as a working actor—something only a tiny percentage of Screen Actors Guild members are able to do. Leilani, his wife, is also an actor; she appeared with Miguel in a film, *The Harvest*, featuring Miguel's full frontal nudity. I didn't see the picture; I haven't seen Miguel that way since he was six months old. A few years ago, Miguel audited an acting class that Uta Hagen, Joe's first wife, was teaching. She stopped the class early; like Phyllis Hill, she was upset at seeing Miguel. "I couldn't continue," she admitted to him. "You look too much like Joe."

Gabri was five years old when Joe directed Pat Boone in a remake of the musical *State Fair*. Gabri grew up to marry Pat's daughter Debby, who's sung with me at some of my performances. When Debby signed for her first television special, she wanted Edith Head to design her wardrobe; Edith had retired, so I called her at home. "I have a big favor to ask you, darling," I began. "I know you're not working anymore, but I need something special." Edith interrupted. "Don't tell me you're pregnant again!"

Just as his brothers followed in their father's acting footsteps, Gabri has inherited Joe's talent for painting. His work has been exhibited often, including at Lincoln Center. He's the assistant rector of All Saints Episcopal Church in Beverly Hills, where he preaches sermons that manage to be both funny and profound. And he has absolutely no compunction about "borrowing" lines from my act to use in them.

When Linda Ronstadt sent me the last album she'd done with Nelson, she included a note. "Because you are one of the singers who created this vocal style, I don't know if you understand what it was like as a rock 'n' roll singer to be up to my knees in such brilliant lyrics and subtle melodic nuances. After twenty years of singing 'Ooh-loppa-doo,' as much as I like rock 'n' roll, it was like finding an oasis in the desert."

When she came to dinner, I knew at once we'd be close friends. She brought the former governor of California, Jerry Brown; we talked for hours at the dining room table about being Catholic, our work, politics, music. Linda had appeared on Nick's TV show in Cincinnati, putting her rock career together, the same year I was falling apart. She told him she felt she'd arrived in the Velveeta Belt; when she got home, Nick sent her a big block of Velveeta, a jar of mayo, and a loaf of white bread.

"Nelson talked about you," she told me, putting her hand over mine. "At Radio City, we were so nervous we held hands backstage, and he showed me his cuff links. 'Rosemary gave them to me,' he said. 'I always wear them on important occasions, for good luck.' "

Given Linda's success as a rock 'n' roll performer, I wondered what appeal my kind of music had for her. When she explained, I understood. "I come from a different culture, so I have a different view of the material," she said. "I want to sing not just the ingenue stuff, the courtship stuff, but the kind of music you do—the cumulative impact of your life."

More and more, I felt that was what I was doing: not just singing a song, but singing my life. The focus of my yearly albums had begun to shift. I'd made a series of tributes to songwriters—Cole Porter, Harold Arlen, Irving Berlin, Jimmy Van Heusen, Johnny Mercer, Rodgers, Hart, and Hammerstein—but now I was putting together records with themes that resonated with my own history.

Do You Miss New York? "Me, too," I told the microphone in a near-whisper. *Still on the Road* relived my travels and the road tradition, highlighted by "Let's Get Away from It All." *Dedicated to Nelson* spoke for itself. Released in my fiftieth year as a performer, *Demi-Centennial* spanned it all. On *Girl Singer*, "Straighten Up and Fly Right" included an excerpt from the recording made at WLW when Betty and I auditioned in the spring of 1945. Tony Bennett did the cover, a pen-and-ink sketch of me onstage, microphone in one hand, the other extended toward the audience—signed, as always, BENEDETTO. And I added a note: "This album is dedicated to Dante, my last love, for all his kindnesses." I was able to make records like that because I'd earned a freedom, an artistic authority, that I'd never dared to imagine. Now I picked songs, and the arranger said to me, "How do you want it? How do you see it?" Nobody ever asked me that at the beginning of my career.

Gradually I assembled a fine group of musicians whose interests and talents dovetailed with mine. My old friend Gene Cipriano, whom I hadn't seen since Tony Pastor days, played saxophone on several of my recordings. And I met new men: Warren Vaché, a highly trained and skilled horn player, and tenor sax man Scott Hamilton, less formally schooled but phenomenally intuitive—one of the finest musicians I've ever worked with.

I got to know my musical director, conductor, and arranger John Oddo in 1983 when I made my first Concord album backed by a big band: *My Buddy*, with Woody Herman's orchestra. I'd met John briefly when I went to hear Woody at Fat Tuesday's; now he impressed me as an excellent accompanist and a good jazz player, polite and very reserved. We ran over the music together in about forty-five minutes before each recording session—not much time, but enough, because we clicked right away.

John was a rigorously schooled musician, too; when I heard he'd gotten his master's degree from the Eastman School of Music, I raised an eyebrow, remembering another alumnus, Mitch Miller. But Mitch had been the best thing that could have happened to me in that particular place and time—why not John now?

In the finest Kentucky tradition, I'm blessed with a family of strong women. When I made my *Mothers and Daughters* album in 1997, I wanted to use the language of music to convey to them all how important they are to me. I sang Billie Holiday's "God Bless the Child," Irving Berlin's "Always." From a 1954 recording, we retrieved my duet with Betty, the irrepressible "Sisters"—I kept picturing Bing and Danny with their blue feather fans. I sang "Baby Mine" and, as a duet with Keith Carradine, the achingly poignant "Turn Around."

The women in my life contributed their words and their portraits to the liner notes: my daughters-in-law, my three granddaughters, my sister Gail, my sister-in-law Nina, and my own two daughters. When I recorded "Maria" for the album, of course I sang it for my first-born daughter. She lives on a ranch in the hills of Santa Ynez, where she breeds and trains fine Arabian horses. Early on, she'd studied acting at Catholic University, and appeared in a Dino De Laurentiis film, *Fighting Back*. But her main artistic interest was in design; self-taught, she's licensed belts, ties, shoes, and scarves all over the world. Gail is happily married to Chris Darley, son of Dick Darley, who directed my television show.

With Monsita, I share the defining experience of being a mother. She had just finished high school when Terry Botwick—now a vice president of CBS—knelt on the floor before me and asked my permission to marry her. "I will give you my permission," I said, "if you wait one year from this day." Monsita went off to Skidmore College; exactly one year later, she reminded me of my promise. I know Monsita considers it her most important work in life to keep her marriage strong and her children's lives whole and happy; I respect her deeply for that and admire her success. I was moved when she wrote of me in the *Mothers and Daughters* notes: "She is a warrior for her children, fearless and relentless. Always in our corner, always on our side, and always, always there."

Nina and Nick moved to Augusta, Kentucky, in 1974. After years of moving wherever Nick's radio and TV career took him, they wanted a home, and they found it in a perfect Andy Hardy house with a shady back-yard and a porch swing. Augusta is a tiny town, population 1,400—a storybook river town halfway between Cincinnati and Maysville, so picturesque that the television miniseries *Huckleberry Finn* was filmed there. Nina's served on the Augusta town council; when she ran for mayor in 1998, she lost by fifteen votes. An unnecessary loss, I told her. "With our big family, we could have *mailed* in fifteen votes." Their daughter Ada and her husband, Norman Zeidler, live not far away, in Petersburg, Kentucky—another little river town—with their children, Allison and Nicholas.

Nina and Nick bought a parcel of land across the street from the elementary school and dedicated it as George Marshall Park, with benches and flowers and a graven honor roll, named for the World War II general whose parents came from Augusta. "This is for those kids," Nick said in his dedication speech, pointing at the school, "so they will know what happened."

Nick is still on television, as a host on American Movie Classics, his days of chatting with veteran actors like Thomas Mitchell and Walter Abel coming in very handy. He writes a column for the *Cincinnati Post* on whatever he chooses to write about, from the ethical intricacies of the death penalty to his efforts to dissuade his son George from following a show business career.

Happily, those efforts were not successful. George treated acting like a profession, nothing more—but nothing less—and that perspective gave him staying power. After ten years of going to classes, taking small parts in small projects, persistently showing up, he found his own superstar niche as Dr. Doug Ross on NBC's hit series "ER." We've never sat down and talked about it, but George says he's been helped by watching me, learning the things I had to learn firsthand, often painfully. Not to be seduced or overwhelmed by early success. Not to be devastated when success starts to ebb—not to believe people when they say you don't have it anymore, because you believed them when they said you *did*. And to always, always keep control of your checkbook.

⌒

For the Duration summed up an experience both devastating and unifying. Thinking of the old Zenith crackling with the inescapable news, I sang the old songs: "The White Cliffs of Dover," "I'll Be Seeing You." On the cover, Uncle George grins winningly under his jaunty pilot's cap. I remember how he laughed when Betty and I were frightened of our first plane ride. *At least nobody's shooting at us!*

Uncle George had tremendous promise. He'd been a war hero, dated Miss America, seemed poised to make it big in some interesting way. But he never did. He'd gotten heavily involved in horse racing, first as a breeder and trainer—raising Thoroughbreds with names like Jamboree Jones, after a Johnny Mercer tune—then as a kind of track Gypsy, drifting around without much aim. One spring Miguel and my nephew George went to River Downs racetrack in Ohio and picked Uncle George up out of the tack room, where he'd been sleeping over the winter, unkempt and unwell. They cared for him, got him back together, and took him to Augusta; Nick and Nina found him a place of his own, where he settled in for the duration.

His little house, comfortably ramshackle, had been knocked off its foundation in the flood of 1937—the flood that ruined Papa Clooney's store—and it had been put back askew, so that everything inside was slanted. Nick called it "the Popeye house," and Uncle George loved it. He loved Nina's cooking, too, especially her chocolate pie. He would call her and say, "My taster is set for . . ." and whatever he said, she would cook. I saw him whenever I was in Kentucky, but he never wanted to talk about what had happened in the past, so we never did.

On the day that Nina drove him to the hospital, they stopped for a bite at Caproni's, right by the railroad station in Maysville, and sat at a table where he could watch the river. He ate hardly anything. "I'm a little off my feed," he said. On the hospital gurney, he was still wearing his porkpie hat and black shoes, trying to keep everyone's spirits up. "I'm going to be okay—I got on my dancing shoes!"

He was dying of cancer. He drifted in and out of consciousness as family members came. George was sitting with him, holding his hand, when Uncle George opened his eyes and said very clearly, "What a waste." George thought he might have meant his smoking, but something broader, too—the idea that his life hadn't been successful, that his time hadn't been put to good use. George would have liked to tell him that it wasn't true, that he was leaving a legacy of warmth and fun to the children. He'd always been a wonderful storyteller, a magnet for kids. All our children—Nick's, Betty's, mine—had spent summers with him, unforgettable times around horses and jockeys, the farm and the track.

He was obviously in great distress, and everybody knew he wouldn't have wanted to linger that way. But the nurse said she wasn't allowed to give him any more morphine. "It would slow his breathing, and it's already slowed enough." Then the doctor came in—a young man with understanding enough to grasp the situation and deal with it. He explained how the morphine drip worked, then left. "I'll see you guys later." That evening, Uncle George's breathing slowed to a stop. He was sixty-eight years old.

After we buried him in St. Patrick's cemetery, I walked among the stones. *Well, hello, Aunt Ann, Grandma and Grandpa, Uncle Chick. Hello, Mama.* Her full name was etched there: MARIE FRANCES STONE, MARCH 25, 1909–DECEMBER 13, 1973.

We had placed a stone here in memory of Betty. But she is buried in Las Vegas, where her children live. I've kept our big brown dime-store scrapbook:

THE CLOONEY SISTERS
OUR LIFE WITH TONY PASTOR'S ORCHESTRA
JULY '46 TO ?

No ending date.

I remembered how hard Betty had worked with Carlos on his dramatic monologue when he was applying to Carnegie-Mellon. "Pray he gets in," she'd asked me, and he got the acceptance letter just two weeks after Betty died. But she had asked him to take care of his youngest sister—the last thing she'd ever ask, the last words he'd ever hear from her—and he felt he couldn't keep that promise if he went away to school.

He and Cathi and Cari and Cristina have all made Las Vegas their home, and stayed wonderfully close. There's a cul-de-sac on the edge of the city with six houses on it; four of them belong to Betty's children and their families, a little Clooney compound. I know Betty would be proud and glad of their closeness and of the bright, warm people they've grown to be. We always knew the sibling relationship was the one that would stick.

Monsita and Terry have three boys: Nathaniel, Harry, and Theodore. Miguel and Leilani have two: Rafael and Lukas. Gabri and Debby's son Jordan, my oldest grandchild, is in college; their daughters, Dustin, Gabrielle, and Tessa Rose, wrote me loving messages that grace the *Mothers and Daughters* notes. They call me Grammy, and they call Dante Papa, as I called my father's father, Papa Clooney. They're crazy about Dante, although some of the younger ones seemed confused about our household setup. "Are you sure Papa's your *roommate?*"

He's taught the younger ones to tap-dance, the older ones to do what is now called swing. "If I worked out, Ann Miller and I could still knock your socks off," Dante says. "I'd have to darken my hair, though." My old pal Merv Griffin has opened a new Coconut Club at his Beverly Hilton Hotel. "It's all back, exactly what we used to do," Merv said. "Only we called it jitterbug. Sing with the band—the kids are out there dancing, mixing with the older people—it's the most wonderful crossover of demographics you've ever seen." As *The New York Times* confirmed recently: With swing dancers, "there is absolutely no pattern or stereotype of race, age, sex, dress, or affectation."

Every Sunday, when I'm in town, the Beverly Hills house is the gathering place for my kids, their kids, and assorted friends. The house is too big for me now, takes too much maintenance, and is too filled with memories for me to move. Dante's T-Bird and my Corvette are still side by side, parked in the garage. The olive tree has a touch of crown rot, but Dante's determined to keep it alive. The little camellia bush that Dr. Shulman gave me when I was trying so hard to become pregnant now brushes the second-story window. "The August tree" blooms faithfully, on schedule. The Isolette that Joe donated to celebrate Gabri's life is still in use at St. John's.

Gavin de Becker tells me that his work with me, as a seventeen-year-old road manager, helped him forge his dynamic career in safety issues and logistics for public figures, heading a 100-person consulting firm that advises the CIA and the United States Supreme Court. The Vine Lodge is still open for business, $128.99 a week. Father O'Reilly is now Monsignor O'Reilly in Oak Park; I often think of what he said about the woman at the well, who was healed—not cured, but healed—and went out to tell the village what she had experienced so that others might be helped, too. I go to Mass at St. Patrick's Cathedral when I'm in New York and talk with Cardinal O'Connor. I'm back in the fold to stay—I say the Act of Contrition a lot!

Dante has formed easy relationships with my children, because he knew how to be their friend without trying to replace their father. The kids appreciated that; they always kept in touch with Joe. Rafi was with him on his birthday in 1992, just three weeks before he died.

It was typical of Joe to refuse to let illness keep him from his work. He wouldn't admit that there was any need to slow down, let alone take time for treatment. He'd been looking forward to appearing in *Conversations with My Father* with Judd Hirsch on Broadway; he was still rehearsing a week before his death from prostate cancer on January 26, 1992.

The children went to Joe's funeral in Florida. His wife had told his friends all around the country and the world that the cremation would take place at exactly 5:15 P.M. Eastern standard time, so they could have Joe in their thoughts then and know they were sharing in that central moment. So Rafi knocked on the plain pine casket the way the stage manager knocks on a dressing room door, and gave Joe his call: "Fifteen minutes, Mr. Ferrer."

I was invited to Joe's funeral, but I didn't want to go. Instead, I sat all afternoon in the den in his burgundy leather chair. *How do you separate the present from the past?* Friends came, unasked, one after the other. Nobody had to say a thing. They understood. They knew. *A little place no one can see, a tiny part, deep in my heart, that stays in love with you.*

◯⟋⟍

I've come to a point in my life when the awards are piling up. When I learned I was to receive the Smithsonian Medal, I laughed. "You know what this means, don't you?" I said to a friend. "They think the banshees are wailing." On "ER," I played a woman with Alzheimer's who could only communicate in song. I was nominated for an Emmy in 1995, but I didn't win. George didn't win, either.

When I was given the Ella Lifetime Achievement Award by the Society of Singers in 1998, Patti Page came to sing with me; I'm not mad at her anymore. Debby Boone wore the black velvet dress Edith Head made for me nearly forty years ago when I opened at the Copa. "If I looked as good in black velvet as you do," Liberace said to me that long ago night, "I'd never have to wear spangles."

I've brushed the silver screen again, with songs on two movie soundtracks—"Mambo Italiano" bouncing along under the opening credits of *Married to the Mob*, "Fools Rush In" for *Midnight in the Garden of Good and Evil*. In July 1998, *Life* did a layout from the book *Shooting Stars: Favorite Photos Taken by Classic Celebrities*. The photo Joe took of me in Maidenhead—pregnant with Gabri, eyeing an uninvolved swan—got a full page.

My early work is getting a new hearing: *Blue Rose* has been reissued, and the Reprise label has brought back *Love*. Even "Come On-a My House" is still on the air—most recently, in a Target ad for holiday homeware. I never liked to think that lightweight tune was the hallmark of my career. But Nat Cole helped me past that block. At one of the dinner parties Joe and I gave, I'd asked Nat to sing "That's My Girl," and he said, "Sure, I'll do it," but I noticed he was not too happy about it.

"Listen," I said, "don't do it if you don't want to. Don't you like it?"

He said, "It doesn't matter whether I like it or not. It's your memory, and I respect that, and I'll do it for you as well as I can." So when I sing "Come On," it's no longer a song I like or dislike—it's somebody's memory, summer of '51, on some beach somewhere—it's a part of their youth that they're remembering.

A little perspective can work wonders on a piece of music. Sometimes it's not the material that's changed, but the context. A young woman came up to me after a recent concert in which I'd sung "Don't Fence Me In." Very earnestly, she said, "I didn't know Cole Porter wrote a feminist song!" I was glad she'd never heard "Without Love." *What is a woman? A zero in a void.*

My albums have even started to top the charts again. *A White Christmas* was number one on the Billboard chart in 1996, *Mothers and Daughters* in 1997.

My name keeps turning up for a Grammy award in the Traditional Pop category. In 1992, I was nominated for *Girl Singer.* Tony Bennett won.

In 1993, I was nominated for *Do You Miss New York?* Tony Bennett won.

In 1996, I was nominated for *Dedicated to Nelson.* Tony Bennett won.

In 1997, I was nominated for *Mothers and Daughters.* Tony Bennett won.

In the summer of 1997, our annual family trip in honor of Betty took us on a cruise of the Greek islands, then to Rome. For the Pope's weekly outdoor audience, I dressed in what seemed appropriately modest attire: long-sleeved black wool dress, kerchief, black flat-heeled shoes. Dante wore a baggy black suit. Nick said we looked like a couple of fifteenth-century peasants trudging down from the hills.

As we waited in line to meet the Pope, under the merciless midsummer sun, I was wilting in my long-sleeved black wool. I'd been right about the color, though: the woman ahead of me wore black—crisp, cool linen, just to the knee, sleeveless, with a light shawl to throw over her shoulders in the Pope's presence. She carried an armful of yellow roses to give to him. Just as she moved on, and I stepped up to greet the Pope, he sneezed.

Not a small sneeze, but a full-fledged, high-profile *ah-CHOO!* As some-one handed him a handkerchief, I blurted out, without thinking, "God bless you." The Pope wiped his nose and smiled at me. "No, no," he said. "*I* bless *you.*"

After the trip, we went to Kentucky with Nick and Nina. We visited Blanchie Mae Chambers, still living on a steep little street leading down to the river, still my best friend; she'd become active in All Saints Episcopal Church in Maysville, with a devout, engrossing spiritual life, and she always came to see me when I was singing nearby. When her mother died, Nick gave the eulogy. He talked about the kind and gracious lady Miss Lizzie had been, about the influence she'd had on those who knew her. "She taught us that friendship has no color."

We shopped at Traxel's, the jewelry store in Maysville around the cor-ner from Papa Clooney's old shop, where they're still using the work-bench he'd said he wanted them to have when he was gone. I bought Tessa Rose a pretty birthstone ring, and Dante bought me an emerald ring encir-cled with diamonds, from the estate collection. I liked thinking someone had once worn it happily.

That night we had dinner at Caproni's with Nick and Nina and sev-eral friends, including Blanchie Mae. "Is that an engagement ring?" some-one asked lightly.

I looked at Dante. He looked right back. "Well, is it?" he asked.

There was only one possible answer. This time it was also the right answer.

"Yes," I said.

⌣

Whoever said Catholicism was all sackcloth and ashes? I flew the pastor of St. Patrick's Church in Maysville to New York in October 1997. I booked him into a suite at the Surrey, where he heard my confession, then came to my show at Rainbow and Stars.

I married Dante DiPaolo on November 7 at St. Patrick's in Maysville. "We're doing it for the grandchildren," we explained. When people won-dered why I hadn't married in New York or Beverly Hills, I wondered why they would think I'd marry anywhere except my hometown church.

As a kid, on the way home from school, I'd sometimes stop in for a while—I found a kind of peace there, without even knowing what I was looking for.

I wore dark green velvet; my attendants were my grandchildren. I may have been the only sixty-nine-year-old bride with an eleven-year-old maid of honor. Our wedding turned into a reunion of family and far-flung friends: all my children; Bob and Dolores Hope; Bismarck Irving from Rainbow and Stars; Michael Feinstein; Jackie Rose with her daughter Kathy, from Vermont; Ann Rutherford, who still lives near me in Beverly Hills. Aunt Jeanne was too sick to come from San Diego, but Uncle Roy came, with my cousin Michael; my cousins Pat and Joe Breslin and Tom Anderson; Uncle William and his wife Phyllis from Florida. Ron and Phyllis Shaw from Connecticut, where Ron is the CEO of Pilot Pens—he sends an annual contribution to the Betty Clooney Center, along with all the pens we can use. He said the Olympia Theater, renamed, was still standing in Miami: NO HELLS OR DAMNS IN YOUR ACT PLEASE. My wedding cake came from Magee's; along with elaborate dishes at the reception, there was a tableful of White Castle burgers—still called sliders, no longer three for a quarter.

At my Christmas show in Atlantic City that year, I caught up with another old friend, Stan Weiss of Tony Pastor days, and his wife Jeannette. "Remember that show with fifteen acts, mostly monkeys?" Stan groaned. "And, ah, Montreal—oceans of chicks winking at us like they all had dust in their eyes."

Dean Martin once said to me, "You know, I'm getting to the point where I have more friends on the other side than here." I thought of that when Stan told me that Sy Berger, whom I'd once loved, had just died.

I thought of it when I sang at Dean's funeral in 1995. Peter Matz and I got to the little chapel early, to check out the piano; Edie and Lew Wasserman were already there, sitting quietly in the dimness. Shirley MacLaine gave a funny talk: "I was just speaking to Dean . . ." I was very fond of Dean, though I never belonged to the Rat Pack. Sammy Davis was always a little touchy with me, and I never knew why. But Dean was one of the sweetest, funniest men I knew. I felt very close to him without it being for a moment romantic—it was Jerry Lewis, not Dean, who'd chased me around the Paramount lot.

I thought of it when I lost two friends from my Paramount days. Danny Kaye had worked hard for UNICEF for years; I saw him last on "The Merv Griffin Show," when Danny conducted the audience in "We Wish You a Merry Christmas." My *Red Garters* pal Guy Mitchell had stayed a happy singing cowboy; he was living with his wife Betty on a ranch in Nevada when he died in the summer of 1999.

I thought of it when Ira Gershwin died. When I saw the ambulance outside Ira's house, I called Michael Feinstein, who'd been working with him on his archives. Michael sat in my living room and played "Our Love Is Here to Stay" on the Steinway in the Gershwin spot. He hadn't been able to release any emotion over Ira's death, but now, as he played, he cried. I held him tight. "From now on," I told him, "you're my sixth child."

And I thought of it when Dietrich died. She'd always told her daughter, Maria Riva, "I leave you the truth." So Maria's book about her mother was straightforward and candid, especially about Dietrich's bisexual romances. I told Maria I was surprised that, considering the time Dietrich and I had spent alone together, she'd never made a pass at me. Maria said she wasn't surprised. "My mother was a perfect gentleman."

My brand-new husband and I spent a marvelous family Christmas at home in Beverly Hills, the tree in the marble entrance hall extending to the ceiling, just as it did when the children were small, lined up on the stairs on Christmas morning. I was happier than I'd been for a long time. I was married to a wonderful man who loved me for myself. I had the faith of my childhood restored. I was enjoying my work as I hadn't enjoyed it since the very beginning; I was booked at Carnegie Hall on February 11, 1998. The New Year was brimming with promise.

At first, nobody took it seriously. Just a low-grade fever, some bronchial thing. But to sing poorly at Carnegie was never an option. On February 9, Allen announced a postponement.

Gabri was in New York both for the Carnegie evening and to plan an exhibit of his artwork in the fall. On Friday the 13th, the day he was to fly home, Allen called him. "Your mother's not feeling well," he said in deliberately calming understatement. "She's seeing the doctor this afternoon. Better wait around, see what the doctor says, take a later flight."

Even when Dante called an ambulance to take me to Lenox Hill Hospital, nobody was greatly worried. I had a temperature of 101, obviously some kind of infection. At the hotel, I'd been shaky and a little incoherent; Dante hadn't wanted to wait for my doctor's appointment. But when I was admitted to the hospital, it was into a regular room, not an emergency.

Then, on Saturday, Valentine's Day, my temperature began creeping up. I'd been breathing on my own, but by midnight my fever had spiked to 107; I was put on a ventilator, placed under an ice blanket, and moved to intensive care. A spinal tap showed viral meningitis that had reached the brain: encephalitis. "This is as serious as it gets," the doctor told Gabri. "There's nothing we can give her to fix it. All we can do now is give her body the best chance we can to heal itself. The next forty-eight hours will tell the tale."

For me, those hours were easy and painless, because I was unconscious. For my family, they were a nightmare. Dante stayed at the hospital until someone forced him to go back to the hotel and get some sleep. Nick and Nina came. Rafi and Heather came at once, along with Gabri and friends Deborah Grace Winer and her sister Jessica; their father had been a cardiologist at Lenox Hill for forty-two years, so they were closely linked to the medical community there. My children in California got phone calls on Sunday at two o'clock in the morning. Monsita was so paralyzed by the news that not only wouldn't she leave the house all day, she wouldn't let the children leave the house, or watch TV, or turn on the radio. I was struck by her reaction, so much like my immobilizing fear for Betty when she lay dying. Monsita just kept thinking, *Is the phone going to ring? Is the phone going to ring? If the phone rings, it means Mama died.*

My nephew George called the hospital to find out how I was. They don't give out information on a patient's condition over the phone, but George was persistent. He said to the nurse, "Do you recognize my voice?" Yes, she did. "Ma'am," he said, "I just need to know what I should do. If I got on a plane tomorrow, would that be too late?"

"I'm not allowed to tell you her condition," the nurse insisted.

"Okay," George said. "I'm asking you, if I got on a plane tomorrow, would you think that would be too late?"

And the nurse said, "I would be almost positive that that would be too late."

The signature song on my seventieth birthday album is "The Secret of Life." Never have I found a lyric more meaningful than I do now, with that song. *The secret of life is enjoying the passage of time . . . isn't it a lovely ride?* I read someplace that the only thing we can give back to God is gratitude. Not just for major gifts—a life saved—but for small things. Gratitude for an ordinary day. It's impossible to be grateful and unhappy at the same time.

I was on the brink for about two days and two nights. My family had been allowed into the ICU to see me, wearing masks and gloves, while I lingered on. When I began to awaken, sometime on Monday, I was still on a ventilator, still in some strange mental place—I saw Harry Crosby at the foot of my bed and told him to put out his cigarette. Then, sometime on Tuesday, I came fully awake, looked around me, and asked the classic question: "Where am I?"

Just before I went home two weeks later, my doctor came in and spoke in a low sheepish tone. "We're not supposed to ask this," he said, "but— I wonder—did you see a white light? A long tunnel, maybe, and a white light?"

"No, I didn't," I said. "But I'll tell you what I did see. I saw myself standing on a stage, winning the Grammy. And the prize was handed to me by Tony Bennett. And not just one Tony Bennett, but fourteen or fifteen Tony Bennetts, standing in a semicircle."

I wasn't making it up. I really did have that Grammy dream, and I told that story to the real Tony Bennett three months later when he came to Rainbow and Stars for my seventieth birthday party. Again, all my children showed up, along with Nick and Nina and some very dear friends, including Carol Burnett and Beverly D'Angelo with Al Pacino. Harry Crosby played the guitar, with his amazing mother beaming at him.

Amazing because Kathryn Crosby had just come back from seven months in Siberia, where she played in *The Lion in Winter* at the Red Torch Theater in Novosibirsk, without knowing the language, having memorized the script *phonetically*. Dolores Hope sang "It Had to Be You."

Tony Bennett let loose with "Who's Got the Last Laugh?" Considering my Lenox Hill adventure, I figured I did.

Then the cake was carried in, blazing with candles. HAPPY BIRTH-DAY!

I thought of wishing that everything would be perfect in my life, all conflicts settled, all issues resolved. But that's not a realistic wish, maybe not even a worthwhile one. Maria says that everything that's happened in our lives has made her stronger, convinced she can handle absolutely anything that comes along. Maybe that kind of knowing is better than perfect. Maybe the secret of life—of my life, anyway—is learning to live with unresolved issues. Maybe there's only one way I can do that: not with an armored heart, but with an awakened heart.

"I am 108 days late," I told my audience at Carnegie Hall. It was June 1, 1998—Nelson's birthday—and I was determined to prove whatever might have needed proving.

I carried the lyrics to the songs onstage with me, without being the least bit embarrassed. I sang Nick's song "It Happened to Happen to Me," which embarrasses him, but I sing it anyway. I sang with my regular combo, then I did four numbers with the Count Basie Orchestra. It was like old times, those crazy trumpeters with their beat-up mutes, dented from a lifetime of one-nighters. I sang a wonderful song by Dave Frishberg, "I Want to Be a Sideman," in honor of the big band days. But I closed with a ballad. Always finish with a rousing uptempo number is the rule. But I sang "In the Wee Small Hours of the Morning."

I'd recently seen Tina Sinatra at La Dolce Vita, the Italian restaurant on Little Santa Monica. "He's fine," she told me. "As cantankerous as ever." When I saw him on a PBS rerun in April, I sent him a fax: DAMN, YOU'RE CUTE. When he died in May, it was the first time in my life I'd be singing in a world without Frank Sinatra. I didn't talk a lot about him onstage; I just said what Woody Herman said when Duke Ellington died. "I really don't have to believe it if I don't want to. I just think of him as being somewhere on the road."

When Nicky was six, he was in a parade in Ironton, Ohio, an unfamiliar town. Dressed in white pants, red jacket, a tall plumed hat with chinstrap that Grandma had stuffed with tissue paper to keep it from falling down over his eyes, he played the triangle. We cheered him as he passed, without any of us realizing that a parade doesn't return to its starting point, but disbands at the end of the route. So Nicky found himself alone in a strange place, no idea where he was. But he knew what to do. He walked around until he saw the river. If he had to, he could follow it until it led him home. He was sitting on the bank calmly, skipping stones, when Uncle Chick found him.

I've always felt that way about the river as a centering place. Grandma Guilfoyle did, too. She never got the house she longed for, directly on the river, on moving water. So I'd asked Nina to find me such a house in Augusta. My extraordinary sister-in-law can do what can't be done. An old house right on the river had been vacant for twenty years. People who'd tried to buy it were always told that the owner, who lived in Cincinnati, was angry at the town of Augusta and would never sell. Nina had lunch with the owner, who, at the end of the meal, accepted a check. The full price was just $20,000 because, in the words of the sign the town had hammered to the front door, that now hangs in my front hallway, the house was UNFIT FOR HUMAN HABITATION.

Nina supervised its stripping to bare skeleton, then its yearlong rehabilitation. It's not a mansion, just a very pleasing house—late-nineteenth-century, pale yellow brick, a fireplace, shutters at the windows.

From the porch, I can smell the river, keen and fresh. I know now that the faraway places the river suggests are not just around the bend, but faraway beyond imagining—knotted places in the mind and heart. But I can always follow the river safely home.

Acknowledgments

⁓

*L*oving thanks to my husband, Dante DiPaolo, without whom nothing would be possible.

*M*any members of my family shared memories and perceptions on behalf of this book. I know that some of them would have preferred to remain silent, but because they spoke out for my sake, I am especially grateful to Monsita Ferrer Botwick, Gabriel Ferrer, Maria Ferrer, Rafael Ferrer, Nick Clooney, Nina Warren Clooney, George Clooney, Ada Clooney Zeidler, Bridget Clooney, Tom Anderson, Pat Breslin, Carlos Campo, Cathi Campo-Muckle, Roy Dudenhoeffer, Michael Dudenhoeffer, William Guilfoyle, Phyllis Guilfoyle, Phyllis Middleman Holvey, Sherman Holvey, Cari Campo Leary, and Cristina Campo Stretz.

Acknowledgments

$\mathcal{M}$y book would have been seriously incomplete without the generosity of these friends and associates: Rosemary Riddle Acerra, Tony Bennett, Ian Bernard, Rae Bernson, Carol Burnett, Margaret Calvert, Blanche Chambers, Gene Cipriano, Maria Cole, Betty Comden, Kathryn Crosby, Gavin de Becker, Stanley Donen, Charlie Einstein, Pat Jones Faust, Michael Feinstein, Stan Freeman, Will Friedwald, Gary Giddins, Shecky Greene, Merv Griffin, Skitch Henderson, Janet Leigh, A. C. Lyles, Peter Matz, Mitch Miller, Guy Mitchell, Betty Mitchell, Paul Moer, Bess Moer, John Oddo, Monsignor Peter A. O'Reilly, Linda Ronstadt, Jacqueline Sherman Rose, Bob Rose, Ann Rutherford, Rose Marie, Arnold Scaasi, Jonathan Schwartz, Joey Scognamillo, Mark Sendroff, Ron Shaw, Herb Steinberg, Bob Thompson, Paula Thompson, Roger Vorce, Lew Wasserman, Hal Webman, Stan Weiss, Jeannette Weiss, Jerry White, Margaret Whiting, Deborah Grace Winer, Jessica Winer, and Mary Wood.

$\mathcal{I}$'ve been a fervent reader since I was seven years old, so I'm aware of my indebtedness to those in publishing involved, beginning with Arlene Friedman. And to all those at Doubleday: Judith Kern, my editor; Steve Rubin, my publisher, and to everyone in sales and marketing: Jackie Everly, Laurie Matranga, Suzi Zengo, and Suzanne Herz. Sincere thanks also to Linda Michaels, Mark Hurst, and my agents, Linda Chester and Joanna Pulcini, who gave their all to make this project so special, as well as Gary Jaffe and the staff at Linda Chester and Associates. But most of all to my manager and friend, Allen Sviridoff, and my cowriter, Joan Barthel, whose writing is certain to become part of my legacy.

$\mathcal{F}$or indispensable research help, I am much obliged to Anne Barthel, Linda Dozoretz Communications, Production Central, Evalyn Rodin, and to the knowledgeable staff at the Academy of Motion Picture Arts and Sciences, Margaret Herrick Library; Mason County Museum; the New York Public Library; Nevada Historical Society, and the Library of the University of Nevada at Las Vegas.

Selected Discography
Michael Feinstein

⁓

*T*his is a select discography dictated by several factors. It is a personal list and for the sake of saneness had to be limited in various ways. In the section listing single recordings, I have chosen to list discs that are significant because of content, performance, collaborating artist, songwriter, commercial success, or other mitigating factor. Single discs are generally not listed when they were also originally released on LP albums. Rosemary's myriad recordings of children's songs are also omitted.

For the years 1946–49, when Rosemary and her sister Betty sang with the Tony Pastor Band, I did not include Clooney Sisters duets; instead, I have listed Rosemary's significant solo vocal records that foreshadowed her subsequent career. A CD containing Clooney Sisters duets can be found in the Compact Disc listings. I also chose not to include international CD releases because they are very difficult to locate and many are out of print. Bootleg releases and those of inferior technical quality and artistic compromise have also been omitted.

Michael Feinstein
April 1999

Single Recordings

All are 10-inch 78 rpm discs unless otherwise noted. Columbia singles were issued in both 78 and 45 rpm format beginning approximately 1949. All discs issued after 1958 are issued as 45's only (see page 313).

May 1946. Vocal with Tony Pastor Band.
"Sooner or Later" (Woolcot–Gilbert). From *Song of the South*. Cosmo Records 721.
NOTE: Rosemary's first solo performance on record.

June 5, 1947. Vocal with Tony Pastor Band.
"I'm Sorry I Didn't Say I'm Sorry When I Made You Cry Last Night" (Roberts–Lee). Columbia Records CO 37562.

September 29, 1947. Vocal with Tony Pastor Band.
"Grieving for You" (Gold–Gibson–Ribaud). Columbia CO 38383.

December 23, 1947. Vocal with Tony Pastor Band.
"You Started Something" (Rinker–Huddleston). Columbia CO 38297.

March 3, 1949. Vocal with Tony Pastor Band.
"When You're in Love" (O'Connor–Fields–John). Columbia CO 38454.

March 28, 1949. With Tony Pastor and His Orchestra.
"Cabaret" (Russell–Cowan). Columbia CO 38501.
"Bargain Day" (William Roy). Columbia CO 38501.
NOTE: Rosemary's first official solo recording.

September 14, 1949. With Orchestra and Chorus Conducted by Hugo
Winterhalter.
"Don't Cry Joe" (Marsala). Harmony HA 1071.
"There's a Broken Heart for Every Light on Broadway"
(Fisher–Johnson). Harmony HA 1074.
"Oh You Beautiful Doll" (Brown–Ayer). Harmony HA 1071.
"The Kid's a Dreamer" (Snider–Snider). Columbia CO 38678.
"Chicago" (Fisher). Harmony HA 1074.

March 9, 1950. Percy Faith Orchestra and Chorus.
"I Found My Mama" (Holmes). Columbia CO 38766.
"Me and My Teddy Bear" (Coots–Winters). Columbia CO 38766.
NOTE: These titles were the first of over two dozen highly successful
children's songs recorded over the next five years.

April 8, 1950. Duet with Frank Sinatra. George Siravo, Conductor.
"Peachtree Street" (Saunders–Mason–Sinatra). Columbia CO 38853.
NOTE: A recording that Rosemary (justifiably) dislikes, notable only
because it is sung with "Ol' Blue Eyes."

June 21, 1950. Percy Faith Orchestra.
"Why Fight the Feeling?" (Frank Loesser). Columbia CO 38900.

August 23, 1950. Percy Faith Orchestra.
"Where Do I Go from You?" (Kaye–Coquatrix–Marcland).
Columbia CO 38983.

October 21, 1950. Duet with Guy Mitchell. Percy Faith, Conductor.
"Marrying for Love" (Irving Berlin). Columbia CO 39052.
"You're Just in Love" (Berlin). Columbia CO 39052.
"The House of Singing Bamboo" (Warren–Freed). Columbia CO
39054.

December 11, 1950. Duet with Frank Sinatra. Alex Stordahl, Conductor.
"Love Means Love" (Lake–Sigman). Columbia CO 39141.

"Cherry Pies Ought to Be You" (Cole Porter). Columbia CO 39141.
NOTE: See "Peachtree Street," April 8, 1950.

December 30, 1950. Duet with Tony Pastor. Tony Pastor, Conductor.
    "Sentimental Music" (Wayne–Care). Columbia CO 39158.

January 27, 1951. Mitch Miller, Conductor.
    "Beautiful Brown Eyes" (Smith–Delmore). Columbia CO 39212.
    "Shot Gun Boogie" (Tennessee Ernie Ford). Columbia CO 39212.

February 22, 1951. Percy Faith, Conductor.
    "Mixed Emotions" (Louchheim). Columbia CO 39333.

June 5, 1951. Mitch Miller, Conductor. Mundell Lowe, Guitar.
    Terry Snyder, Bass. Stan Freeman, Piano.
    "The Lady Is a Tramp" (Rodgers–Hart). Columbia 10-inch LP: CL
    2525.
    "I'll Be Around" (Wilder). Columbia 10-inch LP: CL 2525.
    NOTE: "Come On-a My House" was supposed to be recorded this
    day, but the rented harpsichord never arrived. Rosemary and the
    boys improvised the above titles, creating the finest single record-
    ings of her Columbia tenure. They were issued in 1954.

June 6, 1951. Mundell Lowe, Guitar. Frank Carroll, Bass.
    Jimmy Crawford, Drums. Stan Freeman, Harpsichord.
    "Come On-a My House" (Saroyan–Bagdasarian). Columbia CO
    39467.

August 23, 1951. Percy Faith Orchestra.
    "Half as Much" (Williams). Columbia CO 39710.

November 21, 1951. Percy Faith Orchestra.
    "Be My Life's Companion" (Hilliard–DeLugg). Columbia CO
    39631.
    "Tenderly" (Gross–Lawrence). Columbia CO 39648.

April 8, 1952. Mundell Lowe, Guitar. San Salvador, Guitar.
Frank Carroll, Bass. Terry Snyder, Drums.
Stan Freeman, Harpsichord.
"Botch-a-Me" (Stanley–Morbelli–Astore). Columbia CO 39767.
"On the First Warm Day" (Howard). Columbia CO 39767.
Duet with Marlene Dietrich:
"Too Old To Cut the Mustard" (Carlisle). Columbia CO 39812.

April 25, 1952. Percy Faith Orchestra.
"Blues in the Night" (Mercer–Arlen). Columbia CO 39813.

May 19, 1952. Duet with Marlene Dietrich. Jimmy Carroll, Conductor.
"Good For Nothin'" (Wilder–Engvick). Columbia CO 39812.

June 20, 1952. Duet with Gene Autry. Carl Cotner, Conductor.
"The Night Before Christmas Song" (Marks–Moore). Columbia
CO 39876.
"Look Out the Window" (Porter–Mitchell). Columbia CO 39876.
NOTE: On second title, Rosemary steadfastly sings "window" to
Gene Autry's "winder."

September 12, 1952. Due with George Morgan. Marvin H. Hughes,
Conductor.
"Withered Roses" (Kay). Columbia CO 21071.
"You Love Me Just Enough to Hurt Me" (Tillman). Columbia CO
21071.

December 9, 1952. Paul Weston, Conductor.
*"Haven't Got a Worry" (Livingston–Evans). Columbia CO 39943.
*"I Do, I Do, I Do" (Livingston–Evans). Phillips B1618 (England).
*"Lovely Weather for Ducks" (Livingston–Evans). Columbia CO
39943.
"What Would You Do (If You Were in My Place)" (Adler–Ross).
Columbia CO 39931.
NOTE: First three titles* are from *The Stars Are Singing,* Rosemary's
first motion picture.

February 3, 1953. Percy Faith, Conductor.

"It Happened to Happen to Me" (Clooney). Columbia CO 40003.

NOTE: This song was written by Nick Clooney, Rosemary's brother.

February 17, 1953. Duet with Marlene Dietrich. Jimmy Carroll, Conductor.

"Dots Nice Donna Fight" (Showalter–Bagdasarian). Columbia CO 39980.

"It's the Same" (Wright–Forrest). Columbia CO 39980.

September 17, 1953. Paul Weston, Conductor.

"Happy Christmas" (Rodgers–Hammerstein II). Columbia CO 40102.

"We'll Be Together Again" (Laine–Fischer). Columbia CO 40361.

November 8, 1953. Paul Weston, Conductor.

"When You Love Someone" (Livingston–Evans). Columbia CO 40142.

NOTE: This song is from *Here Come the Girls*, Rosemary's second motion picture.

December 10, 1953. Norman Leyden, Conductor.

"You Make Me Feel So Young" (Myrow–Gordon). Phillips B1896 (England).

Duet with José Ferrer:

"Man (Uh-Huh)" (Gleason–McKean). Columbia CO 40144.

"Woman (Uh-Huh)" (Gleason). Columbia CO 40144.

NOTE: Rosemary's first recorded duet with her husband, José Ferrer.

December 15, 1953. Percy Faith, Conductor.

"What Is There to Say?" (Harburg–Duke). Columbia 10-inch LP: CL2525.

February 10, 1954. Wally Stott, Conductor.

"While We're Young" (Engvick–Wilder–Palitz). Phillips B1895 (England).

"Love Is a Beautiful Stranger" (Frings–Ferrer). Phillips B1932 (England).

NOTE: Orchestral tracks recorded in London on above date. Vocals recorded by Rosemary in Los Angeles on May 3, 1954.

May 3, 1954. Percy Faith, Conductor.
"Younger Than Springtime" (Rodgers–Hammerstein II). Columbia 10-inch LP: CL 6297.
"Hello Young Lovers" (Rodgers–Hammerstein II). Columbia CO 40723.

May 22, 1954. Paul Weston, Conductor.
"Hey There" (Adler–Ross). Columbia CO 40266.
"This Ole House" (Hamblen). Columbia CO 40266.
Duet with Marlene Dietrich:
"Besides He's a Man" (Wilder–Engvick). Phillips PB 314 (England).

May 27, 1954. Duet with Marlene Dietrich. Paul Weston, Conductor.
"Land, Sea and Air" (Gilkyson). Phillips PB 314 (England).

June 11, 1954. Duet with José Ferrer. Adolph Deutsch, Conductor.
"Mr. and Mrs." (Romberg–Wood). MGM 12-inch LP E3153.
NOTE: This performance was taken from the soundtrack of the MGM musical film *Deep in My Heart,* starring José Ferrer as Sigmund Romberg. It was issued as part of the *Deep in My Heart* soundtrack and has been reissued on Compact Disc as part of a 6-CD set called *That's Entertainment* (Rhino R2 72182).

June 23, 1954. Paul Weston, Conductor.
"A Touch of the Blues" (Wilcox–George) Columbia CO 40498
Duet with Betty Clooney:
"Sisters" (Irving Berlin). Columbia CO 40305.
NOTE: Above title from *White Christmas* (Paramount, 1954).

Selected Discography

July 2, 1954. Duet with José Ferrer. Paul Weston, Conductor.
"Mr. and Mrs." (Romberg–Wood). Columbia CO 40407.
NOTE: This title from *Deep in My Heart* (MGM, 1954).

September 23, 1954. Paul Weston, Conductor.
"Mambo Italiano" (Merrill). Columbia CO 40361.

January 13, 1955. Orchestra Conducted by Buddy Cole.
"Where Will the Dimple Be" (Hoffman–Merrill). Columbia CO
40434.
"Love Among the Young" (Gimbel–Wilder). Columbia CO
40498.

January 20, 1955. Paul Weston, Conductor.
"Easter Parade" (Irving Berlin). Columbia CO MJV234.

September 19, 1955. With Ray Conniff and His Orchestra.
"Pet Me Poppa" (Frank Loesser). Columbia CO 40579.

February 27, 1956. Johnny Bond, Conductor. The Tunesmiths with Carl
Smith, Gene Autry, Don Cherry, and the Collins Kids.
"You Are My Sunshine" (Davis–Mitchell). Columbia CO 40760.

March 3, 1956. With Paul Weston Orchestra.
"I've Grown Accustomed to Your Face" (Lerner–Loewe).
Columbia CO 40676.
"I Could Have Danced All Night" (Lerner–Loewe). Columbia CO
40676.

June 29, 1956. "Frank Comstock," Conductor.
"Come Rain or Come Shine" (Mercer–Arlen). Columbia CO 40774.
NOTE: Nelson Riddle actually orchestrated and conducted this track
and the following six, but was under exclusive contract to Capitol
Records and could not be given credit.

September 24, 1956. "Frank Comstock," Conductor. "Joe Seymour" Orchestra.

"(Don't That Take the) Rag Offen the Bush" (Mercer–DePaul). Columbia CO 40812.

"That's How It Is" (Livingston–Evans). Columbia CO 40981.

"It's a Nuisance Having You Around" (Mercer–DePaul). Columbia CO 40774.

NOTE: See note for June 29, 1956.

November 24, 1956. "Frank Comstock," Conductor.

"Love Is a Feeling" (Gimbel–Charlap). Columbia CO 40812.

"Mangos" (Wayne–Libbey). Columbia CO 40835. "Independent (On My Own)" (Comden–Green–Styne). Columbia CO 40835.

NOTE: See note for June 29, 1956.

June 1, 1957. With Frank DeVol Orchestra.

"(You Can't Lose the Blues with) Colors" (Irving Berlin). Columbia CO 40981.

NOTE: This song was written by Berlin especially for Clooney. It's a mediocre song.

October 18, 1957. With Frank DeVol Orchestra.

"Tonight" (Sondheim–Bernstein). Columbia CO 41053.

January 7, 1958. With Frank DeVol Orchestra.

"You Don't Know Him" (Livingston–Evans). Columbia CO 41107.

"Surprise" (Livingston–Evans). Columbia CO 41107.

NOTE: The above two titles were Rosemary's last two issued singles for Columbia.

Singles Released as 45's Only

November 21, 1958. Buddy Cole Orchestra.

"Love Look Away" (Rodgers–Hammerstein). Coral 62064.

December 1, 1958. Sy Oliver Orchestra.

"Flattery" (Gimbel–Charlap). (Duet with José Ferrer.) MGM X1651 (EP).

"Love Eyes" (Gimbel–Charlap). MGM X1651 (EP).

"Sorry for Myself" (Gimbel–Charlap). MGM X1651 (EP).

"What I Mean to Say" (Gimbel–Charlap). MGM X1651 (EP).

NOTE: Above four songs from Broadway musical *Whoop Up*. They were issued on an MGM Records Extended Play 45 disc.

March 25, 1959. Duet with Bob Hope. Gus Levene, Conductor.

"Ain't-A-Hankerin" (Burston–Altman). RCA 47-7517.

Protection (Burston–Altman). RCA 47-7517.

NOTE: Above two songs from film *Alias Jesse James*.

February 15, 1960. With Perez Prado Orchestra.

"Summertime Love" (Loesser). RCA 47-7707.

November 7, 1960. Jimmie Haskell, Conductor.

"What Takes My Fancy" (Coleman–Leigh). RCA 47/61-7819.

"Hey Look Me Over" (Coleman–Leigh). RCA 47/61-7819.

April 18, 1961. Nelson Riddle, Conductor.

"The Wonderful Season of Love" (Waxman–Webster). RCA 47/37-7887.

"Without Love" (Porter). RCA 47/37-7887.

July 25, 1963. Duet with Frank Sinatra. Morris Stoloff, Conductor.

"Some Enchanted Evening" (Rodgers–Hammerstein). Reprise FS2018 (LP).

July 25, 1963. Morris Stoloff, Conductor.

"How Are Things in Glocca Morra" (Lane–Harburg). Reprise FS2015 (LP).

"Look to the Rainbow" (Lane–Harburg). Reprise FS2015 (LP).

NOTE: Above two tracks from *Finian's Rainbow*.

March 12 and 26, 1968. Shorty Rogers, Conductor.

"Let Me Down Easy" (Stillman–Simon). Dot 17100.

"One Less Bell to Answer" (Bacharach–David). Dot 17100.

NOTE: Above two selections were Rosemary's last recordings made before her nervous breakdown. She was in very good vocal form at this last session, better than she had been for several years.

Long Playing Albums (33 1/3 rpm)

Albums listed are originally conceived as LP releases, unless the word "compilation" is listed in parentheses, meaning that the disc is compiled from single tracks. (Concord Jazz releases are listed chronologically under compact disc listings, since they are all currently available in that format.)

—*Hollywood's Best*. With Harry James Orchestra. Recorded May 1952. Columbia 10-inch LP CL 6224.

NOTE: This was Rosemary's first issued LP recording consisting of a selection of Academy Award-winning songs.

—*Red Garters*. Soundtrack and Studio Recordings. Recorded May, June, and December 1953. Columbia 10-inch LP CL6282.

NOTE: Album of songs by Livingston and Evans from film starring Rosemary, Guy Mitchell, and Jack Carson.

—*While We're Young*. Recorded May and June 1954. Columbia 10-inch LP CL6297.

NOTE: Collection of eight songs with "young" in the title.

—*White Christmas*. Recorded May, June, and September 1954. Columbia 10-inch LP CL6338.

NOTE: Album of songs by Irving Berlin from film starring Rosemary, Bing Crosby, Danny Kaye, and Vera-Ellen. Includes "Sisters," performed by Rosemary and Betty Clooney (their last recording together).

—*Tenderly*. Compilation. Columbia 10-inch LP CL 2525.
NOTE: Includes several previously unreleased tracks including "I'll Be Around" and "The Lady is a Tramp"—both among Rosemary's most sublime work.

—*Rosemary Clooney On Stage*. Recorded June, July, and August 1955. Columbia 10-inch LP CL2581.
NOTE: This recording consists of three studio recordings (in Los Angeles) and three live recordings taken from Rosemary's London Palladium Concert (July 19–August 1, 1955). It was reissued on a Reader's Digest Collection titled *Rosemary Clooney: Her Greatest Hits and Finest Performances*. Reader's Digest Music (3 CD's) RC7-122.

—*Rosemary Clooney Live at the London Palladium*.
Phillips 10-inch LP BBR 8073 (England).
NOTE: Complete Recording of Rosemary's London Palladium Concert taken from two separate shows recorded July 19–August 1, 1955.

—*Date with the King*. With Benny Goodman Trio and Sextet. Recorded November 14, 1955. Columbia 10-inch LP CL 2572.
NOTE: Of the six tracks on the disc, Rosemary performs three songs (including a vocal duet with Benny Goodman on Cole Porter's "It's Bad for Me").

—*Blue Rose*. With Duke Ellington Orchestra. Recorded January and February 1956. Columbia 12-inch LP CL872.
NOTE: An essential recording containing some of Rosemary's most sublime singing. The Ellington band recorded the accompanying tracks on January 23 and 27 and Clooney's vocals were added on February 8 and 11. Two tracks not included on the original LP have been added to the subsequent CD reissues.

—*Clooney Tunes*. Compilation. Columbia 12-inch LP CL969.
NOTE: A wonderful collection of twelve of Rosemary's children's

recordings, including "Teddy Bear's Picnic," "The Syncopated Clock," and "On the Good Ship Lollipop." Sony is planning a CD reissue.

—*Ring Around Rosie*. With the Hi-Lo's. Recorded February 14 and 16, 1957. Columbia 12-inch LP CL1006.
NOTE: All songs on this album were originally performed on the television series, "The Rosemary Clooney Show" (1956–57 season). The Hi-Lo's were regulars on the show and this album consists of four solo numbers sung by the Hi-Lo's, four solos by Rosemary, and four duets. Nelson Riddle was the musical director of the show, even though this album lists Frank Comstock as its conductor.

—*The Ferrers: Rosemary Clooney and José Ferrer Sing Selections from the Broadway Musical "Oh Captain."* Recorded March 14–17, 1958. MGM 12-inch LP SE3687.
NOTE: This was an album of duets with José Ferrer of songs from the Livingston and Evans Broadway show that was directed by Ferrer. Rosemary sings two solo numbers: "The Morning Music of Montmartre" and "Keep It Simple."

—*The Story of Celeste*. Recorded June 15, 1958. MGM 12-inch LP E3709.
NOTE: Rosemary narrated this children's story written by Paul Tripp and George Kleinsinger.

—*Fancy Meeting You Here*. Duets with Bing Crosby. Recorded July and August 1958. Billy May, Conductor. RCA 12-inch LP LSP1854.
NOTE: This album is Rosemary's favorite recording. A clever concept album, it was arranged and conducted by Billy May and is an essential Clooney album, even though it was not considered successful when initially released. Crosby and Clooney were a supreme combination. Sammy Cahn created the concept.

—*Swing Around Rosie*. Recorded December 26, 1958. With Buddy Cole Trio. Coral 12-inch LP CRL7-57266.
NOTE: Buddy Cole was Rosemary's longtime pianist and conductor. They recorded literally hundreds of songs for Rosemary's various radio shows from mid-1955 through the early 60s. That they recorded this entire album in one day is proof of their easy working relationship. The Japanese CD reissue featured two previously unissued tracks.

—*Hymns from the Heart*. Recorded June 4–6, 1959. Buddy Cole, Conductor. MGM 12-inch LP SE3782.
NOTE: An album of hymns primarily arranged by Ralph Carmichael and featuring his chorus on five of the fourteen tracks.

—*How the West Was Won*. Recorded July 1959. Bob Thompson, Conductor. RCA 12-inch LP's LS06070.
NOTE: A concept album featuring Clooney performing four solos and six duets with Bing Crosby of American folk songs. Other performers included Jimmy Driftwood, Sam Hinton, and the Mormon Tabernacle Choir.

—*A Touch of Tabasco*. Recorded July and August 1960. With Perez Prado Orchestra. RCA 12-inch LP LSP 2123.
NOTE: A delightful album of Latin and American standards performed with imaginative arrangements (and vocal punctuations) provided by Prado.

—*Clap Hands! Here Comes Rosie*. Recorded February 18, 23, and 27, 1960. Bob Thompson, Conductor. RCA 12-inch LP LSP2212.
NOTE: Rosemary's first solo album for RCA, featuring a very 60s vocal chorus on many of the tracks.

—*Rosemary Clooney Swings Softly*. Compilation. MGM 12-inch LP SE3834.
NOTE: An interesting disc culled from five unreleased Columbia tracks (1954–58) arranged by Paul Weston, Nelson Riddle, and Frank

DeVol, plus one track from MGM's *Oh Captain* album and two tracks from the "Whoop Up" (EP). Add to this, four new tracks recorded April 29, 1960, with composer/arranger Ian Bernard and you have an album listing no arranger or conductor credits! Rosemary's vocals are uniformly pleasing.

—*Rosie Solves the Swingin' Riddle*. Recorded May and June, 1960. Nelson Riddle, Conductor RCA 12-inch LP LSP2265.
NOTE: A superb collaboration that is perhaps Rosemary's best-loved LP recording. Every track is perfection and Riddle was at his zenith. The perfection was the result of hard work: some tracks required up to twelve takes to perfect. Happily reissued on CD: Koch Koc-CD-7991.

—*Love*. Recorded March 6, 21, and 24, 1961. Nelson Riddle, Conductor. Reprise 12-inch LP RS6088.
NOTE: Another classic Riddle/Clooney collaboration that was recorded by RCA in 1961 but not released until 1963 by Reprise Records. The Riddle arrangements clearly reflect his love for Vaughn–Williams. Though Rosemary isn't in perfect voice on every track, it hardly matters; her interpretations are spot-on and timeless. The CD reissue has too much echo on it, but is still worth having: Reprise 9-46072-2.

—*Rosemary Clooney Sings Country Hits from the Heart*. Recorded March and July 1962. Floyd Cramer and Don Gibson, Conductors. RCA 12-inch LP LSP2565.
NOTE: A pleasant album produced in Nashville by Dick Pierce and Chet Atkins. Rosemary clearly is at home with material that takes her back to her Kentucky roots.

—*Thanks for Nothing*. Recorded September, October, and November 1963.
Bob Thompson, Conductor. Reprise 12-inch LP RS6108.
NOTE: Rosemary isn't very fond of this album because the stresses of her personal life are audible on many of the tracks.

—*That Travelin' Two Beat*. Recorded August and December 1964. Duets with Bing Crosby. Billy May, Conductor. Capitol 12-inch LP ST2300.

NOTE: A concept album fashioned by Livingston and Evans in an attempt to recreate the atmosphere of *Fancy Meeting You Here*. It is a fun Dixieland romp and Rosie and Bing were both in fine fettle.

—*Look My Way*. Recorded June 1975. United Artists UAS29918 (England).

NOTE: Even though this album was recorded in Nashville, it was not released in the United States save for a 45 rpm single of two songs on the Apco label. This was Rosemary's first released album after a long hiatus and she resumed her rightful place at the microphone with her usual ease.

—*Nice to Be Around*. Recorded 1975. Del Newman, Conductor. United Artists UAS3008 (England).

NOTE: This album is a cult favorite of those lucky enough to own it. Rosemary's renditions of several 1970s pop classics, including "The Hungry Years," "All By Myself," and "Fifty Ways to Leave Your Lover" imbue them with a depth and seriousness that dims the memory of other interpretations.

—*Bing Crosby Live at the London Palladium*. Recorded June 24 and 25, 1976. Pete Moore, Conductor. KTEL Records (two LP's) NE951 (England).

NOTE: Rosemary's segment at this concert included a duet with Bing ("On a Slow Boat to China") plus the following solos: "By Myself"; "Tenderly"; "Fifty Ways to Leave Your Lover"; "Just One of Those Things," and "A Song for You." She is in very good form and one can feel the warmth of the audience. The recording has been reissued in Britain on Compact Disc: EMI 7243-8-57547-2-2. The single track of "A Song for You" has been separately issued on a three-CD Bing Crosby compilation called *The Complete United Artists Sessions:* EMI 7243-8-59808-2-4.

Compact Discs

—*16 Most Requested Songs.* Columbia CK44403.
NOTE: A basic greatest hits collection with a few classic pop standards added for good measure.

—*The Essence of Rosemary Clooney.* Columbia/Legacy CK53569.
NOTE: A ten-track, well-programmed collection consisting largely of ballads beautifully sung.

—*Rosemary Clooney Sings Songs from "White Christmas" and Other Yuletime Favorites.* Columbia/Legacy CK65278.
NOTE: All of Rosemary's Christmas songs recorded for Columbia (1950–56) have been collated for this sixteen-track compendium. Some of the songs are creaky, but all in all it's a nice atmospheric holiday collection.

—*Tenderly.* Sony Music Special Products A22542.
NOTE: A mindlessly chosen twenty-eight-minute collection containing a few hits ("This Ole House," "Hey There"), some standout classics ("Sisters," "Just-a-Sittin' And-a-Rockin'") and several schlock pop songs that should have stayed buried. (And the sound quality ain't so great either.)

—*Blue Rose.* Columbia/Legacy CK 65506. (See note on page 316.)

—*Rosemary Clooney and Tony Pastor—You Started Something.* Sony Music Special Products A26085.
NOTE: A representative sampling of the Clooney Sisters' early years with Tony Pastor. Contains three standout solos ("You Started Some-

thing," "When You're in Love," "Grieving for You"), as well as three Clooney Sisters' tracks. Total running time is less than thirty minutes.

—*Tony Pastor and His Orchestra: 1945–1950.* Circle CCD-121.
NOTE: Taken from radio transcriptions, this wonderful collection imparts a real feeling for the Pastor band's energy and talent. Contains twenty-two tracks, with twelve of them featuring either Rosemary or the Clooney Sisters.

—*The Uncollected Rosemary Clooney: 1951–1952.* Hindsight HCD 234.
NOTE: A meticulously engineered collection of radio transcriptions featuring the Earl Sheldon Orchestra. Rosemary sounds vibrant and fresh on all fourteen tracks.

—*Everything's Rosie.* Hindsight HCD 255.
NOTE: This collection duplicates seven of the more famous songs from *The Uncollected Rosemary Clooney* (HCD 234) but adds seven new tracks from 1959 radio broadcasts featuring Buddy Cole at the keyboard.

—*Rosemary Clooney: Her Greatest Hits and Performances.* Three-CD collection. Reader's Digest Music 122C.
NOTE: A well-organized collection touching on almost every phase of Rosemary's recording career, it contains several hard-to-obtain performances. Well worth having, even though the sound quality is uneven on many vintage tracks.

—*Rosie Solves the Swingin' Riddle.* Koch KOC-CD-7991.
(See note on page 319.)

—*Love.* Reprise 946072-2.
(See note on page 319.) CD reissue contains two tracks from "Thanks for Nothing" LP.

—*Marian McPartland's Piano Jazz with Guest Rosemary Clooney.* The Jazz Alliance TJA-12003.
NOTE: A CD release of Rosemary's appearance on the National

Public Radio series, recorded October 14, 1991. Rosemary sings four songs with the delightful accompaniment of McPartland and engages in warm conversation for the better part of an hour. Charming!

—*A Tribute to Duke.* Concord Jazz CCD-4050.

NOTE: Rosemary's guest appearance on this album in 1977 cemented her relationship with Concord Jazz, the label she currently records with. She sings "I'm Checking Out—Goom Bye" and "Sophisticated Lady," both knowingly reprised from the 1956 *Blue Rose* album. Other participants included Bing Crosby (his last American recording), Tony Bennett, and Woody Herman.

Concord Jazz Compact Discs

Rosemary has currently recorded albums for Concord Jazz with each annual addition eagerly anticipated by her fans. Her releases, beginning in 1977, are listed in chronological order.

—*Everything's Coming Up Rosie.* 1977. CCD-4047.
—*Rosie Sings Bing.* 1978. CCD-4060.
—*Here's to My Lady.* 1979. CCD-4081.
—*Rosemary Clooney Sings the Lyrics of Ira Gershwin.* 1980. CCD-4112.
—*With Love.* 1981. CCD-4144.
—*Rosemary Clooney Sings the Music of Cole Porter.* 1982. CCD-4185.
—*Rosemary Clooney Sings the Music of Harold Arlen.* 1983. CCD-4210.
—*My Buddy.* With the Woody Herman Band. 1983. CCD-4226.
—*Rosemary Clooney Sings the Music of Irving Berlin.* 1984. CCD-4255.
—*Rosemary Clooney Sings Ballads.* 1985. CCD-4282.
—*Rosemary Clooney Sings the Music of Jimmy Van Heusen.* 1986. CCD-4308.
—*Rosemary Clooney Sings the Lyrics of Johnny Mercer.* 1987. CCD-4333.
—*Show Tunes.* 1989. CCD-4364.

—*The Music of Rodgers, Hart & Hammerstein*. 1990. CCD-4405.
—*For the Duration*. 1991. CCD-4444.
—*Girl Singer*. 1992. CD-4496.
—*Do You Miss New York?* 1993. CCD-4537.
—*Still on the Road*. 1994. CCD-4590.
—*Demi-Centennial*. 1995. CCD-4633.
—*Dedicated to Nelson*. 1996. CCD-685.
—*White Christmas*. 1996. CCD-4719.
—*Mothers and Daughters*. 1997. CCD-4754-2.
—*Rosemary Clooney '70*. 1998. CCD4804-2.
—*at long last*. With the Count Basie Orchestra. 1998. CCD-4795-2.

Bear Family Collection

—*The Complete Recordings of Rosemary Clooney.*
  Three Volumes (1946–68).
  Volume One: Come On-a My House. Bear Family Records. Seven
  C.D.'s. BCD 15 89.
  Volume Two: Memories of You. Bear Family Records. Seven C.D.'s.
  BCD 15 914.
  Volume Three to be released in early 2000.

NOTE: This gargantuan collection contains a complete documentation of
the Clooney career in sound, text, and pictures. Each set contains a beautifully illustrated hardcover book with a biographical article by Deborah
Grace Winer. There are many rarities and unreleased demos, as well as
two discs collating all of the children's recordings (on *Box Two*) and one
disc with all Clooney soundtrack performances (on *Box One*). These
sets, however, are pressed only in Germany and are not generally available in the United States.

Index

Academy Awards ceremonies,
  99–100, 137–38
Agents and managers
  J. Sherman, 59–64, 83–84
  J. Shribman, 33, 45–46, 50, 51,
    81, 204
  A. Sviridoff, 273–79
  Uncle George Guilfoyle,
    21–23, 27–28, 36, 38,
    43–46
Allen, Bea, 90, 109
Ambassador Theater, 255–57
Anderson, Tom (cousin), 14
Arlen, Harold, 265
Arrangers, musical, 21, 151,
  153–54, 281–82
"Arthur Godfrey's Talent
  Scouts," show, 43

Astaire, Fred, 90
Asthma, 178
Atlantic City debut, 26–27
Augusta home, 301
Awards, 43, 143, 173, 293–94

Bacall, Lauren, 143
Bagdasarian, Ross, 72
Balaban, Barney, 49
Balaban, Judy, 49, 67, 101, 112
Ballard, Kaye, 275
Bangkok, 208
Bankhead, Tallulah, 61, 62
Barkley, Alben, 177
Barry, Gene, 95
Beatty, Warren, 167
Beaulieu, France, 120–22

Becker, Gavin de, 232, 292
"Bell Telephone Hour, The," 184
Bennett, Tony, 43, 53–54, 69, 262, 286, 294, 299–300
Berger, Sy, 32, 40–41, 185
Bergman, Ingrid, 87
Berlin, Irving, 108–9
Bernard, Ian, 90, 106, 186
Bernson, Rae, 202–3, 214, 216
Betty Clooney Center, 279
Betty Clooney Foundation for Persons with Brain Injury, 278–79
Beverly Hills homes, 88–89, 101, 103–4, 106–8, 291–92
Big band career with Tony Pastor's Orchestra, 20–46
    audition, 20–21
    end of, 45–46
    first performance, 25–27
    recording, 29–30, 37–38, 44, 71
    relationship with Betty during, 25, 29
    romantic interests during, 35–39, 40–41, 42–43
    touring, 28–35, 39–45
    Uncle George as chaperone and agent, 21–23, 27–28, 36, 38, 43–46
Big bands, 30, 50
Bloomingdale, Betsy and Alfred, 167
Blue Rose (album), 293
Bogart, Humphrey, 127, 132, 143, 179
Boone, Debby, 278, 285, 293
Botwick, Terry, 287
Brando, Marlon, 61, 63, 68, 101, 143
Breakdown, psychotic, 213–22, 225, 246
Brown, Jerry, 285
Brynner, Yul, 61
Burke, Johnny, 260
Burma Shave signs, 42

Burnett, Carol, 178, 213, 299
Burton, Richard, 221

Cambridge, Godfrey, 209
Campo, Cari, 226, 253, 254, 291
Campo, Carlos, 226, 230, 248, 254, 290–91
Campo, Cathi, 226, 247, 254, 278–79, 291
Campo, Cristina, 226, 291
Campo, Pupi, 136, 142, 231
Capitol Records, 265
Carnegie Hall, 48, 248, 281–82, 297, 300–1
Cash Box magazine, 91
Cavanaugh, Dr., 132
Censorship, 88, 110, 150–51
Chambers, Blanchie Mae, 8–9, 22, 96, 210, 295
Chambers, Lizzie, 8, 22–23
Charity events, 278–79
Children's recordings, 56
Christy, June, 36–37
Cincinnati homes, 12–23, 41–42
Cipriano, Gene, 41–42, 43, 286
Clark, Dick, 172
Clift, Montgomery, 49
Clooney, Ada Frances, 167, 288
Clooney, Andrew (father)
    death of, 244–45
    early life with, 3, 9–10, 16–17, 18
    and funeral of ex-wife, 237
    remarriage of, 170
Clooney, Betty (sister)
    big band career with (see Big band career with Tony Pastor's Orchestra)
    charity named for, 278–79
    children of, 167, 226
    Clooney Sisters comeback plans, 247–49
    Clooney Sisters act, 17–20

Index

death of, 252–55
early life of, 4–5, 12–13
end of big band career, 45
life in Beverly Hills, 229–31
loss of falsies during performance,
    39–40
marriage of, to Pupi Campo,
    136–37, 142
memorial stone for, 290
mother's death, 237
recording with, 44, 71
F. Sinatra and, 71–72
stage career of, 56–57, 71
television career of, 135–37, 165,
    224–29
Clooney, Bridget (half sister),
    244–45
Clooney, Celeste (half sister), 244
Clooney, Crescentia Koch
    (grandmother), 5–6, 9, 10
Clooney, George (nephew), 12, 167,
    225, 266, 268, 288–89, 298–99
Clooney, Joe (half brother), 244
Clooney, Nick (brother)
    Armed Forces Network career,
        139
    call to, from White House, 191
    and R. Clooney's drug addiction,
        233–35
    early life of, 12–13, 301
    Hollywood career of, 158
    life saved by D. DiPaolo, 102
    marriage and children of, 167, 268
    opinion of J. Ferrer, 168
    radio career of, 165
    relationship of, with D. DiPaolo,
        90–91
    songwriting of, 11, 55
    television career of, 165, 224–29,
        288
    touring with big band, 39
    travel with, 279, 294–95
    visit to New York, 58–59

Clooney, Nina, 167, 279, 287, 288, 301
Clooney, Olivette (aunt), 6
Clooney, Papa, 3, 5–6, 7–9, 22, 41, 177
Clooney, Rosemary
    agents and managers (see Agents
        and managers)
    birth of, 3
    brother (see Clooney, Nick
        (brother))
    careers (see Big band career with
        Tony Pastor's Orchestra; Film
        career; Radio career; Recording
        career; Stage career; Television
        career)
    Clooney Sisters act, 17–20
    Clooney Sisters comeback plans,
        247–49
    early life in Cincinnati, Ohio,
        12–23
    early life in Maysville, Kentucky,
        1–12
    father (see Clooney, Andrew
        (father))
    finances (see Financial concerns)
    first hit recording, 78–79
    first performances, 6–7
    half sister Gail (see Darley, Gail
        (half sister))
    health concerns (see Health
        concerns)
    homes (see homes)
    marriages, 102, 295–96 (see also
        DiPaolo, Dante (husband);
        Ferrer, José (husband))
    mother (see Guilfoyle, Frances
        (mother))
    political activities, 7–9, 100, 177,
        189–92, 194–95, 210–13
    religious life, 9, 40, 134–35, 202–4,
        294–95, 295–96
    romantic interests (see Romantic
        interests)
    sister (see Clooney, Betty (sister))

Clooney Sisters act, 17–20, 247–49.
  See also Big band career with
  Tony Pastor's Orchestra
Cockleshell Heroes (Ferrer film), 138
Cocoanut Grove, 126
Cole, Nat and Maria, 124–25, 173,
  293–94
Columbia Records, 37, 45, 48–49, 69,
  173–74
Columbo, Russ, 105
"Come On-a My House" record,
  72–79, 215
Commercials, 174, 268–69
Concannon, Monsignor, 135, 203
Concord Jazz, 261–62, 264
Congressional hearings on
  Communism, 128–29
Conrad, Jerry, 224
Cooper, Gary and Rocky, 126
Copenhagen, Denmark, 235
Coward, Noel, 140–41, 194–95, 196
Crosby, Bing
  R. Clooney house and, 105
  concert with, 247, 249–50
  death of, 258–61
  first meeting with, 85–86
  Papa Clooney as fan of, 6
  recording with, 166
  television specials with, 161–62,
    255–58
  touring with, 250–51
  White Christmas film with, 101, 108–14
Crosby, Gary, 136
Crosby, Harry, 256, 299
Crosby, Kathryn, 112, 168, 256,
  259–60, 300
Crosby, Lindsay, 86
Crosby, Mary Frances, 256
Crosby, Nathaniel, 256
Crosby Clambake show, 85
Curtis, Tony, 124, 150
Curtiz, Mike, 111

Dakota apartments, 174–76
Dancing, 109–10
D'Angelo, Beverly, 299
Darley, Chris, 287
Darley, Gail (half sister)
  B. Clooney's death and, 253
  living with, 116–17, 127
  marriage of, 287
  recording with, 133
  television shows with, 150, 165
  visiting R. Clooney, 65–66
Davis, Sammy, 296
Day, Doris, 17, 18, 20
Decoupage, 224
Dedicated to Nelson (album), 286
Deep in My Heart (film), 129
Demi-Centennial (album), 286
De Mille, Cecil B., 88, 95, 158
Democratic Party, 7, 177
Denmark, 235
Desmond, Johnny, 50
Diet plan, 269–70
Dietrich, Marlene, 61–63, 114–15, 140,
  141, 159–61, 251, 297
DiPaolo, Dante (husband)
  album dedication to, 286
  film career of, 94, 241
  first meetings with, 89–91
  grandchildren and, 291
  living with, 245–46
  marriage to, 295–96
  meeting with, 138–39
  performing with, 251–52
  reunion with, 238–44
  saving life of N. Clooney, 102
  Seven Brides for Seven Brothers film,
    94
  seventieth birthday party, 284
  touring with, 267
Divorce, 182–84, 186–88, 196
Donen, Stanley and Marion, 124,
  129–30, 134

Index

Dorothy Chandler Pavilion, 249–50, 278–79
Dorsey, Tommy, 71–72, 172
Dressing rooms, 88
Drug addiction, 192, 196, 198–99, 201–18, 233–35
Dudenhoeffer, Michael, 230
Dudenhoeffer, Roy and Jeanne, 13, 14, 15, 18, 19, 26, 41, 158

Edsel (car), 161–62
"Ed Sullivan Show, The," 51
Education, 19–20
Elizabeth, Queen of England, 250–51
Ellington, Duke, 125, 152–53
Empire Theater, 139–40
Encephalitis, 297–99
England, 115–17, 140–42, 159–61, 162, 250
"ER" television show, 288
Everything's Coming Up Rosie (album), 261–62

Fabian, 171
Faith, Percy, 56, 59, 71, 91–92
Fan clubs, 60, 77–78
Fancy Meeting You Here (album), 166, 260
Farrow, Mia, 258
Feinstein, Michael, 297
Ferrer, Gabriel Vicente (son), 159, 164, 240, 267–68, 285, 291, 297–98
Ferrer, Heather, 284
Ferrer, José (husband)
    on "Come On-a My House" song, 75
    death of, 292–93
    M. Dietrich and, 160
    divorce from, 182–84, 186–88, 196

film with, 129
first meetings with, 65–68
Girl Who Came to Supper, The film, 194–96
house purchased by, 103, 106
infidelities of, 98–99, 121–22, 124, 156–57, 168–69
insecurity of, 167–68, 196–97
life in Hollywood with, 125–28
marriage to, 102
meeting with, in Copenhagen, 235
Mitch Miller's opinion of, 155–57
Monday night dinner parties with, 123–25
morals clause of film contract and, 86–88
Moulin Rouge film, 84, 99–100
offices of, 33–34
post-divorce relationship with, 267–68
reconciliation with, 192–94
recording with, 113–14, 133
remarriage of, 199
singing of, 105–6, 114
television special with, 177–78
testimony before Congress, 128–29
travels with, 115–22
Ferrer, Leilani, 284
Ferrer, Maria Providencia (daughter), 154, 181–83, 210–13, 240, 287
Ferrer, Mel, 113
Ferrer, Miguel José (son), 134–35, 223, 240, 243, 251, 267–68, 284–85, 291
Ferrer, Monsita Teresa (daughter), 166, 223, 235, 240, 287–88, 291
Ferrer, Rafael Francisco (son), 176, 216, 284
Film career
    film with J. Ferrer, 129
    first film "The Stars Are Singing," 86, 95–98

Index

Here Come the Girls film, 90
morals clause, 86–88
Red Garters film, 94–95, 116
soundtrack songs, 293
television movies, 276–77
White Christmas film, 108–14
Financial concerns, 28–29, 48, 50,
    106–7, 112, 170–71, 186–87, 197,
    204–5, 274–75, 276, 277–78
Fischer, Bobby, 130
Fitzgerald, Ella, 30, 34–35
Flanagan, Ralph, 21
Flon, Suzanne, 118
Flood in Maysville, 10–11
Fonda, Henry, 126
Ford television special, 161–62
Fortas, Abe, 129
For the Duration (album), 14, 289
Four Girls Four act, 263–76
France, 119–22
Freed, Alan, 172
Freeman, Frank, 86–87
Freeman, Stan, 63, 75–76, 151
Friend, Arthur, 129

Gardner, Ava, 53, 80–81, 257–58
Garland, Judy, 88–89, 153–54, 263
Garroway, Dave, 60
"Garry Moore Show, The," 194
Gaynor, Mitzi, 273
Gershwin, George, 104
Gershwin, Ira and Leonore, 104–5,
    127, 297
Gielgud, John, 115
Gillespie, Dizzy, 80
Girl Singer (album), 286
Girl Who Came to Supper, The (Ferrer
    film), 194–96
Glasgow, Scotland, 139–40
Goldwyn, Jennifer and Sammy Jr.,
    160

Goodman, Benny, 147–48
Gordon, Ruth, 116
Grammy awards, 294
Grant, Kathryn, 112
Green, Shecky, 216
Gregory, Danny, 31
Grier, Roosevelt, 210–11
Griffin, Merv, 44–45, 67, 126, 245–47,
    291
Guarnieri, Johnny, 54, 75
Guilfoyle, Ada (grandmother), 2–3,
    9–10, 41, 70, 96–97, 169
Guilfoyle, Ann (aunt), 3, 6, 93
Guilfoyle, Chick (uncle), 11, 14
Guilfoyle, Christine (aunt), 3,
    14, 28
Guilfoyle, Frances (mother)
    daughter Gail, 29
    death of, 236–38
    early life with, 3–4
    living with R. Clooney, 142, 157,
        201–2
    Dr. Monke and, 236–37
    moving without R. Clooney,
        14–16
    refusal of, to talk, 170, 222–23
Guilfoyle, George (uncle)
    as agent and chaperone, 21–23,
        27–28, 36, 38, 43–46, 136
    death of, 289–90
    death of Aunt Ann and, 6
    death of A. Clooney and, 245
    military service, 14
    musical ability of, 11–12
Guilfoyle, Jeanne (aunt), 3. *See also*
    Dudenhoeffer, Roy and
    Jeanne
Guilfoyle, Michael Joseph
    (grandfather), 3
Guilfoyle, Neal (uncle), 11
Guilfoyle, Rose (aunt), 3, 13–14, 41
Guilfoyle, William (uncle), 11, 14

Index

Hagen, Uta, 67, 128, 156–57, 284–85
Hamilton, Scott, 286
Hammer, Victor, 176
Hanna, Jake, 257, 260–61
Hartog, Jan de, 121
Havanna, Cuba, 78
Hayworth, Rita, 94, 126
Head, Edith, 89, 127, 285
Health concerns
  asthma, 178
  drug addiction, 192, 196, 198–99,
    201–18, 233–35
  encephalitis, 297–99
  miscarriage, 178
  ovarian cyst, 58–59
  pregnancies, 132–35, 149–50, 159,
    165–67, 176, 178
  psychotic breakdown, 213–22, 225,
    246
  weight concerns, 224, 269–70
Henderson, Skitch, 42–43, 57–58, 59
Hepburn, Audrey, 113
Here Come the Girls (film), 90
Here's to My Lady (album), 265
Herman, Woody, 286–87
Hill, Phyllis, 67, 101, 240
Hi-Lo's quartet, 150
Holiday, Billie, 32, 56, 145–49, 154,
  172, 281
Hollywood, 36–39, 83–84, 125–27
Holvey, Sherman and Phyllis, 13–14,
  158, 252, 278
Homes
  in Augusta, 301
  in Beverly Hills, 88–89, 101, 103–4,
    106–8, 291–92
  in Cincinnati, 12, 14, 16, 41–42
  in England, 141
  Grandma Guilfoyle's, 1–2
  Grandmother Clooney's, 5–6
  in Hollywood, 84
  in Maysville, 1–12

  in New York City, 47–48, 60,
    114–15, 174–76
Hope, Bob and Dolores, 90, 126
Hopper, Hedda, 92
Hord, Rebekah, 96
Hunt, Terry, 137
Hussein, King of Jordan, 178
Huston, John, 117–19, 143
Huston, Ricki, 118, 168

Ireland, 117–19
Island Queen (riverboat), 1, 3

Japan, 207–8
Jefferson, Carl, 261–62
Jones, Pat, 16

Kanin, Garson, 116
Kaye, Danny, 109–10, 297
Kelly, Grace, 101, 112, 137–38, 193
Kennedy, John, 177, 190–92, 194–95
Kennedy, Patricia, 177
Kennedy, Robert and Ethel, 177, 191,
  209, 210–13, 215
Kennedy, Ted, 191
Kentucky State Fair, 171
Kern, Betty, 258
Kilgallen, Dorothy, 61, 98
King, Martin Luther, Jr., 209

Laine, Frankie, 61
Las Vegas, 79–81, 137, 166, 224
Lawford, Peter, 177, 190–91
Lee, Hap, 19
Lee, Peggy, 50
Legion of Decency, 88, 110
Leigh, Janet, 93, 112–13, 124, 142, 149,
  168–69

Leigh, Vivien, 115–16, 142
Lewis, Jerry, 296
Lewis, Robert Q., 65–66
Lieberson, Goddard, 173–74
Life magazine, 80, 293
Logan, Josh and Nedda, 106
London, 115–17, 140–42, 162, 250–51
Long, Louise, 137
Losers, The (TV movie), 276–77
Loudon, Dorothy, 194
Love (album), 185–86, 293
Luft, Sid, 127
"Lux Show Starring Rosemary Clooney, The," 163–66
Lyles, A. C., 84–85

McGuire, Phyllis, 62
McNair, Barbara, 263
Magee, Stella, 185
Managers. *See* Agents and managers
Marie, Rose, 263–64, 266, 271, 272, 275
Marine Ballroom, 26–27
Marriages, 102, 295–96. *See also* DiPaolo, Dante (husband); Ferrer, José (husband)
Married to the Mob (film soundtrack), 293
Marshall, George, 95
Martin, Dean, 161, 296
Martinez, Vince, 126
Marvin, Lee, 276–77
Maser, Dave, 28
Mason, James, Pamela, and Morgan, 194
Matz, Peter, 151
Mawley. *See* Clooney, Crescentia Koch (grandmother)
Maysville, Kentucky
  early life in, 1–12
  film premiere in, 95–98
Mercer, Johnny, 265

Miami, Florida, 76–78
Middleman, Isadore and Rose, 13–14, 41
Midnight in the Garden of Good and Evil (film soundtrack), 293
Miller, Mitch
  novelty music of, 53, 72–76, 154–55
  opposition of, to Clooney movies, 84
  recording talents of, 68–70
  recording with, 113–14, 132–33, 173
  resentment of Clooney–Ferrer marriage, 155–57
Miscarriage, 178
Mitchell, Guy, 68, 94, 297
Moer, Paul, 209
Monaco, 193
Monday night dinners, 123–25
Monke, Dr. J. Victor, 220–22, 232–33, 235–37
Monroe, Marilyn, 143
Mooney, Joe, 32
Morals clause, 86–88
Morgan, Al, 126–27
Mothers and Daughters (album), 287–88, 294
Moulin Rouge (Ferrer film), 84, 99–100
Mount Sinai hospital, 218–21
Movies. *See* Film career
Murray, Jan, 54
Musical ability
  of B. Clooney, 43
  of N. Clooney, 11, 55
  of R. Clooney, 28, 30, 43
  of family members, 6, 11
  of J. Ferrer, 105–6, 114
  of B. Kennedy, 211
My Buddy (album), 286–87

New York City, 33–35, 47–48, 114–15, 169–71

Index

Nightclubs. *See also* Stage career
  Hollywood, 126–27
  New York, 57–58
Norman, Milt, 35–39
Novelty music, 53, 75–76, 154–55

O'Connell, Helen, 263–64, 270–71
Oddo, John, 286–87
Olivier, Laurence, 115–16, 142
Olympia Theater, 76–77
Opera, J. Ferrer and, 177–78
O'Reilly, Father Peter, 203–4, 213,
  217–18, 292
Ortega, Frankie, 272
Ovarian cyst, 58–59

Paar, Jack, 135
Pacino, Al, 299
Page, Patti, 50–51, 219–20, 293
Palladium, Hollywood, 36–39
Palladium, London, 140–42, 250–51
Paramount Pictures, 83, 86–87, 92
Paramount Theater, 34
Paris, 119–20, 181
Parsons, Louella, 92–93, 102, 104, 184
Pastor, Tony, 20, 30, 147, 172. *See also*
  Big band career with Tony
  Pastor's Orchestra
Patsy's, 49–50, 284
Pearl Harbor, 14
Peckinpah, Sam, 277
Petering, Billy, 20, 35
Philip, Prince of England, 250
Philippines, 208–9
Political activities, 7–9, 100, 177,
  189–92, 194–95, 210–13
Pope, audience with, 294–95
Porter, Cole, 6, 127
Pregnancies, 132–35, 149–50, 159,
  165–67, 176, 178
Presley, Elvis, 172, 173, 260

Preston, Robert, 63
Prizefights, 126
Psychotic breakdown, 213–22, 225,
  246

Quaglieri, Al, 32

Radio career, 17–20, 54, 77
Radio DJs, 37, 54–55
Rainbow and Stars club, 283–84
Raine, Grace, 18–19
Rapp, Barney, 20
Rascism, 8–9, 125, 165
Ray, Johnnie, 61
Raye, Martha, 275
Reagan, Ronald and Nancy, 167
Recording career
  Blue Rose album, 293
  with B. Clooney, 44, 71
  "Come On-a My House" record,
    72–79
  with Concord Jazz, 261–62, 264–65
  with M. Dietrich, 62
  with D. Ellington, 125, 152–53
  Fancy Meeting You Here album with
    B. Crosby, 166, 260
  with J. Ferrer, 113–14, 133
  film soundtracks, 293
  first contract with Columbia, 45–46,
    48–49
  first hits, 72–79
  first record, 55–56
  For the Duration album, 14, 289
  with half sister Gail, 133
  loss of Columbia contract, 173–74
  Love album with N. Riddle, 185–86,
    293
  with M. Miller, 68–70, 72–76,
    113–14, 132–33, 154–57
  Mothers and Daughters album,
    287–88, 294

pregnancy and, 132–33

reissued albums, 293–94

Rosemary Clooney Sings the Lyrics of Ira Gershwin album, 105

with F. Sinatra, 51–53

Still on the Road album, 283, 286

"Tenderly" with P. Faith, 91–92

with Tony Pastor Orchestra, 29–30, 37–38, 44, 71

tribute albums, 264–65, 286

White Christmas, A album, 294

Red Channels: The Report of Communist Influence in Radio and Television (book), 128

Red Garters (film), 94–95, 116

Reed, Judge Stanley, 7, 190

Religious life, 9, 40, 134–35, 202–4, 294–95, 295–96

Reno, Nevada, 213–17

Retirement, 215

Reviews, 29, 30, 43, 86, 97, 100, 116, 163, 205, 214, 264

Riddle, Chris, 281–82

Riddle, Nelson

　death of, 282–83

　musical arrangements of, 151–52, 153–54, 263, 281–82

　romance with, 184–86, 188–89, 197–99

　L. Ronstadt's work with, 282, 285–86

　F. Sinatra and, 137

　television show with, 150–52

Riva, Maria, 297

Robeson, Paul, 128, 156–57

Rockefeller Center, 283–84

Rock 'n' roll music, 171–74

Rogers, Ginger, 273–74

Rogers, Ken, 256

Romanoff's, 126–27

Romantic interests, 58–59, 206

　S. Berger, 40–41, 185

　D. DiPaolo (*see* DiPaolo, Dante (husband))

　J. Ferrer (*see* Ferrer, José (husband))

　D. Garroway, 60

　S. Henderson, 42–43, 57–58, 59

　M. Norman, 35–39

　B. Petering, 20, 35

　N. Riddle, 184–86, 188–89, 196–99

Ronstadt, Linda, 282, 285–86

Rose, Bob, 176

Rosemary Clooney Fan Club, 60, 77–78

"Rosemary Clooney Show, The," 149–52

Rosemary Clooney Sings the Lyrics of Ira Gershwin (album), 105, 265

Rosemary Clooney Street, 2, 97

Rosie Sings Bing (album), 265

Rutherford, Ann, 84, 94

Sachs, Manie, 45–46, 48–49, 69, 172

Sante Fe, New Mexico, 177–78

Saroyan, William, 72

Schwartz, Jonathan, 282–83

Scognamillo, Joey, 284

Scognamillo, Pasquale and Concetta, 49–50

Scotland, 139–40

Seven Brides for Seven Brothers (DiPaolo film), 94

Shaw, Artie, 20, 81, 147, 257–58

Shaw, Ron, 77–78, 205, 296

Sherman, Jacqueline, 59–64, 83–84, 176

Shore, Dinah, 49, 111

Shribman, Joe, 33, 45–46, 50, 51, 81, 204

Shribman, Sy, 20

Shulman, Dr., 176

Simms, Ginny, 104

Sinatra, Frank
  career of, 34, 48
  B. Clooney and, 71–72
  R. Clooney as fan of, 6, 16, 31
  B. Crosby funeral and, 259
  death of, 300–301
  M. Dietrich and, 160–61
  Ford television special with, 161–62
  From Here to Eternity film, 137
  A. Gardner and, 258
  meeting with, about N. Riddle, 198
  prizefights and, 126
  recording with, 51–53
  relationship with, 57–58
  ridicule of R. Clooney by, 51, 81
Sinatra, Tina, 300
"Singers' Salutes to the Songwriter,"
    278–79
*Sister Margaret and the Saturday Night
    Ladies* (TV movie), 276–77
Smith, Stephen, 190
Stafford, Jo, 50, 133
Stage career
  big band career (*see* Big band career
    with Tony Pastor's Orchestra)
  at Carnegie Hall, 297, 300–301
  charity events, 278–79
  in Copenhagen, 235
  with B. Crosby, 85, 249–51
  with D. DiPaolo, 251–52
  first performances, 6–7, 20
  Four Girls Four act, 263–76
  in Glasgow, 139–40
  in Las Vegas, 79–81, 137, 224
  in London, 140–42
  in Miami, 76–78
  in Maysville, 97–98
  in New York City, 50–51, 57–58,
    283–84
  rebuilding, 231–38
  in Reno, 213–17
Stanley, Kim, 167

Starr, Kay, 275
Stars Are Singing, The (film), 86,
    95–98
Steinberg, Herb, 93, 96
Still on the Road (album), 283, 286
Storm, Tempest, 98
Stravinski, Igor, 177–78
Strayhorn, Billy, 152–53
Sviridoff, Allen, 273–79
Swanson, Gloria, 66

Television career
  T. Bankhead's "The Big Show," 62
  "Bell Telephone Hour, The," 184
  commercials, 174, 268–69
  with B. Crosby, 161–62, 255–57
  with brother Nick, 224–29
  debut, 51
  "ER" show 293
  "Garry Moore Show, The," 194
  M. Griffin's show, 245–47
  R. Lewis's variety show, 65–66
  "Lux Show Starring Rosemary
    Clooney, The," 163–66
  radio/television simulcast with
    T. Bennett, 54
  "Rosemary Clooney Show, The,"
    149–52
  *Sister Margaret and the Saturday
    Night Ladies* movie, 276–77
  Thanksgiving Day special, 178–79
"Tenderly" record, 91–92
Thompson, Bob, 151, 173, 207, 211–12
Time magazine cover photo, 100
Tokyo, Japan, 207–8
Tracy, Spencer, 143–44, 160
Trask, Clyde, 20, 57
Tribute albums, 264–65, 286
Trotta, Charlie, 20–21, 45–46
Truman, Harry, 189
Turner, Lana, 258

Index

Vaché, Warren, 286

Van Dyke, Dick, 178

Van Heusen, Jimmy, 260

Vera-Ellen, 109

Vine Lodge, 36, 248, 292

Virginia Beach, 38–39, 44–45,
251–52

Vlaminck painting, 149, 187, 207,
277–78

Vorce, Roger, 276

WCPO television station, 224–29

Weaver, Leonore, 137–38

Webman, Hal, 276

Wehringer, Marge, 16

Weight concerns, 224, 269–70

Weiss, Stan, 32, 296

West, Mae, 138, 207

Westbrook, Lynn, 107

WFTM radio station, 158

White, Jerry, 272–73

White Christmas (film), 108–14

White Christmas, A (album), 294

Whiting, Margaret, 263–64, 265–66,
267, 270, 271–72

Williams, Joe, 50

With Love (album), 265

WLAP radio station, 165

WLW radio station, 17–20, 57

World War II, 14

Zeidler, Norman, 288

When not performing elsewhere, Rosemary Clooney makes her home in Beverly Hills, California, and Augusta, Kentucky.

Joan Barthel is the author of several award-winning nonfiction books, including *A Death in Canaan*. She lives in St. Louis, Missouri.

Printed in the United States
by Baker & Taylor Publisher Services